Eighth Edition

Assessment in Early Childhood Education

Sue C. Wortham
Professor Emerita University of Texas at San Antonio

Belinda J. Hardin
Associate Professor Emerita The University of North Carolina at Greensboro

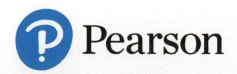

Director and Publisher: Kevin Davis
Executive Portfolio Manager: Aileen Pogran
Managing Content Producer: Megan Moffo
Portfolio Management Assistants: Maria Feliberty
Development Editor: Krista McMurray
Executive Product Marketing Manager: Christopher Barry
Executive Field Marketing Manager: Krista Clark
Manufacturing Buyer: Carol Melville
Cover Design: Pearson CSC
Cover Art: Iam_Anupong/ Shutterstock
Media Producer: Autumn Benson
Full-Service Vendor: Pearson CSC
Full-Service Project Management: Pearson CSC, Rowena Saycon and Kabilan Selvakumar
Printer/Binder: LSC Communications, Inc.
Cover Printer: LSC Communications, Inc.
Text Font: 9.5/13 Palatino LT Pro

Credits and acknowledgments for material borrowed from other sources and reproduced, with permission, in this textbook appear on the appropriate page within the text.

Every effort has been made to provide accurate and current Internet information in this book. However, the Internet and information posted on it are constantly changing, so it is inevitable that some of the Internet addresses in this textbook will change.

Library of Congress Cataloging-in-Publication Data
Wortham, Sue Clark
  Assessment in early childhood education/Sue C. Wortham, Belinda Hardin.—Eighth edition.
    p. cm.
    Includes index.
    ISBN 978-0-13-520652-2—ISBN 0-13-520652-9
1. Educational tests and measurements—United States. 2. Psychological tests for children—United States. 3. Ability in children—United States—Testing. 4. Early childhood education—United States—Evaluation. I. Hardin, Belinda June II. Title.
    LB3060.217.W67 2016
    372.21—dc23   2014040128

4 2020

ISBN-13: 978-0-13-520652-2
ISBN-10:   0-13-520652-9

Brief Contents

Contents

Part II   Standardized Tests

4   How Standardized Tests Are Used, Designed, and Selected   78

5   Using and Reporting Standardized Test Results   106

Part III   Classroom Assessments

6   Data-Driven Decision Making, Assessment, and Documentation   137

About the Authors

SUE CLARK WORTHAM is Professor Emerita of Early Childhood and Elementary Education at the University of Texas at San Antonio. Prior to beginning a teaching career in higher education in 1979, she taught prekindergarten through second grade in public schools, worked as a school district administrator, and was a consultant at an education service center.

She has authored numerous texts, including *Early Childhood Curriculum: Developmental Bases for Learning and Teaching* (5th ed., 2010), Pearson. She coauthored *Play and Child Development* (4th ed., 2012) with Joe Frost and Stuart Reifel, also published by Pearson. Organizational publications include *Childhood 1892–2002*, published by the Association for Childhood Education International, and *Playgrounds for Young Children: National Survey and Perspectives*, coauthored with Joe Frost, published by the American Alliance for Health, Physical Education, Recreation, and Dance (AAHPERD).

In 1992, she served as a Fulbright Scholar in Chile. She was president of the Association for Childhood Education International (ACEI) from 1995 to 1997. Since retirement, she has been very active in the development of the Global Guidelines for Early Childhood Education and Care that resulted from an international symposium held in Ruschlikon, Switzerland, in 1999. Subsequently, she has a leadership role in the development, validation, and implementation of the ACEI Global Guidelines Assessment adapted from the original guidelines. She edited *Common Characteristics and Unique Qualities in Preschool Programs: Global Perspectives in Early Childhood Education* for Springer in 2013, which reported on the use of the *Global Guidelines Assessment* in countries around the world.

Dr. Wortham served as volunteer director of educational programs for World Children's Relief and Volunteer Organization, a small nongovernmental organization (NGO), from 2001 to 2011. She engaged in training teachers and principals in Haiti, Senegal, Burkina Faso, and Sierra Leone.

BELINDA J. HARDIN is an Associate Professor Emerita in the Department of Specialized Education Services at The University of North Carolina at Greensboro. Dr. Hardin completed her PhD in Early Childhood, Families, and Literacy at the University of North Carolina at Chapel Hill. Prior to entering higher education in 2004, she was a public school kindergarten and special education teacher, a Head Start director, and the Director of the Special Projects Division at Chapel Hill Training-Outreach Project.

Her research includes cross-cultural studies investigating the effectiveness of services for young children with and without disabilities in the United States and other countries, particularly in Latin America. She is especially interested in measures of program quality with global applicability and how they are informed by sociocultural context. She served as the Co-Principal Investigator of three national studies in the United States that investigated the reliability and validity of Learning Accomplishment Profile assessment instruments, including a dual-language sample of 2,099 children (half English speakers and half Spanish speakers) to norm the Learning Accomplishment Profile-Diagnostic Edition.

Additionally, Dr. Hardin completed studies investigating the referral, evaluation, and placement of preschool children with disabilities who are English Language Learners and is currently developing a family report questionnaire on preschool language development in English and Spanish. Dr. Hardin has conducted research and professional development activities with professionals and Spanish-speaking families in North Carolina, Guatemala, and the Yucatan Peninsula of Mexico. She was the Co-Principal Investigator of three international studies investigating the reliability and validity of the ACEI Global Guidelines Assessment in multiple countries around the world. Dr. Hardin has served on the Board of Directors for the Association of Childhood Education International and participated in two initiatives spearheaded by UNICEF to improve services for young children in inclusive early childhood settings worldwide.

Preface

Students preparing to become teachers of young children from infancy through the early primary grades must be prepared to measure or evaluate children who are in the period of development called *early childhood*. Tests and other types of assessments designed for young children are different from those intended for children in later grades in elementary school. Because infants and children under age 8 have developmental needs different from those of older children, a textbook that includes discussion of assessment in the early childhood years must be written from a developmental perspective.

In the second decade of the 21st century, early childhood educators have been challenged in their efforts to assess very young children using the most important strategies for their ongoing development. As a result, it is especially important that future teachers and teachers who are struggling with these issues be fully informed about the range of assessment possibilities and when they are the most beneficial for young children.

Traditional and Authentic Assessment Strategies

This book is written for future teachers and current teachers of young children. It includes information about standardized tests and, more importantly, other types of assessments that are appropriate for young children, such as screening tools, observations, checklists, and rating scales. Assessments designed by teachers are explained both for preschool children and for kindergarten and primary-grade children who are transitioning into literacy. With the ever-growing trend toward performance assessment, portfolios, and other methods of reporting a child's performance, chapters describing these strategies have been expanded and enhanced. The approach of this edition is the development of an assessment system that includes traditional as well as authentic assessment strategies in a comprehensive plan. Thus, in this new edition, we seek to inform the reader about all types of assessments and their appropriate use.

New to This Edition

- Search and Share activities in each chapter give students an opportunity to identify pertinent information from the web for further understanding and discussion.

- Chapter 3, Communicating with Families, was previously located as Chapter 11 and has now been moved forward and expanded to increase the role of the family-professional relationship. Parents are recognized as equal partners with their child's teacher.

- Chapter 4, How Standardized Tests Are Used, Designed, and Selected, includes new information about current editions of screening and assessment instruments.

- Chapter 6, Data-Driven Decision Making, Assessment and Documentation, changes the emphasis from classroom assessments in general to specific information on how data from assessments are used to make instructional decisions.

- Relevant information about the Common Core State Standards and Early Learning Standards has been integrated where appropriate throughout the text.

- Expanded information on children with disabilities and English language learners (ELLs) appears in all chapters throughout the text.

How to Assess Young Children

Earlier editions of this book were developed in response to the expressed needs of teachers and graduate students who must understand and use current trends in assessment and put them into perspective within the reality of public schools that are required to focus intensively on standardized tests. Fortunately, commercial publishers of curriculum kits and textbooks for public schools are increasingly including performance assessments along with traditional assessments in their guides for teachers. Portfolios are becoming common as well. Nevertheless, teachers still need help in maintaining a balance between these new strategies and standardized testing.

An important factor in the assessment of young children is determining when and how they should be measured. This is a controversial issue. The strengths and weaknesses of each type of assessment presented are discussed, as is research on the problems surrounding testing and evaluation in early childhood. Because many sources in the literature and other textbooks do not include the limitations in addition to the merits of assessment techniques, this text provides an objective perspective on issues surrounding the efficacy and effectiveness of assessment strategies.

Organization

The book is divided into three parts. Part I provides an introduction to assessment in early childhood in **Chapters 1** and **2**. **Chapter 3** addresses the partnership between families and school professionals. Part II is devoted to standardized tests and how they are designed, used, and reported in **Chapters 4** and **5**. Classroom assessments are discussed in Part III. **Chapter 6** is a new chapter that focuses on data-driven assessment and documentation, while **Chapter 7** includes expanded information on observation. Checklists, rating scales, and rubrics are covered in **Chapter 8**. **Chapter 9** discusses teacher-designed strategies, while **Chapter 10** focuses on performance-based assessment strategies. Finally, **Chapter 11** brings all the assessment strategies together into a portfolio system.

Pearson Enhanced eText

The Pearson Enhanced eText includes the following interactive content that furthers student engagement and comprehension:

- Video links that make it possible for students to see real-life examples of the content in each chapter have been expanded.
- Formative and summative assessments for students include Self-Checks within major sections of each chapter so that students can gauge their understanding as they read and study the material, and an end-of-chapter quiz supports student learning and knowledge retention.
- Application Exercises in each chapter provide practice applying chapter concepts for deeper understanding.

Instructor Supplements

The supplements for this edition have been revised, upgraded, and made available for instructors to download on www.pearsonhighered.com/educators.

- Instructor's Resource Manual This manual contains chapter overviews and activity ideas to enhance chapter concepts.
- Test Bank. The Test Bank includes a variety of test items, including multiple-choice and short-answer items.
- PowerPoint Slides. PowerPoint slides highlight key concepts and strategies in each chapter and enhance lectures and discussions.

Acknowledgments

We would like to thank the reviewers who provided valuable suggestions and feedback for this eighth edition, including Natalie Williams, University of Nebraska-Lincoln; Dr. Sandra Plata-Potter, University of Mount Olive; and Cathy Jones, Coastal Carolina University. Their comments were perceptive and their suggestions constructive. The reviewers were thoughtful in their ideas for how the text could be improved.

It is also important to thank the staff at Pearson, who helped in the conceptualization of important revisions as well as in the production process, including Megan Moffo, content producer; Aileen Pogran, portfolio manager; Krista McMurray, development editor; and Rowena Saycon, who coordinated production at Pearson CSC, Inc.

Chapter 1
An Overview of Assessment in Early Childhood

Suzanne Clouzeau/Pearson Education, Inc.

 ## Chapter Learning Outcomes

As a result of reading this chapter, you will be able to:

1.1 Explain the purposes of assessment in early childhood.

1.2 Describe the history of tests and measurements in early childhood.

1.3 Discuss issues and trends in assessing all young children.

Understanding the Purposes of Assessment in Infancy and Early Childhood

Not too long ago, resources on early childhood assessment were limited to occasional articles in journals, chapters in textbooks on teaching in early childhood programs, and a few small textbooks that were used as secondary texts in an early childhood education course. Very few teacher preparation programs offered a course devoted to assessment in early childhood. Now, in the 21st century, assessment of very young children has experienced a period of rapid growth and expansion. In fact, it has been described as a "virtual explosion of testing in public schools" (Meisels & Atkins-Burnett, 2005, p. 1). Some of the most recent concerns relate to the mandated tests used with the Common Core State Standards Initiative. Other issues arise from the increased use of tests selected by individual school districts (DeWitt, 2014; Lazarin, 2014).

There has also been an explosion in the numbers of infants, toddlers, and preschoolers in early childhood programs and the types of programs that serve them. Moreover, the diversity among these young children increases each year. For example, Head Start programs serve children and families who speak at least 140 different languages. In some Head Start classrooms, 10 different languages might be spoken. Currently, nearly a third of children enrolled in Head Start speak Spanish as their first language (HHS/ACF/OHS, 2017). Head Start teaching teams may be multilingual, also representing growth in the diversity of the U.S. population (David, 2005; HHS/ACF/OHS, 2010).

What Is Assessment?

What do we need to know about all the diverse children found in services for infants and young children from all kinds of families, cultures, and languages? The study of individuals for measurement purposes begins before birth with assessment of fetal growth and development. At birth and throughout infancy and early childhood, various methods of measurement are used to evaluate the child's growth and development. Before a young child enters a preschool program, he or she is measured through medical examinations. Children are also measured through **observations** of developmental milestones, such as saying the first word or walking independently, by parents and other family members. Children might also be screened or evaluated for an early childhood program or service. Assessment is really a *process*. A current definition describes the assessment process as follows: "**Assessment** is the process of gathering information about children from several forms of evidence, then organizing and interpreting that information" (McAfee, Leong, & Bodrova, 2004, p. 3). The U.S. Department of Education describes assessment as a comprehensive system that includes screening measures, formative assessment, measures of environmental quality, and measures of the quality of adult–child interactions (U.S. Department of Education, n.d). The U.S. Department of Education's approach considers factors beyond the child to include the family and other adults that can affect that child.

Assessment of children from birth through the preschool years is different from assessment of older people. Not only can young children not yet write or read, but the assessment of young, developing children also presents different challenges that influence the choice of measurement strategy, or how to measure or assess the children. Assessment methods must be matched with the level of mental, social, and physical development at each stage. Developmental change in young children is rapid, and there is a need to assess whether development is progressing normally. If development is not normal, the measurement and evaluation procedures used are important in making decisions regarding appropriate intervention services during infancy and the preschool years (Jiban, 2013).

The term *assessment* can have different meanings when used with different age groups. An infant or toddler can be assessed to determine instructional needs in Early Head Start programs or to determine eligibility for early intervention services, for example. A preschool child may be assessed to determine school readiness or special education needs. A school-age child may be assessed to understand his or her academic achievement and/or whether the child is ready for the next grade level.

Enhanced eText: Video Example 1.1

Purposes of Assessment

Assessment is used for various purposes. An *evaluation* may be conducted to assess a young child's development overall or in a specific developmental domain such as language or mathematics. Evaluations usually include multiple sources of assessment. When we need to learn more, we may assess the child by asking her or him to describe what she or he has achieved. For example, a first-grade teacher may use measurement techniques to determine what reading skills have been mastered and what weaknesses exist that indicate a need for additional instruction.

Assessment strategies may be used for *diagnosis.* Just as a medical doctor conducts a physical examination of a child to diagnose an illness, psychologists, teachers, and other adults who work with children can conduct an informal or formal assessment to diagnose a developmental delay or causes for poor performance in learning, as well as to identify strengths. Assessment for this purpose may be one part of the initial evaluation process, which may also include observation, a review of medical records, and information from parents to identify their concerns, priorities, and resources.

If medical problems, birth defects, or developmental delays in motor, language, cognitive, or social development are discovered during the early, critical periods of development, steps can be taken to correct, minimize, or remediate them before the child enters school. With many developmental deficits or differences, the earlier they are detected and the earlier intervention is planned, the more likely the child will be able to overcome them or compensate for them. For example, if a serious hearing deficit is identified early, the child can learn other methods of communicating and acquiring information.

Assessment of young children is also used for *placement*—to place them in infant or early childhood programs or to provide special services. To ensure that a child receives the best services, careful **screening** followed by more extensive testing and observation may be conducted before selecting the combination of intervention programs and other services that will best serve the child.

Program planning is another purpose of assessment. After children have been identified and evaluated for an intervention program or service, assessment results can be used in planning the individualized programs that will serve them. These programs, in turn, can be evaluated to determine their effectiveness.

Besides identifying and correcting developmental problems, assessment of very young children is conducted for other purposes. One purpose is *research.* Researchers study young children to better understand their behavior or to measure the appropriateness of the experiences that are provided for them.

Early Intervention for a Child with Hearing Impairment

Julio, who is 2 years old, was born prematurely. He did not have regular checkups during his first year, but his mother took him to a community clinic when he had a cold and fever at about 9 months of age. When the doctor noticed that Julio did not react to normal sounds in the examining room, she stood behind him and clapped her hands near each ear. Because Julio did not turn toward the clapping sounds, the doctor suspected that he had a hearing loss. She arranged for Julio to be examined by an audiologist at an eye, ear, nose, and throat clinic.

Julio was found to have a significant hearing loss in both ears. He was fitted with hearing aids and is attending a special program twice a week for children with hearing deficits. Therapists in the program are teaching Julio to speak. They are also teaching his mother how to make Julio aware of his surroundings and help him to develop a vocabulary. Had Julio not received intervention services at an early age, he might have entered school with severe cognitive and learning deficits that would have put him at a higher risk for failing to learn.

How were these assessment strategies developed? In the next section, we describe how certain movements or factors, especially during the past century, have affected the development of testing instruments, procedures, and other measurement techniques that are used with infants and young children.

Enhanced eText: Self-Check 1.1

The History of Tests and Measurements in Early Childhood

Interest in studying young children to understand their growth and development dates back to the initial recognition of childhood as a separate period in the life cycle. Johann Pestalozzi, a pioneer in developing educational programs specifically for children, wrote about the development of his 3-year-old son in 1774 (Irwin & Bushnell, 1980). Early publications also reflected concern for the proper upbringing and education of young children. *Some Thoughts Concerning Education* by John Locke (1699), *Emile* by Rousseau (1762/1911), and Frederick Froebel's *Education of Man* (1896) were influential in focusing attention on the characteristics and needs of children in the 18th and 19th centuries. Rousseau believed that human nature was essentially good and that education must allow that goodness to unfold. He stated that more attention should be given to studying the child so that education could be adapted to meet individual needs (Weber, 1984). The study of children, as advocated by Rousseau, did not begin until the late 19th and early 20th centuries.

Scientists throughout the world used observation to measure human behaviors. Ivan Pavlov proposed a theory of conditioning to change behaviors. Alfred Binet developed the concept of a normal mental age by studying memory, attention, and intelligence in children. Binet and Theophile Simon developed an intelligence scale to determine mental age that made it possible to differentiate the abilities of individual children (Weber, 1984). American psychologists expanded these early efforts, developing instruments for various types of measurement.

The study and measurement of young children today has evolved from the child study movement, the development of standardized tests, Head Start and other federal programs first funded in the 1960s, the passage of Public Law 94-142 (now called the Individuals with Disabilities Education Improvement Act of 2004), and Public Law 99-457 (an expansion of PL 94-142 to include infants, toddlers, and preschoolers). Most recently, there has been a movement toward more meaningful learning or authentic achievement and assessment (Newmann, 1996; Wiggins, 1993). At the same time, continuing progress is being made in identifying, diagnosing, and providing more appropriate intervention for infants and young children with disabilities (Epstein, Schweinhart, DeBruin-Parecki, & Robin, 2004; Meisels & Fenichel, 1996).

The Child Study Movement

G. Stanley Hall, Charles Darwin, and Lawrence Frank were leaders in the development of the child study movement that emerged at the beginning of the 20th century. Darwin, in suggesting that by studying the development of the infant one could glimpse the development of the human species, initiated the scientific study of the child (Kessen, 1965). Hall developed and extended methods of studying children. After he became president of Clark University in Worcester, Massachusetts, he established a major center for child study. Hall's students—John Dewey, Arnold Gesell, and Lewis Terman—all made major contributions to the study and measurement of children. Dewey advocated educational reform that affected the development of educational programs for young children. Gesell first described the behaviors that emerged in children at each chronological age. Terman became a leader in the development of psychological tests (Irwin & Bushnell, 1980; Wortham, 2002).

Research in child rearing and child care was furthered by the establishment of the Laura Spelman Rockefeller Memorial child development grants. Under the leadership of Lawrence Frank, institutes for child development were funded by the Rockefeller grants at Columbia University Teacher's College (New York), the University of Minnesota, the University of California at Berkeley, Arnold Gesell's Clinic of Child Development at Yale University, the Iowa Child Welfare Station, and other locations.

With the establishment of child study at academic centers, preschool children could be observed in group settings, rather than as individuals in the home. With the development of laboratory schools and nursery schools in the home economics departments of colleges and universities, child study research could also include the family in broadening the understanding of child development. Researchers from many disciplines joined in an ongoing child study movement that originated strategies for observing and measuring development. The results of their research led to an abundant literature. Between the 1890s and the 1950s, hundreds of children were studied in academic settings throughout the United States (Weber, 1984). Thus, the child study movement taught us to use observation and other strategies to assess the child. Investigators today continue to add new knowledge about child development and learning that aids parents, preschool teachers and staff members, and professionals in institutions and agencies that provide services to children and families. In the last decade of the 20th century and in the 21st century, brain research has opened up a whole new perspective of the nature of cognitive development and the importance of the early years for optimum development and later learning (Begley, 1997; National Scientific Council on the Developing Child, 2004, 2010; Shore, 1997). These new findings have caused early childhood educators to reflect on the factors that affect early development and the implications for programming for children in infancy and early childhood. Recent research has focused on longitudinal studies of children as they grow up, children's development globally, and psychophysiological and neuroscience experiments to measure influences on child growth and development.

Standardized Tests

Standardized testing also began around 1900. When colleges and universities in the East sought applicants from other areas of the nation in the 1920s, they found the high school transcripts of these students difficult to evaluate. The *Scholastic Aptitude Test (SAT)* was established to permit fairer comparisons of applicants seeking admission (Cronbach, 1990).

As public schools expanded to offer 12 years of education, a similar phenomenon occurred. To determine the level and pace of instruction and the grouping of students without regard for socioeconomic class, objective tests were developed (Gardner, 1961). These tests grew out of the need to sort, select, or otherwise make decisions about both children and adults.

The first efforts to design tests were informal. When a psychologist, researcher, or physician needed a method to observe a behavior, he or she developed a procedure to meet those needs. This procedure was often adopted by others with the same needs. When many people wanted to use a particular measurement strategy or test, the developer prepared printed copies for sale. As the demand for tests grew, textbook publishers and firms specializing in test development and production also began to create and sell tests (Cronbach, 1990).

American psychologists built on the work of Binet and Simon in developing the intelligence measures described earlier. Binet's instrument, revised by Terman at Stanford University, came to be known as the *Stanford–Binet Intelligence Scale*. Other Americans, particularly educators, welcomed the opportunity to use precise measurements to evaluate learning. Edward Thorndike and his students designed measures to evaluate achievement in reading, mathematics, spelling, and language ability (Weber, 1984). Because of the work of Terman and Thorndike, testing soon became a science (Scherer, 1999). By 1918, more than 100 standardized tests had been designed to measure school achievement (Monroe, 1918).

The Industrial Revolution in the 1800s was a major influence in the development of standardized tests. School-age children were taken out of factories and farms to attend school. Standardized tests made it possible to assess the new, large numbers of students. The SAT and ACT college entrance exams became the most prevalent standardized tests used to assess college eligibility. The SAT was founded in 1926. It remained largely unchanged until 2005, when a writing section was added. The current version of the SAT, published in 2016, was revised to be more reflective of education in the United States and has received positive reviews by users (The College Board, 2017). The ACT was developed to compete with the SAT in 1959. The ACT assesses accumulated knowledge. Both tests are widely used today (Fletcher, 2009). However, colleges and universities are in the process of developing other measures beyond standardized tests to access other accomplishments that can contribute toward success in higher education.

After World War II, the demand for dependable and technically refined tests grew, and people of all ages came to be tested. As individuals and institutions selected and developed their own tests, the use of testing became more centralized. Statewide tests were administered in schools, and tests were increasingly used at the national level.

The expanded use of tests resulted in the establishment of giant corporations that could assemble the resources to develop, publish, score, and report the results of testing to a large clientele. Centralization improved the quality of tests and the establishment of standards for test design. As individual researchers and teams of psychologists continue to design instruments to meet current needs, the high quality of these newer tests can be attributed to the improvements and refinements made over the years and to the increased knowledge of test design and validation (Cronbach, 1990).

Head Start and the War on Poverty

Prior to the 1960s, medical doctors, psychologists, and other professionals serving children developed tests for use with infants and preschool children. Developmental measures, IQ tests, and specialized tests to measure developmental deficits were generally used for noneducational purposes. Child study researchers tended to use observational or unobtrusive methods to study the individual child or groups of children. School-age children were assessed to measure school achievement, but this type of test was rarely used with preschool children.

After the federal government decided to improve the academic performance of children from low-income homes and those from non-English-speaking backgrounds, test developers moved quickly to design new measurement and evaluation instruments for these preschool and school-age populations.

In the late 1950s, there was concern about the consistently low academic performance of children from poor homes. As researchers investigated the problem, national interest in improving education led to massive funding for many programs designed to reduce the disparity in achievement between poor and middle-class children. The major program that involved preschool children was Head Start. Models of early childhood programs ranging from highly structured academic, child-centered developmental approaches to more traditional nursery school models were designed and implemented throughout the United States (White, 1973; Zigler & Valentine, 1979). Developers of Head Start programs were influenced by the work of Urie Bronfenbrenner, one of the cofounders of Head Start, who studied the impact of environments on children's development and learning (Bronfenbrenner, 2004). The emphasis on family involvement in Head Start was largely due to Bronfenbrenner's work (1995, 2004).

All programs funded by the federal government had to be evaluated for effectiveness. As a result, new measures were developed to assess individual progress and the programs' effectiveness (Laosa, 1982). The quality of these measures was uneven, as was comparative research designed to examine the overall effectiveness of Head Start. Nevertheless, the measures and strategies developed for use with Head Start projects added valuable resources for the assessment and evaluation of young children (Hoepfner, Stern, & Nummedal, 1971).

Other federally funded programs developed in the 1960s, such as bilingual programs, Title I, the Emergency School Aid Act, Follow Through, and Home Start, were similar in effect to Head Start. The need for measurement strategies and assessment tools to evaluate these programs led to the improvement of existing tests and the development of new ones to evaluate their success accurately.

Legislation for Young Children with Disabilities

Efforts to improve education for children who do not experience typical development were a major focus in the last three decades of the 20th century. Prior to legislation to address atypical development, young children with disabilities were served in separate classrooms in special education programs. The first law passed in 1975 started a new approach to identifying children with special needs and designing individual plans for their education. A series of laws were passed to develop suitable programs for these children. Later, infants and toddlers were also included to provide early identification and efforts to minimize the disabilities.

PL 94-142   Perhaps the most significant law affecting the measurement of children with disabilities was Public Law (PL) 94-142, the Education for All Handicapped Children Act, passed by Congress in 1975. This law mandated that all children ages 6 to 21 with special needs receive services within public schools. The law further required the use of nondiscriminatory testing and evaluation of these children.

PL 99-457   Many of the shortcomings of PL 94-142 for young children were addressed in PL 99-457 (Education of the Handicapped Act Amendments), passed in 1986. The newer law authorized two new programs: the Preschool Grant Program, mandated for children 3 to 5 years old, and the Early Intervention State Grant Program for infants and toddlers. Under PL 94-142, the state could choose whether to provide services to children with disabilities between ages 3 and 5. Under PL 99-457, states had to prove they were meeting the needs of all children with disabilities ages 3 to 21 if they wished to receive federal funds under PL 94-142. These two laws were later amended, combined, and renamed the Individuals with Disabilities Education Act (IDEA).

INDIVIDUALS WITH DISABILITIES EDUCATION IMPROVEMENT ACT OF 2004

The U.S. Congress reauthorized the Education for All Handicapped Children Act of 1975 in 1997 (IDEA). The reauthorization of the 1997 law required special education students to participate in state tests, and states were to report the results of those tests to the public. Many states were slow to comply with the law, and there were no consequences for states that did not comply. The most recent amendments to IDEA were passed in December 2004, called the Individuals with Disabilities Education Improvement Act of 2004 (IDEA 2004). Final regulations were published in 2006 that included Part B for children ages 3 to 21 and, in September 2011, Part C regulations for infants and toddlers (National Dissemination Center for Children with Disabilities, 2012).

IDEA 2004 guarantees all children 3 to 21 years old with disabilities the right to a free, appropriate public education and placement in the least restrictive learning environment under the Part B program. This means that preschool services must also be provided for children under age 6. For these children, the public schools have the legal responsibility for implementing early childhood programs for children with disabilities, whether the services take place in a public school or another setting such as private child-care centers or Head Start (Guralnick, 1982; Spodek & Saracho, 1994; U.S. Congress, 2004).

The law also includes the Part C program, or Early Intervention Program, ensuring early intervention services for all children with disabilities from birth through age 2 and their families. All participating states must provide intervention services for every eligible child (McCollum & Maude, 1993; Meisels & Shonkoff, 1990; Shackelford, 2006).

Enhanced eText: Video Example 1.2

The implications of these laws were far reaching. Testing, identification, and placement of students with intellectual disabilities and other disabilities were difficult. Existing tests were no longer considered adequate for children with special needs. Classroom teachers had to learn the techniques used to identify students with disabilities and determine how to meet their educational needs (Kaplan & Saccuzzo, 1989). Measures had to be revised or developed to assess infants, toddlers, and preschool children.

One Family's Experience with Head Start

Rosa is a graduate of the Head Start program. For 2 years, she participated in a class housed in James Brown School, a former inner-city school that had been closed and remodeled for other community services. Two Head Start classrooms were in the building, which was shared with several other community agencies serving low-income families. In addition to learning at James Brown School, Rosa went on many field trips, including trips to the zoo, the botanical garden, the public library, and a nearby McDonald's restaurant.

This year, Rosa is a kindergarten student at West Oaks Elementary School with her older brothers, who also attended Head Start. Next year, Rosa's younger sister, Luisa, will begin the program. Luisa looks forward to Head Start. She has good memories of the things she observed Rosa doing in the Head Start classroom while visiting the school with her mother.

Luisa's parents are also happy that she will be attending the Head Start program. Luisa's older brothers are good students, which they attribute to the background they received in Head Start. From her work in kindergarten, it appears that Rosa will also do well when she enters first grade.

The law requires that a team of teachers, parents, diagnosticians, school psychologists, medical personnel, specialists (e.g., occupational or physical therapists), school administrators, and perhaps social workers or representatives of government agencies or institutions be used to determine eligibility and placement of children with disabilities. When appropriate, the child must also be included in the decision-making process. Once a child is determined to be eligible for the Part C program (for infants and toddlers) or the Part B program (for children 3 to 21 years of age), an individualized plan is developed by the team. For infants and toddlers, this plan is called the Individualized Family Services Plan (IFSP). For children in the Part B program, it is called the Individualized Education Program (IEP).

MAINSTREAMING, LRE, INCLUSION, AND NATURAL ENVIRONMENTS The term **mainstreaming** came to define the requirement that a child be placed in the **least restrictive environment (LRE)**. This meant that as often as possible, a child would be placed with children with typical development, rather than in a segregated classroom for students in special education. How much mainstreaming was beneficial for the individual student? The question was difficult to answer. In addition, the ability of teachers to meet the needs of students with and without disabilities simultaneously in the same classroom is still debated. Nevertheless, classroom teachers were expected to develop and monitor the educational program prescribed for students with disabilities (Clark, 1976).

The PL 94-142 amendments required that the individual educational needs of young children with disabilities must be met in all early childhood programs (Deiner, 1993; McCollum & Maude, 1993; Wolery, Strain, & Bailey, 1992). These laws advance the civil rights of young children and have resulted in the inclusion of young children with disabilities in preschool and school-age programs. As a result, the concept of mainstreaming has been replaced by integration, or **inclusion**, whereby all young children learn together with the goal that the individual needs of all children will be met (Krick, 1992; Wolery & Wilbers, 1994). The efforts of these programs and their services must be assessed and evaluated to determine whether the needs of children are being met effectively (Early Head Start National Resource Center, 2011).

> Early childhood inclusion embodies the values, policies, and practices that support the right of every infant and young child and his or her family, regardless of ability, to participate in a broad range of activities and contexts as full members of families, communities, and society. The desired results of inclusive experiences for children with and without disabilities and their families include a sense of belonging and membership, positive social relationships and friendships, and development and learning to reach their full potential. The defining features of inclusion that can be used to identify high quality early childhood programs and services are access, participation, and supports (DEC/NAEYC, 2009, p. 2).

The term *inclusion* for infants and toddlers means that early intervention services should be provided in the most *natural environment.* Natural environments may include a child's home, a child-care center, or any other setting in which infants and toddlers typically participate.

The identification and diagnosis of students with disabilities is the most complex aspect of IDEA 2004. Many types of children need special education, including students with intellectual disabilities, physical disabilities, vision disabilities, speech impairments, auditory disabilities, learning disabilities, emotional disturbances, and autism, as well as students who are gifted. Children may have a combination of disabilities. The identification and comprehensive testing of children to determine what types of disabilities they have and how best to educate them requires a vast array of assessment techniques and instruments. Teachers, school nurses, and other staff members may be involved in initial screening and referral, but the extensive testing used for diagnosis requires professionals who have been trained to administer assessment tools in a variety of areas including psychological tests, developmental assessments, and vision and hearing screenings (Mehrens & Lehmann, 1991).

How to measure and evaluate young children with disabilities and the programs that serve them is a continuing challenge (Cicchetti & Wagner, 1990). The design of measures to screen, identify, and place infants and young children in intervention programs began with the passage of PL 94-142 and was extended under PL 99-457. Many of these instruments and strategies, particularly those dealing with developmental delay, were also used with preschool programs serving children with typical development.

As children with disabilities were served in a larger variety of settings, such as preschools, Head Start programs, child-care settings, early intervention programs, and hospitals, early childhood educators from diverse backgrounds became more involved in determining whether infants and young children were eligible for services for special needs. Many questions were raised about appropriately serving young children with diverse abilities. Meeting the developmental and educational needs of infants and preschool children with disabilities and at the same time providing inclusive services was a complex task. How should these children be grouped for the best intervention services?

When children with and without disabilities were grouped together, what were the effects when all of them were progressing through critical periods of development? Not only was identification of young children with disabilities more complex, but evaluation of infant and preschool programs providing intervention services was also more challenging.

PL 101-576   The Americans with Disabilities Act (ADA), passed in 1990 (Stein, 1993), had an additional impact on the education of young children with disabilities. Under the ADA, all early childhood programs must be prepared to serve children with special needs. Facilities and accommodations for young children, including outdoor play environments, must be designed, constructed, and altered appropriately to meet the needs of young children with disabilities.

Enhanced eText: Self-Check 1.2

Issues and Trends in Assessment in Early Childhood Education

The 1980s brought a new reform movement in education, accompanied by a new emphasis on assessment. The effort to improve education at all levels included the use of standardized tests to provide accountability for what students are learning. Minimum competency tests, achievement tests, and screening instruments were used to ensure that students from preschool through college reached the desired educational goals and achieved the minimum standards of education that were established locally or by the state education agency. As we continue in a new century, these concerns have increased.

In the 1990s, many schools improved the learning environment and achievement for all children; nevertheless, a large percentage of schools were still low performing in 2000 and 2001. Inadequate funding, teacher shortages, teachers with inadequate training, aging schools, and poor leadership affected the quality of education (Wortham, 2002).

During the 2000 presidential campaign, candidate George W. Bush named quality education as one of the goals of his presidency. After his election, President Bush worked for legislation that would improve education for all children. After months of dialogue and debate, Congress passed a new education act in December 2001. The No Child Left Behind Act (NCLB), formerly known as the Elementary and Secondary Education Act (ESEA), was signed into law on January 8, 2002, and had an impact on testing required by individual states. In addition to other provisions, all states were required to administer tests developed by the state and to set and monitor adequate yearly progress (Moscosco, 2001; Wortham, 2002).

President Bush was also committed to strengthening early childhood programs. The early childhood education projects initiated by the Bush administration in 2002 stressed the importance of improving early childhood programs. Fortunately, child-outcome standards were also developed by professional organizations in addition to state education agencies. For example, the National Council for the Social Studies (1994) issued *Curriculum Standards for the Social Studies*. Improved Head Start Performance Standards published in 2009 included children from birth to age 5 (Head Start, 2009). Current Head Start Performance Standards (HHS/ACF/OHS, 2016) clarify that eligibility requirements apply to infants and toddlers under age 3 and preschoolers from age 3 to the age required

Search and Share 1.1

New Head Start Performance Standards

Explore the "Policy & Regulations" page of the Head Start website by searching for "Head Start" online; then, on the home page of the website, select the "Policy & Regulations" tab toward the top of the screen. On this page, you can learn more about the new Head Start Performance Standards. Share three regulations that are new to you with a classmate. How might they affect services for young children in Head Start?

for school entrance. These standards and others provide guidelines for early childhood educators as they strive to improve programs and experiences for young children.

By 2005, standards that included early childhood were available in many states. Some were in response to NCLB, but others were part of the emerging efforts to establish state and national standards for development and learning (Seefeldt, 2005). During the following decade, NCLB was used as a blueprint for proposed revisions by President Barack Obama's administration. On December 10, 2015, the Every Student Succeeds Act (ESSA) was signed by President Obama, which reauthorized the ESSA. Two provisions of ESSA included sustaining and expanding early childhood education and annual statewide assessment of all students (U.S. Department of Education, 2017b).

Issues in a New Century: The Accountability Era

The major issue in education today is the idea of accountability. Even before the rules and regulations surrounding the legislation for NCLB were issued, there were growing concerns about accountability. The interest in developing more responsibility for student results evolved from a perception that states had been evaluating school systems based on available resources rather than student performance. NCLB addressed student performance, public reporting of achievement results, consequences for poor student performance, and continuous improvement. Individual states were also responding to the need for accountability by moving from a focus on curriculum offerings and funding levels to standards-based accountability. States had set standards, developed assessment systems, and assigned responsibilities for meeting the goals and designating rewards and sanctions to achievement levels. If states wanted to continue getting benefits under NCLB, they had to follow the new policies for accountability (National Council of State Legislatures, 2009).

ISSUES WITH NCLB   The requirements of NCLB were to be implemented by 2006. In the summer of 2006, it was evident that there were difficulties in complying with the law. An early issue was the requirement that schools report test scores by racial subgroup. Nearly two dozen states had been granted waivers in reporting by subgroups. Other schools avoided the problem by determining that the numbers of students in racial subgroups were too small to be statistically significant; their scores were not included (Rebora, 2006).

The law also provided that states would implement standards-based assessments in reading and math by 2006. States were required to test students in reading and math annually in grades 3 to 8 and once again in grades 10 to 12 (New America Foundation Feedback, 2013). Ten states were notified in 2006 that a portion of state administrative funds would be withheld for failing to comply fully with NCLB. Twenty-five states

Assessments can be conducted while young children engage in classroom activities.

might also lose a portion of their aid if they did not comply fully with NCLB and comply with the testing requirement by the end of the school year. The monetary penalties caught many states by surprise. In addition, states had difficulty providing the extensive documentation required to demonstrate that the tests met that state's academic standards (Olson, 2006). Further, states had to demonstrate how they were including students with disabilities and English language learners (ELLs) in their testing system. This included developing alternative assessments when needed. When combined with concerns about testing young children in the early childhood years, NCLB had an impact on all populations of students, including those in the preschool years.

The reauthorization of NCLB was due in 2007. Congress had already blocked action on the reauthorization until after the 2008 election. The Obama administration indicated in 2009 that the rewriting of the law would focus on teacher quality and academic standards, and that more attention would be given to help failing schools and students. The Commission on No Child Left Behind (2009) urged Secretary of Education Arne Duncan to retain some core elements of NCLB. Regardless of the direction of continuing reform in education, the federal government continued to expand its influence on accountability and has also encouraged the movement from individual state standards to national standards (Dillon, 2009; *The New York Times*, 2009).

No changes were made to NCLB until 2014. States were increasingly concerned about the requirement that 100 percent of students be proficient in English language arts and math by 2014. In response to educators' concerns, then U.S. Education Secretary Arne Duncan allowed some states to have waivers from some requirements of NCLB. The resignations of key players in Congress who supported a strong role for the government in education and anxiety about the election in 2016 led to the passage of the Every Student Succeeds Act (ESSA). Subsequently, NCLB was replaced by ESSA in December 2015 (Tooley, 2015). The requirements under ESSA are similar to the policies expected that are on waivers under NCLB. States are allowed to develop their own accountability rating systems, but states were expected to help struggling schools.

Concerns about Assessing Infants and Toddlers

Screening of infants and toddlers in the early months is very important to monitoring development. Likewise, early identification of developmental delays or disorders is critical to the well-being of infants and their families. Delayed development may indicate an increased risk of other medical conditions or disorders.

There are challenges in early identification of disabilities, as early detection rates are lower than their actual numbers. One possible cause is that few pediatricians use effective strategies to screen their patients for developmental problems (American Academy of Pediatrics [AAP], 2002). The AAP recommended a process in 2006 for health care professionals to develop a practice to conduct surveillance screening from birth to beyond age 3. Development would be given attention at regular pediatric appointments (Pinto-Martin, Dunkle, Fliedner, & Landes, 2005).

Parents have a critical role in developmental screening. Consultants working with infant and toddler caregivers can provide training for observing children's development and communicating with parents about questions they may have about their child's development.

Enhanced eText: Video Example 1.3

Parents can be taught to engage in screening activities in the home. If a child is showing signs of hearing loss, for example, the parent can follow steps to determine whether the child is hearing adequately. Parents can also be given information on developmental guidelines so that they can contact their health care professional if they notice signs of delay (Ferrara, 2013).

Concerns about Assessing Young Children in Early Childhood Settings

The increased use of testing at all levels has been an issue in American education, but the assessment of young children is of particular concern. Standardized tests and other assessment measures are now being used in preschool, kindergarten, and primary grades to determine whether children will be admitted to preschool programs, promoted to the next grade, or retained. During the late 1980s and early 1990s, tests were used to determine whether students should be promoted from kindergarten to first grade or placed in a "transitional" first grade. Although this practice is now less popular, it persists in some school districts and states (Smith, 1999). In 2000, the National Association of Early Childhood Specialists in State Departments of Education (NAECS/SDE) was concerned about the continuing trend to deny children's entry to kindergarten and first grade. They issued a position statement, "Still! Unacceptable Trends in Kindergarten Entry and Placement" (NAECS/SDE, 2000). This continuing effort to advocate appropriate assessment of very young children was endorsed by the Governing Board of the National Association for the Education of Young Children (NAEYC, 2001).

By 2006, states used a wide range of types of screenings and assessments with young children entering public school. Screening tests were used in most states for hearing and vision, as were developmental screenings and readiness tests. Behavior screenings are also widely used as part of the preschool and kindergarten entrance activities. Many states conduct screening to identify children at risk for failing to succeed in school and/or for referral to determine developmental disorders or disabilities. Some states met the criteria for developmentally appropriate assessments first discussed by NAEYC, whereas others did not. For example, California required observation and portfolio materials in preschool assessments. On the other hand, Georgia students were tested for first-grade readiness at the end of the kindergarten year to determine grade placement (Education Commission of the States, 2006). More information on these topics is provided in later chapters.

The announcement by President Bush in 2003 that all Head Start students would be given a national standardized test assessment raised new concerns. At issue were the validity and reliability of tests for preschool children (Nagle, 2000) and whether such "high-stakes" testing should be used to evaluate the quality of Head Start programs (Shepard, Kagan, Lynn, & Wurtz, 1998). Policy makers had to address these and other concerns about appropriate assessment of young children in their decisions about how to evaluate preschool programs that receive federal funding (McMaken, 2003).

In February 2003, a large group of early childhood experts wrote to their congressional representatives to express their concerns about the impending test. They made the following points:

1. The test is too narrow.

2. The test may reduce the comprehensive services that ensure the success of Head Start.

3. The test is shifting resources away from other needs within Head Start.

4. Testing should be used to strengthen teaching practices, not to evaluate a program, and should in no way be linked to program funding (Fair Test, 2003; NAEYC, 2004).

In September 2003, the new test, the *National Reporting System (NRS)* (U.S. Department of Health and Human Services Head Start Bureau, 2003), was administered by the Head Start Bureau in the Department of Health and Human Services (HHS) Administration for Children and Families to more than 400,000 children ages 4 and 5; it continued to be administered each year. In 2005, when Head Start funding was being considered, the Government Accountability Office (GAO) issued a report on the NRS. The report stated that the NRS had not shown that it provided reliable information on children's progress during the Head Start program year, especially for Spanish-speaking children. Moreover, the NRS had not shown that its results were valid measures of the learning that took place in the program. In its recommendations, the GAO required that the Head Start Bureau establish validity and reliability for the NRS. As a result, the NRS was not to be used for accountability purposes related to program funding (Crawford, 2005; Government Accountability Office, 2005). Because the Bush administration reportedly intended to use the NRS to establish accountability requirements similar to those for NCLB, this GAO finding essentially halted the use of the test for that purpose. The NRS was suspended in 2007.

Concerns about Assessing Young Children with Cultural and Language Differences

A concurrent concern related to current trends and practices in the assessment of young children is the question of how appropriate our tests and assessment strategies are in terms of the diversity of young children attending early childhood programs. Socioeconomic groups are changing dramatically and rapidly in our society, with an expansion of families living in poverty and a corresponding shrinking of the middle class. At the same time, an increase in minority citizens has occurred as the result of the continuing influx of people from other countries, especially those in Southeast Asia and Latin America. The National Center for Educational Statistics (NCES) reports that in the 2014–15 school year, 9.4% of students (or 4.6 million students) were English language learners (ELLs), of which 16.7% were in kindergarten (NCES, 2017). In addition, approximately 460 languages are represented in schools and programs in the United States (Biggar, 2005; Lopez, Salas, & Flores, 2005). Currently, the most prevalent languages are Spanish, Arabic, Chinese, Vietnamese, Hmong, and Somali (NCES, 2017). Assessment of the developmental progress of children from these groups is particularly important if their learning needs are to be identified and addressed.

Evidence shows that standardized test scores are highly correlated to parents' occupations and level of education, the location of the student's elementary school, and the family's income bracket. Moreover, students from limited English backgrounds tend to score lower on reading and language fluency tests in English. They typically perform better on computational portions of mathematics tests (Wesson, 2001) because math tests may be less dependent on English fluency. The fairness of existing tests for children who are school disadvantaged and linguistically and culturally diverse indicates the need for alternative assessment strategies for young children (Biggar, 2005; Goodwin & Goodwin, 1993, 1997). A major issue in the 21st century is appropriate measurement and evaluation strategies that will enhance, rather than diminish, their potential for achievement.

The history of assessment of minorities who are bilingual students or learning English as a second language is one of potential bias. Children have been, and continue to be, tested in their nondominant language (English) or with instruments that were validated on Anglo, middle-class samples of children. As a result, many Hispanic preschool children were and are still regularly diagnosed as being developmentally delayed or speech/language delayed or as having some other type of disability and placed in special education (Lopez et al., 2005). The issue of appropriate assessment of these children was addressed by court cases such as *Diana v. California State Board of Education* (1968) and *Lau v. Nichols* (1974). More recently, NCLB and Head Start have addressed the issue of testing ELLs (Crawford, 2005; David, 2005; Government Accountability Office, 2005).

The disproportionality of minority students in special education is often related to language and cultural differences. Some of the issues addressed in the rising numbers of minority children being referred to special education include inconsistent methods of determining home language and English proficiency, confusion about the purpose of language screening instruments, and a need for more teacher training in meeting the needs of culturally and linguistically diverse children and families (Abebe & Hailemariam, 2008; Hardin, Roach-Scott, & Peisner-Feinberg, 2007). Most recently, researchers have advocated for systemic change in the public school system that would support a more equitable approach for identifying and placing children in special education (Sullivan, Artiles, & Hernandez-Saca, 2015). The model they propose is built around Bronfenbrenner's theoretical model (Bronfenbrenner, 1995, 2004) and would include a leadership consulting team to work with local stakeholders (e.g., teachers, administrators) to understand the local system of services and then design and implement changes that would ensure greater equity.

Increasing concerns about overidentification of minority children is addressed in two significant books. *Why Are So Many Minority Students in Special Education? Understanding Race and Disability in Schools* (Harry & Klingner, 2005) is one effort to explain the problem. The authors address the issue of the disproportionate representation of minorities in special education. *Racial Inequity in Education* (Losen & Orfield, 2002) addresses many factors, including language, high-stakes testing, inappropriate and inadequate special education for minority children, and the role of the federal government.

On December 19, 2016, the U.S. Department of Education published final regulations to address this disparity and establish greater equity as an amendment under IDEA 2004, which went into effect on January 18, 2017. The new regulation, *Assistance to States for the Education of Children with Disabilities; Preschool Grants for Children with Disabilities*, describes a standard methodology for states to:

> . . . determine whether significant disproportionality based on race and ethnicity is occurring in the State and in its local educational agencies (LEAs); clarify that States must address significant disproportionality in the incidence, duration, and type of disciplinary actions, including suspensions and expulsions, using the same statutory remedies required to address significant disproportionality in the identification and placement of children with disabilities; clarify requirements for the review and revision of policies, practices, and procedures when significant disproportionality is found; and require that LEAs identify and address the factors contributing to significant disproportionality as part of comprehensive coordinated early intervening services (comprehensive CEIS) and allow these services for children from age 3 through grade 12, with and without disabilities (U.S. Department of Education, 2016, p. 92376).

Another concern about testing children with cultural and language differences is the process of screening preschool children who fit into this category. A problem of correctly screening young children who are learning English may lead to the underidentification of children who have special needs or to the overidentification of special needs because English language delays are misdiagnosed as a disability (NAEYC, 2005a). Recommendations were made by NAEYC and the Division for Early Childhood of the Council for Exceptional Children (2007), and other national organizations for appropriate screening and assessment procedures and program accountability.

The impact of NCLB on testing ELLs resulted in the development of new English language proficiency tests based on new standards adopted by each state. More importantly, the tests measured the reading, writing, speaking, and listening skills of ELLs (Zehr, 2006). In the summer of 2006, five states had failed to meet the U.S. Department of Education's deadline to have tests in place. While some states designed their own tests, other states adopted tests designed by consortia or testing corporations. Nevertheless, because test development and implementation were still in the beginning stages, little was known about the validity and reliability of the tests and whether the tests met the requirements of the law. The New York example reveals the complexity of the assessment of ELLs. The New York State test was designed to measure language acquisition, whereas the tests meeting NCLB requirements measured English language skills. This was true for bilingual and ELL programs throughout the United States prior to NCLB. It would take many years to develop and validate tests that would resolve how to assess the language skills of limited-English speakers that were comparable with tests for English-speaking students.

When the NCLB was scheduled for reauthorization in 2007, it was estimated that ELL students' performance was 20% to 30% below that of non-ELL students. Legislators proposed giving schools more time for ELLs to meet the standards. As the numbers of ELLs continued to increase, constant changes meant the ELL students' status was unstable. ELL students' status changed as new language learners entered school. Differences in learning rates in acquiring English made proficiency a complex issue (DeVoe, 2007).

By 2011, four consortia of states developed ELL tests to rigorous state content standards. The tests were very similar. As some states implemented these tests, the issues of adequate English mastery continued. However, because the tests emphasized formative development, educators had hopes that test results would be constructive in determining student strengths and needs (Bunch, 2011).

Assessment of young children who are from families that are culturally and linguistically diverse must include many dimensions of diversity. The many variations within communities and cultures must be considered, among them the educational background of the parents and the culture of the immediate community of the family. These **funds of knowledge** can help the assessment process be more authentic because they contribute information that the children and families bring with them to the education settings (Moll, Amanti, Neff, & Gonzalez, 1992). Congruence between the individual cultural perceptions of the assessors and the children being assessed, even when both are from the same culture or language population, must also be considered in order to have more authentic information about children's skill development (Barrera, 1996). Many types of information, including the child's background and the use of assessments, must be combined to determine a picture of the child that reflects individual, group, and family cultural characteristics (Lopez et al., 2005).

Enhanced eText: Application Exercise 1.1

Concerns about Assessing Young Children with Disabilities

The use of testing for infants and young children with disabilities cannot be avoided. Indeed, Meisels, Steele, and Quinn-Leering (1993) reflected that not all tests used were bad. Nevertheless, Greenspan, Meisels, and the Zero to Three Work Group on Developmental Assessment (1996) believed that assessments used with infants and young children were borrowed from assessment methodology used with older children that does not represent meaningful information about their developmental achievements and capacities. Misleading test scores were being used for decisions about services, educational placements, and intervention programs. These developmental psychologists propose that assessment should be based on current understanding of development and use structured tests as one part of an integrated approach that includes observing the child's interactions with trusted caregivers. Assessment should be based on multiple sources of information that reflect the child's capacities and competencies and better indicate what learning environments will best provide intervention services for the child's optimal development.

Play-based assessment is one major source of information among the multiple sources recommended. Play assessment is nonthreatening and can be done unobtrusively. Moreover, during play, children can demonstrate skills and abilities that might not be apparent in other forms of assessment. Children's ability to initiate and carry out play schemes and use play materials can add significant information (Fewell & Rich, 1987; Segal & Webber, 1996). In transdisciplinary play-based assessment, a team that includes parents observes a child at play. Each member of the team observes an area of development. During the assessment, the child's developmental level, learning styles, patterns of interaction, and other behaviors are observed (Linder, 1993, 2008).

NCLB and ESSA have had an impact on curriculum and assessment of children with disabilities. Although identification of children can begin very early in life, the needs of the children as they enter public education are not usually identified until first grade. However, during the last 10 years, the nature and objectives of kindergarten have changed because of advances in knowledge about what young children are capable of learning and the advent of the standards-based accountability movement. Kindergarteners are taught and tested on the mastery of academic standards. This change in expectations has affected the kindergarten year for children at risk for learning disabilities. The kindergarten year formerly was used to work with at-risk children and refer them for testing at the end of the year. When they reached first grade, they would be referred for identification and possible special education services. Children with disabilities or those who are at risk for learning problems now need identification and services earlier than first grade. Identification of disabilities and referral for services should now be considered for the kindergarten year, even if some disabilities are difficult to identify in early childhood (Litty & Hatch, 2006). While the policies for identifying and serving young children with disabilities under IDEA 2004 have not changed, the Office of Special Education Programs issued a statement in January 2017 that outlined in detail the importance of examining the individual needs of young children and securing the most appropriate free public education needed for school success (U.S. Department of Education, Office of Special Education Programs, 2017).

NCLB, and subsequently ESSA, also added accountability measures to IDEA. School districts must test at least 95% of students with disabilities and incorporate their test scores into school ratings. There has been strong public reaction to the inclusion of special education students in state testing and reporting. Some policy makers see this provision as an important step in every child receiving a high-quality education. Critics worry that the law is not flexible enough to meet the individual needs of students with disabilities. Many teachers feel that special education students should not be expected to meet the same set of academic content standards as regular education students. These issues were yet to be resolved when the final regulations for IDEA 2004 were published in August 2006 (*Education Week*, n.d.; U.S. Department of Education, 2006).

Since 2006, work has continued to address the issue of identifying and serving students with learning disabilities. The focus of this effort has been to find more flexible and research-based strategies for both identifying students who need intervention services and better serving students with quality instruction and evaluation (Division for Early Childhood of the Council for Exceptional Children, 2007). Two models for a more inclusive instructional process for all students are Response to Intervention (RTI) and Universal Design for Learning (UDL).

RTI addresses all student needs regardless of whether students have been identified as learning disabled. It is a schoolwide, multilevel prevention system to improve student achievement and reduce behavior problems. Although its first component is to identify students at risk of poor success in learning, it is a prevention program for all students (Burns & Coolong-Chaffin, 2006; Millard, 2004). There are three levels of prevention in RTI, and states, districts, and schools can have multiple tiers within these three levels of instruction to meet the needs of students. All students begin at the first tier. Students who need more targeted education are served in the second tier. Students who need intensive intervention are served in the third tier. This third tier can include special education services.

The RTI model seeks to match students with the most effective instruction. The core features of RTI are high-quality classroom instruction, research-based instruction, classroom performance, universal screening, continuous progress monitoring during interventions, and fidelity measures (Millard, 2004). The essential components of the RTI system are screening, progress monitoring, the schoolwide system prevention system discussed earlier, and data-based decision making where the information from screening and prevention efforts is used to adjust the type of responsiveness based on

Search and Share 1.2

Response to Intervention in Early Childhood

Search online for the NAEYC website. On the NAEYC website's home page, select the tab "Topics" toward the top of the screen. Then, from the dropdown menu, select "Response to Intervention" to learn about the components of the *Frameworks for Response to Intervention in Early Childhood: Description and Implications*. What do you think is the most important aspect of RTI for young children? Why?

the student's response to instruction (National Center on Response to Intervention, n.d.). In 2013, a joint position statement titled *Frameworks for Response to Intervention in Early Childhood: Description and Implications* was issued by leading early childhood professional organizations (Division for Early Childhood of the Council for Exceptional Children [DEC], National Association for the Education of Young Children [NAEYC], & National Head Start Assocation [NHSA], 2013). This statement outlines the components of RTI and describes how they interface with early childhood education services to promote positive outcomes for children.

UDL also seeks to include all kinds of students, including those with learning disabilities, English language barriers, emotional or behavior problems, lack of interest or engagement, or sensory and physical disabilities. UDL is based on the need for multiple approaches to instruction that meet the needs of diverse students (Center for Applied Special Technology [CAST], 2009). It applies recent neuroscience research and uses technology to make learning more effective for all students. The curriculum includes customized teaching that implements multiple means of representation, multiple means of action and expression, and multiple means of engagement (CAST, 2009).

Trends in a New Century

Current practices for assessing young children have evolved over time. Technology, new and updated assessment tools, and evidence indicating the best approach to assessing children have brought about new trends. Some of the key trends are described below.

AUTHENTIC AND PERFORMANCE ASSESSMENT Assessment is in a period of transition. Teachers of young children are moving from more traditional strategies of assessing for knowledge and facts to assessing the students' ability to reason and solve problems. Despite the demands for accountability for addressing early childhood standards, assessments provide a variety of methods for children to demonstrate what they understand and can do.

A broader view of assessment has incorporated a multidimensional approach to measurement, as described earlier in the sections on concerns about assessment of children from diverse populations and children with disabilities. It is now felt that too much attention has been given to the use of standardized tests, rather than to a multidimensional approach that uses many sources of information. The more inclusive practice of assessment, which includes work samples, observation results, and teaching report forms, is called **alternative assessment**. These alternatives to standardized tests measure how students can apply the knowledge they have learned (Blum & Arter, 1996; Maeroff, 1991). Within this evolution in the purposes for assessment and interpretation of assessments is the move to authentic and performance assessments.

Authentic assessments must have some connection to the real world; that is, they must have a meaningful context. They are contextual in that they emerge from the child's accomplishments. **Performance assessments** permit the child to demonstrate what is understood through the performance of a task or activity (Wortham, 1998).

Performance assessment as applied through the use of portfolios provides a multi-faceted view of what the young child can understand and use. Performance assessment is used because teachers in early childhood programs seek information about the child's development and accomplishments in all domains. Performance assessment combined with other assessments provides a longitudinal record of change in development, rather than an assessment of a limited range of skills at a particular time. It is appropriately used with infants, young children, school-age children, children from diverse populations, and children with disabilities (Barrera, 1996; Meisels, 1996; Wortham, 1998).

Pedagogical documentation is another form of performance assessment. First developed in Reggio Emilia schools in Italy and now widely used in the United States, pedagogical documentation is a process of collecting and displaying children's work on projects to assess their skill development and instructional needs (Wurm, 2005). More about pedagogical documentation is discussed in Chapter 8.

This broader view of assessment in early childhood programs is echoed by the organizations that endorsed and supported the *Guidelines for Appropriate Curriculum Content and Assessment in Programs Serving Children Ages 3 through 8*, a position statement of the NAEYC and the NAECS/SDE adopted in 1990 and renewed in 2000 and 2001 (NAEYC, 1992; NAECS/SDE, 2000). These guidelines proposed that the purpose of assessment is to benefit individual children and to improve early childhood programs. Appropriate assessment should help enhance curriculum choices, help teachers collaborate with parents, and help ensure that the needs of children are addressed appropriately. Rather than being narrowly defined as testing, assessment should link curriculum and instruction with program objectives for young children (Hills, 1992). Authentic and performance assessments provide dynamic assessment approaches that benefit the child, parents, caregivers, and teachers.

Finally, studies conducted by the Division for Early Childhood of the Council for Exceptional Children, the National Research Council, the National Goals Panel, and the National Association for the Education of Young Children focused on three big ideas shared by the organizations. The first big idea was that assessment must be purposeful. This was in response to assessments that were used for purposes for which they were not designed. The second big idea was that assessment should be aligned with instruction. This included alignment with curriculum standards. The third big idea was related to the benefits of assessment. Assessments should justify the time taken from instruction and not result in negative consequences for some children (Jiban, 2013).

STANDARDS FOR BEGINNING TEACHERS   The era of accountability includes expectations for the appropriate preparation of teachers. Just as states set standards for student curriculum and assessment for diverse children, there are standards for preparing and assessing whether teachers and other professionals are qualified to educate young children.

The Interstate New Teacher Assessment and Support Consortium (INTASC) includes state education agencies and national education organizations. The consortium believes that each state's education system should have a teacher licensing policy that requires teachers to know how and be able to effectively help all students achieve the state standards for students (Council of Chief State School Officers, 2007, 2009).

The Mission of INTASC

The mission of INTASC is to provide a forum for its member states to learn and collaborate in the development of

- Compatible educational policy on teaching among the states.
- New accountability requirements for teacher preparation programs.
- New techniques to assess the performance of teachers for licensing and evaluation.
- New programs to enhance the professional development of teachers (Council of Chief State School Officers, 2007, p. 1).

The *INTASC Model Core Teaching Standards: A Resource for State Dialogue* (INTASC, 2011) discussed what all teachers across all grade levels should know and be able to do to be effective teachers. Subsequently, in 2013, the *INTASC Model Core Teaching Standards and Learning Progressions for Teachers 1.0: A Resource for Ongoing Teacher Development* (INTASC, 2013) was released. This tool described the increasing complexity of teaching practice so that educators could understand effective practice across three developmental levels.

The licensing standards for early childhood teachers have been addressed by three organizations: the Association of Teacher Education (ATE), the National Association for the Education of Young Children (NAEYC), and the Association for Childhood Education International (ACEI). A position statement on early childhood teachers was issued by ATE and NAEYC in 1991 (ATE & NAEYC, 1991). The position statement also calls for state early childhood organizations and agencies to develop policies leading to certification that are distinct from policies related to elementary and secondary certification. In addition, policies for early childhood teachers should be congruent across the 50 states.

The *Position Paper on the Preparation of Early Childhood Education Teachers* was issued by ACEI in 1998 (ACEI, 1998). It calls for early childhood specialization to be developed within broader policies for teacher preparation. Early childhood teachers should have a broad and liberal education. Experiences should also include foundations of early childhood education, child development, the teaching and learning process, and provisions for professional laboratory experiences.

NAEYC also developed a position statement on ethical conduct (NAEYC, 2005b). Standards of ethical behavior by early childhood care and education teachers are based on a commitment to

- Appreciate childhood as a unique and valuable stage of the human life cycle.
- Base our work on knowledge of how children develop and learn.
- Appreciate and support the bond between child and family.
- Recognize that children are best understood and supported in the context of family, culture, community, and society.
- Respect the dignity, worth, and uniqueness of each individual (child, family member, and colleague).
- Respect diversity in children, families, and colleagues.
- Recognize that children and adults achieve their full potential in the context of relationships that are based on trust and respect (NAEYC, 2005b, p. 1).

The most recent effort to establish standards for beginning teachers was made by the Council for the Accreditation of Educator Preparation (CAEP). Although the council is charged with accrediting institutions that prepare teachers, the standards themselves are focused on student outcomes. The five standards are as follows:

- Standard 1: Content and Pedagogy
- Standard 2: Clinical Partnerships and Practice
- Standard 3: Candidate Quality, Recruitment, and Selectivity
- Standard 4: Program Impact
- Standard 5: Provider Quality Assurance and Continuous Improvement

The standards are complementary with INTASC standards. The relationship between teacher preparation and the impact of teacher instruction is basic to both INTASC and CAEP (CAEP, 2013).

COMMON CORE STANDARDS   The Common Core Standards were developed as a result of organizational concerns that test scores for graduation varied widely from state to state. Moreover, students' performance on state tests differed from performance on the National Assessment of Educational Progress (NAEP). Two organizations, the National Governor's Association and the Council of Chief State School Officers, decided to work together to develop a single set of standards and common grading criteria. In 2009, all but four states signed on to the Common Core Standards and promised to help create and implement them by 2014 (Common Core State Standards Initiative, 2010). In 2013, the reviews of the standards were mixed. Some teachers using the standards had positive opinions. One observed that Common Core Standards set standards that were higher than the ones individual states had established on their own. Others praised the standards for being based on the highest-quality research in the field (Toppo, 2012).

There were also many criticisms. Diane Ravitch, a leader in educational reform, suggested that there was no convincing evidence that students would be better prepared for college and success because of the Common Core Standards. She proposed that developers of Common Core Standards made many promises that contained no evidence that the standards could be achieved. She joined others in pointing out that where students were already taking Common Core Standards tests, their scores had plummeted. As well, only 5% of students were able to pass the test (Han, 2013; Ravitch, 2013; Rich, 2013).

Critics also pointed out that a large number of states signed up for the new standards because they were seeking waivers from NCLB or funding for the new program Race to the Top (discussed in the next section).

States complained that preparing teachers for the challenges of preparing students for a more difficult curriculum were such that they needed more time before their professional evaluations reflected the new test scores. Responding to this and other complaints, Secretary of Education Arne Duncan postponed making career decisions about teachers based on the new tests until 2016–17 (Rich, 2013).

In the fall of 2013, some states had pulled out of the Common Core Standards program for various reasons. There were now several sources of tests, leading to some concerns that student achievement could not be compared across states. States were also finding that the new tests were more costly than previous ones, and some states felt that financial restrictions would prevent them from compliance with the technology required by the program. The Common Core Standards curriculum was destined to face serious challenges as it approached its first year of full implementation in 2014 (Ujifusa, 2015).

RACE TO THE TOP   The Race to the Top program was another effort to improve education outcomes that was funded by the American Recovery and Reinvestment Act of 2009. The legislation was designed to stimulate the economy, support job creation, and invest in education. The Race to the Top Fund was a competitive grant for secondary education to reward states that are developing and using innovative strategies that will improve student learning and result in closing achievement gaps, improving high school graduation rates, and preparing students for college.

Race to the Top has four education reform areas:

- Adopting standards and assessments that prepare students to succeed in college and the workplace and to compete in the global economy;
- Building data systems that measure student growth and success, and inform teachers and principals about how they can improve instruction;
- Recruiting, developing, rewarding, and retaining effective teachers and principals, especially where they are needed most; and
- Turning around our lowest-achieving schools (U.S. Department of Education, 2009).

There were 12 recipients in the first group of states that received grants in the first round of grants. At the end of the 2012–13 school year, 6 of the 12 recipients had fully implemented their programs, including teacher and principal evaluation systems. However, as with the difficulties experienced with teacher evaluation in the Common Core Standards program, some states were experiencing delays in developing and putting their teacher and evaluation systems in place. The original states reported teacher concerns with the new evaluation system. However, participating states reported high confidence in the support given to them by the Department of Education. They felt that the Department of Education's role in monitoring and helping recipients was very successful (Klein, 2013; U.S. Department of Education, 2009).

The Race to the Top – Early Learning Challenge (RTT-ELC) was directed at early childhood programs. This program, related to the Race to the Top program, first accepted applications in 2013. The awards were to go to "states that are leading the way with ambitious yet achievable plans for implementing coherent, compelling, and comprehensive early learning education reform" (U.S. Department of Education, 2013).

The U.S. Department of Education issued a report on Race to the Top in 2015. In that report, a positive overview of Race to the Top focused on success stories, including rising graduation rates and higher passing rates by students taking advanced placement stories (Ujifusa, 2015; U.S. Department of Education, 2015). However, the report neglected to address the issues with teacher evaluations. Declining scores on the National Assessment of Educational Progress (NAEP) were also a problem. A study conducted by the Economic Policy Institute in 2013 examined progress with Race to the Top in the third year of implementation. Among their findings were that the grantee states promised to raise student achievements to unrealistic levels and had to delay design and implementation of teacher evaluation systems due to time factors that prevented their development (Weiss, 2013).

The 2016 election brought a new direction in education at all levels. The new president, Donald Trump, selected Betsy DeVos, a strong supporter of charter schools, as Secretary of Education. In the fiscal year 2018 budget, some existing programs were eliminated or given reduced funding. A stated goal for the Department of Education was to return decision making to the states and give parents more control over their children's education. The budget included a $167 million increase for the Charter Schools Program as well as funding for innovative initiatives. More than 30 programs were reduced or eliminated after being designated as better addressed at the state or local level. Secretary DeVos proposed that every state should provide choices and equal opportunity to meet the needs of that state's children (U.S. Department of Education, 2017b).

Enhanced eText: Self-Check 1.3

Summary

The measurement and assessment of children begins very early in the life span. Newborns are tested for their neonatal status, and infant tests designed to assess development begin the trend for testing and assessment in the early childhood years. Assessments in the early childhood years have many purposes; some are beneficial for young children, and others are detrimental.

The advent of measures to assess and evaluate young children's development and learning occurred at the beginning of the 20th century. As the decades passed, significant trends in the study of young children and services and programs implemented for young children have driven the need to develop standardized tests and other measures to evaluate children's progress and program effectiveness.

Many issues surround the testing of young children. Some educators question the validity and reliability of standardized tests used with young children, as well as the purposes for administering tests to children who are culturally and linguistically diverse. At the same time, the use of individual testing and evaluation to identify children with disabilities and provide services for them continues to serve a valuable purpose.

The 21st century brought new issues and trends. The No Child Left Behind (NCLB) law was intended to raise student achievement through policies established when the law was initiated; however, there were difficulties with achieving goals set by NCLB. The ongoing issues with NCLB delayed reauthorization of the law. In the meantime, Common Core Standards that overlap NCLB were developed. The Common Core Standards also encountered difficulties in evaluating teachers and conflicts about waivers related to NCLB. Yet another program, Race to the Top, introduced a competitive grant program to reward schools with innovative strategies to increase student learning. The first cohort of 12 school districts had mixed success at the end of the first year.

The presidential election of 2016 brought major changes to the U.S. Department of Education. With a Republican president and both houses of Congress under Republican control, the future of public education seemed headed in a new direction. In 2017, the implications for the future of education were still unclear, with many factors affecting how children would be taught. Studies of national programs implemented to improve the educational outcomes of minority and low-income students showed that lower achievement in this population of students persisted regardless of what type of effort was funded at the federal level. The efforts of the Department of Education to return reform efforts to the state and local levels made it unclear how educational transformation would fare. The new Secretary of Education, Betsy DeVos, proposed that any options for improving education should be accountable directly to parents and communities, not to Washington, DC (U.S. Department of Education, 2017a).

Enhanced eText: Self-Check: Chapter Review

Suggested Activities

1. Review a recent journal article on a topic related to current issues in the testing and assessment of young children. The article should have been published within the past 5 years. Describe the major points in the article and your response. Be prepared to share your findings in small groups.

2. What policies are followed in your state regarding the use of standardized tests? What tests are administered in the primary grades? How are they chosen? How are the results used?

3. How does the school district in your community screen preschool children for possible disabilities? What types of assessments are used? If children need further testing to identify specific needs, what process is used? Who conducts the tests with the child?

Key Terms

alternative assessment 20

assessment 2

authentic assessment (authentic performance assessment) 21

funds of knowledge 18

inclusion 10

least restrictive environment (LRE) 9

mainstreaming 9

observation 2

pedagogical documentation 21

performance assessment 21

screening 3

Selected Organizations

Search for the following organizations online:

National Child Care Information and Technical Assistance Center

National Conference of State Legislatures

Association for Childhood Education International

National Association for the Education of Young Children

Council of Chief State School Officers

Division for Early Childhood/Council for Exceptional Children

---

References

Abebe, S., & Hailemariam, A. (2008). Factors influencing teachers' decisions to refer students for special education evaluation. Retrieved July 15, 2009, from http://ERICWebPortal/custom/portlets/recordED503139

American Academy of Pediatrics (AAP). Medical Home Initiatives for Children with Special Needs Project Advisory Committee. (2002). The medical home. *Pediatrics, 10,* 184–186.

Association for Childhood Education International (ACEI). (1998). ACEI position paper: Preparation of early childhood education teachers. Retrieved July 16, 2009, from http://www.acei.org/prepec.htm

Association of Teacher Educators (ATE) & National Association for the Education of Young Children (NAEYC) (1991, July/August). *Early childhood teacher certification: A position statement of the Association of Teacher Educators and the National Association for the Education of Young Children.* Washington, DC: NAEYC.

Barrera, I. (1996). Thoughts on the assessment of young children whose sociocultural background is unfamiliar to the assessor. In S. J. Meisels & E. Fenichel (Eds.), *New visions for the developmental assessment of infants and young children* (pp. 69–84). Washington, DC: Zero to Three: National Center for Infants, Toddlers, and Families.

Begley, S. (1997, Spring/Summer). How to build a baby's brain. *Newsweek Special Edition,* 28–32.

Biggar, H. (2005). NAEYC recommendations on screening and assessment of young English-language learners. *Young Children, 60*(6), 44–47.

Blum, R. E., & Arter, J. A. (1996). Setting the stage. In R. E. Blum & J. A. Arter (Eds.), *A handbook for student performance assessment in an era of restructuring* (pp. I:1–I:2). Alexandria, VA: Association for Supervision and Curriculum Development.

Bronfenbrenner, U. (1995). The bioecological perspective from a life course perspective: Reflections of a participant observer. In P. Moen, G. H. Edler, & K. Luscher (Eds.), *Examining lives in context* (pp. 549–618). Washington, DC: American Psychological Association.

Bronfenbrenner, U. (2004). *Making human beings human: Bioecological perspectives on human development.* Thousand Oaks, CA: Sage Publications.

Bunch, M. B. (2011, July). Testing English language learners under No Child Left Behind. *Language Testing, 28,* 323–331.

Burns, M. K., & Coolong-Chaffin, M. (2006, November). Response to intervention: The rate of and effect on school psychology. *School Psychology Forum: Research in Practice, 1,* 3–15.

Center for Applied Special Technology (CAST). (2009). What is universal design for learning? Retrieved July 15, 2009, from http://www.cast.org/research/wd/index.html

Cicchetti, D., & Wagner, S. (1990). Alternative assessment strategies for the evaluation of infants and toddlers: An organizational perspective. In S. J. Meisels & J. P. Shonkoff (Eds.), *Handbook of early childhood intervention* (pp. 246–277). New York, NY: Cambridge University Press.

Clark, E. A. (1976). Teacher attitudes toward integration of children with handicaps. *Education and Training of the Mentally Retarded, 11,* 333–335.

Commission on No Child Left Behind. The Aspen Institute. (2009, July 13). Commission urges Duncan to uphold core NCLB elements in the law. Retrieved July 21, 2009, from http://www.aspeninstitute .org/2009/07/13/commission

Common Core State Standards Initiative. (2010). Implementing the Common Core State Standards. Retrieved August 28, 2013, from http://www .corestandards.org

Council for the Accreditation of Educator Preparation (CAEP). (2010). CAEP standards for accreditation of educator preparation. Retrieved September 24, 2013, from http://www.caepsite .org/standards/html

Council of Chief State School Officers. (2009). INTASC standards development. Retrieved July 16, 2009, from http://www.ccsso.org/projects/ Interstate_new_teacher_assessment

Council of Chief State School Officers. (2011). Interstate New Teacher Assessment and Support Consortium (INTASC). Retrieved from https:// ccsso.org/sites/default/files/2017-11/InTASC_ Model_Core_Teaching_Standards_2011.pdf

Crawford, J. (2005, May/June). Test driven. *NABE News, 28,* 1.

Cronbach, L. J. (1990). *Essentials of psychological testing* (5th ed.). New York, NY: Harper & Row.

David, J. (2005). Head Start embraces language diversity. *Young Children, 60*(6), 40–43.

DEC/NAEYC. (2009). *Early childhood inclusion: A joint position statement of the Division for Early Childhood of the Council for Exceptional Children (DEC) and the National Associaiton for the Education of Young Children (NAEYC).* Chapel Hill: The University of North Carolina, FPG Child Development Institute.

Deiner, P. L. (1993). *Resources for teaching children with diverse abilities.* Fort Worth, TX: Harcourt Brace Jovanovich.

DeVoe, J. J. (2007). ELL testing: A state of flux. Retrieved August 11, 2013, from http://www.districtadministration.com/article/ell-testing-state-flux

DeWitt, P. (2014, October 14). 10 critical issues facing education. Retrieved July 18, 2017, from http://blogs.edweek.org/edweek/finding_common_ground/2014/01/10_critical_issues_facing_education.html

Dillon, S. (2009, April 14). Education standards likely to see toughening. *The New York Times*, 1–4. Retrieved July 2, 2009, from http://www.nytimes.com/2009/04/15/education

Division for Early Childhood of the Council for Exceptional Children. (2007). *Promoting positive outcomes for children with disabilities.* Missoula, MT: Author.

Division for Early Childhood of the Council for Exceptional Children (DEC), National Association for the Education of Young Children (NAEYC), & National Head Start Association (NHSA). (2013). *Frameworks for response to intervention in early childhood: Description and implications.* Washington, DC: Authors.

Early Head Start National Resource Center. (2011, February 18). Technical assistance paper no. 4. Retrieved August 9, 2013, from http://ecfacenter.org/topics/earlyed/screeneal.asp

Education Commission of the States. (2006). Kindergarten screening and assessment requirements. Retrieved January 29, 2007, from http://mb2.ecs.org/reports/Report.aspx?id=31

Education Week. (n.d.). *Special education.* Retrieved January 29, 2007, from http://www.edweek.org/rc/issues/special_education

Epstein, A. S., Schweinhart, L. J., DeBruin-Parecki, A., & Robin, K. B. (2004). *Preschool assessment: A guide to developing a balanced approach.* New Brunswick, NJ: National Institute for Early Education Research.

Fair Test. (2003). Head Start letter. Retrieved January 29, 2007, from http://www.fairtest.org/nattest/Head_Start_Letter.html

Ferrara, D. (2013, August). How to test hearing in an infant at home. Retrieved August 17, 2013, from Livestrong.org

Fewell, R. R., & Rich, J. (1987). Play assessment as a procedure for examining cognitive, communication, and social skills in multihandicapped children. *Journal of Psychoeducational Assessment, 2,* 107–118.

Fletcher, D. (2009, December 11). A brief history of standardized testing. Retrieved August 27, 2013, from http://www.time.com/timenation/article/0,8599,1947019.00.html

Froebel, F. (1896). *Education of man.* New York, NY: Appleton.

Gardner, J. W. (1961). *Excellence: Can we be equal and excellent too?* New York, NY: Harper & Row.

Goodwin, W. L., & Goodwin, L. D. (1993). Young children and measurement: Standardized and nonstandardized instruments in early childhood education. In B. Spodek (Ed.), *Handbook of research on the education of young children* (pp. 441–463). New York, NY: Macmillan.

Goodwin, W. L., & Goodwin, L. D. (1997). Using standardized measures for evaluating young children's learning. In B. Spodek & O. N. Saracho (Eds.), *Issues in early childhood educational assessment and evaluation* (pp. 92–107). New York, NY: Teachers College Press.

Government Accountability Office. (2005, May). Further development could allow results of new test to be used for decision making. Retrieved January 29, 2007, from http://www.gao.gov/new.items/d05343.pdf

Greenspan, S. I., Meisels, S. J., & the Zero to Three Work Group on Developmental Assessment. (1996). Toward a new vision for the developmental assessment of infants and young children. In S. J. Meisels & E. Fenichel (Eds.), *New visions for the developmental assessment of infants and young children* (pp. 11–26). Washington, DC: Zero to Three: National Center for Infants, Toddlers, and Families.

Guralnick, M. J. (1982). Mainstreaming young handicapped children: A public policy and ecological systems analysis. In B. Spodek (Ed.), *Handbook of research in early childhood education* (pp. 456–500). New York, NY: Free Press.

Hacker, A., & Deifus, C. (2013, June 8). Who's minding the schools? *The New York Times.* Retrieved September 6, 2013, from NYTimes.com

Hardin, B. J., Roach-Scott, M., & Peisner-Feinberg, E. S. (2007). Special education referral evaluation and placement practices for preschool English language learners. *Journal of Research in Childhood Education, 22,* 39–54.

Harry, B., & Klingner, J. (2005). *Why are so many minority students in special education? Understanding race and disability in schools.* New York, NY: Teachers College Press.

Head Start (2009). *Program Performance Standards for the operation of Head Start Programs 45CFR, Chapter XIII. RTN0970-AC63 Department of Health and Human Services. Part 1302--Program Operations.*

HHS/ACF/OHS. (2010). *Revisiting and updating the multicultural principles for Head Start children ages birth to five.* Washington, DC: Authors.

HHS/ACF/OHS. (2016). *Head Start program performance standards.* Washington, DC: Authors.

HHS/ACF/OHS. (2017, September 6). Office of Head Start—Services snapshot, national all programs (2015–2016). Retrieved from https://eclkc.ohs.acf.hhs.gov/sites/default/files/pdf/service-snapshot-all-programs-2015-2016.pdf

Hills, T. W. (1992). Reaching potentials through appropriate assessment. In S. Bredekamp & T. Rosegrant (Eds.), *Reaching potentials: Appropriate curriculum and assessment for young children* (pp. 43–64). Washington, DC: National Association for the Education of Young Children.

Hoepfner, R., Stern, C., & Nummedal, S. (Eds.). (1971). *CSE-ECRC preschool/kindergarten test evaluations.* Los Angeles, CA: University of California, Graduate School of Education.

Interstate New Teacher Assessment and Support Consortium (INTASC-CCSO) 2013. Learning progressions for teachers.

Irwin, D. M., & Bushnell, M. M. (1980). *Observational strategies for child study.* New York, NY: Holt, Rinehart & Winston.

Jiban, C. (2013, March). *Early childhood assessment: Implementing effective practice.* Portland, OR: Northwest Evaluation Association.

Kaplan, R. M., & Saccuzzo, D. P. (1989). *Psychological testing: Principles, applications, and issues* (2nd ed.). Belmont, CA: Brooks/Cole.

Kessen, W. (1965). *The child.* New York, NY: Wiley.

Klein, A. (2013, September 19). GAO Race to Top states have mixed record on teacher evaluation. Retrieved September 24, 2013, from http://blogs.edweek.org/edweek/campaign-k-12/2013.09

Krick, J. C. (1992). All children are special. In B. Neugebauer (Ed.), *Alike and different: Exploring our humanity with young children* (rev. ed., pp. 152–158). Washington, DC: National Association for the Education of Young Children.

Laosa, L. M. (1982). The sociocultural context of evaluation. In B. Spodek (Ed.), *Handbook of research in early childhood education* (pp. 501–520). New York, NY: Free Press.

Lazarin, M. (2014, October 14). Testing overload in America's schools. Retrieved July 18, 2017, from https://www.americanprogress.org/issues/education-k-12/reports/2014/10/16/99073/testing-overload-in-americas-schools/

Linder, T. (2008). *Transdisciplinary play-based assessment.* Baltimore, MD: Brookes.

Linder, T. W. (1993). *Transdisciplinary play-based assessment (TPBA): A functional approach to working with young children* (rev. ed.). Baltimore, MD: Brookes.

Litty, C. G., & Hatch, A. (2006, February). Hurry up and wait: Rethinking special education identification in kindergarten. *Early Childhood Education Journal, 33,* 203–208.

Locke, J. (1699). *Some thoughts concerning education* (4th ed.). London, England: Churchill.

Lopez, E. J., Salas, L., & Flores, J. P. (2005). Hispanic preschool children: What about assessment and intervention? *Young Children, 60*(6), 48–54.

Losen, D. J., & Orfield, J. (2002). *Racial inequality in special education.* Retrieved July 15, 2009, from https://www.gse.harvard.edu

Maeroff, G. I. (1991, December). Assessing alternative assessment. *Phi Delta Kappan,* 272–281.

McAfee, A., Leong, D. J., & Bodrova, E. (2004). *Basics of assessment: A primer for early childhood education.* Washington, DC: National Association for the Education of Young Children.

McCollum, J. A., & Maude, S. P. (1993). Portrait of a changing field: Policy and practice in early childhood special education. In B. Spodek (Ed.), *Handbook of research on the education of young children* (pp. 352–371). New York, NY: Macmillan.

McMaken, J. (2003, March). *Early childhood assessment.* Denver, CO: Education Commission of the States. Retrieved January 29, 2007, from https://www.ecs.org/html/Document.asp?chouseid=4319

Mehrens, W. A., & Lehmann, I. J. (1991). *Measurement and evaluation in education and psychology* (4th ed.). New York, NY: Harcourt Brace.

Meisels, S. J. (1996). Charting the continuum of assessment and intervention. In S. J. Meisels & E. Fenichel (Eds.), *New visions for the developmental assessment of infants and young children* (pp. 27–52). Washington, DC: Zero to Three: National Center for Infants, Toddlers, and Families.

Meisels, S. J., & Atkins-Burnett, S. A. (2005). *Developmental screening in early childhood: A guide*

(5th ed.). Washington, DC: National Association for the Education of Young Children.

Meisels, S. J., & Fenichel, E. (Eds.). (1996). *New visions for the developmental assessment of infants and young children*. Washington, DC: Zero to Three: National Center for Infants, Toddlers, and Families.

Meisels, S. J., & Shonkoff, J. P. (Eds.). (1990). *Handbook of early childhood intervention*. New York, NY: Cambridge University Press.

Meisels, S. J., Steele, D. M., & Quinn-Leering, K. (1993). Testing, tracking, and retaining young children: An analysis of research and social policy. In B. Spodek (Ed.), *Handbook of research on the education of young children* (pp. 279–292). New York, NY: Macmillan.

Millard, D. (2004). Understanding responsiveness to intervention in learning disabilities determination. Retrieved July 15, 2009, from http://www.wrightslaw.com/infor/rti.index.htm

Moll, L., Amanti, C., Neff, D., & Gonzalez, N. (1992). Funds of knowledge for teaching: Using a qualitative approach to connect homes and classrooms. *Theory Into Practice, 31*(2), 132–141.

Monroe, W. S. (1918). Existing tests and standards. In G. W. Whipple (Ed.), *The measurement of educational products: 14th yearbook of the National Society for the Study of Education, Part II* (pp. 71–104). Bloomington, IL: Public School.

Moscosco, E. (2001, December 14). New federal education law passes. *Austin American-Statesman*, p. A4.

Nagle, R. J. (2000). Issues in preschool assessment. In B. Bracken (Ed.), *Principles and recommendations for early childhood assessments*. Washington, DC: National Goals Panel.

National Association for the Education of Young Children and the National Association of Early Childhood Specialists in State Departments of Education. (1992). Guidelines for appropriate curriculum content and assessment in programs serving children ages 3 through 8. In S. Bredekamp & T. Rosegrant (Eds.), Reaching potentials: Appropriate curriculum and assessment for young children (pp. 9–27). Washington, DC: Author.

National Association for the Education of Young Children (NAEYC). 1992.

National Association for the Education of Young Children (NAEYC). (2001). Still! Unacceptable trends for kindergarten entry and placement. *Young Children, 56*, 59–61.

National Association for the Education of Young Children (NAEYC). (2004, February 26). Early education experts highlight concerns about new nationwide test of four-year-olds in Head Start. Retrieved January 29, 2007, from http://www.naeyc.org/about/releases/20040226.asp

National Association for the Education of Young Children (NAEYC). (2005a, Summer). *Screening and assessment of young English-language learners*. Washington, DC: Author.

National Association for the Education of Young Children (NAEYC). (2005b). *NAEYC code of ethical conduct and statement of commitment* (revised). Washington, DC: Author.

National Association for the Education of Young Children & National Association of Early Childhood Specialists in State Departments of Education. (2009).

National Association of Early Childhood Specialists in State Departments of Education (NAECS/SDE). (2000). *Still! Unacceptable trends in kindergarten entry and placement*. Washington, DC: Author.

National Center for Educational Statistics (NCES). (2017, September 6). English language learners in public schools. Retrieved from https://nces.ed.gov/programs/coe/indicator_cgf.asp

National Center on Response to Intervention (n.d.). *Transcript: What is RTI?* Retrieved September 12, 2013, from http://www.rti4success.org/pdf/transcript-WhatisRTI.pc

National Council for the Social Studies. (1994). *Curriculum standards for social studies*. Silver Spring, MD: Author.

National Council of State Legislatures. (2009). Testing, standards, and accountability: Overview. Retrieved July 9, 2009, from http://www.ncsl.org/IssuesResearch/Education/Testing.Standard

National Dissemination Center for Children with Disabilities. (2012). *Early intervention, then and now.* Retrieved from https://www.parentcenterhub.org/ei-history/

National Scientific Council on the Developing Child. (2004). Young children develop an environment of relationships: Working paper no. 1. Retrieved from http://www.developingchild.net

National Scientific Council on the Developing Child. (2010). Early experiences can alter gene expression and affect long-term development: Working paper no. 10. Retrieved from http://www.developingchild.net

New America Foundation Feedback. (2013, July 1). No Child Left Behind—Overview. Retrieved August 3, 2013, from http://www.newamerica.org

Newmann, F. M. (1996). Introduction: The school restructuring study. In F. M. Newmann & Associates, *Authentic achievement: Restructuring schools for intellectual quality* (pp. 1–16). San Francisco, CA: Jossey-Bass.

Olson, L. (2006, July 12). Department raps states on testing. *Education Week, 25*(42), 1, 36–37.

Pinto-Martin, J. A., Dunkle, M. E., Fliedner, D., & Landes, C. (2005). Developmental stages of developmental screening: Stages to implementation of a successful program. *American Journal of Public Health, 95*, 1928–1932.

Ravitch, D. (2013, August 24). *The biggest fallacy of the Common Core Standards*. Retrieved August 24, 2013, from https://www.huffingtonpost.com/diane-ravitch/common-core-fallacy_b_3809159.html

Rebora, A. (2006, April 19). NCLB's counting problems, textual artifacts, and going nuclear. *Teacher Magazine*.

Rich, M. (2013, June 18). Education chief lets states delay use of tests in decisions about teachers' jobs. *The New York Times*. Retrieved June 21, 2013, from NYTimes.com

Rousseau, J. J. (1911). *Emile, or On education*. (B. Foxley, Trans.). London, England: Dent. (Original work published 1762).

Scherer, M. (1999). Perspectives/measures and mismeasures. *Educational Leadership, 56*, 5.

Seefeldt, C. (2005). *How to work with standards in the early childhood classroom*. New York, NY: Teachers College Press.

Segal, M., & Webber, N. T. (1996). Nonstructured play observations: Guidelines, benefits, and caveats. In S. J. Meisels & E. Fenichel (Eds.), *New visions for the developmental assessment of infants and young children* (pp. 207–230). Washington, DC: Zero to Three: National Center for Infants, Toddlers, and Families.

Shackelford, J. (2006). State and jurisdictional eligibility definitions for infants and toddlers with disabilities under IDEA. *NECTAC Notes* (21), 1–16. Chapel Hill, NC: National Early Childhood Assistance Center.

Shepard, L., Kagan, S. L., Lynn, S., & Wurtz, E. (1998). *Principles and recommendations for early childhood assessments*. Washington, DC: National Goals Panel.

Shore, R. (1997). *Rethinking the brain*. New York, NY: Families and Work Institute.

Smith, S. S. (1999). Reforming the kindergarten round-up. *Educational Leadership, 56*, 39–44.

Spodek, B., & Saracho, O. N. (1994). *Dealing with individual differences in the early childhood classroom*. New York, NY: Longman.

Stein, J. U. (1993). Critical issues: Mismanagement, informed consent, and participant safety. In S. J. Grosse & D. Thompson (Eds.), *Leisure opportunities for individuals with disabilities: Legal issues* (pp. 37–54). Reston, VA: American Alliance for Health, Physical Education, and Dance.

Sullivan, A. L., Artiles, A. J., & Hernandez-Saca, D. I. (2015). Addressing special education inequity through systemic change: Contributions of ecologically based organizational consultation. *Journal of Educational and Psychological Consultation, 25*, 129–147.

The College Board. (2017). One year since first administration in March 2016, students say the new SAT makes it easier to show their best work. Retrieved from https://www.collegeboard.org/releases/2017/new-sat-easier-to-show-best-work

The New York Times. (2009, July 21). The No Child Left Behind Act news. Retrieved July 21, 2009, from http://topics.nytimes.com/top/reference/timestopics/subjects

Tooley, M. (2015, December 24). No Child Left Behind is gone, but will it be back? Retrieved August 14, 2017, from https://www.theatlantic.com/education/archives/2015/12/no-child-left-behind

Toppo, G. (2012, May 1). Common Core Standards drive wedge in education circles. *USA Today*. Retrieved September 12, 2013, from https://usatoday30.usatoday.com/news/education/story/2012-04-28/common-core-education/54583192/1

Ujifusa, A. (2015, November 12). What the Ed. Dept's new Race to the Top report reveals, and what it avoids. Retrieved August 3, 2017, from http://blogs.edweek.org/edweek/campaign-k-12/2015/11/what_the_new_race_to_the_top_r.html

U.S. Congress. (2004). Individuals with Disabilities Education Improvement Act (PL 108-446), 108th U.S.C., Stt. 2647, et. Seq.

U.S. Department of Education. (n.d.). Definitions. Retrieved July 17, 2017, from https://www.ed.gov/early learning/elc-draft-summary/definitions

U.S. Department of Education. (2006, August 3). *IDEA 2004 news, information, resources.* Washington, DC: Author.

U.S. Department of Education (2009). Race to the Top Program Executive Summary. Washington DC.

U.S. Department of Education. (2013). Race to the Top Application for Initial Funding.

U.S. Department of Education. (2015, November). *Fundamental change: Innovation in America's schools under Race to the Top: Executive Summary.* Washington, DC: Author.

U.S. Department of Education. (2016, December 19). *Assistance to states for the education of children with disabilities: Preschool grants for children with disabilities.* 34 CFR Part 300. Final Regulations, *81*, 243.

U.S. Department of Eduation (2016). Race to the top. Retrieved from https://www.edreform.com/issues/federal-polidcy/race-to9-the-top

U.S. Department of Education (2017a, June 2). *Ed. review.* Retrieved August 4, 2017, from https://www2.ed.gov/news/newsletters/edreview/2017/0602.html

U.S. Department of Education. (2017b, September 5). *Every student succeeds act (ESSA).* Retrieved from https://www.ed.gov/essa

U.S. Department of Education, Office of Special Education Programs. (2017, January 9). *Dear colleague: Preschool LRE.* Retrieved from https://www2.ed.gov/policy/speced/guid/idea/memosdcltrs/preschool-lre-dcl-1-10-17.pdf

U.S. Department of Health and Human Resources Head Start Bureau. (2003). *National Reporting System.* Washington, DC: Author.

Weber, E. (1984). *Ideas influencing early childhood education: A theoretical analysis.* New York, NY: Teachers College Press.

Weiss, E. (2013, September 12). Mismatches in Race to the Top educational improvements. Retrieved August 2, 2017, from http://www.epi.org/publication/race-to-the-top-goals/

Wesson, K. A. (2001). The "Volvo effect"—Questioning standardized tests. *Young Children, 56*(2), 16–18.

White, S. H. (1973). *Federal programs for young children: Review and recommendations* (Vol. 13). Washington, DC: U.S. Government Printing Office.

Wiggins, G. P. (1993). *Assessing student performance.* San Francisco, CA: Jossey-Bass.

Wolery, M., Strain, P. S., & Bailey, D. B. (1992). Reaching potentials of children with special needs. In S. Bredekamp & T. Rosegrant (Eds.), *Reaching potentials: Appropriate curriculum and assessment for young children* (pp. 92–112). Washington, DC: National Association for the Education of Young Children.

Wolery, M., & Wilbers, J. S. (Eds.). (1994). *Including children with special needs in early childhood programs.* Washington, DC: National Association for the Education of Young Children.

Wortham, S. C. (1998). Introduction. In S. C. Wortham, A. Barbour, & B. Desjean-Perrotta, *Portfolio assessment: A handbook for preschool and elementary educators* (pp. 7–13). Olney, MD: Association for Childhood Education International.

Wortham, S. C. (2002). *Childhood 1892–2002* (2nd ed.). Olney, MD: Association for Childhood Education International.

Wurm, J. P. (2005). *Working in the Reggio way.* St. Paul, MN: Redleaf Press.

Zehr, M. A. (2006, July 12). New era for testing English-learners begins: Federal officials to review exams developed to meet requirements of NCLB. *Education Week.* Retrieved July 12, 2006, from https://www.edweek.org/ew/articles/2006/07/12/42english.h25.html

Zigler, E., & Valentine, J. (Eds.). (1979). *Project Head Start: A legacy of the War on Poverty.* New York, NY: Free Press.

Chapter 2
How Infants and Young Children Should Be Assessed

Jules Selmes/Pearson Education Ltd

 ## Chapter Learning Outcomes

As a result of reading this chapter, you will be able to:

2.1 Define the principles of assessment recommended for all children.

2.2 Explain how infants and young children are assessed.

2.3 Explain how assessment results are used for instruction and to evaluate the instructional program.

2.4 Explain challenges and guidelines in assessing for standards.

In this chapter, appropriate methods of assessing infants and young children will be explained. The focus will be on the future and what assessment should do, as well as how assessments should be conducted and used. Principles and characteristics of quality assessments are described also. A description of how these varied assessment practices can be organized into a comprehensive plan for evaluation, also called an assessment system, will be discussed, followed by how assessment results are used in infant, preschool, and school settings.

The Principles of Assessment for All Children

The goal of the discussion in this part of the chapter is to address the concerns and issues raised about assessing and evaluating infants and young children and to set criteria for higher goals of the process. The objective is not to eliminate established methods and replace them with new ones, but to formulate how to use each method most effectively to serve the needs of individual children. First, criteria for optimal approaches to assessment will be described generally, followed by how assessment should be used for the benefit of infants and young children specifically.

Assessment Should Use Multiple Sources of Information

No matter what strategy is used for assessment, a single method for gathering information is insufficient (Elicker & McMullen, 2013; NAEYC, 2017; Morrison, 2017). Each assessment strategy has strengths and limitations; moreover, a single method provides only one portion of what needs to be known about a child. A variety of strategies provides a comprehensive picture of the child's development and learning from different perspectives, such as that of parents, teachers, and specialists (Feld & Bergan, 2002). Multiple observations are better than a single observation, and other inputs about a child's development, such as parents' and caregivers' views of the child, provide a more complete picture of the child's current functioning and progress. Infant assessment should be meaningful and focus on individual rates of development, interests, and learning styles observed in the child (Elicker & McMullen, 2013; National Research Council, 2008). The child's development and behaviors should be observed in various settings (Caspe, Seltzer, Kennedy, Cappio & DeLorenzo, 2013; Gonzalez-Mena & Stonehouse, 2008).

For older children who have entered school, learning achievement becomes important. The kindergarten and school-age child should be able to demonstrate learning in more than one way and on more than one occasion. Use of a variety of measures of learning ensures an accurate view of the child's accomplishments (McAfee, Leong, & Bodrova, 2004; Morrison, 2017; National Research Council, 2008; Popham, 2013; Shepard, 1989; Wiggins, 1993).

ASSESSMENT SHOULD BENEFIT THE CHILD AND IMPROVE LEARNING   The purpose of assessing infants and toddlers is generally to determine whether the child is developing as expected or exhibits delays and therefore needs assistance or intervention. Thus, the purposes of assessment are to benefit the child. Appropriate assessment of infants and toddlers is based on strengths and builds on capabilities rather than what the child cannot do (Moreno & Klute, 2011).

Mara Larson—Kindergarten

The children in Mara's classroom enjoy the center activities that follow each day's math lesson. They don't know that when they are playing counting and number games, Mara is assessing their progress. For example, when they are learning about numerals, Mara might have a lesson in which children use counters to place the correct number of objects under numeral cards up to 10. In another activity, children take turns throwing dice, counting the total, and selecting the correct numeral. A third game is a game board with a spinner. The child spins the wheel and counts out the correct number to match the numeral where the spinner lands. If the answer is correct, the child advances one square on the game board. At first, Mara guides small groups of children in the math activities. When she observes children who have mastered the math objective of the game, she allows them to play the game independently. Mara continues to guide the children she observes having difficulties with the skills used in the activities. Mara also observes children as they participate in math lessons and assigns other tasks that serve as assessments.

When young children enter school, however, assessments can have negative purposes that are not related to the needs and interests of the child. As is discussed elsewhere in this text, tests are sometimes administered to young children to determine whether they can be admitted to a preschool program or promoted in grade. In the primary grades, tests are administered to determine the child's achievement during a school year. When such tests are given to determine the child's progress and to plan appropriate instruction based on what the child has accomplished, the purpose will benefit the child and improve learning. On the other hand, when such tests are used merely for evaluation of the school program and have no implications for how the child will be served, they do not benefit the child and should not be used. Whatever

Gloria Fuentes—Toddler Class

Several weeks into the school year, two children in Gloria's class still speak very little in school. Gloria has questions about their language development. She schedules conferences with parents to get their help in assessing their child's language ability. As a result of the conversations with parents, she discovers that one of the children readily speaks at home but is still shy and uncertain about school. Another child comes from a home where English is not spoken. From her discussions with these parents, Gloria knows more about the children's language needs. Different approaches will be used with each child to help him or her use more language. One will need much attention and emotional support each day to ensure that he or she is confident and secure enough to talk in class. The other will need daily opportunities to learn and use new English words in classroom activities.

assessment strategies are used, the information should be used to guide the child and enhance learning (Copple & Bredekamp, 2009; Guss, et al., 2013; Popham, 2013; Wiggins, 1993, 1998).

ASSESSMENT SHOULD INVOLVE THE CHILD AND FAMILY   The family has an important role in assessment. Infants and toddlers are unable to understand their own developmental progress; however, their parents and caregivers are primary sources of information. Although tests can be administered to measure development, a parent's knowledge about the child is essential for a true understanding of the child's developmental characteristics (Darragh, 2009; Popper, 1996; Rocco, 1996). The relationship between caregivers and parents should be collaborative, with all participants contributing to the information about the child and sharing views and concerns that add to the knowledge about the child (Desired Results Access Project, 2015; Elicker & McMullen, 2013; Weiss, Caspe, & Lopez, 2006). Moreover, relationships between caregivers and parents can foster "goodness of fit" or compatibility of child-rearing practices between the school and the home that will benefit the child (Tanyel, 2017).

Enhanced eText: Video Example 2.1

Preschool, kindergarten, and primary-grade children are more able to understand what they know and what they are able to do. This ability increases with the child's age and maturity. For example, by the time the child is in the primary grades, self-assessment improves. Students can evaluate their progress and have a voice in how they can best succeed in mastering learning objectives. Assessment is not just administered to children, but accomplished with active participation by the students, parents, and teachers.

ASSESSMENT SHOULD BE FAIR FOR ALL CHILDREN   In Chapter 1 we pointed out that many tests are inappropriate for children who are culturally or linguistically diverse. In addition, educators must evaluate children with disabilities accurately and fairly. Because tests may not reflect a child's culture or language, other, more effective methods must be employed. As was mentioned earlier, a variety of strategies can overcome the limitations of a single method or test. The person administering the evaluation must be alert to limitations and have other strategies to acquire the needed information (Mattix-Foster & Ramos, 2017). This is especially important in the case of children who are culturally and linguistically diverse or whose abilities are outside normal developmental ranges (Barrera, 1996; Genishi & Dyson, 2009; Goodwin & Goodwin, 1993). Recommendations for assessing culturally and linguistically diverse children fairly include:

- Use assessment tools that are culturally and linguistically appropriate. Are the terms, pictures, and items familiar to children from the culture of the child being assessed? Is the instrument available in the child's home language?

- For standardized tools, review the test manual to make sure the instrument was standardized with samples of children similar to the children being assessed.

- If there is uncertainty about how well a child speaks and understands English, administer a language proficiency test before assessing a child to determine if he or she can speak and understand English proficiently.

- Administer the assessment in the home language of children who are non-English speakers or English Language Learners to capture a true understanding of their development.

- If the assessment is not available in the home language, a trained interpreter should assist with the assessment. At a minimum, the interpreter should be as familiar with key terms in the assessment tool and the process used to administer it as a speaker of the child's home language would be.

- Talk with family members of the child being assessed for additional information about the child's background and development.

(Espinosa & López, 2007; NAEYC, 2009)

Similarly, assessment of children with disabilities should be developmentally, culturally, and individually appropriate. Assessment of these children often leads to a diagnosis of the child's disability and/or determination of an infant or young child's eligibility for receiving special services. Additionally, assessment information can inform professionals about the types of early intervention services needed for infants and toddlers with developmental delays or other special needs and instructional needs for older children. Family partnerships are essential to understanding the strengths and needs of children with potential disabilities, and federal law requires their involvement in the assessment process. Assessment tools should be tailored to understanding the type of disability or delay the child is experiencing. For example, if the child has motor challenges, it would be important to gather assessment information using a standardized tool that has a motor section, health records, parent input, and observations. Together, this process is called an **evaluation** because assessment information is being gathered from multiple sources to determine the child's current functioning, and to determine what should happen next in regards to a child's educational and/or developmental needs (DEC/CEC, 2007).

Principles of Assessment for Young Children

The previous section described principles for assessing all children. As a follow-up to that information, we can address how those principles are applied to young children. Principles for early childhood assessments are not just relevant for the assessment of children, but also have implications for program evaluation and quality (Epstein, Schweinhart, DeBruin-Parecki, & Robin, 2004). In the early childhood years, assessment of development is the primary focus. The NAEYC position statement calls for sound assessment that reflects how young children grow and learn. Sound assessment is described through a series of statements of principles (Copple & Bredekamp, 2009, pp. 21–22):

Search and Share 2.1

Fair Assessment for Children with Disabilities

Search the web to learn more about what the **Individuals with Disabilities Education Improvement Act (IDEA, 2004)** requires to help ensure fair testing of children with disabilities. Share one aspect of the law you think is particularly important to fair testing. What strategies would you use to ensure fair testing of children with disabilities?

Margie Phillips—First Grade

Two boys in Margie's first-grade class are having trouble copying information from the board. As a result, they are not having success in completing board assignments. Margie feels that the boys are not paying attention; however, she talks to the parents and suggests that the parents seek professional help to determine whether there is a problem. The parents of the boys take them to a local university to be tested by an early childhood diagnostician. After the assessment, the specialist calls Margie and explains that the boys have difficulty transferring information from the board to paper. They are unable to remember the written material between seeing it on the board and then looking down to their paper. Both boys need to have the information written on paper and placed on their desks for easy referral. Although Margie feels that changing her methods for the two boys is unnecessary and shows favoritism, she follows the specialist's recommendations. When she tries placing the information on the boys' desks, she is surprised to see that the boys improve in completing assignments.

A. Assessment of young children's progress and achievements is ongoing, strategic, and purposeful. The results of assessment are used to inform the planning and implementation of experiences, to communicate with the child's family, and to evaluate and improve teachers' and the program's effectiveness.

B. Assessment focuses on children's progress toward goals that are developmentally and educationally significant.

C. There is a system in place to collect, make sense of, and use the assessment information to guide what goes on in the classroom (formative assessment). Teachers use this information in planning curriculum and learning experiences and in moment-to-moment interactions with children—that is, teachers continually engage in assessment for the purpose of improving teaching and learning.

D. The methods of assessment are appropriate to the developmental status and experiences of young children, and these methods recognize individual variation in learners and allow children to demonstrate their competence in different ways. Methods appropriate to the classroom assessment of young children, therefore, include results of teachers' observations of children's work samples, and their performance on authentic activities.

E. Assessment looks not only at what children can do independently but also at what they can do with assistance from other children or adults. Therefore, teachers assess children as they participate in groups and other situations that are providing scaffolding.

F. In addition to this assessment by teachers, input from families as well as children's own evaluations of their work are part of the program's overall assessment strategy.

G. Assessments are tailored to a specific purpose and used only for the purpose for which they have been demonstrated to produce reliable, valid information.

H. Decisions that have a major impact on children, such as enrollment or placement, are never made on the basis of results from a single developmental assessment or screening instrument/device but are based on multiple sources of relevant information, including that obtained from observations of and interactions with children by teachers and parents (and specialists as needed).

I. When a screening or other assessment identifies children who may have special learning or developmental needs, there is appropriate follow-up, evaluation, and, if indicated, referral. Diagnosis or labeling is never the result of a brief screening or one-time assessment. Families should be involved as important sources of information.

(Copyright ©2009 NAEYC®. Reprinted with permission)

The NAEYC position statement demonstrates how appropriate assessment is tailored to the changing developmental needs of young children. As children go through developmental differences, assessments that best measure the variations in development are employed. In the next section we will discuss how appropriate assessment is conducted with infants, toddlers, and preschool children.

Enhanced eText: Self-Check 2.1

How Infants and Young Children Are Assessed

The early sections of this chapter have discussed reasons for measuring and evaluating infants and young children, and various methods available to accomplish this. Sometimes we measure a child informally. We might look for characteristics by watching a child's behaviors at play or in a setting arranged for that purpose. A pediatrician may observe a baby walk during an examination to determine whether he or she is progressing normally. In a similar fashion, a teacher may observe a child playing to determine how he or she is using language. A second-grade teacher who constructs a set of subtraction problems to evaluate whether his or her students have mastered a mathematics objective is also using an **informal assessment**. Observation, which is defined by Mindes & Jung (2015) as any systematic method for gathering information about children by watching them, is also considered informal assessment.

Formal assessment occurs when standardized instruments are used for the measurement and evaluation of children's development and progress. These measures are designed by experts who then try them out with a large number of children to ensure the instruments are reliable and valid. This process ensures that educators can depend on the information gained each time the test is given to an individual child or group of

Observation a

Observation b

Observation c

Monkey Business/Fotolia

children. This type of test is called a **standardized assessment** because it has specific administration procedures and criteria to judge a child's performance and it has been shown to be reliable and valid. Formal assessments can be administered by trained teachers or other education personnel. Some require certification.

Why do we measure the development of infants and young children? The most common purpose is to assess development. Soon after a child's birth, for example, an **obstetrician** or **pediatrician** evaluates the newborn by using the *Apgar scale* (Apgar, 1975) to determine whether he or she is in good health. Thereafter, at regular intervals, parents, doctors, and teachers follow the baby's development by using standardized tests and informal assessment strategies (Greenspan, Meisels, & the Zero to Three Work Group on Developmental Assessment, 1996; Wodrich, 1984). The screening test for phenylketonuria (PKU) may also be administered to detect the presence of the enzyme phenylalanine, which can cause mental retardation if not managed through diet. In addition, there are newborn screening tests for hearing, cystic fibrosis, sickle cell disease, congenital hypothyroidism, and many others (American Academy of Pediatrics, 2017; Widerstrom, Mowder, & Sandall, 1991). The specific screening tests administered to newborns vary by state.

But what if development is not progressing normally? How can assessment measures be used to help the young child? In recent years, researchers, medical specialists, and educators have learned how to work with children at increasingly younger ages to minimize the effects of delays in growth or other problems that retard the child's developmental progress. Various strategies and instruments are now available. For instance, a **neonatologist** conducts a comprehensive evaluation on a premature baby to determine what therapy should be initiated to improve the infant's chances for survival and optimal development. The child who does not speak normally or who is late in speaking is referred to a speech pathologist, who assesses the child's language and prescribes activities to facilitate improved language development. Similar screenings and assessments occur in other developmental areas.

During a child's infancy and toddler years, child development specialists initiate therapy when development is not typical (Meisels, 1996). During the preschool years, this effort includes assessing and predicting whether the child is likely to experience difficulties in learning. Tests and other measures are used to help to determine whether the child will develop a **disability** and how that disability will affect his or her success in school. Again, when problems are detected, individualized plans are developed, with input from family members and professionals, to address the child's needs in a timely manner to optimize his or her development in preparation for school entry. The child may have a vision impairment, difficulty in hearing, developmental delays, or a diagnosed disability that may interfere with learning. The assessment measures used will help identify the exact nature of the problem. In addition, test results will be used to help determine what kind of intervention will be most successful (Wodrich, 1984).

During the preschool period or even earlier, a developmental difference may emerge. Parents or other adults who interact with the child may observe that he or she demonstrates a learning ability or potential that is much higher than the average range. A more formal evaluation using standardized tests may confirm these informal observations. Plans then can be made to facilitate the child's development to help him or her to achieve full potential for learning.

Enhanced eText: Application Exercise 2.1

Although potential for learning may be assessed at a very early age in the child who is gifted or talented, learning aptitude may also be evaluated in the general population during the preschool and primary school years. Educators wish to determine children's learning abilities and needs, as well as the types of programs that will be most beneficial for them. Informal strategies and formal tests are used with individual children and groups of children to assess what and how much they have already learned and to evaluate weak areas that can be given special attention. Informal and formal strategies are also used to evaluate the success of programs that serve children, as well as to provide indicators for how programs can be improved.

Assessment for Risk in Developmental Status

When Sarah was 6 months old, her teenage mother gave her up for adoption. Because Sarah's father could not be located to agree to release her for adoption, Sarah was placed temporarily in a foster home.

Prior to placement with the foster family, Sarah had lived with her mother in her maternal grandparents' home. In addition to Sarah's mother, six other children were in the family. Both grandparents were employed. Sarah's primary caregiver had been an aunt with intellectual disabilities who was 12 years old.

For the first few days after Sarah was placed in the foster home, she cried when the foster parents tried to feed her. She sat for long periods of time and stared vacantly, without reacting to toys or people. She had no established patterns for sleeping and usually fretted off and on during the night.

When a pediatrician examined Sarah, she was found to be malnourished, with sores in her mouth from vitamin deficiencies. As determined by the *Denver Developmental Screening Test*, she was developing much more slowly than normal.

A special diet and multivitamins were prescribed for Sarah. Members of the foster family patiently taught her to enjoy eating a varied diet beyond the chocolate milk and cereal that she had been fed previously. Regular times for sleeping at night gradually replaced her erratic sleeping habits. Her foster family spent many hours playing with her, talking with her, and introducing her to various toys.

By age 11 months, Sarah had improved greatly. She was alert, ate well, began to walk, and said a few words. Her development was within the normal range, and she was ready for adoption.

Sarah had benefited from being placed in a home where she received good nutrition, guidance in living patterns, and stimulation for cognitive, physical, and social development. Without early intervention, Sarah's delay in development might have become more serious over time. Adaptability to an adoptive home might have been difficult for her and her adoptive parents. If she had been unable to adjust successfully with an adoptive family, she might have spent her childhood years in a series of foster homes, rather than with her adoptive family. She also would have been at risk for not learning successfully beginning in the first years of schooling.

Combating Limitations in Vocabulary and Concept Development

Micah, who is 4 years old, is the sixth child in a family of seven children. Both he and his younger brother are cared for by a grandmother during the day, while their parents are at work. Although Micah's parents are warm and loving, their combined income is barely enough to provide the basic necessities for the family. They are unable to buy books and toys that will enhance Micah's development. Because the family rarely travels outside the immediate neighborhood, Micah has had few experiences that would broaden his knowledge of the larger community.

Fortunately, Micah's family lives in a state that provides a program for 4-year-old children who can benefit from a prekindergarten class that stresses language and cognitive development. The program serves all children who come from low-income homes or who exhibit language or cognitive delay.

In response to a letter sent by the school district, Micah's grandmother took him to the school to be tested for the program. Micah's performance on the test showed that he uses a limited expressive vocabulary and lacks many basic concepts. When school begins in late August, Micah will start school with his older brothers and sisters and will be enrolled in the prekindergarten class.

Micah will have the opportunity to play with puzzles, construction toys, and other manipulative objects that will facilitate his cognitive development. Stories will be read and discussed each day, and Micah will be able to look at a variety of books. Micah's teacher will introduce learning experiences that will allow Micah to learn about shapes, colors, numbers, and many other concepts that will provide a foundation for learning in the elementary school grades.

Micah will also travel with his classmates to visit places that will help him learn about the community. They may visit a furniture or grocery store or a bread factory. Visitors to the classroom will add to the students' knowledge about occupations and cultures represented in the community. The children will have opportunities to paint, participate in cooking experiences, and talk about the new things they are learning. They will dictate stories about their experiences and learn many songs and games. When Micah enters kindergarten the following year, he will use the knowledge and language he learned in prekindergarten to help him to learn successfully along with his 5-year-old peers.

Elements of a Comprehensive System of Assessment for Children of All Ages

Not only do teachers need to understand what strategies and tools are available and how to use them, but they also need to have a systematic plan for conducting assessments that includes both formal and informal components (Bowers, 2008; National Association for the Education of Young Children, 2017). There are many types of assessment systems. Chapters 9 and 10 describe some systems that are currently used in early childhood programs. All systems use most of the elements described next.

Components of an Assessment System for Infants and Toddlers

Teachers and caregivers who work with infants and toddlers engage in the process of documenting development. They collect data from daily interactions with the very young to form a picture or profile of the child. This collection of information consists of their own experiences with the child as well as the family's experiences. The resulting profile helps them understand the child's changes over time. Elicker & McMullen (2013) suggest the use of anecdotal observations, journals and blogs, and photo documentation in addition to developmental screening and structured assessments. This information should never be used to pressure or stress the child. A developmental profile offers another source of understanding the whole child.

ANECDOTAL OBSERVATIONS   Daily routines and events form the basis for anecdotal observations. What the child ate, how much was eaten, naps, and highlights of the day are recorded by the teacher. These observations are recorded daily.

JOURNALS AND BLOGS   Teachers and families find it helpful to keep a journal that might be sent home weekly with reports of activities, plans for curriculum, and examples of a child's work. Parents can contribute to the journal. Interactive media can also serve the function of a journal, with photos and information exchanged between the infant child-care setting and the home.

PHOTO DOCUMENTATION   Photographs can be taken of group as well as individual activities and accomplishments. Elicker and McMullen (2013) suggest that teachers can make a weekly poster of the class activities to share with the children and their families. Photos can also document class projects, special events, and trips outside the center. For example, an enrichment center for infants and preschool children in Louisiana had videotapes of the day's activities playing on a television set when parents came to pick up their children at the end of the day.

DEVELOPMENTAL SCREENING TOOLS AND STANDARDIZED ASSESSMENTS
Screening instruments are another category of information that includes more formal, standardized examinations of development. Developmental screening tools provide a quick snapshot of a child's development across domains. Developmental screenings and infant and toddler standardized assessments include diagnostic information to support intervention with children who are at risk for developmental delays and disabilities. These practices are discussed in Chapter 4. These reliable and valid tools can contribute to creating a complete picture of the child's development.

DEVELOPMENTAL PROFILE   A child's developmental profile collects data from many sources and helps describe areas of development and learning over a period of time. Sources of information discussed in this section all have a role in the child's profile. This includes observations, photos, journal entries, developmental scales, etc. An example of a developmental profile is given in Figure 2-1.

PORTFOLIOS   Many of the assessment materials and much of the documentation can be organized into a portfolio to make a comprehensive record of infant and toddler development. This strategy is useful both for the teacher and the family.

Figure 2-1 Developmental profile

Name: Audrey B.
Age: 3 years

Elizabeth B. Photography

Physical Development: Large and small muscle control, use of sensory materials

Audrey is very active physically, She enjoys activities that challenge her climbing, jumping, and running skills. At a recent birthday party she explored a variety of blow-up structures and attempted to use a structure designed for older children. She also enjoys tactile experiences such as playing with clay and finger painting.

Social–Emotional Development: Ability to interact with others, enter a play situation, and show empathy for others. Demonstrates management of emotion

Audrey is very confident when entering new group situations. She has been attending a Mother's Day Out preschool program since she was two and from the very beginning was very happy to arrive at the school and go to her classroom. She is demonstrating some confusion in acceptable social behaviors. Her teacher has commented that she plays very rough and pushes children. Audrey is learning that pushing another child is not effective in trying to be accepted as a play partner or in a play group. She is very excitable and sometimes shrieks at home or in the classroom. The teacher and her parents are teaching her when she needs to use "inside voice."

Cognitive Development: Uses problem-solving, creative expression, and progress in levels of cognitive development

Audrey has used planning for her play and cognitive activities. On one occasion at home she was given a wilted rose that was losing its petals. She smelled the rose, felt the petals, and then removed them from the stem. First she made piles of petals and moved them from place to place. Next, she put them in the back of a toy vehicle. After a few minutes she returned to the petals and took them into her play kitchen and put them in a pan on the stove. Finally, she took the petals and put them in her doll buggy. The play ended when her grandmother took the petals, telling her, "These are all used up. Let's throw them away." Audrey persisted by trying to take the buggy and petals outside. Instead the petals were removed from the buggy and Audrey was put in the car to go to a restaurant. Audrey has demonstrated an understanding of classification. At school she was given a small bucket filled with various types of clothespins. She soon put those that were alike together.

Language and Literacy Development: Uses language effectively to communicate with others and enjoys printed materials

Audrey is able to speak in three- and four-word sentences. She can ask simple questions and answer questions. She has many books at home and is read to each night before bed. At school she enjoys story time with the rest of the class. She sometimes selects a book to look at by herself.

Development of Self-Help and Personal Care Skills

Audrey's most important self-help skill has been to initiate potty training. After she was praised for her first successful attempt to use her small potty, she kept trying to use the toilet and do it again. After the initial days of success, she had accidents off and on, but is becoming more reliable each week. She can use a fork and spoon with some success, but sometimes reverts to fingers when the food is difficult to handle. She has not shown interest in dressing herself, but is getting encouragement from her parents to try to put on different items.

Summary

Audrey is a very happy child. She hums and sings songs she has learned at school when the family is riding in the car. She is now adjusting to a new baby brother and occasionally "acts out" according to her mother. She loves to go to different places such as the zoo and play dates. She enjoys her extended family and frequently gets together with cousins from both sides of the family. She is looking forward to moving to the 3-year-old group at the Mother's Day Out Program.

Elements of an Assessment System for Young Children

More assessment strategies, in addition to those described previously, are available to use with children in the preschool and primary-grade years. Both informal and formal assessments should be used to gain a comprehensive picture of a child's skills and development.

> **Enhanced eText:** Video Example 2.2

STANDARDIZED TESTS Standardized tests are designed to measure individual characteristics. The tests may be administered to an individual or to a group. The purpose of standardized tests is to measure abilities, achievements, aptitudes, interests, attitudes, values, and personality characteristics. The results can be used to plan instruction, to study differences between individuals and groups, and for counseling and guidance.

CLASSROOM ASSESSMENT STRATEGIES Standardized tests are not the only tools available for evaluation and assessment. Various types of informal instruments and strategies to determine development and learning are available as well.

School districts often use informal assessments or evaluation strategies developed by local teachers or staff members. In early childhood programs, an informal screening tool may be administered to preschool children at registration to determine their instructional needs. Likewise, the speech teacher may use a simple screening instrument to evaluate the child's language development or possible speech difficulties in addition to standardized tools for diagnosing children with speech and language delays.

> **Enhanced eText:** Video Example 2.3

OBSERVATION One of the most valuable ways to become aware of the individual characteristics of young children is through observation. Developmental indicators in early childhood are more likely to be noted from children's behavior in natural circumstances than from a designed assessment or instrument. Adults who observe children as they play and work in individual or group activities are able to determine progress in all categories of development (Segal & Webber, 1996). The child who shows evidence of emerging prosocial skills by playing successfully in the playground is demonstrating significant growth in social development. Children who struggle to balance materials on both sides of a balance scale demonstrate visible signs of cognitive growth. Physical development can be evaluated by observing children using

Observation is part of an assessment system.

Tudor Photography/Pearson Education Ltd

playground equipment. For example, daily observations of a child may reveal that he or she has progressed from needing adult assistance to independently climbing steps on a sliding board. Because young children learn best through active involvement with their environment, observing the child during periods of activity may assess evaluation of learning most appropriately. Observation records can be used to plan instruction, to report progress in various areas of development, and to track progress in mastery of preschool curriculum objectives.

TEACHER-DESIGNED MEASURES   Teachers have always used informal assessment tools that they have devised to measure the level of learning after instruction. Early childhood teachers are more likely to use concrete tasks or oral questions for informal assessment with young children. Teachers frequently incorporate evaluation with instruction or learning experiences. Activities and games can be used both to teach and to evaluate what the child has learned. Evaluation can also be conducted through learning centers or as part of a teacher-directed lesson. Although pencil-and-paper tests are also a teacher-designed measure, they should not be used until children are comfortable with reading and writing.

CHECKLISTS   **Developmental checklists** or other forms of learning objective sequences are used at all levels of preschool, elementary, and secondary schools. Often referred to as a **scope**, or **sequence of skills**, a checklist is a list of the learning objectives established for areas of learning and development at a particular age, grade level, or content area. Many checklists are standardized by experts, while others are locally developed by a teacher or school district and are not standardized.

Skills continuum are available from many sources. The teacher may construct one, or a school district may distribute checklists for each grade level. Educational textbook publishers frequently include a skills continuum for teachers to use as an instructional guide with the textbook they have selected. State education agencies now publish objectives to be used by all school districts in the state.

RATING SCALES   **Rating scales** are similar to checklists. They contain criteria for measurement that can be based on learning objectives or other factors. The major difference between checklists and rating scales is that rating scales provide for measurement on a continuum. Checklist items are rated with a negative or positive response. Rating scales can be used for many purposes when a range of criteria is needed to acquire accurate information.

RUBRICS   **Rubrics** are developed to evaluate authentic and performance assessments. They include a range of criteria like rating scales, but have indicators that can be used to determine quality of performance or to assign a grade. Rubrics are used most frequently with portfolio assessment, but are appropriate for performance assessment that is not part of a portfolio.

PERFORMANCE AND PORTFOLIO ASSESSMENTS   Additional forms of informal assessments focus on more meaningful types of evaluation of student learning. Sometimes called **performance assessments** or **authentic assessments** (Goodwin & Goodwin, 1993; Wiggins, 1993), these evaluation measures use strategies that permit the child to demonstrate his or her understanding of a concept or mastery of a skill. The evaluation might take the form of a teacher-directed **interview**, in which a dialogue with the child would reveal the child's thinking and understanding. Other procedures might include games, **directed assignments**, or activities related to a project.

Processes for reporting student progress related to outcome-based or authentic assessments are also intended to communicate learning and development from a meaningful perspective. Traditional report cards and standardized test results do not necessarily reflect the whole picture of a student's progress. **Portfolios** with samples of the student's work are one type of reporting of progress that is compatible with outcome-based assessment. A detailed narrative or **narrative report** of the student's progress developed by the teacher is another process that enables the teacher to describe the nature of the child's activities that have resulted in achievement and learning.

TECHNOLOGY-BASED ASSESSMENTS   Early childhood educators in the 21st century have access to computers and assessments that are available online. One source of technological assessment is **assessment software**. Assessments from computer software can be an adaptation of paper-based assessments, such as reading or mathematics checklists, or assessments that are linked to a specific curriculum. Other software can be acquired that permits teacher design of activities and lesson plans or continuous revision of assessment tools.

Assessment software companies abound on the Internet. In addition to electronic educational software for elementary and secondary schools, there are also resources available for higher education. Publishers of textbooks for school-age children also have their own systems of online assessment and reporting available for teachers and families.

In recent years commercial developers have developed software for preschool children. Some of the programs include a combination of curriculum and assessment. The programs are intended for use by young children with some assistance from adults. One such program is *ABC Mouse.com*. It is designed for children ages 2 to 7. The child can use a smartphone, tablet, or computer to participate (The Age of Learning.com, 2017). *Preschool First.com* is a web-based preschool curriculum for use in the classroom. *Preschool First.com* is aligned with Head Start standards, NAEYC accreditation standards, and state standards. The system is comprehensive with curriculum, assessments, and reporting progress built in (The Source for Learning, Inc., 2018).

Enhanced eText: Self-Check 2.2

Using Assessment Results for Instruction and to Evaluate the Instructional Program

Earlier in the chapter, we discussed the kinds of assessments that are needed for a new century. Components of a comprehensive system of evaluation were described. Now we will summarize how and when the system of assessment should be used. The discussion will relate to preschool and primary-grade children rather than infants and toddlers. In keeping with the premise that assessment should benefit the child and improve learning, three primary purposes for comprehensive assessment throughout the year are planning for instruction, reporting progress, and evaluating the instructional program continuously from the beginning until the end of the school term.

Using Assessment Results to Plan for Instruction

If assessments should benefit the child, then assessments in preschool and primary-grade settings should be linked to learning experiences and instruction. If they are to be fair and authentic for all children, they need to include strategies that generate a comprehensive picture of each child's progress and needs. The teacher selects assessment methods that are relevant to the information needed and uses the results in planning for curriculum and instruction. This assumes that the teacher is concerned with individual rates of development and learning and is prepared to address individual differences. The learning activities that are available in the classroom and through teacher instruction reflect not only curriculum goals established by the school, but also how each child can best achieve these goals.

Using Assessment Results to Report Progress

The limitations of report cards were discussed earlier in relationship to the broader information provided by performance assessments. Just as we need multiple assessment strategies to assess young children, these assessment strategies should be used to report how the child has developed and what has been learned. If the assessment system is comprehensive, the method to report the child's progress should also be comprehensive and provide many examples of how the child demonstrated growth and achievement. Often, parents receive limited information from reports that rate a child average, above average, or below average in preschool settings. Likewise, a report that indicates that the child's progress is satisfactory or unsatisfactory tells little about the child's learning experiences and accomplishments. Rather than a snapshot of progress, a comprehensive picture of the child should be conveyed in the progress report, regardless of whether the child is in preschool or in the primary grades.

Using Assessment Results to Evaluate the Instructional Program

The assessment process includes evaluation of the effectiveness of the teacher's instruction and the activities and materials used with children. The teacher uses assessment information to determine whether instructional strategies were successful for children to learn new concepts and skills or whether new approaches are needed. The teacher might ask the following questions about the success of the instruction: Were the children interested and engaged in the materials or activities? Did the children demonstrate a deeper understanding of concepts as a result of an instructional activity? Was the activity the right length of time? Too short? Too long? What changes might be made to improve the effectiveness of the activity?

With this type of evaluative reflection, the teacher demonstrates that assessment should focus not on student achievement, but, rather, on how well students are progressing and the role that the quality of instruction has on this progress. If some students need additional opportunities to learn information and skills, the teacher considers how more varied activities might accomplish the goal. Should the concepts be incorporated into different types of activities, or should they become a part of a continuum that includes a new direction or focus? Young children need many opportunities to learn new skills, and encountering concepts in new contexts provides meaningful routes to understanding and the ability to use what is being learned.

Environmental Assessment

When assessment of the instructional program is discussed, child progress is part of the purpose; nevertheless, the teacher is also being evaluated. Assessment of the environment also informs how well the instructional program serves young children. Both the indoor and outdoor environments can be evaluated. The *Environment Rating Scales* are used to assess elements of the indoor environment, as well as how teachers function in the environment. *The Early Childhood Rating Scale, Third Edition (ECERS-3)* (Harms, Clifford, & Cryer, 2014) and *Infant/Toddler Environment Rating Scale, Revised Edition* (Harms, Cryer, Clifford, & Yazejian, 2017) are representative of appropriate environmental assessments.

The *Classroom Assessment Scoring System* (CLASS) was developed by The Center for Advanced Study of Teaching and Learning at the University of Virginia. It is an observational teacher assessment tool to measure the quality of educational settings in PK–12 by observing teacher–student interactions in the classroom and the relationship between effective teacher interactions and student achievement. According to the Center for Advanced Study of Teaching and Learning (Rector and Visitors of the University of Virginia, 2013, p. 2), CLASS provides programs, schools, and districts with reliable, valid data on teacher effectiveness. The CLASS:

- Creates a common language about effective teaching practices across subject areas and grade levels.
- Helps teachers better understand how their interactions in the classroom affect student learning.
- Documents improvements in the effectiveness of teachers' interactions with students.

There are four levels of the class scoring system for young children, including the *CLASS Infant, CLASS Toddler, CLASS Pre–K, and CLASS K–3* (Pianta, La Paro, & Hamre, 2008; La Paro, Hamre, & Pianta, 2012; Rector and Visitors of the University of Virginia, 2013).

The ACEI *Global Guidelines Assessment–Third Edition* (GGA) (ACEI, 2011) is an international, evidence-based assessment tool for evaluating early childhood care and education environments. It was designed for emerging countries that wanted to assess their preschool program or needed technical assistance in initiating new programs in their country. The tool was based on global guidelines developed at a symposium held outside Zurich, Switzerland, in 1999 by 80 early childhood specialists representing 27 countries. The third edition of the GGA contains 76 items across five program areas, including (a) Environment and Physical Space (b) Curriculum Content and Pedagogy (c) Early Childhood Educators and Caregivers (d) Partnerships with Families and Communities and (e) Young Children with Special Needs (Barbour, Boyer, Hardin, & Wortham, 2004; Rentzou, 2010; Sandell, Hardin, & Wortham, 2010; Hardin, Bergen, & Hung, 2013; Hardin, Bergen, Busio, & Boone, 2017). The ACEI Global Guidelines Assessment is now available in 15 languages at acei.org.

Search and Share 2.2

Quality Rating and Improvement System (QRIS)

Search the web to find information about the Quality Rating and Improvement System (QRIS). What is the purpose of the QRIS system? What are two examples of how this system works? Does your state have a QRIS system?

How the Assessment Process Should Be Implemented During the School Year with School-Age Children

We proposed earlier that assessment occurs throughout the school year for preschool and school-age children. In this section, we will describe how a process of assessment proceeds from the beginning of the school year until the final evaluation at the end of the year. Ongoing assessment is complemented by periodic assessment for reporting periods.

Preassessment

At the beginning of the year, teachers begin the process of understanding children's development by observation, reviewing health and developmental records, talking with parents, and other informal activities. This process helps teachers and parents understand a child's strengths and needs and whether a child should be assessed using more formal procedures.

AT THE BEGINNING OF THE YEAR   Each year, when a teacher receives a new group of students, the first task is to learn about individual differences and determine each child's current developmental level. Young children have uneven rates of development. Each domain in development—physical, social, cognitive, and language—develops differently within and between children. Development occurs in spurts and may lag for a period of time. The teacher might use observation, checklists, and discussions with the child and parents to determine each child's current status. This initial evaluation provides the teacher with a starting place for planning learning experiences and activities. This step in the assessment process is also called **preassessment** because the teacher is conducting assessment prior to planning curriculum based on individual needs.

The teacher uses preassessment whenever a new cycle of learning is initiated. For example, if a teacher is planning for a new unit of study with students, a preassessment might be conducted to find out what children already know about the topic. If the teacher has taught all of the shapes and now wants to use them all together, a group preassessment might be conducted to determine if the children are still familiar with the individual shapes.

Ongoing Assessment

Ongoing assessment is conducted continuously throughout the year. In the course of group lessons, activities in learning centers, and observation of play, the teacher notes the child's progress or difficulties that might be impeding progress. Notation of this information is made in anecdotal records or some other type of record-keeping system, so that the information can be used for planning.

The process of ongoing evaluation can be accomplished through **formative assessment** and **summative assessment**. Formative assessments are the strategies the teacher uses to monitor a child's progress in mastery of information or skills during a series of learning activities. Formative assessment is used during instructional periods to monitor how children are progressing and serves as a planning tool based on individual children's needs.

Assessment at the End of Instructional Cycles

Summative assessment is used at the end of a cycle of instructional experiences to confirm mastery of information or skills. Summative assessment assures the teacher that the children understand the concept being taught and that it is time to move on to the next stage of instruction. These two types of assessments will be explained further in Chapter 9.

Enhanced eText: Video Example 2.4

END OF GRADING PERIOD ASSESSMENT   Generally, at the end of a period of several weeks, teachers are asked to evaluate a child's progress and accomplishments. At this time, the teacher might record the child's progress for the period of time, as well as plans for the child in the next reporting period. Because some type of report, either oral or written, is made to parents at the end of the reporting period, the teacher might include documentation of the child's work and/or a written summary of progress. In addition to observing the child, the teacher might use specific tasks to document acquisition of a concept or skill. The teacher might interview the child to determine how the child perceives and uses information introduced in classroom activities. In addition, the child might have the opportunity to self-evaluate, and parents can describe their observations of the child's progress.

End of the School Year Assessment

The most complete assessment and reporting of progress is conducted at the end of the school year. At this time, the teacher needs to summarize the child's progress for all the reporting periods. In some settings, this summarization occurs at a midpoint in the year, as well as at the end of the year. A variety of strategies might be used to determine progress, including teacher-designed assessments in different content areas, standardized achievement tests, student self-evaluations, and a written narrative of the student's accomplishments. As will be discussed in later chapters, a variety of possibilities exist to document what the student has accomplished during the year. In many school districts, this summative information is passed on to the next teacher to help in the initial assessment at the beginning of the next school year. Some preschools and Head Start use this same process.

Enhanced eText: Self-Check 2.3

Challenges and Guidelines in Assessing Young Children for Standards

This chapter has focused on how infants and young children should be assessed and for what purposes. In this section of the chapter, we will examine the impact of organizational, state, and national standards for the assessment of children in the early childhood years, particularly in the preschool years.

Evolution of Early Learning Standards

Until the last 15 years, the focus on learning and assessment with young children has been on appropriate kinds of assessment. The movement to establish standards was part of a national effort to improve American public schools in the latter decades of the 20th century. The first standards were developed by content-area organizations such as the National Council of Teachers of Mathematics (NCTM), the National Center for History in the Schools (NCHS), and the National Council of Teachers of English (NCTE) (see Chapter 1). By the mid-1990s, standards had been published for all fields of education taught in elementary and secondary schools (Gronlund, 2006; Seefeldt, 2005). The purpose of standards is to provide clarity for curriculum content and to raise expectations for student learning.

In the early years of standards development, educators of preschool children were not included in the standards movement. Standards were considered difficult to establish for young children because of the wide age range and diversity of programs. In addition, early childhood programs were sponsored by different types of organizations and functioned differently from public schools.

When states entered the work of establishing standards, kindergarten and other school-based pre-primary programs were included. Because each state developed its own standards, each one was different. In addition, the quality of the standards varied from state to state (Scott-Little, Kagan, & Frelow, 2006). The state standards became the structure for accountability required by NCLB and called for by professional organizations such as NAEYC and ACEI.

Currently, most states have developed early learning standards for young children. Many states have developed standards for infant and toddler programs also. These standards have become a way to guide the curriculum content for early childhood care and education programs, particularly publicly funded programs. There are important benefits to having and addressing early learning standards. First, they encourage educators to understand the learning potential in the infant, toddler, and preschool child and help develop quality early childhood programs. Second, they establish definite expectations for infants and young children of different ages and provide guidelines for communication of children's accomplishments. Third, they provide for the requirements for accountability for the children's development and achievement as well as program quality (Gronlund, 2006;). Because many states have developed early learning standards to conform to the Common Core, and Common Core is no longer in use, the standards will have to complement the new Every Student Succeeds Act (ESSA) passed in 2015 and in the process of being implemented in 2017 (Persons, 2017).

Challenges When Assessing Young Children to Meet Standards

How do early educators address the assessment of young children to meet expectations and accountability in state standards? Are the principles for appropriate assessment described in this chapter compatible with the assessments needed for early learning standards? They can be, but teachers face challenges in answering the call for greater accountability and the emphasis on achievement of skills (Oliver & Klugman, 2006). Standards require teachers to be more intentional in how they assess young children. In their planning for teaching and assessment, they need to make the link between the learning experiences and the standards very clear. Standards need to be integrated into the existing curriculum and assessments that are proven to be of high quality for young children. Otherwise, they might find themselves narrowing the curriculum, depending on direct teaching, and using inappropriate testing methods (Cress, 2004; Gronlund, 2006; Oliver & Klugman, 2006; Rosen, 2012).

Assessing for Standards in Colorado

The Colorado State Department of Education (2016) has adopted state standards for early childhood education titled *Colorado Early Learning and Development Guidelines*. The standards include a broad description of a child's development using a holistic approach that will lead to creating positive early childhood environments. The age range of the guidelines is birth to age 8. The focus of the standards is on child development rather than on achievement.

Assessing for Standards in Minnesota

The Minnesota Early Childhood Indicators of Progress was developed into two levels. The first level is for children from birth to age 3. The second level is from age 3 until kindergarten entry. Like the Colorado standards, the Minnesota standards are developmental. The developers stress that the Indicators of Progress are not for high stakes for assessment. Rather, they are intended to serve as a guide to help Early Childhood teachers and caregivers design appropriate learning experiences and to be able to share a child's progress with parents (Minnesota State Department of Education, 2016).

Guidelines for Working with Young Children in an Assessment Setting

When teachers and other professionals conduct assessments with infants and young children, they need to be sensitive to the special requirements of working with very young children. They also need to be constantly aware of professional ethics that are necessary when conducting assessments with all children. Confidentiality of information acquired through assessment should be maintained when working with assessment results. Parents should understand the reasons for the assessment, be included as part of the assessment process, and understand assessment results (Darragh, 2009). Young children have very short attention spans and are easily distracted. Administrators of assessment instruments and other strategies will benefit from the following guidelines:

1. Contact the home for parental permission to conduct the assessment.
2. Have all materials ready before the assessment session and review procedures for administering the assessment before the child arrives.
3. If possible, be sure that the child is familiar with the environment when conducting an assessment. For very young children, the session might need to be con-

ducted in their homes. For assessments administered to children entering a group setting, results will be more accurate if the child has been given time to adjust to the school setting. The test administrator should also be familiar to the child.

4. Before beginning the assessment session, develop a rapport with the child. Engage the child in a conversation or introduce a toy before the session begins. Once the child seems comfortable, the first assessment tasks can begin.

5. Be alert to signs of fatigue or behaviors that indicate that the child is no longer responding to assessment tasks. Take a brief break, especially with very young children, to allow them to relax before continuing.

6. Use assessment time efficiently. The child should not be hurried, but assessment tasks should be administered with little lag in time, while the child is alert and attentive.

7. Consider adaptations that might be needed for children with disabilities. Be knowledgeable about how tasks might be adapted within requirements for how standardized tests should be administered. If alternative procedures can be used, permit the child to respond differently to a test item. Caution must be used, however, not to change the intent of the item or the type of response that is appropriate as well as correct.

Assessing Aggie's Knowledge of Concepts

Aggie is 6 years old and entering first grade in an inclusion class. All the children are administered a test of basic concepts that requires the child to mark the correct answer for three pictures given to identify the concept asked for by the teacher. Because Aggie's physical limitations have affected her fine-motor development, she is unable to hold a pencil or crayon or to make a mark on the test. Instead, her teacher conducts the test orally and asks Aggie to indicate which of the three pictures is the correct answer. Aggie can point with some difficulty, so the teacher exposes only one row of pictures at a time and asks Aggie to point to the picture that matches the concept she has described.

Enhanced eText: Self-Check 2.4

Summary

We need to be able to evaluate the growth and development of young children for various purposes. Specialists who work with children from various perspectives have devised formal and informal assessments that can be used with newborns, as well as later in the early childhood years. Members of the medical profession, psychologists, educators, and parents all want to know whether the young child is developing at a normal rate. If development deviates from acceptable progress in some way, tests and other evaluation strategies are available to study the child and to help devise early intervention measures that can minimize or eliminate the developmental problem.

As we work with young children in a new century, we need to consider how the available assessment methods are best used. In view of the many concerns and issues about testing young children, assessment should focus on meeting the child's developmental and learning needs. We should take advantage of the many assessment strategies available but, at the same time, be sure that we understand the purposes, strengths, and limitations of each type when including them in a system for comprehensive evaluation and reporting. All assessments should have a meaningful purpose and method and be related to the child's development and learning. The assessments used to report progress should also be meaningful to parents and other adults who need to understand the child's profile of progress and learning needs. The assessment process should include the child and the child's parents if the process is to be the most comprehensive and informative.

In the next eight chapters, each component of a comprehensive evaluation system will be discussed, beginning with standardized tests. Informal methods will then be discussed, with portfolio assessment serving as a model for the desired comprehensive assessment plan that will best benefit the young child.

Enhanced eText: Self-Check: Chapter Review

Key Terms

assessment software 47

authentic assessment (authentic performance assessment) 46

developmental checklist 46

directed assignment 46

disability (learning disability) 40

evaluation 37

formal assessment 39

formative assessment 50

informal assessment 39

interview 46

narrative report 47

neonatologist 40

obstetrician 40

pediatrician 40

performance assessment 46

portfolio 47

preassessment 50

rating scale 46

rubric 46

scope (sequence of skills) 46

standardized assessment 40

summative assessment 50

Selected Organizations

Search for the following organizations online:

National Institute for Early Education Research

Child Care Exchange

Council for the Accreditation of Educator Preparation

Education Week

References

Age of Learning, Inc. (2017). ABCmouse.com. Early Learning Academy. Retrieved September 25, 2017 from https://www.abcmouse.com/landing/brand:yahoomobile

American Academy of Pediatrics. (2017). *Newborn screening disorders: What parents want to know about newborn screening disorders.* Retrieved from https://www.aap.org/en-us/advocacy-and-policy/aap-health-initiatives/PEHDIC/Documents/Newbornscreeningdisorders.pdf

Apgar, V. (1975). A proposal for a new method of evaluation of a newborn infant. *Anesthesia and Analgesia, 32,* 260–267.

Association for Childhood Education International (2011). *ACEI global guidelines assessment-third edition.Washington, DC: Author.*

Barbour, A., Boyer, B., Hardin, B., & Wortham, S. C. (2004). From principle to practice. Using the global guidelines to assess quality education and care. *Childhood Education, 80,* 327–331.

Barrera, I. (1996). Thoughts on the assessment of young children whose sociocultural background is unfamiliar to the assessor. In S. J. Meisels & E. Fenichel (Eds.), *New visions for the developmental assessment of infants and young children* (pp. 69–84). Washington, DC: Zero to Three: National Center for Infants, Toddlers, and Families.

Bowers, F. B. (2008, November/December). Developing a child assessment plan: An integral part of program quality. *Exchange,* pp. 51–55.

Caspe, M., Seltzer, A., Kennedy, J., Cappio, M., & DeLorenzo, C. (2013). Engaging families in the child assessment process. *Young Children, 68,* 8–14.

Colorado State Department of Education. (2016). Colorado *Early learning and developmental guidelines, birth to age 8.* Retrieved September 29, 2017 from: https://www.cde.state.co.us/early/preschoolstandardsresources.

Copple, C., & Bredekamp, S. (Eds.). (2009). *Developmentally appropriate practices in early childhood programs* (3rd ed.). Washington, DC: National Association for the Education of Young Children.

Cress, S. W. (2004, October). Assessing standards in the "real" kindergarten classroom. *Early Childhood Education Journal, 32,* 95–99.

Darragh, J. (2009, May/June). Informal assessment as a tool for supporting parent partnerships. *Exchange,* pp. 91–93.

Division of Early Childhood/Council for Exceptional Children (DEC/CEC). (2007). Recommendations on early childhood curriculum, assessment, and program evaluation. Retrieved from http://www.decsped.org/uploads/docs/about_dec/position_concept_papers/Prmtg_Pos_Outcomes_Companion_Paper.pdf

Elicker, J., & McMullen, M. B. (2013). Appropriate and meaningful assessment in family-centered programs. *Young Children, 68,* 22–26.

Epstein, A. S., Schweinhart, L. J., DeBruin-Parecki, A., & Robin, K. B. (2004, July). *Preschool assessment: A guide to developing a balanced approach.* National Institute for Early Education Research. Retrieved August 11, 2009, from http://nieer.org/resources/policybriefs/7.pdf

Espinosa, L. M., & López, M. L. (2007, August). *Assessment considerations for young English language learners across different levels of accountability.* Paper presented at The National Early Childhood Accountability Task Force and First 5 LA.

Feld, J. K., & Bergan, K. S. (2002). Assessment tools in the 21st century. *Child Care Information Exchange, 146,* 62–66.

Genishi, C., & Dyson, A. H. (2009). *Children, language, and literacy.* New York, NY: Teachers College Press.

Gonzalez-Mena, J., & Stonehouse, A. (2008). *Making links: A collaborative approach to planning and practice in early childhood programs.* New York, NY: Teachers College Press.

Goodwin, W. L., & Goodwin, L. D. (1993). Young children and measurement: Standardized and nonstandardized instruments in early childhood education. In B. Spodek (Ed.), *Handbook of research on the education of young children* (pp. 441–463). New York, NY: Macmillan.

Greenspan, S. I., Meisels, S. J., & the Zero to Three Work Group on Developmental Assessment. (1996). Toward a new vision for the developmental assessment of infants and young children. In S. J. Meisels & E. Fenichel (Eds.), *New visions for the developmental assessment of infants and young children* (pp. 11–26). Washington, DC: Zero to Three: National Center for Infants, Toddlers, and Families.

Gronlund, G. (2006). *Make early learning standards come alive: Connecting your practice and curriculum to state guidelines.* St. Paul, MN: Redleaf Press.

Guss, S. S., Horm, D. M., Krebiel, S. M., Petty, J. A., Austin, K., Bergen, C., et al. (2013). Using classroom quality assessments to inform teacher decisions. *Young Children 68*, 16–20.

Hardin, B. J., Bergen, D., Busio, D. S., & Boone, W. (2017). Investigating the psychometric properties of the ACEI global guidelines assessment, third edition (GGA) in nine countries. *Early Childhood Education Journal, 45*, 297–312.

Hardin, B. J., Bergen, D., & Hung, H-F. (2013). Investigating the psychometric properties of the ACEI global guidelines assessment (GGA) in four countries. *Early Childhood Education Journal, 41*(2), 91–101.

Harms, T., Clifford, R. M., & Cryer, D. (2014). *Early childhood environment rating scale* (3rd ed) (ECERS-3). New York, NY: Teachers College Press.

Harms, T., Cryer, D., Clifford, R. M., & Yazejian, N. (2017). *Infant/Toddler environment rating scale* (3rd ed.). New York, NY: Teachers College Press.

La Paro, K., Pianta, R. C., & Hamre, B. (2012). *Classroom Assessment Scoring System (CLASS) Toddler.* Baltimore, MD: Brookes Publishing.

Mattix-Foster, A. A., & Ramos, K. A. (2017, Summer). *Advocating for English language learners. Early years bulletin (Vol. 4, No. 4).* Washington, DC: Association for Childhood Education International.

McAfee, A., Leong, D. J., & Bodrova, E. (2004). *Basics of assessment. A primer for early childhood education.* Washington, DC: National Association for the Education of Young Children.

Meisels, S. J. (1996). Charting the continuum of assessment and intervention. In S. J. Meisels & E. Fenichel (Eds.), *New visions for the developmental assessment of infants and young children* (pp. 27–52). Washington, DC: Zero to Three: National Center for Infants, Toddlers, and Families.

Mindes, G., & Jung, L. A. (2015). *Assessing young children* (5th ed.). Upper Saddle River, NJ: Pearson Education, Inc.

Minnesota State Department of Education (2016). Minnesota *Early childhood indicators of progress.* Retrieved September 29, 2017 from https://www.education.state.mn.us/MDE/fam/elsprog/index.htm

Moreno, A. J., & Klute, M. M. (2011). Infant-toddler teachers can successfully employ authentic assessment: The learning through relating system. *Early Childhood Research Quarterly, 26*, 484–496.

Morrison, G. (2017, July 20). *Why is assessment important?* Retrieved September 15, 2017 from https://www.education.com/reference/article/why-assessment-important/

National Association for the Education of Young Children. (2017). *Revised guidance for assessment, a supplement to NAEYC early learning program standards and accreditation criteria.* Retrieved from https://www.naeyc.org/academy/files/academy/Revised%20Criteria%20and%20Guidance%20for%20 Assessment%20April%202017.pdf

National Association for the Education of Young Children. (2009). *Where we stand on assessing English language learners.* Washington, DC: Author.

National Research Council. (2008). *Early childhood assessment: Why, what, and how? Committee on developmental outcomes and assessments for young children,* Catherine E. Snow and Susan B. Van Hemel (eds.). Board on Children, Youth and Families, Board on Testing and Assessment, Division of Behavioral and Social Sciences and Education. Washington, DC: The National Academies Press.

Oliver, S. J., & Klugman, E. (2006, July/August). Play and standards-driven curricula: Can they work together in preschool? *Exchange, 170*, 12–16.

Persons, S. (2017, April 24). Education Secretary says Common Core no longer an issue for schools. *The Washington Times.* Retrieved September 25, 2017 from https://www.washingtontimes.com/news/2017/apr/24/betsy-devos-common-core-no-longer-issue-schools/

Pianta, R. C., LaParo, K. M., & Hamre, B. (2013). *Classroom Assessment Scoring System (CLASS) PreK.* Baltimore, MD: Brookes Publishing.

Popham, W. J. (2013). *Classroom assessment: What teachers need to know.* Pearson Education.

Popper, B. K. (1996). Achieving change in assessment practices: A parent's perspective. In S. J. Meisels & E. Fenichel (Eds.), *New visions for the developmental assessment of infants and young children* (pp. 59–66). Washington, DC: Zero to Three: National Center for Infants, Toddlers, and Families.

Rector and Visitors of the University of Virginia. (2013). *Classroom assessment scoring system.* Charlottesville, VA: Center for Advanced Study of Teaching and Learning.

Rentzou, K. (2010). Using the ACEI Global Guidelines Assessment to evaluate the quality of early child care in Greek settings. *Early Childhood Education Journal, 38*, 75–80.

Rocco, S. (1996). Toward shared commitment and shared responsibility: A parent's vision of developmental assessment. In S. J. Meisels & E. Fenichel (Eds.), *New Visions for the Developmental Assessment of Infants and Young Children* (pp. 55–58). Washington, DC: Zero to Three: National Center for Infants, Toddlers, and Families.

Rosen, S. (2012, March 22). *Aligning early childhood education with the Common Core.* Retrieved from http://www.ecs-commoncore.org/aligning-early-childhood-educ

Sandell, E., Hardin, B., & Wortham, S. (2010). *Using the ACEI Global Guidelines Assessment for improving early education.* Retrieved from www.ed.mnsu./global-guidelines.pdf

Scott-Little, C., Kagan, S. L., & Frelow, V. S. (2006, March/April). State standards for children's learning. *Exchange, 168*, 27–34.

Seefeldt, C. (2005). *How to work with standards in the early childhood classroom.* New York, NY: Teachers College Press.

Segal, M., & Webber, N. T. (1996). Nonstructured play observations: Guidelines, benefits, and caveats. In S. J. Meisels & E. Fenichel (Eds.), *New visions for the developmental assessment of infants and young children* (pp. 207–230). Washington, DC: Zero to Three: National Center for Infants, Toddlers, and Families.

Shepard, L. A. (1989). Why we need better assessments. *Educational Leadership, 46*, 4–9.

Tanyel, N. (2017, Summer). Fostering resilience in infants and toddlers. *Early Years Bulletin (Vol. 4, No. 4).* Washington, DC: Association for Childhood Education International.

The Source for Learning, Inc. (2018). *Preschool First.com.* Retrieved from https://sourceforlearning.org/home

Weiss, H. B., Caspe, M., & Lopez, E. (2006, Spring). Family involvement in early childhood education. Harvard Family Research Project, no 1. Harvard Graduate School of Education.

Widerstrom, A. H., Mowder, B. A., & Sandall, S. R. (1991). *At-risk and handicapped newborns and infants.* Upper Saddle River, NJ: Prentice Hall.

Wiggins, G. P. (1993). *Assessing student performance.* San Francisco, CA: Jossey-Bass.

Wiggins, G. P. (1998). *Educative assessment.* San Francisco, CA: Jossey-Bass.

Wodrich, D. (1984). *Children's psychological testing.* Baltimore, MD: Brookes.

Chapter 3
Communicating with Families

Flashon Studio/Shutterstock

 ## Chapter Learning Outcomes

As a result of reading this chapter, you will be able to:

3.1 Discuss characteristics of family–professional partnerships that promote children's development and learning.

3.2 Explain strategies for establishing and maintaining family–professional partnerships that benefit children.

3.3 Discuss the roles of families in screening and assessment.

3.4 Describe strategies for conducting effective parent conferences.

Parents are children's first and most important teachers. As such, they have a critical role in their child's development and learning. Teachers, administrators, and other early childhood providers understand that children's success as learners depends on parents as well as professionals. A recent report published by the Center on the Developing Child at Harvard University (2016) provides a scientific basis supporting the critical need for positive family–professional partnerships. Entitled *From Best Practices to Breakthrough Impacts: A Science-Based Approach to Building a More Promising Future for Young Children and Families*, this report emphasizes how children's relationships with adults (e.g., parents, caregivers, health providers) impacts all areas of their development—physical, behavior, social-emotional, and intellectual—as well as later outcomes. Their research shows that brain development is directly influenced by both positive and negative interactions with others and the environments in which these interactions take place. Thus, the importance of having parents as partners in early childhood settings is essential to children's individual development as well as the quality of their care and education (Dunst & Trivette, 2012; Schmidt & Matthews, 2013; Turnbull, Turnbull, Erwin, Soodak & Shogren, 2015). Today's children experience a variety of family relationships. Some children live with a single parent or with grandparents. Children may live in blended families where both parents had previous marriages and children from the first and second marriages now live together as one family. Other children live in households with same-sex parents. Still others may live in households that include adults who function as caretakers but are not related. Therefore, the term *families* should acknowledge the expanded roles of parenting to include any persons that function as family in their daily lives. Throughout this book, information related to family partnerships during screening and assessment processes will be discussed. This chapter is devoted to how professionals can engage in meaningful partnerships with adults who serve in parenting roles for children, particularly during the assessment process. Strategies for communicating with families about children's progress will be discussed, including planning and conducting effective family conferences. Information about working with families of children with disabilities and immigrant families will be discussed also.

Family-Professional Partnerships that Promote Children's Development and Learning

Parents have always actively participated in early childhood settings such as childcare centers and schools. When the first author's father was an elementary school student in the early 20th century in Austin, Texas, mothers took turns going to the school to prepare lunch for the children. Traditionally, parents helped with school parties and volunteered in the classroom. Parent–teacher organizations raised money to secure needed books, equipment, and other materials that were not in the school budget.

Today, the idea of a partnership with parents goes beyond helping with school programs toward empowering and engaging families in mutually respectful interactions that benefit children. Fundamental to effective **family–professional partnerships** is the belief that they should be **strengths-based** (built on family resources and assets) and **family-centered** (led by family concerns and priorities) (Dunst & Trivette, 2012). Turnbull et al. (2006; 2015) describe family–professional partnerships as relationships in which families (not just parents) and professionals build on each other's expertise and resources so decisions will benefit children as well as their partnership. They suggest partnerships that support children's well-being and are achieved by applying the following seven principles:

- Communication—ongoing, honest interactions using methods agreed on by both the parents and the professionals
- Professional Competence—well-trained professionals committed to lifelong learning and who have expectations for children
- Respect—regarding each other in high esteem and interactions that promote honesty and dignity
- Commitment—being accessible and sensitive to the needs of families
- Equality—shared power and decision making
- Advocacy—forming alliances based on identified needs and taking action to address them
- Trust—the keystone of strong family–professional partnerships

Numerous professional organizations have published position papers and guidelines that help educators understand essential characteristics of effective family–professional partnerships. For example, the *NAEYC Standards for Initial and Advanced Early Childhood Professional Preparation Programs* describe professional standards for early childhood professionals (NAEYC, 2010). The purpose of these standards is to provide guidance for professionals that reflect the values of inclusive, high-quality early childhood services. Standard 2, *Building Family and Community Relationships*, describes elements of strong family–professional partnerships as follows:

2a: Knowing about and understanding diverse family and community characteristics

2b: Supporting and engaging families and communities through respectful, reciprocal relationships

2c: Involving families and communities in their children's development and learning (p. 30)

David Kostelnik/Pearson Education, Inc.

Parents and teachers are partners in the learning and assessment of young children.

Similarly, the Council for Exceptional Children/Division of Early Childhood published *Initial Level Special Educator Professional Preparation Standards* in 2012 to prepare educators for effectively serving children with disabilities. There are seven main standards and the importance of strong family–professional partnerships is emphasized throughout (CEC/DEC 2012).

In addition, as early learning standards have become an expected aspect of young children's education, national and state organizations have stressed the importance of family partnerships. For example, a joint position statement on early learning standards developed by the National Association for Young Children and the National Association of Early Childhood Specialists in State Departments of Education (2002) describes four conditions needed in the development and implementation of early learning standards. The fourth condition emphasizes the importance of family-professional partnerships: "Early learning standards will have the most positive effects if families—key partners in young children's learning—are provided with respectful communication and support" (p. 8). This position statement and its content are supported by the National Association of Elementary School Principals and other prominent organizations as a unified effort to guide the field toward quality and developmentally appropriate content in standards, including the important role of families. To date, the majority of states have developed early learning standards for early childhood professionals that include families as the primary partner in young children's learning and development. For example, the North Carolina Foundations for Early Learning and Development (North Carolina Foundations Task Force, 2013) specifically state,

> *Foundations* can also be used as a resource for parents and other family members. All parents wonder if their child is learning what's needed in order to be successful in school. Parents will find it helpful to review the Goals and Developmental Indicators to learn what most early educators in North Carolina feel are appropriate goals for young children (p. 2).

Parents and teachers are not the only beneficiaries of a strong, mutually respectful partnership. Children benefit the most! When parents and other significant adults in their lives have a positive relationship with teachers and other education professionals, children feel that they and their family are honored and respected. The better the relationship, the more children feel that they, too, can have a trusting relationship with the teacher. They learn how to conduct social relationships by watching adult relationships. They notice all the nuances of spoken language, body language, and tone of voice that the adults use. They use these positive models to develop their own relationships with others (Keyser, 2006).

Search and Share 3.1

Family Partnerships & Early Learning Standards

Search online to find your state's early learning standards (or a nearby state). How do these standards promote family partnerships and family-centered services? How can you use them in your program to improve family participation?

Enhanced eText: Self-Check 3.1

Strategies for Establishing and Maintaining Family–Professional Partnerships that Benefit Children

Establishing family partnerships requires a commitment within and outside of the classroom setting. Once professional partnerships with families are in place, a variety of methods for ongoing communication throughout the year should occur to ensure the needs of the children are being met.

Establishing Relationships with Families

The importance of a strong partnership with families becomes more evident as we learn more about how children benefit from strong teacher–parent relationships. All parties in the partnership have an equal role. The quality of the partnership affects the child's security and maximizes the child's potential for learning. This quality partnership includes frequent two-way communications, interest in each other's perspectives, and acceptance of the views of the other partner. The partnership grows through mutual consultation both on daily activities and important decisions. It requires working through differences with mutual respect (Keyser, 2006; Lightfoot, 2003; Turnbull et al., 2015).

Professional organizations have published guidelines for establishing and maintaining family–professional partnerships that reflect the diversity of families. For example, the Division of Early Childhood/Council for Exceptional Children (DEC, 2010) published a position paper entitled *Responsiveness to ALL Children, Families, and Professionals: Integrating Cultural and Linguistic Diversity into Policy and Practice*, which includes information about ways to establish and maintain effective family–professional partnerships with diverse families, especially those who have children with disabilities and culturally and linguistically diverse families. This position statement emphasizes the importance of incorporating diverse values, beliefs, and practices in all aspects of early childhood education such as the classroom curriculum, including communicating with families in their home language, both orally and in written documents.

> **Enhanced eText:** Video Example 3.1

Family members and professionals from a variety of cultures, ethnicities, family structures, and levels of income can enrich partnerships. A variety of languages may be spoken, and families might have different views from professionals on how children should be raised. This means that all parties (e.g., schools, centers, services providers, parents) must learn about each other, both at school and at home. Families

Building Bridges with Families of Infants and Toddlers

In 2016, more than 15 million children younger than age 6, who had working mothers, participated in out-of-home care (Child Care Aware of America, 2017). Thirty-eight percent of the children who participated in child care in 2013 were infants and toddlers (Schmitt & Matthews, 2013). These children spend on average 36 hours a

(Continued)

week in child care and often participate in multiple placements. Thus, for many families, the partnership between educational settings and the home begins when their children are infants and toddlers. The development of relationships between the home and facilities or schools is initiated when the child is transitioned from home to a center or other care and/or educational setting. The development of trust and positive, consistent caregiving are important in developing bonds between the caregiver and the child and the caregiver and the parents. Each day the child and family adults go through emotions related to separation when the child is left in the caregiving setting and then another adjustment when they are united at the end of the day. Caregivers and other center personnel who show sensitivity and understanding of unique family characteristics and cultural differences can facilitate the daily transitions and ongoing interactions with the child and family. Families of babies have the same needs for support and communication regarding their child as families of older children in school settings; however, the needs for daily communication and exchange of information about the child are even more crucial for young children.

need to learn about the school culture and how their child fits into a group of diverse children. Likewise, professionals must understand each child's family cultural practices and seek ways to incorporate them in the early childhood setting (Keyser, 2006).

ONGOING COMMUNICATIONS   Informal and formal communication processes, including home visits, are effective methods for establishing positive family–professional partnerships. Continuing conversations and other forms of communication are an important step in establishing a partnership. At times, the teacher initiates the communication, but at other times the parent initiates the contact. Families have different ways to engage in the partnership. The continuum from relationship to partnership is different from family to family. The teacher needs to be sensitive to how best to communicate with families. Written newsletters to parents may not be effective if the parents speak another language and the written materials are not in the parents' home language, for example. Parents may also be very intimidated by requests for them to give information through written notes. Care should be taken, however, to make sure parents who speak a language other than English can read in their home language. The first author's years as a teacher of children from Spanish-speaking families provides another example of how to be sensitive to parents. The principal decided that all newsletters and information sheets would be communicated in both English and Spanish. It took some reflection and awkward interactions before it was understood that the Spanish-speaking families in the school community could not read in Spanish either. Patience and goodwill are necessary for both families and teachers as partnerships develop, especially if there are extenuating circumstances, such as language differences, that may be challenging.

Today, technological advances can be used to enhance communication between parents and educational settings. For example, the teacher can establish a classroom web site where information can be shared and ideas exchanged. Photographs and videos of class work can be posted and opportunities for family comments provided. E-mails to individual families can replace notes with families who have access to a computer. Other families without computers can continue to exchange written notes with the teacher. Cell phone calls can include photographs of the child at school and possibly text messages to keep families informed. The messages can include anecdotes about the child's experiences at school, new accomplishments, or newly developed social skills (Mitchell, Foulger, & Wetzel, 2009).

HOME VISITS   One of the most effective ways to establish a relationship with a child and the family is to make a **home visit** before the child begins attending the center or school. When the teacher visits the home environment, a context for understanding the child and family is established. As young teachers, both authors made home visits at the beginning of every school year. It was very educational to learn how and where the children in our classrooms lived. The first author taught in a bilingual program; as a result, most of the children in the classroom were Hispanic. Many children were from families of migrant workers. A majority of families she visited had a very low income. One family lived out of two cars several miles from the school bus route. The children were dressed and ready to leave by 5 a.m. so that they could walk with their older siblings to the bus stop. In the afternoons, it was almost dark before they reached home again. Another family lived very near the school, but in a very old wood frame house with bare wood floors. The mother got water from the tap outside for cooking and cleaning. She had a history of being abused and beaten by her husband. When the first author visited, the house was very clean, and the mother proudly showed her the room where three of the girls shared a double bed. Later in the year, when the child from that family in her classroom appeared at school with a broken arm, the school nurse was notified to work with child welfare authorities to investigate and assist the mother, if needed.

Families were pleased that the teacher came to their home. The children were always dressed in their best clothes and on their best behavior. Family pictures, the children's toys, and the plants in the yard were often topics of conversation. These initial visits were vital to the parents' feeling comfortable with the teacher, especially since she spoke Spanish, and the parents were able to overcome their hesitations to come to the school for meetings and conferences. Many times, parent conferences were conducted at a parent's place of work because they could not leave their job or did not have transportation to the school. Home visits continued in some situations when the family or the teacher needed support from the other. This experience illustrates how home visits can benefit young children. For children whose language and culture may be unfamiliar, a home visit is a great way to understand more about parent–child interactions and the home environment. For example, perhaps story telling is a big part of the family's culture. If you do not speak the family's home language, a trained interpreter can accompany you to the home visit. The parents could be invited to the classroom to share their stories and perhaps record them for repeated listening. For a child with disabilities, a home visit can help professionals understand a child's strengths rather than only focusing on their disabilities. Parents can share strategies for including their child in typical activities that may otherwise be unknown.

In conclusion, home visits are an effective way to begin and maintain family–professional partnerships as they provide authentic experiences for both the family members and teachers or other professionals. Ongoing communication strategies can grow out of these experiences or other avenues of learning about the types of communication that work best for families.

Using Professional Ethics in School–Family Partnerships

Teachers are responsible for maintaining professionalism in their relationships with parents. Guidelines for teachers are provided by professional education organizations. The Code of Ethical Conduct was first published by the National Association for the Education of Young Children in 1989, and most recently updated in 2011

(NAEYC, 2011). The Code provides guidelines for professional behavior for teachers and caregivers of young children. It describes categories of ethics that provide a framework for how teachers should interact in their positions in early childhood settings. Throughout this Code of Ethics it is stressed that professional ethics includes responsibilities for children, families, communities, and society. The descriptions discuss that professional ethical judgments guide educators as to what they should and should not do as professionals. Section II of the Code is dedicated to ethical partnerships with families. The Code of Ethics is a document that permits the profession to speak as a group. The hope for the future is that the code can be used not only as a basis for advocacy addressing the needs of young children and their families, but also to help early childhood educators to focus on what is best for all young children and their families (Feeney, 2010).

Enhanced eText: Self-Check 3.2

The Role of Families in the Screening and Assessment Process

As discussed previously, **screening** is a brief snapshot of a child's development, whereas assessment is a more in-depth look at a child's development. Often, children are first screened (e.g., a hearing screening test for newborns) and then only assessed in more depth if there is an indication of atypical development. Family members may be less involved in screening tests as they may be a routine part of care or administered to all children in a group setting. For example, pediatricians may administer a developmental screen during routine appointments. Or, all the children in a preschool classroom may be administered a developmental screen upon enrollment or at the beginning of a new year. While parental permission for screenings may not always be required, it is good practice to obtain parental permission so that parents are aware of this process. Parental permission is required for in-depth assessments, particularly for children with disabilities, as it is part of IDEA 2004.

Parents may have questions such as the following: How are screenings administered? How are checklist assessments conducted? What strategies does the teacher use to acquire checklist information? Why are observation reports important? What does the teacher learn about the child by doing observations? What do the summaries of the child's advances and accomplishments mean when compared with a traditional report card? How does a rubric, an instrument used to measure authentic and performance assessments, work? How does the teacher design written tests for primary-grade children? The teacher should be able to explain during the conference how and why assessments are used so that parents understand the assessment process. Parents will vary in how they understand technical information. The teacher needs to be prepared to help interpret screening results with individual families.

The same is true of assessment materials shared at parent–teacher conferences. One method of summarizing the child's progress and overall evaluation is to have a summary report or narrative report for the parents. The teacher goes over the report with the parents, helping them understand the relationship between the assessment resources and the child's overall evaluation. If a summary report is not used, the

Search and Share 3.2

Understanding Developmental Screening Tools

Search online to find information on developmental screening tools and how to explain screening results to parents. How will you explain the positive aspects of screening results to parents? How will you explain the need for further testing to parents?

teacher must have an overall evaluation ready to share with the parents. The assessments and work samples must be explained, with their implications for the child's progress and future needs for instructional experiences.

Soliciting Parental Input for Assessment and Planning

Practices established for families in the assessment process apply to all children. Home visits with parents before the beginning of school can initiate the process of gathering information about the child. Parents can participate in the assessment process through the teacher's ongoing efforts to solicit information from parents, participating in conferences when the child's progress is reported, and contributing information about the child's progress within the conference, through written responses submitted to the teacher, and by telephone or e-mail messages (Gilkerson & Hanson, 2000).

Opportunities for parental input into the assessment and planning process should be built into each aspect of the process. Parental input can be obtained informally through home visits or individual family meetings. More formal methods of gathering information include surveys, questionnaires, and other written documents. If parents do not voluntarily reflect on the child's progress and make suggestions, the teacher should be ready to solicit input. As the teacher completes the evaluation report, parents can give their own views about progress and concerns they might have about the child. Older children may also discuss progress and how learning might be improved. As the teacher discusses the next steps in planning for the child, parents can give their suggestions of what might be helpful for the child. Also, the teacher and parents can discuss what the parents might do to help the child at home. The important point is that parents and children need to feel that they are a vital part of the evaluation process and not mere recipients of the evaluation report. Although the teacher may need to discuss improvements that the child needs to make, parents should also be encouraged to look at problems and suggest solutions. If a true partnership has been established, parents will be able to address the child's needs and help plan ways to guide the child without feeling that they are being judged.

Families from Diverse Cultures

Obtaining parental input during the assessment process is especially important for children who are English Language Learners (ELLs) and whose home cultural practices may differ from early childhood professionals. Both the overall assessment process and specific assessment tools rely heavily on language and cultural practices. Learning about the cultural practices of the families in the classroom can help professionals gain insight into child-rearing practices and ways to respectfully approach

Search and Share 3.3

Supporting Families of Diverse Cultures

Search online to find strategies for establishing partnerships with families of young children from diverse cultures. Share two or three strategies with other professionals and discuss how to implement them in your local setting.

communication with families. Learning a few words or phrases in a family's home language, for example, can demonstrate a commitment to listening to the family's perspective about their child's education and development. Likewise, including an interpreter in oral communications and/or a translator for written communications sends a clear message of sensitivity for the family and child. Professionals should include photographs and other visual items that illustrate the concepts they are communicating to family members along with oral descriptions to help facilitate their understanding. By doing background research on a specific culture, a family's local community, and/or a specific family's history, professionals not only are more effective communicators, but also can avoid offending families due to a lack of knowledge about their cultural practices. Lastly, be careful to avoid prejudice and stereotypes in communicating with families. Each family is unique! It is always best to ask questions to clarify information rather than to make assumptions.

Families of Children with Disabilities

Families of children with disabilities have unique knowledge about their child's behaviors and development. If their child has already been diagnosed with a disability, parents also know what strategies for learning and daily functioning work best. Make sure to gather this information not only for a specific evaluation process or assessment, but also on an ongoing basis to ensure an accurate picture of the child's strengths and needs.

When parents discover that their infant, toddler, or young child has a delay or disability, they soon understand the important role of assessment in the child's life. They experience conflicting emotions about what the assessment will reveal. One mother described her reaction (Rocco, 1996):

> When assessments emphasize deficits and diminished expectations for future success, we parents generally begin to look for a way to thwart these negative prognostications. At the very best, we want a miracle cure. At the least, we want professionals to "fix" our children . . . . We believe that professionals have all the answers, and therefore, all the power. (p. 56)

The extent of the family's participation affects the child's performance and the relevance of the child's assessment in guiding intervention services (Berman & Shaw, 1996; Bruder & Dunst, 2015; Dunst & Trivette, 2012; Ray, Pewitt-Kinder, & George, 2009). Dunst and Trivette (2012) describe the assessment process as family-directed or family-centered, with the child and family's concerns, priorities, resources, and values as most important in planning for the child. Reasons for a family-centered approach include:

- Following legal mandates—The Individuals with Disabilities Education Improvement Act of 2004 (IDEA, 2004) requires that families be a team member and partner in the assessment, decision making, and activities planned for addressing the child's needs (U.S. Congress, 2004).

- Focusing on the child as part of a family system—Children are part of a family system that impacts the child's developmental progress. Likewise, the needs of a child with disabilities may reshape how the family system works. Thus, it is important to understand how the child functions within the family system.

- Ensuring individualizing services—IDEA 2004 requires an individual plan for each child. By focusing on the family's concerns, priorities, and resources, individual services will be more likely to meet the needs of the family and the child.

- Identifying family's need for services—Conferences with families who have a child with a disability are more complex than parent–teacher conferences for children with typical development. For example, parents may hear new test results for the first time and need to process how this information could impact their child's services or their family routines at home.

- Identifying family's strengths—Building on family strengths helps ensure greater success in both the assessment process itself and the subsequent intervention plan. For instance, the family may live close to extended family members who can provide additional time to reinforce the goals or outcomes on a child's individual plan.

An Individualized Family Service Plan (IFSP) is developed specifically for children and families participating in the Early Intervention Program (Part C of IDEA 2004). A team of intervention providers that might include therapists, early intervention specialists, teachers, and family members are involved in both planning for the family and child's needs and later assessing progress on the IFSP with the family (Ray, Pewitt-Kinder, & George, 2009). For children ages 3–21 (Part C of IDEA 2004), an Individual Education Program is developed with a similar team but with a larger focus on learning and academic skills.

Enhanced eText: Video Example 3.2

All the assessment strategies discussed in this text apply to children with disabilities. Some types of assessments may have to be modified, especially for children who have a cognitive delay or physical disability. Nevertheless, children with disabilities should not be excluded from **performance assessments,** in which a child demonstrates knowledge by applying it to a task or problem-solving activity, and portfolios. **Portfolios** include a child's work samples, the teacher's assessments for a child, and other documents that demonstrate a child's progress. These children should have ongoing opportunities to demonstrate what they understand and can use. Teachers and parents will need to be creative in finding ways for children to engage in their own assessment if they are unable to participate in the same manner as children without disabilities. Computers and other types of assistive technologies can be used, as well as photographs, videotapes, and audiotapes. The important point is that children with disabilities should be included in the assessment and planning process to the best of their abilities. Bridging their disabilities with alternative assessment strategies will complete their inclusion as full members of the classroom (Jarrett, Browne, & Wallin, 2006; McLean, Wolery, & Bailey, 2004; Zero to Three, 2010).

Parent Partnership in Portfolio Assessment

The principal, teachers, and parents at Thomas Jefferson Kindergarten and Primary School discussed portfolio assessment at school council meetings for several months. Teachers and a principal from a school in a nearby community were invited to attend the council meeting and talk about their experiences in starting portfolio assessment. In April, the council decided to implement portfolios the following year. As training sessions were held for the teachers at the end of the school year, newsletters were sent to parents informing them of the change in reporting using portfolios and of evening sessions that would be held to share how the teachers were preparing for using portfolios.

During the summer months, teacher training continued. At the beginning of the school year, an open house was held to further explain how the portfolio process would be used and the rationale for moving to this type of assessment and reporting. Following a general meeting in the multipurpose room of the school, parents visited their child's classroom, where the teacher showed a model of the portfolio that would be used in the classroom and how parents could contribute to the information that would be included in the portfolio. Questions about the portfolio assessment process were answered.

At the first parent–teacher conferences, portfolio assessment to report student progress was used for the first time. Parents were invited to reflect on what the child had accomplished. In some classrooms, the child participated in the conference and discussed why some entries were important. Following review of the portfolios, both the parents and teacher discussed how to plan for the child's learning experiences based on the progress made during the first part of the school year.

Some teachers found the move to the portfolio process easier than others. Likewise, some parents understood and supported portfolio assessment more quickly than others. The principal provided troubleshooting sessions for teachers, and the school council discussed how to continue to improve the process.

Enhanced eText: Self-Check 3.3

Conducting Effective Parent Conferences

Whatever approaches a teacher uses to assess children, a report is made to communicate with the parents about the child's developmental advances and learning accomplishments. The assessments that have been made are evaluated to determine what will be in the report. Families are given the opportunity to share their ideas about the child's growth and progress and to respond to the report that the teacher has developed. Although written reports and portfolios are helpful assessment systems to use when sharing information with families, **parent conferences** permit families and teachers to interact directly.

Types of Parent Conferences

In addition to traditional teacher-led conferences, other options for conducting parent conferences include three-way conferences, student-led conferences, and parent group meeting conferences. Each of these types of conferences are described in the following section.

THREE-WAY CONFERENCES
In the **three-way conference**, the student, parent, and teacher all participate. The student has an opportunity to present and discuss his or her work through a portfolio, the parent has an opportunity to introduce relevant information about the child's progress, and the teacher has the opportunity to summarize what has been accomplished during the time period. All participants plan together for future goals, projects, and general learning. All participants discuss how the home and the school can work together to accomplish the child's learning goals.

STUDENT-LED CONFERENCES
Students can be taught to conduct a conference with the family, called **student-led conferences** (Cromwell, 2010). Using a showcase or evaluative portfolio, the student and parent study portfolio contents and discuss the student's work. The teacher can join the conference later and answer questions the parent might have or elicit the family's ideas for the child's further progress (Stiggins, 2005). Regardless of the approach to be used for the parent conference, the conference should follow the assumption that families are partners in the process:

> The inclusion of families in the overall assessment is critically important. They need to be involved in more than just the final stage of the process if they are to see all the skills and strategies that their children are developing and to assist their children along the way.

Family involvement with portfolios can take many forms, including holding three-way conferences that include students, teachers, and parents. Parents may also respond in writing to the work in the portfolio. They can complete a questionnaire about their perceptions of the student's work and provide examples they think are indicative of growth (Lescher, 1995, p. 28).

PARENT GROUP MEETING CONFERENCES
When circumstances do not permit conferences with individual families, a **parent group meeting conference** for all parents might be considered. In this type of conference, the teacher spends time explaining to all the parents the assessments that have been used, the nature of those assessments, and information on projects or thematic study topics. Classroom documentation in various forms is explained and parents are invited to spend time looking at them. The teacher can make opportunities for individual questions and for parents with concerns to stay after the group meeting to discuss these with the teacher. Arrangements might be made for individual phone calls or other communications when needed to discuss future questions or issues.

Preparing for Family Conferences

The teacher or other professional must prepare the information that is to be shared prior to conducting a conference with a family. Some of the information should involve input from the parents and the child. As part of the preparation, the teacher selects the assessments that will be used for reporting progress and develops a profile or some type of encapsulation that summarizes the child's evidence of development and learning.

SELECTING OPTIONS FOR REPORTING PROGRESS If the teacher uses portfolio assessment, the process of preparing the portfolio contents for the child's evaluation becomes the vehicle for reporting. If a portfolio is not used, the teacher gathers and organizes examples of the child's work, assessments that have been conducted, and some type of report on the child's evaluation that has been determined by the teacher.

DEVELOPING A PROFILE FOR THE CHILD USING ASSESSMENT RESULTS Portfolios include assessment results and other evidence of the child's work that permit an evaluation to take place. Materials in the portfolio, when combined with a narrative report, provide a profile of progress. A profile can also be developed using checklist assessments, samples of the child's work, and a summary report, as in *The Work Sampling System, 5th edition* (Meisels, Marsden, Jablon, & Dichtelmiller, 2014), and the checklist and anecdotal records used in the Preschool Child Observation Record (COR) (High/Scope Educational Research Foundation, 2003). Given the many types of assessments and record-keeping strategies described in earlier chapters, the teacher has a variety of ways to organize assessment and evaluation into a comprehensive profile of the child to share with parents. This report may also include the results of standardized tests in the primary grades.

CONSIDERING INDIVIDUAL FAMILY BACKGROUNDS AND NEEDS As the teacher prepares for the conference with the parents, the backgrounds, concerns, priorities, resources, and needs of parents are considered. Parents must feel comfortable and relaxed when they come for the conference. A trained interpreter should be provided for parents who speak a language other than English. The environment for the conference should be welcoming. Some teachers provide refreshments and decorate the area with flowers and student work.

When preparing for a conference, the teacher must consider the diverse backgrounds of the children also. The children may come from different religions, cultures, languages, and family practices. For example, in some cultures the father takes the lead in participating in the conference, with the mother taking a secondary role. In other cultures, especially traditional American groups, both parents participate equally, or the mother takes the lead.

If language is an issue, provisions should be made for a trained interpreter to assist with the meeting, if the teacher does not speak the home language of the family. It is important to have trained interpreters who understand that their role is to serve as a conduit for delivering information from the teacher, parent, student, or other person involved in the conference without judgment or prejudice. Interpreters should be clear about confidentiality and key terminology. Avoid asking a friend, family member, or other person who is not a professional interpreter. The American Speech-Language-Hearing Association (ASHA, 2014) recommends the following considerations when selecting an interpreter to assist with assessment:

- Determine the interpreter's level of proficiency in English and in the home language used by the child and family.
- Examine the interpreter's educational background and experience.
- Determine the interpreter's communication style to ensure it will work with that of the teacher, child, and parents.
- Try to use the same interpreter for multiple assignments so that you may establish an effective working relationship.

Additional tips for using an interpreter effectively before, during, and after the conference can be found on the ASHA website.

> **Enhanced eText:** Video Example 3.3

Sometimes parents are intimidated by the teacher and other professionals and are uncomfortable attending a conference at the school. Parents may feel inadequate or have bad memories from their own school experiences. Teachers need to be very sensitive to these situations and be ready to help these parents feel welcome and appreciated (Kersey & Masterson, 2009).

Another factor to consider is parental awareness of how assessments are conducted and explained, particularly in the case of standardized test results. Some families may be very familiar and comfortable in understanding the meaning of different terms used in standardized test reports. Others may be totally bewildered when a child's test profile is discussed. The teacher will want to vary how these tests are discussed and what explanations might be necessary. Standardized tests and test reports are discussed in Chapter 4. The teacher will want to understand test reports and how to interpret them to parents from diverse backgrounds.

Conducting Family Conferences

Once the parents or other family representatives have arrived and the conference is ready to begin, the teacher keeps three guidelines in mind when conducting a successful experience for the parents and child, if the child is to participate, including: (1) helping parents understand evaluation information, (2) helping parents interpret evaluation information accurately, and (3) soliciting parental and child input for assessment and planning for the child. If standardized test results are used, these guidelines are especially important.

STEPS IN PREPARING TO CONDUCT CONFERENCES WITH FAMILIES   The teacher can also think through best strategies that will ensure a positive conference result. Following are some measures teachers take to conduct successful conferences:

- *Start and end on a positive note.* It was mentioned earlier that parents should feel welcomed by the teacher. The teacher can share the child's strengths and examples of the child's positive experiences at school.

- *Encourage parents to share information about their child.* Early in the conference, parents are asked about their child. The teacher may ask questions about how the child and family interact at home. The objective is to have the parents take the lead in the discussion about their child.

- *Discuss relevant information about the child's progress.* Important information about the child's accomplishments is discussed with the parents, using portfolio examples, various assessments, and standardized test results, when appropriate. Parents are included in the discussion throughout this part of the conference. Their questions are answered, and the teacher asks questions to extend the information.

- *Discuss the child's needs or issues about progress.* Difficulties the child might be experiencing at school are discussed objectively. The teacher focuses on the most important difficulties that a child might be experiencing. The teacher asks the parents for help in addressing the child's needs. The parents and teacher discuss how they might help the child. The teacher asks the parents for suggestions about how the child might be better helped in school. If possible, the parents and teacher set a plan for the child to be addressed in a follow-up conference or other communication (Kersey & Masterson, 2009).

- *End the conference on a positive note.* The teacher closes the conference by again focusing on the child's positive attributes. The teacher thanks the parents for attending and being helpful in providing needed information. The teacher stresses that the family–professional relationship is a partnership to further positive feelings with parents or family representatives.

Enhanced eText: Application Exercise 3.1

HELPING PARENTS INTERPRET EVALUATION INFORMATION   When parents encounter a collection of work examples of the children and teacher assessments that form the basis for a child's evaluation, they may feel a bit overwhelmed when they compare this type of reporting with a report card. If the teacher and school have prepared the parents for the use of portfolios and performance assessments, they will appreciate understanding how the materials they are seeing form a picture of what the child has learned; nevertheless, they are likely to have questions about assessments and the meaning of the child's work. The teacher needs to be prepared to volunteer information about the assessment strategies used and why the collection of the child's work provides evidence of learning.

A Group Conference for a Child with ADHD

Miles Clark is a third grade child who was identified as having ADHD (attention deficit hyperactivity disorder) in the first grade. He was evaluated and received special education classification at that time. He has received the help of a resource teacher for the past two years. The purpose of the conference is to determine how Miles should be served as he moves to fourth grade. The conference includes Miles's parents, his grandmother, the regular classroom teacher, the school counselor, the resource teacher, and the principal. The conference has been called at the request of Miles's mother, who is concerned about the possible end of services by the resource teacher.

Each member of the teaching and support staff presents an assessment of Miles's progress. At the end of each presentation, the parents and other members of the group are invited to comment or ask questions. The classroom teacher and resource teacher present examples of work that Miles has been able to complete on his own, without assistance. Each member of the group is asked about Miles's ability to work independently, without a resource teacher to assist with assignments. School staff members believe that their plan to transition Miles to working without assistance is showing good progress. Miles's mother is not convinced and insists that Miles is entitled to the continued services of the resource teacher because of his designation as having ADHD.

At the end of the conference, each member of the conference group summarizes his or her current assessment of Miles and what future planning is appropriate for his continued progress. The school counselor summarizes the events of the conference and asks the parents for their assessment. Miles's mother strongly supports the continuation of assistance for Miles. The school staff reluctantly agree to continue the use of the resource teacher during the next school year.

> **Enhanced eText: Self-Check 3.4**

Summary

Assessment in early childhood education includes opportunities and challenges for interactions with parents and other family members. Parents want teachers to explain the use of assessments and changes in student progress reports that accompany the use of these assessments. Teachers want parents to have input during the assessment process and subsequent individual plans. In addition, teachers want to be confident that they have the skills to use and interpret assessment results with parents. Strong, family-centered partnerships benefit all involved, most of all children. Through ongoing communication and mutual respect, parents and professionals can identify strengths and needs of individual children and then build early childhood services that speak to them.

> **Enhanced eText: Self-Check: Chapter Review**

Key Terms

Family-centered 60

Family–professional
partnerships 60

Home visit 65

Parent conferences 70

Parent group meeting
conferences 71

Performance assessment 69

Portfolio 69

Screening 66

Strengths-based 60

Student-led conferences 71

Three-way conferences 71

Selected Organizations

Search for the following organizations online:
American Speech-Language-Hearing Association
Beach Center on Disability
Center for Law and Social Policy
Child Care Aware of America

National Coalition for Parent Involvement in
Education (NCPIE)
Parent Teacher Association
TeacherVision
Wrightslaw

References

American Speech-Language-Hearing Association. (2014). *Tips for working with an interpreter*. Retrieved from http://www.asha.org/practice/multicultural/issues/interpret.htm

Berman, C., & Shaw, E. (1996). Family directed child evaluation and assessment under the Individuals with Disabilities Education Act (IDEA). In S. J. Meisels & E. Fenichel (Eds.), *New visions for the developmental assessment of infants and young children* (pp. 361–390). Washington, DC: Zero to Three: National Center for Infants, Toddlers, and Families.

Bruder, M. B., & Dunst, C. J. (2015). Parental judgments of early childhood intervention personnel practices: Applying a consumer science perspective. *Topics in Early Childhood Special Education, 34,* 200–210.

Center on the Developing Child at Harvard University. (2016). *From best practices to breakthrough impacts: A science-based approach to building a more promising future for young children and families*. Retrieved from http://www.developingchild.harvard.edu

Child Care Aware of America. (2017). *Checking in: A snapshot of the child care landscape*. Retrieved from http://usa.childcareaware.org/wp-content/uploads/2017/07/FINAL_SFS_REPORT.pdf

Council for Exceptional Children/Division of Early Childhood. (2012). *CEC Professional Preparation Standards and DEC EI and ECSE Specialty Sets*. Author.

Cromwell, S. (2010). *Student-led conferences: A growing trend*. Retrieved from http://www.educationworld.com/a_admin/admin/admin112.shtml

Division of Early Childhood. (2010). *Responsiveness to ALL children, families, and professionals: Integrating cultural and linguistic diversity into policy and practice*. Author.

Dunst, C. J., & Trivette, C. M. (2012). Capacity-building family-systems intervention practices. *Journal of Family Social Work, 12,* 119–143.

Feeney, S. (2010, March). Ethics today in early care and education. *Young Children, 65,* 72–77.

Gilkerson, D., & Hanson, M. F. (2000). Family portfolios: Involving families in portfolio documentation. *Early Childhood Education Journal, 27,* 197–201.

High/Scope Educational Research Foundation. (2003). *Preschool child observation record*. Ypsilanti, MI: Author.

Jarrett, M. H., Browne, B. C., & Wallin, C. M. (2006). Using portfolio assessment to document developmental progress of infants and toddlers. *Young Exceptional Children, 10,* 22–32.

Kersey, K. C., & Masterson, M. L. (2009). Teachers connecting with families—In the best interest of children. *Young Children,* 34–38.

Keyser, J. (2006). *From parents to partners*. St. Paul, MN: Redleaf Press.

Lescher, M. L. (1995). *Portfolios: Assessing learning in the primary grades*. Washington, DC: National Education Association.

Lightfoot, L. S. (2003). *The essential conversation: What parents and teachers can learn from each other*. New York, NY: Ballantine Books.

McLean, M., Wolery, M., & Bailey, D. B. (2004). *Assessing infants and preschoolers with special needs* (3rd ed.). New York, NY: Pearson.

Meisels, S. J., Marsden, D. B., Jablon, J. R., & Dichtelmiller, M. (2014). *The work sampling system®*. San Antonio, TX: Pearson.

Mitchell, S., Foulger, T. S., & Wetzel, K. (2009, September). Ten tips for involving families through Internet-based communication. *Young Children, 65,* 46–49.

National Association for the Education of Young Children. (2011). *NAEYC code of ethical conduct and statement of commitment*. Washington, DC:Author.

National Association for the Education of Young Children. (2010). *NAEYC Standards for early childhood professional preparation*. Washington, DC:Author.

National Association for the Education of Young Children & National Association of Early Childhood Specialists in State Departments of Education. (2002). *Early learning standards: Creating the conditions for success*. Washington, DC: National Association for the Education of Young Children.

North Carolina Foundations Task Force. (2013). *North Carolina foundations for early learning and development*. Raleigh, NC: Author.

Ray, J. A., Pewitt-Kinder, J., & George, S. (2009, September). Partnering with families of children with special needs. *Young Children, 64,* 16–22.

Rocco, S. (1996). Toward shared commitment and shared responsibility: A parent's vision of developmental assessment. In S. J. Meisels & E. Fenichel (Eds.), *New visions for the developmental assessment of infants and young children* (pp. 55–58). Washington, DC: Zero to Three: National Center for Infants, Toddlers, and Families.

Schmidt, S., & Matthews, H. (2013). *Better for babies: A study of state infant and toddler child care policies*. Washington, DC: Center for Law and Social Policy.

Stiggins, R. J. (2005). *Student-involved assessment for learning* (4th ed.). Upper Saddle River, NJ: Merrill Prentice Hall.

Turnbull, A., Turnbull, H. R., Erwin, E. J., Soodak, L. C., & Shogren, K. A. (2015). *Families, professionals, and exceptionality: Positive outcomes through partnerships and trust*. Upper Saddle River, NJ: Pearson.

Turnbull, A., Turnbull, H. R., Erwin, E. J., Soodak, L. C., & Shogren, K. A. (2006). *Families, professionals, and exceptionality: Positive outcomes through partnerships and trust*. Upper Saddle River, NJ: Pearson.

U.S. Congress. (2004). Individuals with Disabilities Education Improvement Act (PL 108-446), 108th U.S.C., Stt. 2647, et. Seq.

ZERO TO THREE. (2010). *Infant/toddler development, screening, and assessment*. Washington, DC: Author.

Chapter 4
How Standardized Tests Are Used, Designed, and Selected

Mangostock/Shutterstock

⌄ Chapter Learning Outcomes

As a result of reading this chapter, you will be able to:

4.1 Discuss how standardized tests are used with infants and young children.

4.2 Describe the steps in standardized test design.

4.3 Explain the differences between test validity and test reliability.

4.4 Describe considerations for selecting and evaluating standardized tests.

In this chapter, we will look at ways standardized tests are used with infants and young children. Specific examples of standardized tests and their purposes will be discussed. A description of how standardized tests are designed and verified to make sure they measure the desired characteristics is included in this chapter also. Test validity and reliability are explained, as well as their effects on the dependability of the test. Finally, we will discuss how to select and evaluate screening and assessment instruments.

How Standardized Tests Are Used with Infants and Young Children

Standardized tests are used to understand skill development of infants, toddlers, and young children as well as academic achievement for school-age children. They are also used to determine eligibility for children who have developmental delays or disabilities. Types of standardized tests are discussed below.

Types of Standardized Tests

Many types of standardized tests are available for use with infants and young children. All are psychological tests, whether they measure abilities, achievements, aptitudes, interests, values, or personality characteristics.

Ability refers to the current level of knowledge or skill in a particular area. Three types of psychological tests—**intelligence tests**, **achievement tests**, and **aptitude tests**—are categorized as ability tests because they measure facets of ability. Young children are often assessed to determine the progress of their development. This type of measure may assess ability in motor, language, social, or cognitive skills. *Bayley's Scales of Infant Development, Third Edition (BSID-III)* (Bayley, 2005), for example, is used to diagnose delays in development. More recently, the BSID-III was designed to learn about a child's overall development. Children with intellectual disabilities might be assessed for adaptive functioning, which is focused on how well a child manages everyday tasks. Instruments such as the *Vineland Adaptive Behavior Scales, Third Edition (Vineland-3)* (Sparrow, Cicchetti, & Saulnier, 2016) are administered through parent and primary caregiver reports to determine communication, social, and daily living skills.

Achievement is the extent to which a person has acquired certain information or has mastered identified skills. An achievement test measures ability in that it evaluates the child's achievement related to specific prior instruction. The *Peabody Individual Achievement Test—Revised-Normative Update (PIAT-R/NU)* (Markwardt, 1997) is a measure of achievement in mathematics, reading recognition, reading comprehension, spelling, and general information, for example.

Aptitude is the potential to learn or develop proficiency in some area, provided that certain conditions exist or training is available. An individual may have a high aptitude for music or art, for example. Like achievement tests, aptitude tests also measure learned abilities. An aptitude test measures the results of both general and incidental learning and predicts future learning.

Intelligence tests are ability tests in that they assess overall intellectual functioning. They are also aptitude tests because they assess aptitude for learning and problem solving. *The Stanford-Binet Intelligence Scales, Fifth Edition (SB-5)* (Roid, 2003) is an

Teachers use standardized test results to design instruction for individual needs.

example of an intelligence scale that also measures individual aptitude.

Personality tests measure a person's tendency to behave in a particular way. Such tests are used to diagnose children's emotional strengths and needs. Because an inventory is used to assess personality characteristics, the test is quite lengthy, usually containing several hundred items in a true–false format. Test items are answered by the parent or child or by both together and are analyzed to determine whether the child has certain personality traits.

Interest inventories are used to determine a person's interest in a certain area or vocation and are not used with very young children. A school-age child may be given a reading interest inventory to provide the teacher with information that will serve as a guide when helping the child select reading material. For example, perhaps a first grade child indicated a strong interest in grasshoppers. The teacher could incorporate grasshoppers into reading (e.g., books on insects), math (e.g., word problems with grasshoppers), science (e.g., look up information about their habitats on the web for a report on grasshoppers), and so forth.

Tests for Infants

Various tests have been constructed for infants and young children. Examples that have been discussed previously are the *Neonatal Behavioral Assessment Scale (NBAS)* (Brazelton & Nugent, 2011) and the *Communication and Symbolic Behavior Scales Developmental Profile (CSBS DP)* (Prizant & Wetherby, 2002). They are examples of tests that have been normed. Such tests are challenging because of the child's developmental limitations. Babies are particularly difficult to evaluate because of their short attention span. Their periods of alertness are brief, and they have their own schedules of opportune moments for testing. In addition, developmental changes occur rapidly, making test results unreliable for more than a short time. Generally, because of these limitations, the validity and reliability of infant scales are questionable. The tests are difficult to administer and interpret. Nevertheless, they are useful in evaluating the status of newborns and infants (Campbell, Kolobe, Osten, Lenke, &

Search and Share 4.1

Standardized Test Types

Search online to find a standardized assessment that is used to evaluate young children's intelligence, achievement, or aptitude. Which type of assessment tool is it and how might it help parents and professionals understand their child's abilities?

Tyler Olson/Shutterstock

Girolami, 1995; Hack et al., 2005; Wodrich, 1997). To better understand the types of infant and toddler measures, the following section is organized into neonatal status, infant and toddler development, and diagnostic tests.

NEONATAL STATUS   The status of a newborn can be determined using various measures. The *Apgar Scale* (Apgar, 1975), administered one minute and five minutes after birth, assesses the health of the newborn by evaluating the heart rate, respiratory effort, muscle tone, body color, and reflex irritability. Each characteristic is scored on a scale of 0 to 2 for a maximum score of 10 points. A score of 7 to 10 indicates the infant is in good condition; a score of 5 may indicate developmental difficulties; and a score of 3 or below is very serious and indicates an emergency concerning the infant's survival. The *Brazelton Neonatal Behavioral Assessment Scale,* another neonatal test (Als, Tronick, Lester, & Brazelton, 1979), measures temperamental differences, nervous system functions, and the capacity of the neonate to interact. Its purpose is to locate mild neurological dysfunctions and variations in temperament. A newer scale, the *Neonatal Behavioral Assessment Scale (NBAS)* (Brazelton & Nugent, 2011), is used with newborns from the first day of life through the end of the first month. In this test, the infant's competence is measured through behavioral items. In addition to identifying the infant's performance, if administered with the parents present, it can be used to help parents understand their infant's signals and skills. This knowledge of a child's development generally, and a baby's competence specifically, can facilitate improvement in parenting skills (Widerstrom, Mowder, & Sandall, 1991). An adaptation of the NBAS to assess preterm infants came through the design of the *Assessment of Preterm Infants' Behavior (APIB)* (Als, Butler, Kosta, & McAnulty, 2005). It includes many of the items in the NBAS, but refined them to be able to observe the preterm infant's functioning. *The Ounce Scale* (Meisels, Marsden, Dombro, Weston, & Jewkes, 2008) is another developmental scale suitable for parents, child-care personnel, and Early Head Start teachers to administer. Used with children from birth to 3.6 years old, *The Ounce Scale* is organized around six developmental domains and helps parents observe developmental milestones.

Enhanced eText: Video Example 4.1

INFANT AND TODDLER DEVELOPMENT   Infant development scales go beyond measuring neonatal status to focusing on development from 1 month to 2 years. The *Gesell Developmental Schedules* (Ball, 1977) were the first scales devised to measure infant development. Gesell designed them to detect infants who were delayed in development and might need special services. More recently, the *Bayley Scales of Infant Development, Third Edition (BSID-III)* (Bayley, 2005) were designed to learn about infants' overall development, while the *Communication and Symbolic Behavior Scales Developmental Profile (CSBS DP™)* (Prizant & Wetherby, 2002) are used to assess communicative and symbolic development, including symbolic play and constructive play. The *Mullen Scales of Early Learning* (Mullen, 1995) measure cognitive functioning in infants, toddlers, and young children from birth to 68 months. The assessment measures intellectual development through the child's response to prepared activities. The Gesell and Bayley instruments are challenging to administer because of their length; however, because they are used to diagnose children with special needs, it is important to examine developmental milestones thoroughly. All of these instruments can indicate a child's functioning in various developmental domains. For instance, if a child's score is below his or her age level in gross motor, this would indicate a potential delay and further observation and testing of the child's skills would be needed.

The *Devereux Early Childhood Assessment for Infants and Toddlers (DECA-I/T)* (Powell, MacKrain, & LeBuffe, 2007) is an assessment designed to understand the social and emotional development of infants and toddlers. There are two forms, the Infant Form for children 1–18 months old, and the Toddler Form for children 18–36 months old.

The *Denver II* (Frankenburg, Dodds, Archer, Shapiro, & Bresnick, 1992) is a simple screening instrument designed to identify children who are likely to have significant delays and need early identification and intervention, while the *Adaptive Behavior Assessment System, Third Edition (ABAS-3)* (Harrison & Oakland, 2015) assesses the strengths and weaknesses in adaptive skills. The *Early Coping Inventory (ECI)* (Zeitlin, Williamson, & Szczepanski, 1988) assesses how well infants and toddlers 4–36 months of age react and cope with different situations; in addition, the *Infant/Toddler Symptom Checklist: A Screening Tool for Parents* (DeGangi, Poisson, Sickel, & Wiener, 1999) screens infants and toddlers who show disturbances in sleep, feeding, and self-calming. Used with children from 7 to 30 months old, it can be administered by a parent or caregiver.

DIAGNOSTIC TESTS   There are diagnostic tests for infants to identify developmental or physical disorders. As with developmental assessments and screening tests for infants and toddlers, it is very difficult to accurately acquire the needed information. The strategies for measuring lung function, for example, can be considered to be intrusive for infants (Panitch, 2004). Likewise, babies who have experienced a life-threatening event (ALTE) present challenges in determining what tests should be used, how to interpret the results, and how well the tests or assessment procedures will contribute to the many factors that can cause ALTE (Brand, Altman, Puttill, & Edwards, 2005). Observational measures to assess children with spinal cord injury can result in lack of agreement among the observers (Calhoun, Gaughan, Chafitz, & Mulcahey, 2009). Regardless, specialists in infant screening and diagnosis continue to research methods that provide the desired testing with minimal invasive methods and more dependable results. Figure 4-1 describes neonatal and infant tests.

Tests for Preschool Children

Professionals have designed a variety of tests to evaluate development and to detect developmental problems during the preschool years. Just as the testing of infants and toddlers presents challenges to test administrators because of the children's developmental circumstances, the evaluation of preschool children under age 6 must also be conducted with their developmental characteristics in mind. Instruments that assess characteristics used to identify developmental delays or to diagnose sources of disabilities that affect the child's potential for learning are administered to one child at a time. Test items are concrete tasks or activities that match the child's ability to respond; nevertheless, validity and reliability are affected by such factors as the child's limited attention span. As children enter the preschool years, more instruments are available for examining development and identifying potential developmental delays. To better understand the various types of measures, preschool tests are organized into screening, diagnostic, language, and achievement tests.

Figure 4.1 Neonatal and infant tests

NAME	LEVEL	TYPE	PURPOSE
Apgar Scale	Neonate	Birth status	Assess health of the newborn infant
Brazelton Neonatal Behavioral Assessment Scale	Neonate	Neonatal status	Locate mild neurological dysfunctions and variations in temperament
Neonatal Behavioral Assessment Scale (NBAS), Fourth Edition	First month		Identify the infant's ability to modulate its behavioral systems in response to external stimuli
Adaptive Behavior Assessment System, Third Edition (ABAS-3)	Infant and preschool	Adaptive skills	Assess strengths and weaknesses in adaptive skills
Assessment of Preterm Infant Behavior (APIB)	Preterm infants	Preterm development	Identify current status and intervention targets
Bayley Scales of Infant Development (BSID-III)	Infant	Intelligence	Diagnose developmental delays in infants
Devereux Early Childhood Assessment for Infants and Toddlers (DECA-I/T)	Infant and toddler	Development	Supports social and emotional development
Denver II	1 month to 6 years	Developmental screening	Identify developmental delays
Communication and Symbolic Behavior Scales Developmental Profile (CSBS DP)	Infants, toddlers, pre-schoolers	Language development	Assess communication and symbolic development
Infant/Toddler Symptom Checklist: A Screening Tool for Parents	7 to 30 months old	Development	Screens for regulatory, attentional, and sensory problems
Mullen Scales of Early Learning	Birth to 68 months	Intellectual development	Assess cognitive functioning
The Ounce Scale	Birth to 3.6 years	Six developmental domains	Helps parents observe developmental milestones

SCREENING TESTS **Screening tests** provide a snapshot of children's development that indicates when a child might have a developmental problem that needs further investigation. Screening tests can be global, screening multiple areas of development such as motor, cognitive, language, and social/emotional skills. Or, they may be domain-specific, screening one area of development such as behavior, language, vision, or hearing (Weitzman & Wegner, 2015). Screening tests can be contrasted with assessments which examine development in more depth to help determine strengths and possible difficulties, as well as to determine what strategies need to be taken to address the child's needs. Screening young children using a variety of tools (e.g., global developmental screening tests, hearing screening tools) is essential for early detection of potential problems. Early detection can reduce or eliminate developmental challenges and later school performance issues. A toolkit of materials for professionals and parents, entitled *Birth to 5: Watch Me Thrive!*, emphasizes the need for early detection and the positive benefits of screening and assessment (U.S. Department of Health and Human Services & U.S. Department of Education, 2014). Following are examples of global screening tools.

The *Denver II* (Frankenburg et al., 1992) was discussed earlier as a screening tool that can be used with infants and older children. It is administered by a professional such as a pediatrician or educator. In contrast, the *Ages and Stages Questionnaires, Third Edition (ASQ-3™)* (Squires & Bricker, 2009) uses parental reporting to screen a child's development. The parent can complete the questionnaire or participate in an interview with a professional. It is administered for children ages 1 month to 66 months.

The *AGS Early Screening Profiles* (Harrison, Kaufman, & Kaufman, 1990) can be administered from ages 2 years to 6 years 11 months. They include parent–teacher questionnaires as well as profiles in cognitive language, motor, and social development.

The *Developmental Indicators for the Assessment of Learning™, Fourth Edition (DIAL™-4)* (Mardell & Goldenberg, 2011) is also used to flag potential developmental delays. Administered to children ages 2 years 6 months to 5 years 11 months, it includes direct observation and tasks presented to the child. The *Early Screening Inventory—Revised (ESI-R)*, 2008 edition (Meisels, Marsden, Wiske, & Henderson, 2008) has two forms: the ESI-P for ages 3 to 4.4 years, and the ESI-K for ages 4.5 to 6 years. It is used to screen developmental domains and uses cutoff scores to determine whether the child needs to be referred for further evaluation. A parental questionnaire is used to provide supplementary information. The *Brigance Early Childhood Screens III* (Brigance, 2013) include three screening tools to examine development in the domains of physical development, language, academic/cognitive, self-help, and social-emotional. The three tools are an *Infant & Toddler Screen* for children 0–35 months; an *Early Preschool, Preschool Screen* for children 3–5 years old; and a *K & 1 Screen* for children in kindergarten and first grade. Finally, the *FirstStep™: Screening Test for Evaluating Preschoolers* (Miller, 1993) has 12 subtests grouped into cognitive, communicative, and motor categories. There is also an optional social-emotional scale and adaptive behavior checklist. *First Step* has three levels: Level 1 is administered to children from ages 2 years 9 months to 3 years 8 months; Level II is for children 3 years 9 months to 4 years 8 months; and Level III is administered to children 4 years 9 months to 6 years 2 months. A newer Gesell Institute instrument, the *Gesell Developmental Observation—Revised* (2011), is used with 2½- to 6-year-old children. It measures child growth, academic achievement, and social and emotional development.

The screening tests just discussed cover various domains of development. The screening tools discussed next focus solely on social-emotional development. These screening instruments look at social behaviors and require sensitive and careful collaboration between the home and school because children's behaviors are affected by environmental differences. Although this type of screening is difficult to do accurately, social-emotional competence is very important and should be monitored (Meisels & Atkins-Burnett, 2005).

The *Early Screening Project (ESP)* (Walker, Severson, & Feil, 1995) is administered to children ages 3 to 6 years in three stages. Children are ranked in social interaction, adaptive behavior, emotional problems, aggressive behaviors, and reactions to critical

Baker School for Early Learning

Baker School is a community school that targets services for toddlers and preschool children from a nearby public housing development. The children in the housing development represent a variety of ethnic groups and languages. Some are from families that recently emigrated from another country. Teachers in the program need input from parents on their child's current stage of development prior to entering the program. Parents can fill out the *Ages and Stages Questionnaire* with information about their child. The form includes questions about behaviors, speaking abilities, and physical skills, as well as other indicators of development. Because the teachers are sensitive to possible language and literacy limitations, they are available if the parents need help filling in the information. In many cases, they read the questions to the parents and record their responses on the test form.

events. A parent questionnaire looks at how the child plays with other children, how the child interacts with caregivers, and social problems such as difficulties with self-esteem or social avoidance. An instrument that uses parent ratings is the *PKBS–2: Preschool and Kindergarten Behavior Scales, Second Edition* (Merrell, 2003). Administered to children ages 3 to 6 years, it examines positive and problem behaviors. (Figure 4-2 provides examples of items on screening tests.)

Enhanced eText: Video Example 4.2

DIAGNOSTIC TESTS   After a child has been screened and there are indicators that further evaluation is needed, tests for diagnostic assessment can be administered. Adaptive behavior instruments attempt to measure how well the young child has mastered everyday living tasks such as toileting and feeding. The *Vineland Adaptive Behavior Scales, Third Edition (Vineland-3)* (Sparrow, Cicchetti, & Saulnier, 2016) assesses the everyday behaviors of the child that indicate level of development. The scale determines areas of strengths and needs in communication, daily living, socialization, and motor skills. Another instrument, the *ABS-S:2™ Adaptive Behavior Scale—School 2nd Edition™* (Lambert, Nihira, & Leland, 2008), assesses adaptive behavior for children 3–16 years old in 16 domains for social competence and independence. Figure 4-3 describes categories of adaptive behaviors.

Preschool intelligence tests and adaptive behavior scales are used to diagnose children with intellectual disabilities. Although intelligence measures during the preschool years are generally unreliable because children's IQs can change enormously between early childhood and adolescence, they are used with young children to measure learning potential.

The *Stanford–Binet Intelligence Scales (SB5), Fifth Edition* (Roid, 2003), the original IQ test, was designed to assess general thinking or problem-solving ability. It is valuable in answering questions about developmental delay and retardation. Another

---

Figure 4.2 Examples of items on screening tests

Motor Skills
Gross Motor: Jumping, skipping, hopping, catching, walking a straight line
Fine Motor: Building with cubes, cutting, copying forms, writing name and copying words, drawing shapes

Cognitive Development
Pointing to body parts
Rote counting
Counting objects
Sorting and classifying pictures
Identifying and naming colors and shapes
Answering simple questions about concepts

Language Development
Identifying correct item in an array of pictures
Answering personal questions
Identifying objects and pictures
Placing object using positional words (*under, over, in*, etc.)

Figure 4.3 Some categories assessed in adaptive behaviors

Independent Living Categories	Social Behavior Categories
Physical development	Social engagement
Language development	Conformity
Independent functioning	Trustworthiness
	Disturbing interpersonal behavior
	Hyperactive behavior
	Self-abusive behavior
	Stereotyped behavior

instrument, the *Wechsler Preschool and Primary Scale of Intelligence™, Fourth Edition (WPPSI™-IV)* (Wechsler, 2012), is useful in identifying signs of uneven development for children ages 2 years 6 months to 7 years 3 months.

Other instruments address all domains of development. The *Kaufman Assessment Battery for Children, Second Edition (KABC™-II)* (Kaufman & Kaufman, 2004) and its update titled the *Kaufman Assessment Battery for Children, Second Edition Normative Update (KABC™-II NU)* (Kaufman & Kaufman, 2018), as well as the *Battelle Developmental Inventory™, Second Edition (BDI-2™)* (Newborg, 2004), and the *Bracken Basic Concept Scale, Third Edition: Receptive (BBCS-3:R)* (Bracken, 2006) have comprehensive assessments of development. Additionally, the *Brigance Inventory of Early Development III (IED III)* (Brigance, 2013) is an assessment used with children from birth through developmental age 7 years. There are two versions of the *IED III*, one which is criterion-referenced, and the *IED III-Standardized*, which is norm-referenced. The *Woodcock-Johnson IV Tests of Early Cognitive and Academic Development (WJ IV ECAD™)* (Schrank, McGrew, & Mather, 2015b) is a new addition to the Woodcock-Johnson battery of tests. The *WJ IV ECAD* assesses general intellectual ability, early academic skills, and expressive language skills for children ages 2 years 6 months through 7 years 11 months as well as children with cognitive developmental delays through age 9 years.

The *Devereux Early Childhood Assessment Preschool Program, Second Edition (DECA P-2)* (LeBuffe & Naglieri, 2012) is a strengths-based assessment system designed to promote resilience and positive social/emotional development for children ages 3–5 years. It can be administered through classroom observations. It has items that examine positive and negative behaviors such as attention problems, aggression, depression, and emotional control.

LANGUAGE TESTS   The category of language tests for preschool children is very important because many children are at risk for school readiness because they have language deficits or their first language is not English. While some language tests for at-risk children are in English, others are available in both English and Spanish, and occasionally other languages. The *Preschool Language Scale, Fifth Edition (PLS-5)* (Zimmerman, Steiner, & Pond, 2011) and *Peabody Picture Vocabulary Test, Fourth Edition (PPVT-4)* (Dunn & Dunn, 2007) provide information on a child's language ability, which can help determine whether a child will benefit from a language enrichment program.

With the expanding numbers of English Language Learners (ELL) who are living in many states, language assessment tests are growing in importance. Children who have limited English proficiency may be served in a bilingual program or ELL program. The *Pre-LAS, Pre-IPT*, and *Woodcock-Muñoz Language Survey* (discussed next) are available in English and Spanish editions. There are also forms of these tests for school-age children.

The *preLAS Observational Assessment*™ measures oral language proficiency for 3-year-olds and the *preLAS* measures language development in both the first and second language (English and Spanish) for young children (Data Recognition Corporation |CTB, 2016).

The *preLAS* has two editions that measure the same concepts, including the *PreLAS Oral* for children 3- to 6-years-old and the *PreLAS Pre-Literacy* for children 4- to 6-years-old (Data Recognition Corporation |CTB, 2016). It is also used to make

Figure 4.4 Categories and characteristics of preschool tests

NAME	LEVEL	TYPE	PURPOSE
Screening Tests			
Ages and Stages Questionnaires, Third Edition (ASQ-3™)	4–60 months	Developmental screening	Measure cognitive, language, motor, and social development
AGS Early Screening Profiles	2–6 years	Developmental screening	Measure cognitive, language, motor, self-help, social acculturation, and health development
Developmental Indicators for the Assessment of Learning™, Fourth Edition (DIAL™-4)	2–6 years	Developmental screening	Assess motor, language, and cognitive development
Early Screening Inventory—Revised (ESI-R)	3–6 years	Developmental screening	Assess developmental domains with cutoff scores for referrals
First Step Screening Test for Evaluating Preschoolers	2 years 9 months to 6 years 2 months	Developmental screening	Assess five developmental domains to identify preschoolers at risk for -developmental delay
Social Emotional Screening			
Devereux Early Childhood Assessment Preschool Program, Second Edition (DECA-P2)	2–5 years	Social-emotional screening	Examine positive and negative social-emotional behaviors
Early Screening Project (ESP)	3–6 years	Social-emotional screening	Rank children in social interaction, adaptive behavior, maladaptive behaviors, and aggressive behaviors
PKBS–2: Preschool and Kindergarten Behavior Scales, Second Edition	3–6 years	Social-emotional screening	Examine positive and problem behaviors through parent ratings
Brigance Early Childhood Screens III	Birth to 5 years	Social-emotional screening	Examine positive and negative behaviors
Adaptive Behavior Tests			
Vineland Adaptive Behavior Scales, Third Edition (Vineland-3)	3–16 years	Adaptive behavior	Measure weaknesses and strengths in everyday-living tasks
ABS-S:2™ Adaptive Behavior Scale—School 2nd Edition™	3–16 years	Adaptive behavior	Assess adaptive behavior in terms of personal independence and development; can be compared to norms for children developing normally, with retardation, and with severe retardation
Diagnostic Tests			
Stanford–Binet Intelligence Scales (SB5), Fifth Edition	2 years to adult	Global intelligence	Detect delays and intellectual disabilities
Wechsler Preschool and Primary Scale of Intelligence™—Fourth Edition (WPPSI™-IV)	4–6 years	Intelligence	Identify signs of uneven development, detect overall delay
Kaufman Assessment Battery for Children, Second Edition (KABC™-II)	3–18 years	Comprehensive developmental assessment	Assess developmental delay and plan for instruction

(Continued)

Figure 4.4 (Continued)

NAME	LEVEL	TYPE	PURPOSE
The Kaufman Assessment Battery for Children, Second Edition Normative Update (KABC™-II NU)	3–18 years	Comprehensive developmental assessment	Culturally fair test of cognitive ability
Battelle Developmental Inventory™, Second Edition (BDI-2™)	Birth to 8 years	Comprehensive developmental assessment	Identify child's strengths and weaknesses and plan for intervention or instruction
Bracken Basic Concept Scale, Third Edition: Receptive (BBCS-3:R)	2 years 5 months to 7 years 11 months	Basic concept development	Quickly identify or comprehensively diagnose basic concept development
Woodcock-Johnson IV Tests of Early Cognitive and Academic Development (WJ IV ECAD™)	2 years 6 months to 7 years 11 months	Comprehensive developmental assessment	Assess intellectual, achievement, and language skills
Language Tests			
Preschool Language Scale, Fifth Edition (PLS-5)	Birth to 7 years 11 months	Language	Measure receptive and expressive language
Peabody Picture Vocabulary Test, Fourth Edition (PPVT-4)	2 years 5 months to 18 years	Vocabulary	Measure receptive vocabulary for Standard American English
Pre-Language Assessment Survey (pre-LAS) (English and Spanish)	4–6 years	Language	Measure oral language proficiency and assess learner needs
IDEA Proficiency Tests (Oral Pre-IPT), Fifth Edition	3–5 years	Language	Identify children for placement in LED programs
Woodcock-Muñoz Language Survey®—Third Edition (WMLS III)	3 years to adult	Language	Measure language proficiency in English or Spanish; determine eligibility for bilingual programs or readiness for English instruction

language placement decisions, monitor progress over time, and identify learner needs. The *IDEA Proficiency Tests (Pre-Oral IPT), Fifth Edition* (Ballard & Tighe, 2016) are designed to evaluate language, reading, and writing skills in Spanish and English for children in pre-K to 12th grade. The *Pre-Oral IPT* is administered to 3- to 5-year-olds and can be used to determine when children are ready to be released from ELL programs. The *Woodcock-Muñoz Language Survey—Third Edition® (WMLS™ III)* (Woodcock, Alvarado, Ruef, & Schrank, 2017) can be administered to students ages 3 to 22.11 years. Figure 4-4 lists different categories of preschool tests.

Enhanced eText: Video Example 4.3

Tests for School-Age Children

For the child old enough to attend preschool and elementary school, many tests are available for use by teachers, school psychologists, program evaluators, and other personnel with responsibilities for students and the early childhood curriculum. In addition to preschool programs for children with disabilities, many states conduct programs for 4-year-old and kindergarten children as well. Descriptions of some of these assessments were included in the previous section on preschool tests. Likewise, some of the assessments in this section include prekindergarten and kindergarten children. Although individual tests are available for some purposes in school-age programs, group testing is also used. Group tests require the child to use paper and pencil; therefore, test results may be affected by the child's ability to respond in this manner. Test validity and reliability may be affected by the child's ability both to respond in a group setting and to use a pencil to find and mark responses on the test. As students move into the primary grades, these factors become less important. The tests discussed in this section do not include the many tests designed by individual states to meet the grade testing requirements of federal legislation. Instead, they address tests for understanding strengths and possible delays in language, cognitive, and motor development as children move into the primary grades.

Many public school programs are designed for children at high risk for disabilities. A number of programs are available, including bilingual and English language programs for children whose first language is not English, intervention programs for children with a physical or intellectual disability, and preschool programs for children from low-income homes who lack the early childhood experiences that predict successful learning. These programs may include a screening instrument to determine which children are eligible for special services. The *Wechsler Intelligence Scale for Children®, Fifth Edition (WISC®-V)* (Wechsler, 2014) and the *Bender Visual-Motor Gestalt Test, Second Edition (Bender-Gestalt-II)* (Bender, 2003) may be administered by a school psychologist or school diagnostician to determine whether the child needs educational services for children with disabilities. Poor performance on the *Bender-Gestalt-II* by a school-age child indicates the need for further evaluation of the child. The *Beery-Buktenica Developmental Test of Visual-Motor Integration, Sixth Edition (BEERY™ VMI)* (Beery, Buktenica, & Beery, 2010) is a similar test.

Achievement tests are useful when making decisions about instruction. If a child is exhibiting learning difficulties, a psychologist might administer the *Peabody Individual Achievement Test—Revised Normative Update (PIAT-R/NU)* (Markwardt, 1997) or the *Wide Range Achievement Test 4 (WRAT 4)* (Wilkinson & Robertson, 2006) to gain information about children's math, reading, and spelling skills. The teacher might administer the *Boehm Test of Basic Concepts, Third Edition (Boehm-3)* (Boehm, 2000) to

St. Pius Preschool

Areas of southwest Arkansas are experiencing an influx of people from Mexico and Central America who work at a large local paper factory. Many of these families in one community attend St. Pius Catholic Church, and parishioners have seen the need to provide English classes and other services for the parents as they adjust to a new country and language. As the parents found work, church members also recognized a need for child care. They decided to include a concentrated English language development program when they added a child-care center to their outreach activities.

As they began the program, the parishioners realized they needed to find a test that would indicate the children's progress in learning English as well as provide a language assessment to send to local Head Start, preschool, and kindergarten programs when the children were transitioning out of the St. Pius school. They learned about the *Pre-Language Assessment Survey (Pre-LAS)* from public school colleagues. After learning how to use the instrument, they were ready to start implementing the test to better help their very young students learn English.

young children to determine their need for instruction in basic concepts or to assess successful learning of concepts previously taught.

Primary-grade teachers may also need specific information about a child having difficulties in the classroom. Diagnostic tests such as the *Spache Diagnostic Reading Scales* (Spache, 1981) can be administered by classroom teachers to pinpoint skills in which students need additional instruction. The *Child Observation Record Advantage (COR Advantage)* developed by the HighScope Educational Research Foundation (HighScope Educational Research Foundation, 2014) can be used to assess children birth through kindergarten. It is comprised of eight areas focused on children's growth and development plus an additional area for English Language Learners. Figure 4-5 includes examples of items from COR Advantage. The checklists can also be used in Head Start programs and child-care centers and with children who speak English as a second language.

Group achievement tests are used to evaluate individual achievement, group achievement, and program effectiveness. All new tests developed by individual states to provide accountability for student achievement are group achievement tests.

Figure 4.5 Examples from COR Advantage

APPROACHES TO LEARNING
A. Initiative and planning
0. Child turns toward or away from an object or person.
1. Child moves with persistence until reaching a desired object or person.
2. Child indicates an intention with one or two words.
3. Child expresses a plan with a simple sentence and follows through.
4. Child makes and follows through on two or more unrelated plans.
5. Child stays with his or her plan for a substantial part (at least 20 minutes) of work time (choice time, free play time).
6. Child plans and follows through on a project that takes more than two days to complete.
7. Child uses outside resources to gather information needed to complete his or her plan.
B. Problem solving with materials
0. Child moves his or her eyes, head, or hand toward a desired object or person.
1. Child repeats an action, even when it isn't working, to solve a problem.
2. Child asks for help in solving a problem with materials.
3. Child verbally identifies a problem with materials.
4. Child persists with one idea or tries several ideas until he or she is successful at solving a simple problem with materials.
5. Child helps another child solve a problem with materials.
6. Child anticipates potential problems with materials in play and identifies possible solutions.
7. Child coordinates multiple resources (materials and/or people) to solve a complex problem with materials.
C. Reflection
0. Child returns his or her attention to an object or event of interest.
1. Child indicates he or she wants something to happen again.
2. Child returns to where something he or she wants or has played with is located.
3. Child says one thing he or she did soon after the event.
4. Child recalls three or more things that he or she did and/or the details of something that happened.
5. Child recalls, without prompting, the sequence of three or more things he or she did or that happened.
6. Child says the reason why an experience happened to him or her as it did and what he or she would do the same or differently next time.
7. Child recalls another person's experience and uses what he or she observed in a similar situation.

SOURCE: COR Advantage, Desk Reference. (2014). HighScope® Educational Research Foundation 2014, used with permission.

A school district may administer achievement tests every year to determine each student's progress, as well as to gain diagnostic information on the child's need for future instruction. The same test results can be used at the district level to give information on student's progress between and within schools and to determine the effectiveness of the district's instructional program.

Instructional effectiveness may also be evaluated at the state or national level. A state agency may administer statewide achievement tests to work toward establishing a standard of instructional effectiveness in all schools within the state. Test results can identify school districts that both exceed and fall below the set standard. Indicators of poor instructional areas in many school districts pinpoint weaknesses in the state's instructional program and facilitate specific types of improvement. The Common Core of State Standards was developed in an effort to measure achievement in all states (NAEYC, 2012). National assessments are made periodically to pinpoint strengths and weaknesses in the educational progress of U.S. children in different subject areas. These findings are frequently compared with achievement results of students in other countries. Figure 4-6 lists tests for school-age children.

Enhanced eText: Video Example 4.4

In this section, we discussed how standardized tests are used. Although the tests described include various types with different purposes, the process used for their development is essentially the same. The next part of the chapter will focus on how standardized tests are designed; that is, the steps followed in the development of all standardized tests.

Figure 4.6 School-age tests

NAME	LEVEL	TYPE	PURPOSE
Bilingual Syntax Measure II	Kindergarten to grade 2	Language	Determine language dominance
Wechsler Intelligence Scale for Children®, Fifth Edition (WISC®-V)	6.0–16.11 years	Intelligence	Measures child intellectual ability; includes verbal and performance subscales
Bender Visual Motor Gestalt Test, Second Edition (Bender-Gestalt-II)	4–10 years	Visual-motor functioning	Assess perceptual skills and hand–eye coordination; identify learning disabilities
Test of Visual-Motor Integration	4–17 years	Visual-motor functioning	Assess visual-motor ability
Peabody Individual Achievement Test—Revised Normative Update (PIAT-R/NU)	Kindergarten to grade 12	Individual achievement	Assess achievement in mathematics, reading, spelling, and general information
Boehm Test of Basic Concepts, Third Edition (Boehm-3)	Kindergarten to grade 2	Cognitive ability	Screen for beginning school concepts
Brigance Comprehensive Inventory of Basic Skills II	Pre-kindergarten to grade 9	Academic achievement	Assess academic skills and diagnose learning difficulties in language, math, and reading
Spache Diagnostic Reading Skills	Grades 1 to 8 reading levels	Diagnostic reading test	Locate reading problems and plan remedial instruction
Child Observation Record, (COR Advantage)	Birth through kindergarten	Comprehensive developmental assessment	Provide appropriate assessment using developmental checklist

Enhanced eText: Self-Check 4.1

Steps in Standardized Test Design

Test designers follow a series of steps when constructing a new test. These steps ensure that the test achieves its goals and purposes. In planning a test, the developers first specify the purpose of the test. Next, they determine the test format. As actual test design begins, they formulate objectives; write, try out, and analyze test items; and assemble the final test form. After the final test form is administered, the developers establish **norms**, statistics that supply a frame of reference based on the actual performance of test takers in a norm group, and determine the validity and reliability of the test. As a final step, they develop a test manual containing procedures for administering the test and statistical information on standardization results.

Specifying the Purpose of the Test

Every standardized test should have a clearly defined purpose. The description of the test's purpose is the framework for the construction of the test. It also allows evaluation of the instrument when design and construction steps are completed. The *Standards for Educational and Psychological Testing* (AERA, APA, & NCME, 2014) has established guidelines for including the test's purpose in the test manual. Test designers should be able to explain what construct or characteristics the test will measure, how the test results will be used, and who will take the test or to whom it will be administered.

The population for whom the test is intended is a major factor in test design. Tests constructed for infants and young children are very different from tests designed for adults. As test developers consider the composition and characteristics of the children for whom they are designing the test, they must include variables such as age, intellectual or educational level, socioeconomic background, language and cultural background, and whether the young child can read.

Determining Test Format

Test format decisions are based on determinations made about the purpose of the test and the characteristics of the test takers. The test format results from the developer's decision on how test items will be presented and how the test taker will respond (Kaplan & Saccuzzo, 2013). One consideration is whether the test will be verbal or written. Although adults are most familiar with written tests, infants and young children are unable to read or write. Tests designed for very young children are usually presented orally by a test administrator. An alternative is to use a psychomotor response in which the child is given an object to manipulate or is asked to perform a physical task. For example, to test a child's understanding of colors, a set of colored cubes could be placed in front of the child. Next, the person giving the test asks the child to hand her a block of a particular color. A more recent approach is to conduct assessments during play or daily routines (Linder, 2008). In this approach, children are assessed in a room that has many play materials geared toward different developmental domains (e.g., markers for fine motor or a ball to examine gross motor skills).

As the child interacts with the materials, the assessor records his or her skills on a checklist. For instance, was the child able to write his or her name or bounce the ball? Recent research indicates that although play-based assessments are less structured than clinical one-on-one tools, they can effectively indicate developmental strengths and needs of young children, though some tools may need further investigation of their reliability and validity (O'Grady & Dusing, 2015).

For older children, high school students, and adults, other test formats are possible. Test takers may respond to an alternative-choice written test such as one with true–false, **multiple-choice**, or matching items. The test may be given as a **group test** rather than administered as an **individual test** to one person at a time. Short-answer and essay items are also possibilities.

After the test designers have selected the format most appropriate for the test's purpose and for the group to be tested, actual test construction begins. Experimental test forms are assembled after defining test objectives and writing test items for each objective.

Developing Experimental Forms

In preparing preliminary test forms, developers use the test purpose description as their guide. Test content is then delimited. If an achievement test for schoolchildren is to be written, for example, curriculum is analyzed to ensure that the test will reflect the instructional program. If the achievement test is to be designed for national use, then textbook series, syllabi, and curricular materials are studied to check that test objectives accurately reflect curriculum trends. Teachers and curriculum experts are consulted to review the content outlines and behavioral objectives that serve as reference points for test items.

The process of developing good test items involves writing, editing, trying out, and rewriting or revising test items. Before being tried out, each item for an achievement test may be reviewed and rewritten by test writers, teachers, and other experts in the field. Many more items than will be used are written because many will be eliminated in the editing and rewriting stages (Mehrens & Lehman, 1991).

A preliminary test is assembled so that the selected test items can be tried out with a sample of students. The experimental test forms resemble the final form. Instructions are written for administering the test. The sample of people selected to take the preliminary test is similar to the population that will take the final form of the test.

The tryout of the preliminary test form is described as *item tryout and analysis.* **Item analysis** involves studying three characteristics of each test question: difficulty level, discrimination, and grade progression of difficulty (McMillan, 2013). The *difficulty level* of a question refers to how many test takers in the tryout group answered the question correctly. *Discrimination* of each question involves the extent to which the question distinguishes between test takers who did well or poorly on the test. Test takers who did well should have been more successful in responding to an item than test takers who did poorly. The item differentiates between people who have more or less knowledge or ability. The *grade progression of difficulty* refers to tests that are taken by students in different grades in school. If a test question has good grade progression of difficulty, a greater percentage of students should answer it correctly in each successively higher grade (Mehrens & Lehman, 1991; McMillan, 2013).

Purpose of, and Rationale for, Selected Tests

The statement of purpose of a test describes the framework that will be used in designing the test. Two examples follow.

The *Neonatal Behavioral Assessment Scale (NBAS)* represents a guide that helps parents, health care providers, and researchers understand the newborn's language. The Scale looks at a wide range of behaviors and is suitable for examining newborns and infants up to 2 months old. By the end of the assessment, the examiner has a behavioral "portrait" of the infant, describing the baby's strengths, adaptive responses, and possible vulnerabilities. The examiner shares this portrait with parents to develop appropriate caregiving strategies aimed at enhancing the earliest relationship between babies and parents (Brazelton & Nugent, 2011, p. 1).

The *Vineland-3* is an individually administered, norm-referenced measure of adaptive behavior or "personal and social self-sufficiency" for individuals ages birth–90 years. It is appropriate for educational, social services, health care, criminal justice, or military settings. The *Vineland-3* helps measure adaptive behavior of individuals with intellectual disability, autism spectrum disorders (ASDs), attention deficit/hyperactivity disorder (ADHD), post-traumatic brain injury, hearing impairment, dementia, Alzheimer's disease, and other conditions (Pepperdine & McCrimmon, 2017; Sparrow, Cicchetti, & Saulnier 2016).

Assembling the Test

After item analysis is completed, the final form of the test is assembled. As a result of item analysis, test items have been reexamined, rewritten, or eliminated. Test questions or required behaviors to measure each test objective are selected for the test. If more than one test form is to be used, developers must ensure that alternative forms are equivalent in content and difficulty. Test directions are made final with instructions for both test takers and test administrators. In addition, information for test administrators includes details about the testing environment and testing procedures.

Standardizing the Test

Although test construction is complete when the final form is assembled and printed, the test has not yet been standardized. The final test form must be administered to another, larger sample of test takers to standardize each item. There are two types of standardized tests: criterion-referenced and normed-referenced. **Norm-reference tests** are tools whereby children's performance can be compared with the performance of a reference group. **Criterion-referenced tests** provide a description of mastery for each item.

A reference group that represents the children for whom the test has been designed is selected to take the test for the purpose of establishing norms or criterion mastery. The performance of the reference or sample group on the final test form during the standardization process will be used to evaluate the test scores of individuals or groups who take the test in the future.

The norming group is chosen to reflect the makeup of the population for whom the test is designed. If a national school achievement test is being developed, the standardization sample consists of children from all sections of the country to include such variables as gender, age, community size, geographic area, socioeconomic status, and ethnic factors. For other types of tests, different characteristics may be used to match the norming sample with future populations to be tested.

Various kinds of norms can be established during the standardization process. Raw scores of sample test takers are converted into derived scores or standard scores for purposes of comparison. Standard scores are achieved by calculating the **raw score**, or the number of items answered correctly, into a score that can be used to establish a norm. Various types of standard scores can be used to compare the people selected to standardize the test with future populations that will be given the test. Each type of **grade norm** allows test users to interpret a child's test scores in comparison with the scores of children used to norm the test (Miller, Linn, & Gronlund, 2012; Payne, 1997). For example, an age score is established by determining the norms for age groups when the test is given to the norming sample. The age norms describe the average performance of children of various ages. Likewise, grade norms or grade-equivalent norms are established by determining the average scores made by children at different grade levels in the norming group (Kaplan & Saccuzzo, 2013; McMillan, 2013).

Developing the Test Manual

The final step in test design is development of the test manual. The test developer describes the purpose of the test, the development of the test, and the standardization procedures. Information on test validity and reliability is also included to give test users information on the dependability of the test. When explaining standardization information in the user's manual, test developers describe the method used to select the norming group. The number of individuals included in standardizing the test is reported, as well as the geographic areas, types of communities, socioeconomic groups, and ethnic groups that they represent.

Enhanced eText: Self-Check 4.2

Differences between Test Validity and Test Reliability

Norm information is important for establishing confidence in analyzing and interpreting the significance of test scores. Test users also need information demonstrating that the test will be valuable for the intended purposes. Therefore, the test manual must provide information on validity and reliability. Both types of dependability indicators are equally important in determining the quality of the test. **Validity** is the degree to which the test serves the purpose for which it will be used; **reliability** is the extent to which a test is stable or consistent. Test validity can be determined through content validity, criterion-related validity, or construct validity.

When first designing a test, the developers describe its purpose. Test objectives or the test outlines provide the framework for the content of the test. When a manual provides information on **content validity**, the test developers are defining the degree to which the test items measured the test objectives and fulfilled the purpose of the test. Thus, for example, on an achievement test, content validity is the extent to which the content of the test represents an adequate sampling of the instructional program it is intended to cover. The content validity of a reading test would be based on how well the test items measured the reading skills examined in the test. The content validity of a mathematics test would look at the content of the objectives on the test and assess how well the test items measured that content.

Criterion-related validity is concerned with the validity of a test. Rather than analyzing course content, test items focus on skills or tasks that predict future success in some area. The estimates of predictive validity are concerned with stability over time. For example, an **intelligence quotient (IQ)** test might be predictive of school achievement. Likewise, Scholastic Aptitude Test scores may predict whether high school students will be successful in college. Validity is predictive because the criteria for success are the future grades the student will earn in college or the student's future grade-point average.

Criterion-related validity may be **concurrent validity**, rather than predictive validity. Instead of using a future measure to determine validity, current measures are used. The outside criterion is assessed when the test is standardized. The developer of an intelligence test may cite an existing intelligence test as the criterion to measure validity. The developer administers both intelligence tests to the sample group. If the new test scores correlate highly with scores on the existing test, they may be used to establish concurrent validity.

If a test measures an abstract psychological trait, the user's manual will describe how the sample group was tested to establish construct validity. **Construct validity** is the extent to which a test measures a relatively abstract psychological trait such as personality, verbal ability, or mechanical aptitude (Miller, Linn, & Gronlund, 2012). Rather than examining test items developed from test objectives, one examines construct validity by comparing test results with the variables that explain the behaviors. For example, suppose the construct is believed to include certain behavioral characteristics, such as sociability or honesty. An instrument's construct validity can be checked by analyzing how the trait is affected by changing conditions. Alternatively, an instrument may measure level of anxiety; its construct validity is determined by creating experiments to find out what conditions affect anxiety (Miller, Linn, & Gronlund, 2012).

The validity of a test is the extent to which the test measures what it is designed to measure. Test users, however, are also interested in a test's dependability or stability in measuring behaviors. Test developers, therefore, also establish and report on the reliability of the instrument as part of the standardization process.

Test reliability is related to test item discrimination. When test items are analyzed after the initial item tryout, they are examined for discrimination power. After the final test form is administered to a norming sample, the items are analyzed again to ensure that the instrument is fairly reliable. The whole test is analyzed, rather than individual test items. The test manual reports the test's reliability as determined by using alternative-form, split-half, or test–retest reliability measures. A test's *reliability coefficient* describes the degree to which a test is free from error of measurement. If **alternative-form reliability** strategies are used, test developers construct two **equivalent forms** of the final test. Both forms are administered to the norming group within a short period. The correlation between the results on the two different forms measures the coefficient of reliability. For example, standardized achievement tests are published using several different forms of the test. To measure reliability, the norming group takes two forms of the test and then the results are compared to see if the performance on each of the tests was the same or very similar.

If a **split-half reliability** coefficient is used to establish reliability, the norming group is administered a single test, and scores on half of the test are correlated with scores on the other half of the test. Split-half reliability is determined from the contents of a single test. A test with split-half reliability is also considered to have **internal consistency**; that is, the items on each half of the test are positively correlated in measuring the same characteristics.

Test–retest reliability is also derived from the administration of a single test form. In this case, however, the test is administered to the norming group and then is administered again after a short interval. The two sets of scores are compared to determine whether they were consistent in measuring the test objectives.

Factors That Affect Validity and Reliability

Despite the measures and procedures that are used to ensure validity and reliability in standardized tests, other factors can affect test outcomes. Some common factors are reading ability, the physical condition of the testing room, memory, and the physical condition of the individual taking the test. Thus, if the testing room is uncomfortably warm or a student had inadequate rest the night before the test, scores will be affected. Lack of adherence to time limits and lack of consistency in test instructions affect test scores. Other factors are inconsistency in the rating of essays from individual to individual and student guessing of test answers (Payne, 1997).

Validity is affected by such factors as unclear directions, difficulty of reading vocabulary on the test, and test items that are not appropriate for the test objectives (Miller, Linn, & Gronlund, 2012). Reliability is affected by the number of test items or the length of the test, lack of inter-rater reliability, and extraneous events that affect the testing situation (Miller, Linn, & Gronlund, 2012; McMillan, 2013).

These and other factors affect the possible errors on a test and the quality of the test. This variation in testing quality is accounted for in the **standard error of measurement**, discussed next.

Standard Error of Measurement

No matter how well designed, no test is completely free from error. Although there is a hypothetical **true score**, in reality it does not exist. The reliability of the test depends on how large the standard error of measurement is after analysis of the chosen method of determining reliability. If the reliability correlations are poor, the standard error of measurement will be large. The larger the standard error of measurement, the less

Search and Share 4.2

Test Validity and Reliability

Search online to find two of the assessments mentioned in this chapter. Compare the validity and reliability information reported for each one. Which one would you choose to use and why?

reliable the test. Standard error of measurement is the estimate of the amount of variation that can be expected in test scores as a result of reliability correlations.

Several variables that are present during standardization affect test reliability, as discussed earlier. First is the size of the population sample. Generally, the larger the population sample, the more reliable the test will be. Second is the length of the test. Longer tests are usually more reliable than shorter tests. Longer tests have more test items, resulting in a better sample of behaviors. The more items that measure a behavior, the better the estimate of the true score and the greater the reliability. Strict adherence to test directions by test administrators contributes to higher reliability, whereas variations in test instructions or the coaching of students can distort the reliability of test results.

The third variable that can affect standard error of measurement is the range of test scores obtained from the norming group. The wider the spread of scores, the more reliably the test can distinguish among them. Thus, the range of scores demonstrates how well the test discriminates between good and poor students (Miller, Linn, & Gronlund, 2012). The spread of test scores can be related to the number of students taking the test. The larger the testing sample, the more likely there will be a wider spread of test scores.

Enhanced eText: Self-Check 4.3

Considerations in Selecting and Evaluating Standardized Tests

Whenever a private school, public school district, preschool, or child-care center decides to use a test to evaluate children, educators must decide how to select the best test for that purpose. Those who select the test must determine the relevant questions to ask about the test. Brown (1983) identifies various factors that test users must consider: (1) the purpose of the testing, (2) the characteristics to be measured, (3) how the test results will be used, (4) the qualifications of the people who will interpret the scores and use the results, and (5) any practical constraints. All these factors are important in selecting tests for young children. Because of the developmental limitations of young test takers, test formats must be compatible with their ability to respond. Developmental limitations include short attention span, undeveloped fine-motor skills, inability to use reading skills for test responses, and poor performance on group tests. Limitations in training and experience in those who administer the test are also factors in test selection.

Other relevant concerns, particularly in selecting tests for young children, are the costs involved, testing time, and ease of scoring and using test results (Kaplan & Saccuzzo, 2013). The test must be reasonable in cost, and the time needed to administer the test should be suitable for young children. In addition, tests need to be culturally sensitive given the diverse society in which they are used. Care should be taken to check the sample on which the tool was standardized to make sure it includes a proportional representation of the groups of children that compose the current population. For example, if the test developers say it can be used with children from the Latino community, the standardization sample should include a significant number of

Latino children. Some tools are available in more than one language (e.g., English and Spanish). In these cases, it is important that reliability and validity research has been conducted on a sample of children that speak each language (Guzman-Orth, Lopez, & Tolentino, 2017).

Enhanced eText: Application Exercise 4.1

Finally, it is important to understand adaptations the test may include for assessing children with diagnosed disabilities. Most tests have specific instructions. For example, the *Learning Accomplishment Profile—Third Edition (LAP-3)* describes two ways to determine the starting point of the test for children with diagnosed disabilities. One recommendation is to examine the child's evaluation records and start at the developmental age indicated in the records. Or, the assessor can begin administering each subscale of the test at half of the child's chronological age (Hardin & Peisner-Feinberg, 2004).

A major issue is whether the test has quality. Is it a good test to use with the children? The person searching for an appropriate test will want to examine the test manual for indications of how well the test was designed and normed. The test manual should include information on the following:

1. *Purpose of the test.* The statement of purpose should include the rationale for the test, the characteristics the test is designed to measure, and the uses for the test.

2. *Test design.* The procedures and rationale for selecting test items and the development and trial of test forms should be explained.

3. *Establishment of validity and reliability.* The description should describe the procedures used to establish validity and reliability and include sufficient data on validity, reliability, and norms.

4. *Test administration and scoring.* Specific information should be given on how to administer and score the test and to interpret test results. Information should be adequate for users to determine whether the test is practical and suitable for their purposes. Potential problems should be pointed out that might be encountered when administering and scoring the test (Kaplan & Saccuzzo, 2013). See Figure 4-7 for questions that should be answered in a test manual, including an acceptable coefficient of reliability.

Test users need extensive training in tests and measurements to interpret a test manual adequately. For many users, the explanations and data reported in test manuals are complex and difficult to understand. A reader may have difficulty in deciding whether the reliability coefficient is adequate, whether the size and demographic characteristics of the norming population are appropriate, or whether test content and format are suitable for the intended uses. To obtain additional help in understanding the suitability of the test, test users will want to consult resources for test standards and reviews. The *Standards for Educational and Psychological Testing* (AERA, APA, & NCME, 2014) includes standards for tests, manuals, and reports. It also includes standards for reliability and validity, as well as information that should be included on the use of tests.

The Buros Institute of Mental Measurements is perhaps the most important source in identifying, describing, and evaluating published tests. The series of *Tests in Print* is a comprehensive bibliography of thousands of tests in five volumes. The most recent,

Figure 4.7 Questions for test manuals about the quality of tests

Reliability
1. How was reliability determined for the test? What were the methods used?
2. Does the reliability achieve recommended levels (0.90 or above for tests used to make decisions about individuals or 0.70 or above for research studies)?

Validity
1. Does the test actually measure what it purports to measure?
2. Is the test meaningful for your purposes?
3. How was the test validated? What specific criteria were used?

Standardization Sample
1. Was the number of subjects used to establish reliability, validity, and norms adequate?
2. What kinds of demographic and personal characteristics were included in the group of subjects? Are they similar to the population you will be testing?

Scoring
1. Are scoring keys available?
2. Is the time needed to score reasonable?
3. If the test is machine scored, is the cost reasonable? What sort of report is available? How long does it take for test results to be available?

Other Considerations
1. How long does it take to administer the test?
2. Are the test content and length appropriate for the developmental level if used with young children?
3. Does the test require reading? Is the reading level appropriate for students who will take the test?
4. How much training is required for the test administrator? Can the test be administered by classroom teachers?

Tests in Print IX (Anderson, Schlueter, Carlson, & Geisinger, 2016), consists of two volumes. The tests are listed by type, and basic information is given about each test.

The *Mental Measurements Yearbooks* include descriptive information about tests, plus professional reviews. The content also includes sources of information about test construction, validation, and use. Critical reviews of the tests are included. For example, the *Stanford–Binet Intelligence Scale* (Terman & Merrill, 1973) is the oldest and most highly regarded IQ test used in the United States. However, the fourth edition of the test (Thorndike, Hagen, & Sattler, 1986) was found to be significantly different from the earlier editions. Reviewers pointed out that users are given poor information on the accuracy of reliability scores, the test is less game-like and therefore likely to be less appealing to children, and it overrepresents parents from high occupational and educational levels in the sample of children used for norming (Anastasi, 1989; Cronbach, 1989). The most recent edition is the *Stanford-Binet Intelligence Scales (SB5), Fifth Edition* (Roid, 2003). Educators choosing a test need to be informed of the quality of the test being considered for selection. The most recent yearbook is *The Twentieth Mental Measurements Yearbook* (Carlson, Geisinger, & Jonson, 2017). Test reviews can be accessed online. The Buros Center for Testing provides search engines for *Test Reviews Online*.

Brown (1983) summarized the steps in selecting and evaluating tests as follows:

1. Outline your general requirements: the purpose of testing, the characteristics to be measured, and the nature of the group to be tested. Consider also the qualifications of test users and practical considerations.

2. Identify what tests are available that appear to meet your needs. Here sources such as *Tests in Print*, the *Mental Measurement Yearbooks*, test publishers' catalogs, and test compilations will be most helpful.

3. Obtain further information about these tests from texts, journals, reference books, and consultation with people who have used this type of test.

4. Select the most promising tests. Obtain samples (specimen sets) of these tests.

5. Make a detailed evaluation of these tests, keeping in mind the unique requirements of your situation. On the basis of these evaluations, select the test(s) to be used.

6. If possible, conduct an experimental tryout of the test before putting it to use.

7. Use the test. Constantly monitor and evaluate its usefulness and effectiveness. (p. 463)

Enhanced eText: Self-Check 4.4

Summary

Psychological tests are administered to children of all ages beginning in infancy. The tests can be organized to measure abilities such as achievement, aptitudes, and intelligence. There are also measures to understand interests, attitudes, values, and personality characteristics. These types of assessments have been organized in this chapter according to age level. Thus, there are charts for tests for infants and toddlers, preschool children, and school-age children. Some of the measures, such as interest and attitude tests, are appropriate only for school-age children. The tests vary in quality depending on how they were designed and evaluated for validity and reliability. As a result, the choice of tests for a particular purpose should be examined for established quality indicators.

Despite their shortcomings, standardized tests are useful for test users. Because they have been carefully developed through a series of steps that ensure their dependability, educational institutions, in particular, use them to measure students' characteristics. Good standardized tests are normed by using many individuals from various backgrounds who live in different parts of the United States. As a result, the tests also accurately measure the population to whom the tests are given.

Although the process of developing a standardized test may seem to be unnecessarily tedious, good test design requires careful planning and attention to each step. The ultimate validity and reliability of the test depend on the attention paid to design details, beginning with the definition of the test's purpose and ending with the description of technical data about the test's construction in the users' manual.

Enhanced eText: Self-Check: Chapter Review

Key Terms

achievement test 79

alternative-form reliability 96

aptitude test 79

concurrent validity 96

construct validity 96

content validity 96

criterion-referenced test 94

criterion-related validity 96

equivalent forms 96

grade norm 95

group test 93

individual test 93

intelligence quotient (IQ) 96

intelligence test 79

interest inventories 80

internal consistency 97

item analysis 93

multiple-choice 93

Norm-reference tests 94

norms 92

personality test 80

raw score 95

reliability 95

screening test 83

split-half reliability 97

standard error of measurement 97

test–retest reliability 97

true score 97

validity 95

Selected Organizations

Search for the following organizations online:
Child Care Exchange

Buros Institute of Mental Measurements
Test Reviews Online

References

Als, H., Butler, S., Kosta, S., & McAnulty, G. (2005). The assessment of preterm infants' behavior (APIB): Furthering the understanding and measurement of neurodevelopmental competence in preterm and full-term infants. *Mental Retardation and Developmental/Disabilities Research Reviews, 11*, 94–102.

Als, H., Tronick, E., Lester, B. M., & Brazelton, T. B. (1979). Specific neonatal measures: The Brazelton Neonatal Behavioral Assessment Scale. In J. D. Osofsky (Ed.), *Handbook of infant development* (pp. 185–215). New York, NY: Wiley.

Anastasi, A. (1989). Review of the *Stanford–Binet Intelligence Scale, Fourth Edition.* In J. C. Conoley & J. J. Kramer (Eds.), *The tenth mental measurements yearbook* (pp. 771–772). Lincoln, NE: University of Nebraska Press.

Anderson, N., Schlueter, J. E., Carlson, J. F., & Geisinger, K. F. (Eds.). (2016). *Test in print IX.* Lincoln, NE: Buros Center for Testing.

American Educational Research Association., American Psychological Association., National Council on Measurement in Education., & Joint Committee on Standards for Educational and Psychological Testing (U.S.). (2014). *Standards for educational and psychological testing.* Washington, DC: AERA.

Apgar, V. (1975). A proposal for a new method of evaluation of a newborn infant. *Anesthesia and Analgesia, 32,* 260–267.

Ball, R. S. (1977). The Gesell developmental schedules. *Journal of Abnormal Child Psychology, 5,* 233–239.

Ballard, W., & Tighe, P. (2016). *IDEA Proficiency Tests (Oral Pre-IPT), Fifth Edition.* Brea, CA: Author.

Bayley, N. (2005). *Bayley scales of infant development, third edition (BSID-III).* San Antonio, TX: Pearson Assessments.

Beery, K. E., Buktenica, H., & Beery, N. (2010). *Beery-Buktenica developmental test of motor integration, sixth edition.* San Antonio, TX: Pearson.

Bender, L. (2003). *Bender visual motor Gestalt test for children, second edition (Bender-Gestalt-II).* San Antonio, TX: Pearson Assessments.

Boehm, A. E. (2000). *Boehm test of basic concepts, third edition.* San Antonio, TX: Pearson.

Bracken, B. A. (2006). *Bracken basic concept scale—third edition receptive (BBCS-3:R).* San Antonio, TX: Pearson Assessments.

Brand, D. A., Altman, R. L., Puttill, K., & Edwards, K. S. (2005, April). Yield of diagnostic testing in infants who have had an apparent life-threatening event. *Pediatrics*, *115*, 885–893.

Brazelton, T. B., Berry, T., & Nugent, J. K. (2011). *Neonatal Behavioral Assessment Scale (NBAS)*. Cambridge, England: Cambridge University Press.

Brigance, A. H. (2013). *Brigance early childhood screens, III*. Woburn, MA: Curriculum Associates.

Brown, E. G. (1983). *Principles of educational and psychological testing* (3rd ed.). New York, NY: CBS College Publishing.

Calhoun, C. L., Gaughan, J. P., Chafitz, R. S., & Mulcahey, M. J. (2009, Spring). A pilot study of observational motor assessment in infants and toddlers with spinal cord injury. *Pediatric Physical Therapy*, *21*, 62–67.

Campbell, S. K., Kolobe, T.H.A., Osten, E. T., Lenke, M. L., & Girolami, G. L., (1995). Construct validity of the Test of Infant Motor Performance. *Physical Therapy*, *75*, 585–596.

Carlson, J. F., Geisinger, K. F., & Jonson, J. L. (2017). *The twentieth mental measurements yearbook*. Lincoln, NE: University of Nebraska Press.

Cronbach, L. J. (1989). Review of the *Stanford-Binet Intelligence Scale, Fourth Edition*. In J. C. Conoley & J. J. Kramer (Eds.), *The tenth mental measurements yearbook* (pp. 773–775). Lincoln, NE: University of Nebraska Press.

Data Recognition Corporation | CTB. (2016). *The LAS links suite of assessments and instruction*. Retrieved from https://www.datarecognitioncorp.com/Assessment-Solutions/Documents/LAS%20Links%20Overview%20Brochure%202016.pdf

DeGangi, G., Poisson, S., Sickel, R., & Wiener, A. S. (1999). *Infant/Toddler Symptom Checklist: A screening tool for parents (ITSC)*. San Antonio, TX: Pearson Assessments.

Dunn, L. M., & Dunn, L. (2007). *Peabody picture vocabulary test, fourth edition (PPVT-4)*. San Antonio, TX: Pearson Assessments.

Frankenburg, W. K., Dodds, J., Archer, P., Shapiro, H., & Bresnick, B. (1992). *Denver II*. Denver, CO: Denver Developmental Materials.

Gesell Institute. (2011). *Gesell developmental observation—revised*. New Haven, CT: Author.

Gronlund, N. E. (1990). *Measurement and evaluation in teaching* (6th ed.). New York, NY: Macmillan.

Guzman-Orth, D., Lopez, A. A., & Tolentino, F. (2017). *A framework for the dual language assessment of young dual language learners in the United States* (Research Report No. RR-17-37). Princeton, NJ: Educational Testing Service. https://doi.org/10.1002/ets2.12165

Hack, M., Taylor, H. G., Drotar, D., Schluchter, M., Carter, L., Wilson-Costello, D., Klein, N., Friedman, H., Mercuri-Miinicih, N., & Morrow, M. (2005). Poor predictive validity of the Bayley scales of infant development for cognitive function of extremely low birth weight children. *Pediatrics*, *116*, 333–341.

Hardin, B. J., & Peisner-Feinberg, E. S. (2004). *The learning accomplishment profile-third edition (LAP-3): Examiner's manual and technical report*. Lewisville, NC: Pact House Publishing.

Harrison, P., Kaufman, A. S., & Kaufman, N. L. (1990). *AGS early screening profiles (ESP)*. Bulverde, TX: Pearson Assessments.

Harrison, P., & Oakland, T. (2015). *Adaptive behavior assessment system, third edition (APAS-3)*. Torrance, CA: WPS Publishing.

HighScope Educational Research Foundation. (2014). Child Observation Record Advantage (COR Advantage) Ypsilanti, MI: Author.

Kaplan, R. M., & Saccuzzo, D. P. (2013). *Psychological testing principles: Applications and issues* (8th ed.). Belmont, CA: Wadsworth.

Kaufman, A., & Kaufman, N. (2004). *Kaufman assessment battery for children (K-ABC-II): Sampler manual* (2nd ed.). San Antonio, TX: Pearson Assessments.

Kaufman, A., & Kaufman, N. (2018). *The Kaufman assessment battery for children, second edition normative update (KABC™-II NU)*. San Antonio, TX: Pearson.

Lambert, N., Nihira, K., & Leland, H. (2008). *Adaptive behavior scale-school, second edition (ABS-S:2)*.. North Tonawanda, NY: Multi-Health Systems.

LeBuffe, P. A., & Naglieri, J. A. (2012). *Devereux early childhood assessment preschool program, second edition (DECA P-2)*. Villanova, PA: Devereux Center for Resilient Children.

Linder, T. W. (2008). *Transdisciplinary play-based assessment-2*. Baltimore, MD: Brookes.

Mardell, C. D., & Goldenberg, D. S. (2011). *Developmental indicators for the assessment of learning* (fourth edition). San Antonio, TX: Pearson Assessments.

Markwardt, F. (1997). *Peabody individual achievement test—revised normative update. (PIAT-R/NU)*. San Antonio, TX: Pearson Assessments.

McMillan, J. H. (2013). *Classroom assessment: Principles and practice for effective instruction* (4th ed.). Boston, MA: Allyn & Bacon.

Mehrens, W. A., & Lehmann, I. J. (1991). *Measurement and evaluation in education and psychology* (4th ed.). New York, NY: Harcourt Brace.

Meisels, S. J., & Atkins-Burnett, S. A. (2005). *Developmental screening in early childhood: A guide* (5th ed.). Washington, DC: National Association for the Education of Young Children.

Meisels, S., Marsden, D. B., Dombro, A. L., Weston, D. R., & Jewkes, A. M. (2008). *The ounce scale*. San Antonio, TX: Pearson Assessments.

Meisels, S. J., Marsden, D. B., Wiske, M. S., & Henderson, L. W. (2008). *Early screening inventory—revised (ESI-R)*. New York, NY: Pearson Education.

Merrell, K. W. (2003). *Preschool and kindergarten behavior scales, second edition (PKBS-2)*. Austin, TX: PRO-ED.

Miller, L. J. (1993). *First step: Screening test for evaluating*. San Antonio, TX: Pearson.

Miller, M. D., Linn, R. L., & Gronlund, N. M. (2012). *Measurement and assessment in teaching* (11th ed.). Upper Saddle River, NJ: Pearson.

Mullen, E. M. (1995). *Mullen scales of early learning, AGS edition*. San Antonio, TX: Pearson.

National Association for the Education of Young Children (NAEYC). (2012). *Common Core Standards: Caution and opportunity for early childhood educators*. Washington, DC: Author.

Newborg, J. (2004). *Battelle developmental inventory—II (BDI-II)*. Chicago, IL: Riverside Publishing.

O'Grady, M. G. & Dusing, S. C. (2015). Reliability and validity of play-based assessments of motor and cognitive skills for infants and young children: A systematic review. *Physical Therapy, 95*, 25–38.

Panitch, H. B. (2004). The role of pulmonary testing in infants. *NeoReviews, 5*. Retrieved September 29, 2009, from http://www.neoreviews.aappublications.org

Payne, D. A. (1997). *Applied educational assessment*. Belmont, CA: Wadsworth.

Pepperdine, C. R., & McCrimmon, A. W. (2017). Test review: Vineland adaptive behavior scales, third edition (Vineland-3). *Canadian Journal of School Psychology*, DOI: 10.1177/0829573517733845.

Powell, G., MacKrain, M., & LeBuffe, P. (2007). *Devereux early childhood assessment infant and toddler (DECA-I/T) technical manual*. Lewisville, NC: Kaplan Early Learning Company.

Prizant, B., & Wetherby, A. (2002). *Communication and symbolic behavior scales developmental profile (CSBS DP), first normed edition*. Baltimore, MD: Brookes Publishing.

Roid, G. (2003). *Stanford-Binet intelligence scales (SBS), fifth edition*. Rolling Meadows, IL: Riverside Publishing.

Schrank, F. A., McGrew, K. S., & Mather, N. (2015b). *Woodcock-Johnson IV tests of early cognitive and academic development*. Rolling Meadows, IL: Riverside.

Schrank, F. A., Wendling, B. J., Alvarado, C. G., & Woodcock, R. W. (2010). *Woodcock-Muñoz language survey—revised normative update (WMLS-R NU)*. Rolling Meadows, IL: Riverside Publishing.

Spache, G. D. (1981). *Diagnostic reading scales: Examiner's manual*. Monterey, CA: CTB/McGraw-Hill.

Sparrow, S. S., Cicchetti, D. V, & Saulnier, C. A. (2016). *Vineland adaptive behavior scales, third edition (Vineland-3)*. San Antonio, TX: Pearson.

Squires, J., & Bricker, D. (2009). *Ages and stages questionnaire, third edition (ASQ:3)*. Baltimore, MD: Brookes.

Terman, L. M., & Merrill, M. A. (1973). *Stanford–Binet intelligence scale: Manual for the third revision form L-M*. Boston, MA: Houghton Mifflin.

Thorndike, R. L., Hagen, E. P., & Sattler, J. M. (1986). *Stanford–Binet intelligence scale (fourth ed.)*. Chicago, IL: Riverside.

U.S. Department of Health and Human Services & U.S. Department of Education. (2014). *Birth to 5: Watch me thrive! An early care and education provider's guide for developmental and behavioral screening*. Retrieved from https://www.acf.hhs.gov/sites/default/files/ecd/ece_providers_guide_march2014.pdf

Walker, H. M., Severson, H. H., & Feil, E. G. (1995). *Early screening project (ESP)*. Longmont, CO: Sopris West.

Wechsler, D. (2012). *Wechsler preschool and primary scale of intelligence, fourth edition (WPPSI-IV)*. San Antonio, TX: Pearson.

Wechsler, D. (2014). *Wechsler intelligence scale for children, fifth edition (WISC-V)*. San Antonio, TX: Pearson.

Weitzman, C., & Wegner, L. (2015). *Promoting optimal development: Screening for behavioral and emotional Problems*. American Academy of Pediatrics. Retrieved from http://pediatrics.aappublications.org/content/early/2015/01/20/peds.2014-3716

Widerstrom, A. H., Mowder, B. A., & Sandall, S. R. (1991). *At-risk and handicapped newborns and infants.* Upper Saddle River, NJ: Prentice Hall.

Wilkinson, G. S., & Robertson, G. J. (2006). *Wide range achievement test 4 (WRAT4).* Lutz, FL: Psychological Assessment Resources.

Wodrich, D. (1997). *Children's psychological testing: A guide for nonpsychologists.* Baltimore, MD: Brookes.

Woodcock, R. W., Alvarado, C. G., Ruef, M. L., &
Schrank, F. A. (2017). *Woodcock-Muñoz Language Survey—Revised (WMLS-R).* Houghton Mifflin Harcourt.

Zeitlin, S., Williamson, G. G., & Szczepanski, M. (1988). *Early coping inventory (ECI): A measure of adaptive behavior.* Bensenville, IL: Scholastic Testing Service.

Zimmerman, I. L., Steiner, V. G., & Pond, R. E. (2011). *Preschool language scale, fifth edition (PLS-5).* San Antonio, TX: Pearson.

Chapter 5
Using and Reporting Standardized Test Results

Serhiy Kobyakov/Shutterstock

⌄ Chapter Learning Outcomes

As a result of reading this chapter, you will be able to:

5.1 Explain the distinctions between norm-referenced and criterion-referenced tests.

5.2 Explain how standardized test scores are interpreted.

5.3 Explain how test scores are reported to professionals and to parents.

5.4 Discuss the advantages and disadvantages of using standardized tests with young children.

Tests are administered to young children to acquire beneficial information about them. In Chapter 4 we discussed how tests are planned, designed, and standardized. In this chapter, we discuss in more detail how to use information from children's test scores. In the process of standardizing a test, developers establish the norms that make test score interpretation useful. We not only take a more detailed look at norm-referenced tests, but also study how another type of standardized test, the criterion-referenced test, is used to meet the learning needs of young children. Group test scores can be used to analyze and improve curriculum and instruction at various levels within a school district. Individual test scores can be used by the classroom teacher to organize appropriate learning experiences for individual students or the class as a whole.

We also discuss how individual and group test results are used to report student progress and program effectiveness. Test results are important to teachers, school district administrators, and school boards. Results are reported to each stakeholder in a context that provides meaningful interpretation of the test. Parents are also interested in how their child is progressing in school. Reporting results to parents can be different than information used by school district staff members. Reports to parents can vary depending on parental background and varying needs of their children. Finally, we consider the disadvantages and advantages of using norm- and criterion-referenced tests with young children.

Distinctions between Norm-Referenced and Criterion-Referenced Tests

Norm-referenced and criterion-referenced tests are both standardized instruments. Some standardized tests are designed for norm-referenced results (e.g., standards scores) and others for criterion-referenced results (e.g., results about specific skills). The current trend is to design tests that are both norm- and criterion-referenced. The two types of tests have different purposes, and test items are used differently when measuring student learning or achievement. **Norm-referenced tests** provide information on how the performance of an individual compares with that of others. The person's percentile rank or another type of standard score is obtained to determine the relative standing to a norming group by recording what percentage of the group obtained the same score or a lower/higher score.

In contrast, **criterion-referenced tests** provide information on how the individual performed on some standard or objective (Renaissance, 2017). These test results allow users to interpret what an individual can do without considering the performance of others. Criterion-referenced tests are designed to measure the results of instruction; they determine the individual's performance on specific behavioral or instructional objectives (Brassard & Boehm, 2008; Zucker, 2003). Linn and Miller (2005) describe the difference between the two types of tests as the ends of a continuum: "The criterion-referenced test emphasizes description of performance and the norm-referenced test emphasizes discrimination among individuals" (p. 44).

Regardless of whether tests are norm- or criterion-referenced, the process of their design and development is as described in Chapter 4. They are constructed and standardized through all the steps that will result in validity and reliability (Cohen & Spenciner, 2010). It is important that criterion-referenced tests have validity and reliability if they are to be used to make decisions about young children. Recently, "standards-referenced tests" have been used as a variation on criterion-referenced tests. They are often based on state standards and curriculum. Some standards-referenced state tests have been criticized for being poorly written and biased (FairTest a, 2007).

Norm- and criterion-referenced tests have characteristics in common. Linn and Miller (2005) describe these as follows:

1. Both require a relevant and representative sample of test items.
2. Both require specification of the achievement domain to be measured.
3. Both use the same type of test items.
4. Both use the same rules for item writing (except for item difficulty).
5. Both are judged by the same qualities of goodness (validity and reliability).
6. Both are useful in educational measurement. (p. 14)

Both tests measure what students have learned; nevertheless, the objectives for measurement are different. The norm-referenced test is broad in content. Many aspects of the content are measured. Because the test is concerned with overall achievement, only a small sample of behaviors for each objective can be assessed. The criterion-referenced test focuses on mastery of objectives. Each objective has many test questions to determine whether the objective has been mastered (Zucker, 2003).

An achievement test in mathematics provides a good example. The norm-referenced test for the first grade may have items on addition, subtraction, sets, and all other areas included in the mathematics curriculum. Test items are written to sample the student's overall performance in first-grade mathematics. The student's total raw score is then transformed to compare overall achievement with the test norms. On the criterion-referenced test, student performance on individual curriculum objectives is important. Test items are written to measure whether the child has mastered a particular learning objective in subtraction, addition, or other components of the mathematics curriculum, for example.

Another difference between norm- and criterion-referenced tests also relates to differences in test items. In a norm-referenced instrument, test items must cover a wide range of difficulty. Because the test is intended to discriminate between the performance of individual students and groups of students, the difficulty of test items ranges above the grade level for which the test is intended. Test items designed primarily for criterion-referenced purposes are written specifically for learning tasks. Easy items are not omitted, and the intent is to evaluate how well the student has learned the objectives for one grade level (Dill, 2012; Hambleton, 2009).

Enhanced eText: Video Example 5.1

New standardized tests have been developed with dual referencing; that is, they are designed for both norm- and criterion-referenced assessment. Although it is difficult to develop a single test that works equally well for both types of measurements, obtaining both kinds of performance results is helpful to educators. Compromises in test construction are offset by the more effective use of the test (Popham, 2014). Some criterion-referenced tests have not been standardized. This does not imply that they are not well designed and useful, but readers should be aware of this condition.

Special-Needs Children and Criterion-Referenced Assessments

Children in the primary grades who have special needs might be mainstreamed in the regular classroom. They may have accommodations and modifications written into their IEP plans for test taking. One strategy is having the test read to them or having notes to guide them. Information from criterion-referenced assessments inform the teacher how the student understands the material in content area subjects. The teacher can use this information to provide individual support when needed. For example, limitations in reading and writing abilities may prevent a student from demonstrating understanding. The teacher can provide assistance with reading content and writing skills to permit the student to achieve understanding of the assigned reading sources (Dill, 2012)

Uses of Norm-Referenced Tests and Criterion-Referenced Tests with Infants

Tests used with infants and toddlers are also norm-referenced or criterion-referenced. The *Bayley's Scales of Infant Development, Third Edition (BSID-III)* (Bayley, 2005) is norm-referenced, as is the screening tool, the *Denver II* (Frankenburg, Dodds, Archer, Shapiro, & Bresnick, 1992). *The Early Learning Accomplishment (E-LAP)* (Hardin & Peisner-Feinberg, 2001) is criterion-referenced. All infant tests are administered individually. The process of developing and validating standardized tests for infants and toddlers is the same as for all standardized tests. Procedures used to conduct the tests are adapted to the developmental limits of infants and toddlers, including how they respond to the test administrator.

Uses of Norm-Referenced Tests with Preschool Children

Norm-referenced test scores are used to measure individual achievement within a designated group. Norms are not standards to be reached; they are numerical descriptions of the test performance of a group of students. Norms can be established at a national, state, or local level. Norm-referenced tests are commonly used to measure school achievement, intelligence, aptitude, and personality traits. Formal tests are administered at the preschool level to identify children who need or can benefit from special instruction, as well as to determine the success of an early childhood program.

Measures of intelligence such as the *Wechsler Preschool and Primary Scale of Intelligence™—Fourth Edition (WPPSI™-IV)* (Wechsler, 2012) are norm-referenced instruments that allow test examiners to

Parents need to understand standardized test results.

Suzanne Clouzeau/Pearson Education, Inc.

differentiate the knowledge skills of preschool students. As discussed in Chapter 2, intelligence tests are described as diagnostic because they include comprehensive examination of children who might be mentally or physically delayed or who are at risk for learning disabilities. Other tests in this category include the *Kaufman Assessment Battery for Children, Second Edition (KABC™-II)* (Kaufman & Kaufman, 2005) and *McCarthy's Scales of Children's Abilities* (McCarthy, 1983). In addition to identifying children with disabilities, intelligence tests can be used to identify children who are gifted.

Norm-referenced tests are used with preschool children to measure their present level of knowledge, skills, or performance. In federally funded programs such as Head Start, a norm-referenced measure may be used to evaluate the learning acquired by the children as a result of the program. The *Peabody Picture Vocabulary Test (PPVT-4)* (Dunn & Dunn, 2007) provides a measure for language development. The *Boehm Test of Basic Concepts, Third Edition* (Boehm, 2000) assesses the child's abilities and skills, including the acquisition of concepts.

The *Dynamic Indicators of Basic Early Literacy Skills (DIBELS-NEXT)* (Good & Kaminski, 2012) is an example of an assessment for literacy skills. Figure 5-1 shows a sample of a kindergarten math test. Students are asked to choose the correct answer in response to pictures with a multiple-choice format. Some of the problems have a simple question.

Uses of Norm-Referenced Tests with School-Age Children

After children enter primary school, achievement tests are the most frequently administered norm-referenced tests. Locally developed achievement tests, as well as state and national tests, can be given in order to measure and analyze individual and group performance resulting from the educational program. Children experiencing difficulties in school are evaluated with screening and diagnostic tests, but all students take achievement tests, sometimes as early as kindergarten, more frequently beginning in first grade.

Norm-referenced test results are used for more general comparisons of group test results. One such use is to assess achievement level in subject areas. The achievement of a single class in a school, all classes of a certain grade level in the school, all schools at a grade level in a school district, and all schools within a state with that grade level can be studied to determine general progress in one or more subject areas. The results of batteries of tests can be analyzed for trends in achievement.

In a similar type of analysis, components of an instructional program can be studied by using group test scores. If a new instructional program is to be tried or if an existing method is to be evaluated to help in deciding whether changes are needed, an achievement test can be used to investigate the effectiveness of the program. Particular areas of weakness and strength can be pinpointed, and decisions and plans can be made to improve weak components in the curriculum.

Uses of Criterion-Referenced Tests with Preschool Children

Criterion-referenced test scores are used to describe individual performance on specific objectives. Criterion-referenced measures de-emphasize distinctions among individual performances; rather, they indicate whether the individual has mastered the objectives that were tested. Criterion-referenced tests are used to understand children's development, for **diagnostic evaluation**, and for instructional planning.

Figure 5.1 Examples of easyCBM Math Assessment Items—Kindergarten

Math Numbers and Operations K_1

Student Name: _____   Date: _____

1.

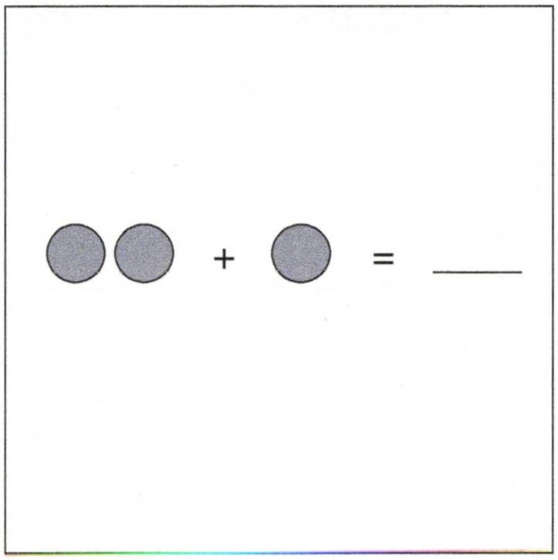

A. 9

B. 5

C. 3

2.

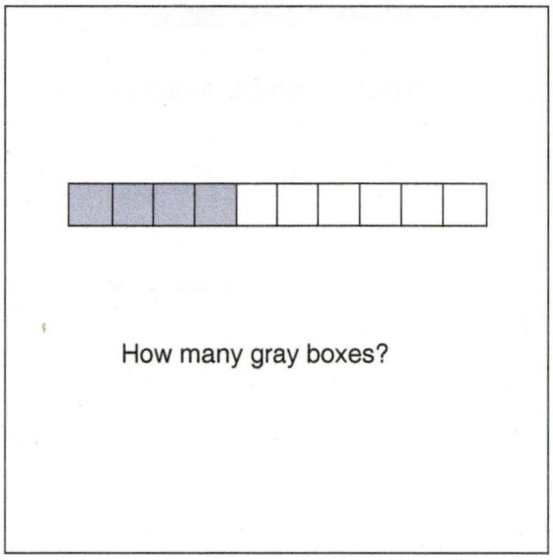

How many gray boxes?

A. 4

B. 2

C. 6

3.

How many?

A. 10

B. 7

C. 6

4.

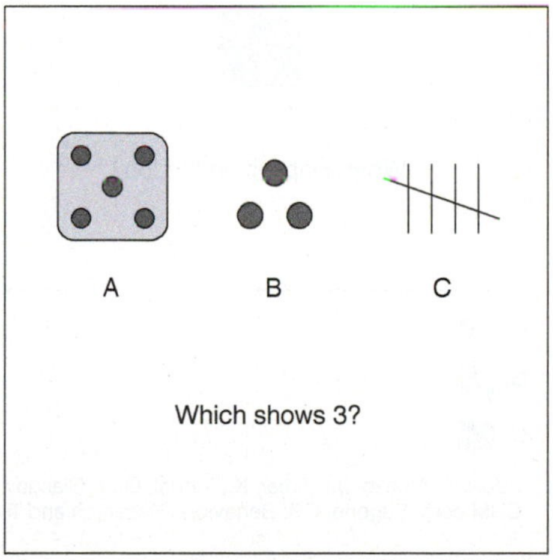

A   B   C

Which shows 3?

A. A

B. B

C. C

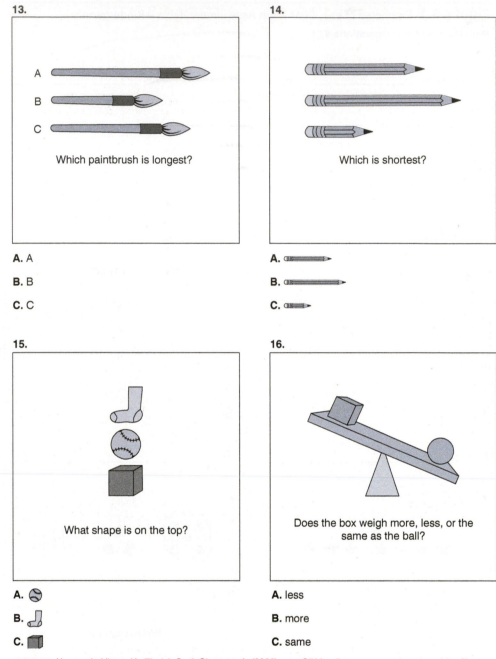

13.

Which paintbrush is longest?

A. A

B. B

C. C

14.

Which is shortest?

A.

B.

C.

15.

What shape is on the top?

A.

B.

C.

16.

Does the box weigh more, less, or the same as the ball?

A. less

B. more

C. same

SOURCE: Alonzo, J., Ulmer, K., Tindal, G., & Glasgow, A. (2006). easyCBM online assessment system. http://easy-CBM.com. Eugene, OR: Behavioral Research and Teaching, University of Oregon. Used by permission.

In the preschool years, developmental and diagnostic assessments are the criterion-referenced tests used most frequently. Although **developmental assessments** are used primarily to identify children who might profit from early education intervention or from special services before kindergarten or first grade, they can also be used as a checkpoint for children who are developing normally (Payne & Miller, 2009).

As introduced in Chapter 2, various screening tests have been developed as a result of Public Law 94–142, now known as the Individuals with Disabilities Education Improvement Act (IDEA, 2004), which required children ages 3 to 21 with disabilities to be placed in the "least restrictive environment" possible. **Developmental screening** tests assess affective, cognitive, and psychomotor characteristics to determine whether further testing evaluation is needed to identify disabilities and strategies for remediation (Payne & Miller, 2009).

Various screening measures have been developed for the preschool child. The *Denver II* (Frankenburg, Dodds, Archer, Shapiro, & Bresnick, 1992) is commonly used by pediatricians and other medical professionals. The *Early Screening Inventory—Revised* (Meisels, Marsden, Wiske, & Henderson, 2008) is used for screening purposes also. Figure 5-2 shows some of the items on the *Early Screening Inventory—Revised, 2008 Edition*.

Enhanced eText: Application Exercise 5.1

Uses of Criterion-Referenced Tests with School-Age Children

Diagnostic evaluation measures are used with school-age children as well as preschool children. Intelligence batteries and diagnostic tests in academic content areas are used with students who demonstrate learning difficulties. In addition, criterion-referenced results are used for instructional planning with children at all levels of learning needs and achievement.

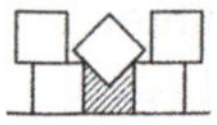

Figure 5.2 Sample of a developmental screening instrument

(Continued)

Figure 5.2 (Continued)

II LANGUAGE AND COGNITION		Circle Points, or F, or R			
		Points	Fail	Refuse	Comments
A	**Number Concept**				
1	**10 Block Counting**				
	Count these blocks. Point to each one and count out loud so that I can hear you. *Place 10 blocks in random order on a piece of construction paper. Blocks should not touch each other. Child may rearrange blocks when counting.*				
	10 Blocks (counting)	2	F	R	
	If child passes, proceed promptly *to All Together*				
	or, if child fails 10 Block Counting — 5 Block Counting				
	Remove 5 blocks. **Count these blocks. Point to each one and count out loud so that I can hear you.**				
	or 5 Blocks (counting)	or 1	F	R	
	If child passes, proceed promptly *to All Together*				
	or, if child fails both counting trials, go directly to Verbal Expression				
2	**All Together**				
	If child passes either counting trial, promptly ask: **How many are there all together?**				
	If child begins counting (again): **Tell me without counting.**				
	10 Blocks *or* 5 Blocks (all together)	1	F	R	

ESI-K   3

SOURCE: *Early Screening Inventory Revised: 2008* by Pearson Education, Inc., publishing as Pearson Early Learning. Used by permission, *Early Screening Inventory, Revised ESI-R, ESI-P, ESI-K,* and the *ESI-R, ESI-P,* and *ESI-K* logos are trademarks of Pearson Education, Inc.

Criterion-referenced scores on achievement tests are used to describe individual performance. Reports of individual performance are then used for instructional planning. Individual performance can also be used in teaching groups of children with the same instructional needs.

Mastery testing is a common criterion-referenced measure in which instructional objectives are assessed. After mastery on a test objective has been achieved, instruction proceeds with a new objective. In the case of an achievement test, performance results may be charted to show which objectives the test taker has mastered and which need further attention. This result can be used in planning instruction for a group of students. In a similar manner, individualized instruction can be initiated as a result of criterion-referenced test results. Figure 5-3 gives examples of criterion-referenced objectives in early achievement tests.

In **individualized instruction**, students are taught singly, on the basis of personal needs, rather than in large groups. Instead of planning learning activities for the class as a whole, instructional groups of different sizes are formed, and the teacher diversifies instruction based on the progress of each student. Criterion-referenced tests are one source of information for individualized instruction.

Minimum-competency testing also uses criterion-referenced test results. In minimum-competency testing, a minimum standard is set regarding competence in achieving test objectives. Individual test scores are interpreted to screen for test takers who have reached or exceeded the established level of competency. Many states have

Search and Share 5.1

Criterion-Referenced Assessments and Instructional Objectives

Search online to learn more about the relationship between criterion-referenced assessments and individual or classroom instructional objectives. What are examples of how criterion-referenced assessments can inform instruction for individual children? For groups of children? What cautions should teachers take to ensure they are not teaching to the test?

instituted minimum-competency tests for students at the elementary school level; the test results help determine promotion or retention.

On a larger scale, criterion-referenced test scores are used for broad surveys of educational accomplishment. Group achievement on a local, state, or national level is assessed to better understand educational progress. The achievement of very large groups of students is analyzed to assess strengths and weaknesses in instruction beyond the level of an individual school district. For example, students tested on a national achievement test in reading were found to be stronger in word identification skills than in comprehension skills. More recently, the National Assessment of Educational Progress (NAEP) report on trends in academic progress found the following:

> Overall, the 2012 long-term trend results show 9- and 13-year-olds scoring higher in both reading and mathematics than students their age in the 1970s. At age 13, the overall average score in each subject was also higher in comparison to the last assessment in 2008. At age 17, however, the 2012 reading and mathematics average scores were not significantly different from those in the respective first assessment year (National Center on Educational Statistics, 2012).
>
> NAEP scores result from testing of fourth- and eighth-grade students. The 2015 Mathematics scores were lower than the average scores in 2012 test results. In reading, the 2015 scores were the same as the 2012 scores in grade 4 and lower in grade 8 than the 2012 scores. (NAEP, 2015)

Figure 5.3 Examples of objectives used in criterion-referenced tests

Criterion-referenced items in beginning reading

1. Matches uppercase and lowercase letters
2. Recognizes uppercase and lowercase letters
3. Matches three-letter words
4. Matches four-letter words
5. Recognizes letters, words, and numbers
6. Recognizes words in context
7. Demonstrates skill in copying letters, numbers, and words

Criterion-referenced items in mathematics

1. Counts to 10
2. Recognizes numbers to 20
3. Recognizes coins
4. Matches number to numeral to 10
5. Adds numbers to 10
6. Subtracts numbers from 10
7. Recognizes basic shapes

Is Poverty the Cause of Poor Student Achievement?

Critics of education in the United States frequently claim that poverty is the cause of poor achievement on standardized tests when compared with students from other advanced countries. And it is true that states that have high rates of poverty do report lower scores for school achievement. However, it is not poverty alone that is the cause. There are other social factors that have an effect. Children in poverty are more likely to live in a single-parent family, and/or families experiencing alcoholism, substance abuse, child abuse, or neglect. It is not poverty alone but poverty-related "risk factors" that affect student achievement. Moreover, it has been found that some countries do better with higher-status children, while other countries do better with lower-status children. The United States does about the same with both higher- and lower-status children. The United States is not especially effective with students from the best-educated or the least-educated parents. It is the children of highly-educated parents who compare poorly in international comparisons. (Brown, 2015; Petrilli & Wright, 2016)

After such information is acquired at a state or national level, curriculum resources and teaching practices can be investigated to correct the problem. The *California Achievement Test (Terra Nova CAT/6)* (2009) is an achievement test that includes criterion-referenced information.

It would be easy to assume that teachers do not need standardized test results because other types of assessment are preferable for classroom use. Information in Chapter 2 stressed that assessments should benefit the child, and standardized tests should be used for instructional planning. Although the prevalent use of standardized tests is for accountability of effective instruction and standards-based evaluation of students, teachers, and schools, standardized test results contain valuable information that the teacher can use to understand student achievement and instructional planning.

Chapter 2 recommended that all assessment be integrated with instruction. However, recent studies have shown that teachers perceived standardized tests as separate from instruction. They did not understand that standardized tests could be helpful in planning for student needs. To the contrary, in spite of many concerns about standardized tests, they can be included as one of many tools for instructional planning when used appropriately and effectively by the classroom teacher.

Enhanced eText: Self-Check 5.1

How Standardized Tests Are Interpreted

A child's performance on a standardized test is meaningless until it can be compared with other scores in a useful way. The raw score must be translated into a score that reports how well the child's performance compares with that of other children who took the same test. In describing the standardization process, we have discussed how norms are set for comparing individual or group test scores on the basis of the scores made by a norming sample. Although several different scoring systems have been established for translating and interpreting raw scores, the bell-shaped normal curve is the graph on which the distribution of scores is arranged by using some type of standard score.

The Normal Curve

The normal curve (Figure 5-4) or bell curve represents the ideal **normal distribution** of test scores of groups of people, as well as the distribution of many other human characteristics. Physical and psychological traits are distributed in a bell-shaped frequency polygon, with most scores clustered toward the center of the curve. If, for example, we were to chart the heights of all adult men in the United States, most heights would be grouped around a mean height, with fewer distributed toward very short and very tall heights.

Ideally, group test scores have a similar distribution, and the normal curve can be used as a reference for understanding individual test scores. Any numerical scale can be used with the normal curve to demonstrate the range of scores on a test instrument.

The midpoint of the curve is the **mean**. Because the curve represents the total number of scores in the distribution of scores on a test, the mean divides the curve into two halves. As many scores are distributed above the mean as below it. The normal curve is used to describe or pinpoint an individual's performance on a standardized test. Derived scores are used to specify where the individual score falls on the curve and how far above or below the mean the score falls (Miller, Linn, & Gronlund, 2012).

If you look at the normal curve, the highest point is the mean and marked as 0. The curve is divided into 8 sections called Standard Deviations. Below the standard deviations are several different types of scores. Some of the scores begin at 0 and range before and after the mean (percentile equivalents and stanines). Others begin at the left-hand side of the curve and spread across the curve from left to right (Z scores and T scores).

The Relationship between the Normal Curve and Norm-Referenced versus Criterion-Referenced Tests

Norm-referenced tests are organized to rank test takers on a normal or bell curve. Test questions are written to show performance differences among test takers. Following the shape of a bell curve, a small percentage of test takers fall in the performing well or performing poorly locations on the curve, while most test takers perform at the average level of the curve. The test is intended to accentuate performance differences among the test takers.

Criterion-referenced tests are used to determine if the test takers have specific learning standards or specific skills and knowledge. Criterion-referenced test results are not arranged on a normal curve. Rather, they are compared to standards or specific skills (FairTest b, 2007; The Glossary of Education Reform, 2014).

Figure 5.4 Normal curve

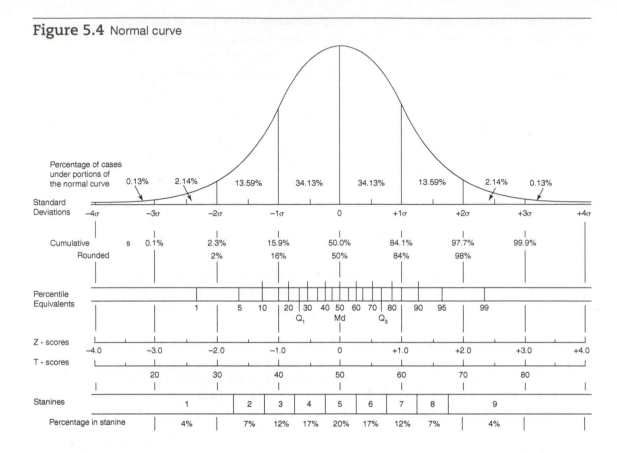

Standard Deviations

The normal curve is divided into eight equal sections called **standard deviations** (designated by a sigma, σ). Standard deviations are used to calculate how an individual scored compared with the scores of the norming group on a standardized test. Standard deviations describe how test scores are dispersed around the mean. For example, an individual score that is one standard deviation above the mean indicates that the individual scored higher than the mean of test scores on the norming sample. Furthermore, the individual scored higher than about 84% of the individuals who normed the test. If we look at the percentage of scores in each standard deviation, we find that about 68% of the scores are found between one standard deviation below the mean and one standard deviation above the mean. The percentage of scores in each successive standard deviation above and below the mean decreases sharply beyond one standard deviation. When raw scores are transformed into percentiles, or standard scores, standard deviations further explain individual scores compared to the normal distribution of scores (Saccuzo & Kaplan, 2013).

> **Enhanced eText: Video Example 5.2**

All scoring scales are drawn parallel to the baseline of the normal curve. Each uses the deviation from the mean as the reference to compare an individual score with the mean score of a group. In the next section, the transformation of raw scores into standard scores is explained in terms of percentile ranks, stanines, and Z scores and T scores, as illustrated in Figure 5-4.

Percentile Ranks and Stanines

After a test is standardized, percentile ranks and stanines may be used as the measures of comparison between the norming sample and individual test scores. Figure 5-4 shows how **percentile ranks** are arrived at by looking at cumulative percentages and percentile equivalents under the normal curve. We already understand that a percentage of the total distribution of scores is arranged within each standard deviation on the normal curve, with a smaller percentage located in each deviation as we move away from the mean. These percentages can also be understood in a cumulative fashion.

Beginning at the negative end of the curve, percentages in each standard deviation can be added together. At the mean, the cumulative percentage is 50%, while 99.9% is reached at three standard deviations above the mean.

Percentile equivalents are derived from the accumulated percentages. If the cumulative percentages represent the percentage of test scores falling into standard deviations along the normal curve, **percentiles** represent a point on the normal curve below which a percentage of test scores is distributed. A score at the 40th percentile equals or surpasses 40% of the scores on the test being used. A student's percentile rank on a test thus indicates the percentage of students who scored at the same percentile or lower in the comparison group. If a student's percentile rank is 60%, the student scored as well or better than 60% of the comparison group who took the test. Most important, the percentile rank is compared to scores of a particular group when the test was standardized and norms were established.

After a percentile rank norm is established for a standardized test, the developers determine how the distribution of scores acquired from the norming sample is arranged on the normal curve. Standard deviations and percentiles calculate the distribution. Future test users can then use these norms as measures of comparison to interpret individual or group scores in comparison with the scores of the original norming group.

Stanines provide another way to understand the distribution of scores. As shown in Figure 5-4, stanines divide the norm population represented by the normal scale into nine groups. Except for stanine 9, the top, and stanine 1, the bottom, each stanine represents half of a standard deviation. Stanines provide a helpful way to compare cumulative percentages and percentile ranks on the normal curve. One can look at the percentage of scores distributed in each stanine and understand how the percentile rank is correlated with the overall distribution. In reporting group test scores, the stanine rank of an individual score measures how the individual is ranked within a group of test takers (Miller, Linn, & Gronlund, 2012). Thus, the stanines clustered at the center of the normal curve represent the highest percentage of scores, while the stanines one or more standard deviations above or below the mean reflect much lower percentages of scores.

Parents usually find stanine results the easiest to understand when looking at their child's performance on a standardized test. They can understand where the child's score falls when described as follows:

9. Very superior
8. Superior

7. Considerably above average

6. Slightly above average

5. Average

4. Slightly below average

3. Considerably below average

2. Poor

1. Very poor (Psychological Corporation, 1980, p. 4)

Z Scores and T Scores

Some standardized test results are reported in terms of Z scores or T scores because they provide a simple way to locate an individual score along the normal curve. **Z scores** and **T scores** are called **standard scores** because they report how many standard deviations a person's transformed raw score is located above or below the mean on the normal curve. A Z score is used to describe an individual's location within a group of scores. A Z score of zero is located at the middle of the normal curve. From there, scores can move by standard deviations below zero or above zero. T scores tell how far an individual score is from the mean. The lowest number is 4 standard deviations below the mean and the highest score falls 4 standard deviations above the mean. Student T scores of 50 fall at the mean of the normal curve. A student with a T score of 30 would be 2 standard deviations below the mean (American Education Agency 267, 2013).

Z scores are considered the most basic of all standard scores and the building blocks for other standard scores. They are used to determine how far above or below the mean a score is located in standard deviation units. Percentile ranks are understood by looking at where cumulative percentages fall on the normal curve. Z scores make a similar comparison; however, with Z scores the standard deviations are used as the criteria for determining where an individual score falls. Z scores are parallel to standard deviations in that the mean is at the center of the normal distribution; if a score falls within one standard deviation above the mean, the Z score is +1. If the score falls two standard deviations below the mean, the Z score is −2.

T scores also report scores that are parallel to standard deviations on the normal curve. Like percentiles, T scores are cumulative along the curve. T scores range from 0 to 100, with a range of 10 points from one standard deviation to the next. T scores are almost the same as Z scores; Z scores have a mean of 0 and a standard deviation of 1.0, while T scores have a mean of 50 and a standard deviation of 10 (Hopkins, 1997; Kubiszyn & Borich, 2013). Various standardized tests use T scores. *McCarthy's Scales of Children's Abilities* (McCarthy, 1983) report T scores, as do IQ tests such as the *Stanford–Binet Intelligence Scales (SB5), Fifth Edition* (Roid, 2003).

Using Achievement Test Results to Improve Teaching and Learning

The school board in Lucky, Ohio analyzed the yearly report on school achievement in their community. Results indicated that students achieved at the national norm through the third grade, but thereafter scores tended to drop off steadily among some groups of students. Minority student scores dropped more signifi

cantly than the scores of Anglo students. Students from low-income homes did less well than those from middle-income homes.

Teachers in the elementary schools studied the criterion-referenced test results to discover whether incorrect student responses on certain objectives were weak and instruction needed to be improved. Consistent indicators of weakness were found in reading comprehension and in problem solving in mathematics. As a group, students in the school district were stronger in word-attack skills in reading and computation in mathematics than they were in higher-order skills that involved analysis and synthesis.

A committee of teachers at each grade level was assigned to search instructional resources to find supplementary materials that would strengthen teaching in those areas. The committees were particularly interested in finding materials that would involve the students in applying what they were learning in mathematics and allow students to engage in meaningful reading experiences.

The grade-level committees first searched through reading and math materials available in their own classrooms. They then surveyed materials available through the school district's central resource center. Finally, they traveled to a regional educational service center, where an educational consultant helped them find additional resources that addressed their students' needs in mathematics and reading. The consultant also worked with the committees in designing workshops to share materials and teaching strategies with the other teachers at each grade level.

The second year after the supplementary materials were included, a small improvement was noted in the test scores. Another gain occurred in the third year.

Now, each year, a committee of teachers studies test results to see where the students are encountering difficulty in order to determine whether the instructional program should be modified. The committee is especially attentive to students who are likely to have lower scores. The school board is pleased with the steady improvement in elementary achievement scores.

Enhanced eText: Self-Check 5.2

How Standardized Test Results Are Reported

After a standardized test has been administered and scored and individual and group scores have been interpreted, test users can use the information to report not only to professionals within the school district, but also to parents of the students. Reporting originates with individual test results, which are then combined and recombined with the scores of other individuals to form class, school, and district reports.

Reporting Standardized Test Results to Professionals

Test results should be reported to professionals in a way that contributes to the overall understanding of a child's learning and development. Standard scores are powerful and caution should be taken to ensure that professionals understand their meaning for each test. Methods for reporting standard scores to professionals are discussed below.

Individual Test Record

The individual test record in Figure 5-5 is from the *Stanford Achievement Test Series, Tenth Edition* (2010). The hypothetical student is in the fourth grade. The test was administered in April, the eighth month of the school year. In this form of the test report, both norm-referenced and criterion-referenced scores are reported. In Figure 5-5, the norm-referenced scores are listed in the section at the top of the page. The criterion-referenced scores are located at the bottom of the page.

Norm-Referenced Scores

The individual record includes the subtests or content areas of the test battery. In this particular test, reading, mathematics, language, spelling, science, social science, listening, and thinking skills are included. Reading, mathematics, and language also have subtests. Within each test and subtest, the scaled score, national percentile rank and stanine, and grade equivalent are reported. The scaled score is a continuous score measured over all grade levels. It indicates the student's progress on the continuum for each category.

To the right of the student's norm-referenced scores is the National Grade Percentile Bands report. In these bands the percentile score is reported as a possible range for the score that accounts for the standard error of measurement on the test. For example, this student's total reading score was in the 65th percentile; however, the percentile band ranged between about the 50th and 68th percentiles. Examination of all scores demonstrates that they generally fall within the range that is close to the mean or above the mean; however, language expression and listening range as low at the 30th percentile.

Criterion-referenced scores are all broken down into subcategories. For example, in the norm-referenced results for mathematics, the overall score was given for mathematical problem solving and mathematics procedures. In the criterion-referenced scores for mathematics problem solving and procedures, scores were given for the categories within each type of scores. In addition to individual national percentile scores, the student was ranked below average, average, or above average on each subtest. This student's scores were predominantly in the average and above average categories.

Class Reports

Figure 5-6 is a class report on the *Stanford Achievement Test, 8th Edition*, also for fourth grade. The norm-referenced scores appear on the top section of the page. The information includes how many were tested (15), the number correct on each test and subtest, and the mean scaled score, national individual percentile range, and median grade equivalent. This class report combines the percentile rank and stanine into one section and also includes the normal curve equivalent scores. The NCE

Figure 5.5 Individual student report

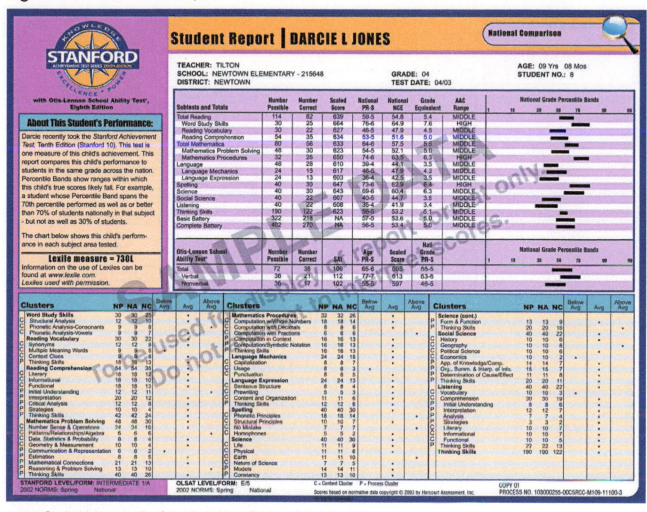

mean score on this test reflects the class average score on the normal curve for each test and subtest.

The National Grade Percentile Ranks appear on the top right of the page. As a class, the percentile ranks were average. There were no strong differences between categories in the National Grade Percentile Ranks.

Criterion-referenced scores are shown at the bottom of the page. Each subtest is represented by the categories or types of questions and the number of test items for each category. The teacher can determine strengths and weaknesses in the class by examining what percentage of the class was below average, average, or above average. The results can be compared with individual reports to determine students who would benefit from additional instruction and those who are ready to move to more advanced learning experiences. Note that the individual student report shown in Figure 5-5 can be compared with the overall grade reports in Figure 5-6 to determine the individual student's learning accomplishments and needs.

Figure 5.6 Group test report

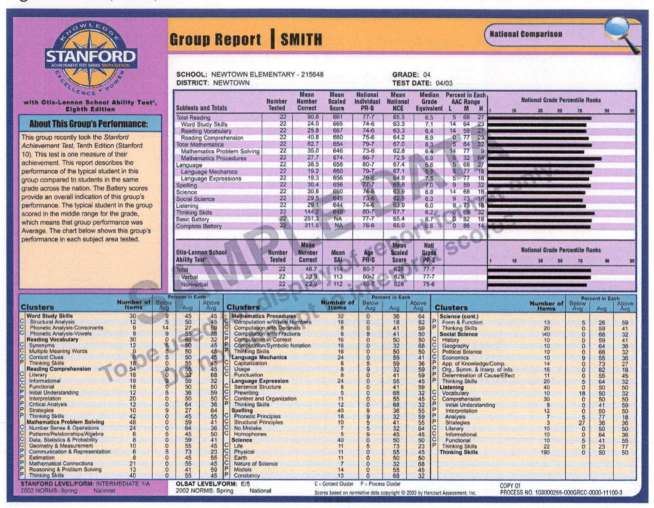

School and District Reports

Summaries of class reports can be grouped to form school and district reports. Both norm- and criterion-referenced information can be organized in a useful form for building principals, school district evaluators, superintendents, and governing boards.

Search and Share 5.2

Reporting Standardized Test Scores

Search online to learn more about reporting standardized test scores in meaningful ways. What are the similarities or differences in summarizing standardized test scores for very young children (e.g., infants or toddlers) versus school-age children? What safeguards do you recommend to ensure appropriate reporting for individual children? Groups of children?

Achievement reports can be studied by grade level, across a school, or among all the schools in the district serving a grade level. Instructional strengths and weaknesses can be analyzed by content areas, as well as by school and grade level. Achievement can be compared over several years to determine long-term improvement or decline in achievement. Each type of analysis must take into account the error of measurement on the test so that realistic conclusions are drawn from the study of test results.

Reporting Standardized Test Scores to Parents

Parents have the right to know about their child's performance in school, and schools have the responsibility to keep parents informed. One method used to report student learning is the standardized achievement test. The school should report the test results in a manner that is helpful to the parents.

Statistical data that are part of standardized test reports can be confusing to parents. Because of the seeming complexity of test reports, it is important to give parents an opportunity to meet with the teacher for an explanation of their child's test results. Test results can be discussed in a parent–teacher conference.

The classroom teacher can have the major responsibility for explaining standardized test results to parents. The teacher not only knows the children from working with them every day, but is also aware of the kinds of information that individual parents will understand and want to acquire. It is helpful for the teachers to explain both the value and the limitations of the test scores. Parents may also benefit from knowing why the test was chosen and how the results will be used. Specialists who work with children may also explain standardized test results along with the teacher.

It may be helpful for parents to understand how the criterion-referenced test results may be used to plan appropriate learning experiences for their child. For example, the teacher may use test results to suggest activities that the parent can use at home to help the child.

The teacher may also advise against the comparison of test scores among children, particularly siblings. Parents can be reassured that individual differences in test scores result from many variables. Comparing test scores of different children is neither accurate nor useful.

After children enter the primary grades, parents are eager to know how well their child is progressing and whether the child is achieving as well as he or she should be at that grade level. Analysis of the results of a standardized test can provide the information that parents need.

After a test has been given at a grade level, the results are compared with test results from grades above and below that grade level. In Figure 5-6, the child's test score for phonetic analysis is 2.5—second grade, fifth month. However, the grade equivalent is 4.4, or fourth grade, fourth month. These test results show that in this category, the child made the same number of correct responses as children in the norming group in fourth grade.

The **grade-equivalent score** indicates whether the child performed above or below average, but it does not indicate grade-level placement in school. If the child's comprehension grade equivalent is compared with the local or national percentile ranks, both show that the child performed well above average in the number of correct responses.

Some test publishers recommend that grade equivalents not be used to report to parents because they can be misunderstood. Parents can understand that the grade-equivalent score is reported in years and months in school, but they may not understand that the score does not mean the child should be placed in a higher or lower grade. The child reflected in the *Stanford Diagnostic Reading Test* was tested in November, the third month of school. All the grade-equivalent scores are higher than 2.3 but do not indicate that the child should be placed at a higher grade level.

The criterion-referenced scores at the bottom of the page are reported in a different format. Each skill is reported in the ovals as the number of correct responses compared to the total number. A shaded oval indicates that the score is at or above a progress indicator cutoff score indicating mastery. A note below the scores indicates that none of the ovals is shaded because the student's scores were higher than the level of the test. In other words, the student mastered all the skills at a high level for second grade.

Sharing Assessment Results with Parents of Children with Disabilities and/or English Language Learners (ELLs)

Special care needs to be taken when sharing assessment results with parents of children with disabilities and English Language Learners. Sharing assessment results with parents should be a collaborative process that builds on family strengths and resources and recognizes and values parents' perspectives on the meaning of the results. Parents and professionals should agree upon how test results will be used for instructional planning or early intervention services. Information about parental participation can be found on the Wrightslaw website, as well as the U.S. Department of Education website.

Similarly, input from parents of ELLs needs to be a part of the assessment process. When sharing results, all written information and verbal descriptions should be presented in the home language of the parents as well as in English. Trained interpreters should be used, if needed. Professionals should ask parents if they understand the assessment results throughout the discussion rather than just at the end of the meeting. Additional information about early intervention or special education services in the schools should be provided, also. A follow-up phone call or meeting for parents to provide additional information about their child or ask for clarification will be important. In this way, parents who are less familiar with English and special services in the United States can have time to review the assessment results and organize their thoughts and questions.

> **Enhanced eText:** Self-Check 5.3

Advantages and Disadvantages of Using Standardized Tests with Young Children

Norm-referenced and criterion-referenced achievement tests can provide valuable information regarding the effectiveness of curriculum and instruction. At the beginning of the school year, such tests can show what children know in relation to an instructional program. Likewise, achievement tests administered at the end of the school year can demonstrate how well children learned the content of a program. Teachers can use the test results to determine how to reteach or change program content or instructional methods. In other words, teachers can use test results to evaluate their program and to make changes to more effectively meet the instructional needs of their students. In the sections that follow, we continue the discussion of the advantages of using standardized tests. Then we discuss the disadvantages of using standardized tests, including concerns regarding their inappropriate use with young children.

Advantages of Standardized Tests

Standardized tests can be described as measuring instruments. Each test is constructed, administered, and scored to measure some human characteristic. An individual's responses to the test items provide samples of his or her behavior, which can be scored and evaluated according to an established standard. In contrast to informal strategies, standardized tests have unique qualities that are advantageous for measuring human behavior. Among these characteristics are uniformity in test administration, quantifiable scores, norm referencing, and validity and reliability.

UNIFORMITY IN TEST ADMINISTRATION   Standardized tests have precise administration procedures. Because the results should be dependable, test designers must be sure that all examiners who give the test to children will follow the instructions exactly. Whether the test is being given in Wisconsin or in Florida, the procedures are the same. Informal methods are less specific; the examiner uses personal strategies for assessment.

QUANTIFIABLE SCORES   Standardized tests are quantifiable because they have numerical scores. The correct answers are totaled to determine the raw score. The raw score is then translated into a derived score, so that the child's performance on the test can be compared with the performance of other test takers. The derived score can be interpreted to evaluate the child's performance when compared to the established standard.

NORM REFERENCING   *Norm referencing* refers to the process of developing a standard for interpreting test scores on a standardized test. To compare a child's performance on a test with the performance of other children, a norm group is selected during the development of the test. The test is administered to that group to determine what normal performance is. The norm group's test responses result in a range of scores with which a child's performance can be compared.

VALIDITY AND RELIABILITY   Unlike informal evaluation and measurement strategies, standardized tests have established dependability through determination of validity and reliability. Reliability is the test's ability to measure the child's characteristics accurately under different conditions. If the child were given the test more than once, would the results be similar?

Validity establishes whether a test measures the characteristics it was designed to measure. If the test is designed to measure intelligence, does it actually yield results that show the child's level of intelligence?

Tests that have proven reliability and validity are dependable. They can be administered to many children, either individually or as a group, and children's scores can be interpreted with confidence that the results accurately reflect each child's behaviors or characteristics.

Improving Shirley's Comprehension Skills

Shirley is in the second grade. Although she is able to use phonics to decode words and has a good vocabulary, she has difficulty demonstrating her understanding of the reading materials she has read. The reading specialist at her school discussed Shirley's lack of progress in reading and administered a diagnostic reading test.

The results of the test showed that Shirley has the most difficulty in answering questions about reading content. The reading specialist and the classroom teacher discussed comprehension strategies that might be used to help Shirley focus on the meaning of what she is reading. Shirley's mother was given activities and tips on how to discuss books that are read to and with Shirley at home.

Validity, reliability, norm referencing, and other test characteristics that contribute to the effectiveness of the standardized test result from careful and thorough test design. Each step in test construction has the goal of producing a dependable test to measure a human characteristic accurately.

In recent years there has been controversy over the use of standardized tests. Advocates believe the tests that measure students' achievement compared to learning standards will ensure that all students have the same standard of instruction. Advocates also say that standardized tests are part of the goal to raise student learning by attaching test scores to teacher evaluations, student promotion, and graduation. Advocates believe that standardized tests measure student achievement with precision.

Disadvantages of Standardized Tests

Concerns about the use of standardized tests were first introduced in the 1970s. Educators were particularly concerned about the poor performance of children from low socioeconomic and minority populations (Wesson, 2001). Another early concern was the control that testing imposed on instruction, labeled by some as *measurement-driven instruction*. In the late 1990s, many of the concerns published in the 1970s persisted, in spite of improvements in test design. New exams were matched to the curriculum, particularly in state achievement tests. In addition, essay questions and short-answer questions were added to the traditional multiple-choice questions (McGinn, 1999). More recently, the *California Achievement Test (Terra Nova CAT/6)* (2009) has added writing tasks and performance assessments, in keeping with advances in assessment. However, on some tests, the results could be based on the answers to a few questions, and time limitations for achievement tests precluded adequate assessment of student achievement (Popham, 1999). Although standardized tests can give accurate information about students' relative strengths and weaknesses across content areas, most tests contain too few items to provide meaningful within-subject comparisons of strengths and weaknesses.

The passage of the No Child Left Behind Act included new requirements for testing. Opposition to standardized tests continued to grow. The program ended in 2016 with the election that returned the control of the presidency and both houses of Congress to the Republican Party. The focus of the Department of Education during the Obama administration rapidly changed in 2017. No Child Left Behind (NCLB) ended, but some of the changes in testing were positive. The accountability required under NCLB resulted in the alignment of instruction with the state curriculum (Haladyna, 2006).

Concerns about standardized testing are continuing today, with new information testing trends. One significant trend is that colleges and universities are using SAT and ACT admission tests less frequently while standardized tests are increasing in public education. Another factor is that accountability that once held schools responsible for student achievement now holds teachers responsible for student achievement (Haladyna, 2006; Roach, 2014).

Critics of standardized tests say that tests can still be culturally biased and contain content unfamiliar to minorities. The format of the test can be unfair to children with disabilities. Critics also believe the practice of punishing schools with low test scores can result in reduction of resources for students who need them the most. There is also concern over narrowing of the curriculum or teaching to the test to raise scores. Critics continue to be concerned about the need for a variety of types of assessment rather than depending on one standardized test to measure student learning (PBS/Frontline, 2002).

High-Stakes Testing

The concerns about high-stakes testing are related to the use of standardized tests to admit children into schools; place them in programs such as special education, ELL, and bilingual programs; promote or retain students; or determine whether they can graduate from high school (Heubert, 2002). Dependence on standardized tests limits teachers, parents, and administrators from including other resources when making program and evaluation decisions with the intent of benefiting the child.

When major decisions are based on the outcomes of a single test, it is known as a high-stakes test. When children are denied promotion to the next grade, entry into school, or exit from high school based on a standardized test, they have had decisions made about their future based on high-stakes testing (American Psychological Association, 2001; FairTest b, 2007; Heubert, 2002).

Measurement Limitations

Standardized tests are limited in what they measure. They are limited in how long they can be and how many learning objectives can be properly evaluated. The organization FairTest b (2007) proposes that standardized tests cannot be a fair and helpful evaluation tool as follows:

> Standardized tests are tests on which all students answer the same questions, usually in multiple-choice format, and each question has only one correct answer. They reward the ability to quickly answer superficial questions that do not require real thought. They do not measure the ability to think or create in any field. Their use encourages a narrowed curriculum, outdated methods of instruction, and harmful practices such as retention in grade and tracking. They also assume all test takers have been exposed to a white, middle-class background. (p. 1)

There are several factors that can affect results of standardized tests. The students themselves can affect test results. When students fail to answer some of the test questions, are not motivated to do well on the test, or have fatigue, test scores are affected. Poor test alignment with curriculum content is a major factor, especially in some tests developed at the state level. Teachers are tempted to coach students or "teach to the test."

Cheating of various types affects test result quality. Poor test security encourages teachers and students to cheat. Teachers or test monitors can cheat by altering test responses. Test monitors might read test questions to the students (Downing & Haladyna, 2006). Other factors can include poorly designed tests, the quality of test items, and differences in test scoring from one state to another on state-designed tests.

Assessment of Students with Disabilities and/or English Language Learners (ELLs)

NCLB required that all students be assessed regardless of their special needs. For decades, these students had not been required to be included in standardized testing because of their limitations. A negative impact of this practice was that these students were also neglected in their opportunities for an education. The Every Student Succeeds Act (ESSA) passed in 2015 made significant positive changes for children with disabilities. ESSA returned control over education policy to state and local authorities. It included less emphasis on testing, and more attention to individual needs. Also, students with disabilities must have access to accommodations such as assistive technology (Alvarez, 2016; ASCD, 2015).

Accommodations also had to be implemented for students who spoke another language or had limited English. Under ESSA, accountability was shifted from annual assessments to Title 1. Schools were permitted to phase in test results for accountability purposes (ASCD, 2015). One group that provided support to states for the implementation of Title III is the World-Class Instructional Design and Assessment (WIDA). WIDA provides English proficiency standards, assessments, and professional development to support English learners in prekindergarten through grade 12. Recently, WIDA added Early English Language Development (E-ELD) and Early Spanish Language Development (E-SLD) Standards that can be used by early childhood educators. According to WIDA, the E-ELD standards are designed for children ages 2.5–5.5 years. Its purpose is to provide a "developmentally sound framework" that supports instruction and assessment of dual language learners (DLLs) (WIDA, 2018). To date, 39 states and territories use the WIDA system. Learning a second language takes time, which is why ongoing assessment of English learners' proficiency is important to providing appropriate instruction. Knowing the English proficiency of a child can help determine the type of accommodations needed during the assessment process and result in a more accurate picture of a child's developmental and/or academic performance.

One benefit of the new policies regarding children with special needs is the increased emphasis on precursors to reading and mathematics at the preschool level. Assessment teams are learning about difficulties that might be encountered in primary grades and interventions that can be used at the preschool level. Building on legal changes, organizations have introduced standards for assessment and intervention at the preschool level (Hooper & Umansky, 2010).

The National Center for Educational Statistics (NCES) has also worked to upgrade policies for NAEP to ensure the needs of students with disabilities and English Language Learners are met. In 2010, the governing board adopted a new policy after working with experts in testing and curriculum. The policy encourages the inclusion of as many students with special needs and students learning to speak English as possible. The policy includes development of uniform national rules, reduction of variation in exclusion rates across states, and maximization of participation of identified students in NAEP (National Center for Educational Statistics, 2010).

Concerns about High-Stakes Testing

The potential problem with the current increased emphasis on testing is not necessarily the test, per se, but the instances when tests have unintended and potentially negative consequences for individual students, groups of students, or the educational system more broadly. But it is also critical to remember that, in many instances, without tests, low-performing students and schools could remain invisible and, therefore, not get the extra resources or remedial help that they need.

SOURCE: American Psychological Association. (2001). *Appropriate use of high-stakes testing in our nation's schools.* Retrieved from http://www.apa.org/pubs/info/brochures/testing.aspx

A Misinterpretation of Julio's Achievement Test Scores

Julio's family recently moved to Florida from Puerto Rico. Julio has been attending a school in Florida for about 2 years. He has now entered fourth grade and is required to take standardized achievement tests as a part of the requirements of NCLB. Julio's scores in reading and math were both very low, although he scored higher in mathematics than in reading. Julio's teacher is considering referring Julio for the special education program. The school counselor, however, realizes that Julio's low scores are due to his limitations in using English rather than a delay or disability. She shows the teacher how Julio's computation skills in mathematics are higher than problem-solving questions. The decision is made to provide additional ESL training and tutoring to address Julio's language limitations.

Enhanced eText: Video Example 5.3

Misapplication of Test Results with Young Children

Early childhood specialists began discussing in the 1980s their concerns about using intelligence tests, developmental screening measures, and school readiness tests to make decisions about school entry and moving from kindergarten to first grade. They pointed out that developmental tests and IQ tests do not differentiate between limited intelligence and limited opportunities to learn. Like readiness tests, IQ tests and developmental tests should not be used to determine school entry (Shepard & Graue, 1993). The use of developmental screening tests was recommended to predict quickly whether a child could profit from special education placement, if such tests have had predictive validity, developmental content, and normative standardization (Meisels, 1987; Meisels, Steele, & Quinn-Leering, 1993). Nevertheless, Meisels stated that developmental screening tests should be used to identify children who need further evaluation. Decisions on such issues as enrollment, retention, and placement in special classes should never be based on a single test score. Other sources of information, including systematic observation and samples of children's work, should be part of the evaluation process (Bredekamp & Copple, 1997; National Association for the Education of Young Children, 1988).

Another concern about misapplication of standardized test results surfaced in 2003. President Bush announced that in the fall of 2003, all Head Start students would be given a national standardized skills assessment test (McMaken, 2003). An immediate issue was whether preschool children should be given a standardized test and whether the test, the National Reporting System, had the desired reliability and validity (Raver & Zigler, 2004). Other issues related to the limitations of the test to measure only cognitive skills and omit measurement of children's competence, emotional development, and cultural diversity (Schumacher, Greenberg, & Mezey, 2003). It was proposed that a narrow test of skills in literacy and math should not be used to measure the overall quality of the Head Start program (Meisels & Atkins-Burnett, 2004).

In succeeding years, improvements were made in the use of standardized tests with young children. FairTest (n.d.) reported that most states had moved away from using tests with kindergarten children and they had been eliminated from use with children earlier than third grade. In addition, more schools were moving to classroom-based assessment that includes performance assessment.

A new direction has been taken to overcome the limitations of standardized tests for identifying and diagnosing children with disabilities. **Play-based assessment**, which uses observation of children's play as the major assessment strategy, is becoming more common as educators of children with disabilities seek more natural approaches to assessment (Linder, 2008).

Play-based assessment is a structured observation of an individual child's play. An adult follows the child engaged in play and talks to and plays with the child, using the toys and activities the child chooses. In four phases of the observation, the child engages in more structured play, child–child play, parent–child interaction, and motor play (Brookes Publishing, 2002; Linder, 2008).

Play-based assessment is used in addition to the administration of standardized tests and other developmental assessments. Play-based assessment will be discussed further in Chapter 6.

Enhanced eText: Self-Check 5.4

Summary

Standardized tests have a role in measuring the development of young children. Many early childhood educators are not opposed to the use of standardized tests per se, but rather to specific tests. While teacher intuition for evaluation can be biased, systematic measurement and evaluation can have advantages. Although there are shortcomings in standardized tests used with young children, more is needed than informal measures and teacher observations, especially for young children with disabilities. The need for appropriate instruments to identify at-risk children and to plan programs for remediation will continue pressures for valid and reliable instruments.

On the one hand, information from norm- and criterion-referenced tests can be very useful in evaluating achievement and in considering instructional improvement. On the other hand, misuse of test results or lack of consideration of test errors and limitations can have a negative impact on instructional decisions affecting preschool and school-age children.

Despite ongoing concerns about their weaknesses, the use of standardized tests is increasing, and new instruments are being developed in response to pressures for accountability for the quality of education and minimum-competency standards for students and teachers. Teachers of young children need to understand how tests are designed and interpreted. The function of the normal curve to chart progress in learning uses various types of measurement tools to record individual learning and comparisons of groups of children. Test results are reported using scores that include stanines, percentile equivalents, Z scores, and T scores.

Increasingly, early childhood educators and specialists are urging the use of a variety of methods to evaluate or test children, particularly preschool children. Standardized tests have a role, but they are only one method that should be used to evaluate young children. Informal methods, such as teacher observation and teacher-designed tasks, can also be used to obtain a more accurate picture of what preschool and primary-grade children have learned and achieved.

Enhanced eText: Self-Check: Chapter Review

Key Terms

criterion-referenced test 107	mean 117	standard deviation 118
developmental assessments 112	minimum-competency testing 114	standard score 120
developmental screening 112	normal distribution 117	stanine 119
diagnostic evaluation 110	norm-referenced test 107	T score 120
grade equivalent score 125	percentile 119	Z score 120
individualized instruction 114	percentile rank 119	
mastery testing 114	play-based assessment 132	

Selected Organizations

Search for the following organizations online:

Pearson Education Assessments
American Psychological Association
FairTest

U.S. Department of Education
World-Class Instructional Design and Assessment (WIDA)
Wrightslaw

References

Alvarez, B. (2016). Promising Changes for Special Education under ESSA. Retrieved from http://neatoday.org/2016/06/30/special-educatioin-essa/

American Education Agency 267 (AEA/267). (2013). Z scores and T scores. Retrieved from http://www.aea267.k12.ia.us/assessment/different-types-of-data-and-scores

American Psychological Association. (2001, May). *Appropriate use of high-stakes testing in our nation's schools.* Retrieved from http://www.apa.org/pubs/info/brochures/testing.aspx

ASCD (2015). *Elementary and secondary education act: Comparison of the No Child Left Behind Act to the Every Student Succeeds Act.* Alexandria, VA: Author.

Bayley, N. (2005). *Bayley Scales of Infant Development, Third Edition (Bayley, III).* San Antonio, TX: Pearson Assessment.

Boehm, A. E. (2000). *Boehm test of basic concepts* (3rd ed.). San Antonio, TX: Psychological Corp.

Brassard, M. R., & Boehm, A. (2008). *Preschool assessment: Principles and practices.* New York, NY: Guilford Press.

Bredekamp, S., & Copple, C. (1997). *Developmentally appropriate practices in early childhood programs* (Rev. ed.). Washington, DC: National Association for the Education of Young Children.

Brookes Publishing. (2002). *Using transdisciplinary play-based assessment: Structuring a play session.* Retrieved from http://www.brookespublishing.com/email/archive . . . july02EC4.hrm/

Brown, E. (2015). U.S. performance slips on national test. Retrieved from https://www.washingtonpost.com/local/education/us-sutent-performance . . .

California Achievement Test (Terra Nova CAT/6) (6th ed.). (2009). Monterey, CA: CTB/McGraw-Hill.

Cohen, L. G. & Spenciner, J. (2010). Excerpt from assessment of children and youth with special needs. Boston.

Dill, M. (2012). *Using Criterion-Referenced Tests' Results.* Retrieved from http://www.brighthubeducation.com/special-ed-inclusion-strategies/ . . .

Downing, S. M., & Haladyna, T. M (eds.). (2006). *Handbook of Test Development.* Mahwah, N.J: Lawrence Erlbaum Associates.

Dunn, L. M., & Dunn, L. (2007). *Peabody Picture Vocabulary Test* (4th ed.) *(PPVT-4).* San Antonio, TX: Pearson Assessments.

FairTest (no date). *Trends show improvement in testing young children.* Retrieved from http://www.fairtest.org/trends-show-improvement-testing-young-children

FairTest a. (2007, August). *Criterion- and standards-referenced tests.* Retrieved from http://www.Fairtest.org/criterion-and-standards-referenced-tests

FairTest b. (2007, December). *What's wrong with standardized tests?* Retrieved from http://www.Fairtest.org/whats-wrong-standardized-test

Frankenburg, W. K., Dodds, J., Archer, P., Shapiro, H., & Bresnick, B. (1992). *Denver II.* Denver, CO: Denver Developmental Materials.

Good, R. H., & Kaminski, R. A. (Eds.). (2012). *Dynamic indicators of basic early literacy skills (DIBELS), administration and scoring guide* (6th ed.). Eugene, OR: Institute for the Development of Educational Achievement.

Haladyna, T. M. (2006). *Perils of Standardized Achievement Testing.* Retrieved from http://w.w.w.files.eric.gov/fulltext/EJ750641.pdf

Hambleton, R. (2009, December 23). Criterion-Referenced Tests. Retrieved from http://www.education.com/reference/article/criterion-referenced-tests1/

Hardin, B. J., & Peisner-Feinberg, E. S. (2001). *The Early Learning Accomplishment Profile (Early LAP) examiner's manual and technical report.* Lewisville, NC: Kaplan Press.

Heubert, J. P. (2002). *High-stakes testing: Opportunities and risks for students of color, English-Language Learners, and students with disabilities.* Wakefield, MA: National Center on Accessing the General Curriculum. Retrieved October 20, 2009, from http://www.cast.org/publications/ncac/ncac_highstakes.html

Hooper, S. R., & Umansky, W. (2010). *Current standards for the assessment process of children with special needs.* Retrieved from https://www.education.com/reference/article/standards-assessment-children-with-special-needs/

Hopkins, K. D. (1997). *Educational and psychological measurement and evaluation* (8th ed.). Upper Saddle River, NJ: Prentice Hall

Individuals with Disabilities Education Act (IDEA). Retrieved from https://www2.ed.gov/policy/sprced/giuid/idea2004.html

Kaufman, A., & Kaufman, N. (2005). *Kaufman assessment battery for children (K-ABC-II).* San Antonio, TX: Pearson Assessments.

Kubiszyn, T., & Borich, G. (2013). *Educational testing and measurement: Classroom application and practice* (10th ed.). Hoboken, NJ: John Wiley & Sons.

Linder, T. (2008). *Transdisciplinary play-based assessment* (2nd ed.). Retrieved from http://www.brookespublishing.com/stor/books/linder-tbai2/

Linn, R. L., & Miller, M. D. (2005). *Measurement and assessment in teaching* (9th ed.). Upper Saddle River, NJ: Merrill/Prentice Hall.

McCarthy, D. (1983). *McCarthy xcales of children's abilities.* San Antonio, TX: Pearson Assessments.

McGinn, D. (1999, September 6). The big score. *Newsweek,* pp. 46–49.

McMaken, J. (2003, March). *Early childhood assessment.* Denver, CO: Education Commission of the United States. Retrieved from http://www.ecs.org/html_IssueSection.asp?issued=77 . . . 0 . . .

Meisels, S. J. (1987). Uses and abuses of developmental screening and school readiness testing. *Young Children, 42,* 68–73.

Meisels, S. J., & Atkins-Burnett, S. (2004, January). The Head Start National Reporting System: A critique. *Young Children, 59,* 64–66.

Meisels, S. J., Marsden, D. B., Wiske, M. S., & Henderson, L. W. (2008). *Early Screening Inventory—Revised.* Ann Arbor, MI: Pearson Early Learning.

Meisels, S. J., Steele, D. M., & Quinn-Leering, K. (1993). Testing, tracking, and retaining young children: An analysis of research and social policy. In B. Spodek (Ed.), *Handbook of research on the education of young children* (pp. 279–292). New York, NY: Macmillan.

Miller, M. D., Linn, R., & Gronlund, N. E. (2012). *Measurement and assessment in teaching—11th Edition.* Upper Saddle River, NJ: Pearson.

National Assessment of Educational Progress (2015). Mathematics and Reading Assessments. The nation's report card. Retrieved from https://nation'sreportcard.gov/reading-math-2015/#=4

National Association for the Education of Young Children. (1988). Position statement on standardized testing of young children age 3 through age 8. *Young Children, 43,* 42–47.

National Center for Educational Statistics (2010). *Current Policy.* Retrieved from https://nces.ed.gov/nationsreportcard/about/inclusion.asp

National Center on Educational Statistics. (2012). The nation's report card: Trends in academic progress 2012. Retrieved from http://nces.ed.gov/pubsearch/pubsinfo.asp?pubid=2013456

Payne, M., & Miller, M. (2009, Spring). A collaborative approach to assessment: *The Assessment and Improvement Management System (AIMS). Issues in Education, 18,* 149–160.

Petrilli, M. J., & Wright, B. L. 2016). America's mediocre test scores. Education crisis poverty crisis. Retrieved from http://educationnext.org/americas-mediocre-test-scores

Popham, W. J. (1999). Why standardized tests don't measure educational quality. *Educational Leadership, 56,* 8–16.

Popham, W. J. (2014). Classroom assessment: What teachers need to know, 7th Ed. Boston: Pearson.

Psychological Corporation. (1980). *On telling parents about test results.* Test Service Notebook 154. New York, NY: Author.

Public Broadcasting System (PBS) Frontline. (2002). Testing our schools: A guide for parents. Retrieved from http://www.pbs.org/wgbh/pages/frontline/shows/schools/etc/guide.html

Raver, C. C., & Zigler, E. F. (2004, January). Another step back? Assessing readiness in Head Start. *Young Children, 59,* 58–63.

Renaissance (2017). Criterion-referenced test. Retrieved from https://www.renaissance.com/edwords/criterion-referenced-test/

Roach, R. (2014). *Concerns about use of standardized tests a constant over the years.* Retrieved from http://diverseducation.com/article/61309/

Roid, G. H. (2003). Stanford-Binet Intelligence Scales, Fifth Edition (SB:V). Itasca, IL: Riverside Publishing.

Saccuzo, D. P., & Kaplan, R. M. (2013). *Psychological testing: Principles and applications, 8th Edition.* Belmont, CA: Wadsworth.

Schumacher, R., Greenberg, M., & Mezey, J. (2003). *Head Start reauthorization: A preliminary analysis of HR 2210, the "School Readiness Act of 2003."* Washington, DC: Center for Law and Social Poli.

Shepard, L. A., & Graue, M. E. (1993). The morass of school readiness screening: Research on test use and test validity. In B. Spodek (Ed.), *Handbook of research on the education of young children* (pp. 293–305). New York, NY: Macmillan.

Stanford Achievement Test Series (10th ed.). (2010). San Antonio, TX: Pearson Assessments.

The Glossary of Education Reform. (2014, August 26). Norm-referenced test. Retrieved from http://edglossary.or/norm-referenced-test/

Wechsler, D. (2012). *Wechsler Preschool and Primary Scale of Intelligence (WPPSI-IV)* (4th ed.). San Antonio, TX: Pearson Assessments.

Wesson, K. A. (2001) The "Volvo effect"—Questioning standardized tests. *Young Children*, *56*(2), 16–18.

World-Class Instructional Design and Assessment (WIDA). (2018). Early language development standards. Retrieved from https://www.wida.us/standards/EarlyYears.aspx

Zucker, S. (2003, December). *Fundamentals of standardized testing*. San Antonio, TX: Pearson, Inc. Retrieved October 19, 2009, from http://www.hemweb.com/libraryresearchreports/index.htm

Chapter 6
Data-Driven Decision Making, Assessment, and Documentation

Benjamin LaFramboise/Pearson Education, Inc.

Chapter Learning Outcomes

As a result of reading this chapter, you will be able to:

6.1 Describe the purposes of assessment in data-driven decision making.

6.2 Discuss the role of documentation for planning effective instruction.

6.3 Explain different types of documentation.

Standardized test reports are one type of data that informs decisions about children's learning and development. However, teachers should use a variety of types of documentation to assess children's progress. Documentation provides a record of what has been accomplished as well as contributes to instructional planning.

In this chapter, we will describe the role of assessment in data-driven decision making that promotes children's learning and development. We will also describe various methods of documentation.

Purposes of Assessment in Data-Driven Decision Making

Without assessment data, decisions about children's learning and development would be guesswork. Both formal assessments, such as standardized tests, and informal assessments, such as teacher-designed tests, provide specific data that contribute valuable information about individual children that guides educational decisions. In this section, the concept of data-driven decision making is discussed, as well as the purposes of assessment data for decision making.

Defining Data-Driven Decision Making

All forms of assessment provide data to help teachers and parents make informed and appropriate decisions about children's development and education. The process of systematically collecting and using data to identify the strengths and needs of children and then applying this information to plan appropriate learning experiences is called **data-driven decision making** (Ikemoto & Marsh, 2007; Mertler, 2018).

The process of data-driven decision making includes multiple steps (Mandinach, 2012). First, data is collected systematically. This process may be informal documentation such as photographing a child's work samples over time for his or her portfolio, or more formal by administering a standardized instrument. Second, data is analyzed in the context of the goal for its collection. For example, the results of a developmental assessment are summarized for an individual child to see if his or her development appears on target. Third, interpretation of the results is completed; and fourth, decisions about the next step in the child's education are made. For example, a child's development may appear to be on target so a typical curriculum is needed. Or, perhaps the assessment data indicate delays and thus a referral for in-depth diagnostic testing is needed. Once these decisions are applied, the cycle begins again.

Standardized tests are one type of data that contributes to data-driven decision making. As discussed previously, standardized tests are used for two purposes: (1) to evaluate achievement or developmental skills in comparison with a norming sample of children (normed-referenced tests); and (2) to measure individual children's achievement or development compared to mastery of specific test criteria to determine the child's strengths and needs. Standardized assessments generate standard scores in the case of normed referenced tests, providing a general picture of a child's development. Criterion-referenced tests provide information about a child's mastery of specific skills typical for particular ages or other group characteristics. Thus, all standardized test results provide data that describes a rough idea of the child's learning strengths and needs. Results of standardized tests are typically compiled and summarized in a formal report that is shared with parents, teachers, or other professionals.

In contrast, **teacher-designed assessments**, measures created by teachers to assess one or more subjects or developmental areas, allow teachers to obtain more specific information about each student's knowledge and skills relative to the instructional objectives of the class. These informal assessments can be used to supplement standardized tests during diagnostic evaluations for placement decisions, for instructional planning, and for formative and summative evaluation (Educational Testing Service, 2002; Snow & Van Hemel, 2008). Teacher-designed assessments are another important part of the data-driven decision-making system because these locally created tools reflect the content being taught in the classroom setting and often state or federal standards requirements (Goldstein & Flake, 2016). For example, early learning standards may suggest that a preschool teacher use items from the local environment (e.g., pine cones, rocks, leaves, etc.) to teach children how to classify similar objects. After doing multiple activities with the objects, the teacher may design an assessment (e.g., a checklist) using the same concrete objects or pictures of similar objects to test the children's comprehension of classifying objects.

> **Enhanced eText:** Video Example 6.1

Purposes of Data-Driven Decision Making

The more specific purposes of the data generated by these types of assessments varies. Some results are used solely for instructional planning while other data contribute to the diagnosis and placement of children with special needs, such as those with disabilities or English Language Learners (ELLs) as described below. Still others may be used for formative and summative evaluations.

PLACEMENT EVALUATION At the beginning of the school year and periodically during the year, preschool and primary-grade teachers must decide how to group children to best meet their instructional needs. This process, called **placement evaluation**, occurs when one or more assessments are completed to determine how to group children for instructional needs. These groupings change as instructional needs change throughout the school year. With preschool children, the teacher needs to know the skills and knowledge of each child. Because the backgrounds of the children can vary widely, the teacher typically evaluates all students to determine how to plan for them in the instructional program.

DIAGNOSTIC EVALUATION **Diagnostic evaluation** is more specific than placement evaluation. When assessing for diagnostic purposes, the teacher investigates the child's ability to accomplish specific objectives. With preschool children, the teacher may assign tasks involving knowledge of colors, for example, to determine which children know the colors and which children need activities to learn them. With school-age children, the teacher may administer a paper-and-pencil test to determine which children have learned to add and which children need to be taught this skill, for example.

Also, the diagnostic evaluation helps determine whether the child is eligible for a special services program. Formal referral and testing is done by a team of professionals for children with suspected developmental delays or disabilities to determine their eligibility for special services. Students with identified delays or disabilities also need individual attention for instructional placement. These children have an individualized education program (IEP) plan, which must be reviewed to determine whether the child has made sufficient progress. Though federal law now allows IEPs to be reviewed every three years, many states opt for IEP reviews to be conducted each new school year so a child's needs are reassessed and adjustments made for maximum progress. Teachers (as part of the IEP team) are responsible for contributing assessment information for special education placements and for supporting adequate improvement each year. Indicators of progress in specific skills are documented and monitored throughout the year. These data are used for individualized instruction, which is adapted as necessary. The teacher may want to use pictures to teach and assess the concept of classifying similar items for a child with autism or sensory differences. Or, for another child who has limited motor abilities, the teacher may want to use a computer or picture board. In all of these examples, the teacher will keep detailed written records of the child's progress and challenges to inform the subsequent learning experiences of the child. These data should also be shared with parents so they can reinforce progress at home using the same or similar strategies.

DATA-DRIVEN DECISION MAKING FOR ELLS When considering children who are English Language Learners (ELLs), teachers need to conduct additional assessments to track progress and determine whether a child needs to continue in an English as a Second Language (ESL) program or if they have completed the program. School districts are responsible for understanding and following federal requirements for providing instruction that will support ELLs in schools as required by *Titles I and III of the Elementary and Secondary Education Act of 1965 (ESEA) and as amended by the Every Student Succeeds Act of 2015 (ESSA)* (U.S. Department of Education, 2016). Because about 10 percent of the student population nationwide are ELLs, it is imperative that teachers monitor their progress. Though school districts certainly use standardized assessments for this purpose, more frequent monitoring tools may be designed by classroom teachers to assess specific skills or content in greater detail.

The same process just described for preschool children is continued for children in elementary grades who are ELLs or have special needs. In addition, teacher-conducted testing may result in a child's placement in a particular group for reading, mathematics, or another academic area. The teacher or team of teachers often administers tests at the beginning of the school year to determine the child's mastery of content objectives; the purpose is to group children with similar learning needs for instruction. This type of evaluation may be repeated whenever teachers believe that regrouping is needed to improve instructional services for meeting the individual needs of the children.

Search and Share 6.1

Advantages and Disadvantages of Data-Driven Decision Making

Search online to locate information about the advantages and disadvantages of assessment as part of the data-driven decision-making process. What are special issues related to children with disabilities, end-of-year testing, and children who are English Language Learners?

FORMATIVE AND SUMMATIVE EVALUATION Formative evaluation and summative evaluation occur after instruction on a particular objective or a series of objectives. **Formative evaluation** is implemented throughout the year. Data generated from formative evaluation during the instructional process provide the teacher with information on the learning progress of the student and the effectiveness of instructional methods and materials. In other words, formative evaluation data informs the teacher on how children are progressing toward mastery of objectives. In individual classrooms, formative evaluation may take place more frequently as students move through specific objectives in the curriculum. After students practice a skill or learn information, the teacher evaluates them to determine which ones have achieved mastery of a particular skill or objective and which children need additional work through differentiated instructional methods or learning experiences. Documentation of the child's progress during formative evaluation is critical and can take place in numerous ways as discussed below.

Summative evaluation is a final assessment of what children have learned for a given objective or time period. In some schools, summative evaluation is conducted every six weeks or every nine weeks for grading purposes. The child receives a grade for performance on the objectives tested, for example. Whether or not grades are used, it is hoped that children who have not mastered the information or skills tested will have more opportunities to learn. Formative and summative evaluation will be discussed in more detail in Chapter 8.

Enhanced eText: Self-Check 6.1

The Role of Documentation

Documentation provides a record of children's learning and development. This record helps to tell the story of children's journeys as capable and competent learners. The adult documents important points about what children understand, what they can do, and how they approach learning. He or she also sometimes records in more detail children's involvement in particular events or activities in order to create a fuller picture of the richness and complexity of their learning and development (National Council for Curriculum and Assessment, 2009, p. 3).

The teacher learns to use documentation over a period of time. Initially, the teacher has to learn habits of documentation. The teacher needs to gather the tools of documentation that she needs and then develop the habit of remembering to document. Because there are many ways to use documentation, the educator new to documentation learns to have documentation possibilities at hand, such as a camera, tape recorder, computer, sticky pads, or pencil and notepad. The newcomer to documenting learns when documentation is needed, what type of documentation is most useful, and how to use documentation strategies effectively (Seitz, 2008; Wein, 2011).

The Influence of Reggio Emilia

To practitioners of Reggio Emilia programs, documentation makes learning visible. The infant–toddler centers and preschools in the city of Reggio Emilia in northern Italy have had a major influence on the practice of curriculum development and

Learning the What, When, and How of Documentation

Dianna Gonzales is a second grade teacher. She has used projects and thematic curriculum in the past. She has been learning about documentation and wants to add this process to her assessment strategies. One of her first steps is to think about topics that can be documented in her classroom. She considers the following possibilities:

- Individual progress in language development
- A list of appropriate play behaviors contributed by members of the class
- A report on the chronology of progress on a curriculum project
- Posted work samples documenting mastery of learning objectives in mathematics
- A list of ideas for future projects

After Dianna started working with her list, she found it was very easy to think of new possibilities for documentation. She began by documenting progress on a current project. She used displays of the children's work to report important accomplishments on the project objectives. Then she worked on assessing the quality of the curriculum using examples of different types of representation of the learning such as children's pictures, language experience, stories about classroom events, and a chart of new words that children were learning to recognize. She labeled objects in the classroom as a part of this activity.

Dianna soon learned that planning for learning from the perspective of documentation included some of the strategies she was already using; in addition, she became more aware of how documentation promoted child-initiated assessments and self-reflections.

documentation in many countries. In Reggio Emilia classrooms, learning is a child-initiated process in which interests develop into processes that evolve into learning. Art is a basic element of the process as children sketch, paint, or use three-dimensional creations to show what they are learning and the strategies they are using to accomplish a learning experience over a period of time (Guyevsky, 2005).

> **Enhanced eText:** Video Example 6.2

In Reggio Emilia schools, the teacher documents the progress of a period of time. Many Reggio Emilia schools have specific forms and procedures for documenting children's progress. The work that the children produce also serves as documentation of what has transpired. The important factor in the documentation is that the teacher is observing from the children's perspective. The teacher needs to:

- observe to see what the children are doing every day,
- see their interactions and hear their real conversations, and
- record children's explorations and share them with parents, other teachers, and children (McDonald, 2006).

Lillian Katz and Sylvia Chard (1996) followed a similar process in the United States, using documentation in a child-centered project approach to learning in early childhood programs. Children planned and carried out interests in learning through a process that included all types of representation, such as drawings, stories, photos, and other representations of what they had learned (Katz & Chard, 1996). Curriculum was based on projects and labeled "The Project Approach." Multiple types of resources were used for documentation similar to the Reggio Emilia documentations. Today, documentation is a very common practice at all ages, from infant–toddler programs through preschool and elementary classrooms.

Developing a system to document children's learning takes time. Wien, Guyevskey and Berdoussis (2011) recommend five aspects of developing documentation as an everyday practice in the following order, including: "(1) developing the habits of documenting, (2) 'going public' with recountings of activities, (3) exploring the visual literacy of graphic displays, (4) making children's theories visible, and (5) sharing visible theories with others for the purpose of further interpretation and curriculum decision making."

The outdoor learning environment is often omitted from discussions about documentation. Yet, the outdoor learning environment can provide numerous opportunities for learning across developmental domains and academic areas. In her research on identifying effective strategies using pedagogical documentation that supports learning, Merewether (2018) found that listening to children's conversations and then asking questions to further their learning was one important strategy. She suggests audio recorders and journals as two ways to document conversations. Photography by children and adults provided another method of documenting outdoor experiences. The simple act of providing cameras to children can spur a world of exploration and new knowledge. Adults can further document and analyze these activities through field notes that describe process and context as well as other forms of written information.

> **Enhanced eText: Self-Check 6.2**

Types of Documentation

The types of documentation used to keep records of children's developmental and learning progress are numerous and depend on the purposes for the documentation. It is not useful to try to document everything that the teacher sees and hears in the classroom. Selections have to be made concerning what information is particularly helpful in understanding the child's developmental growth and progress in developing skills, attitudes, and understanding (National Council for Curriculum and Assessment, 2009).

Documentation of infant and toddler development focuses on visual samples of the child; photos and videos, as well as conversations with parents and anecdotes of daily activities. Documentation of infant and toddler development and learning is conducted by an adult. Figure 6-1 describes some documentation strategies for infants and toddlers.

As children move into the preschool years, their physical, social, and cognitive abilities provide many more types of documentation to tell their stories and provide examples of their speech, explorations, and encounters with others. In the primary grades, they can provide written information about themselves and express themselves through art and other work samples. They will be able to select what kinds of activities they want to use to document their learning accomplishments.

Figure 6-1 Documentation strategies for infants and toddlers

Documentation Strategy	Method
1. Photos and videos	An adult makes photos or videos of important events in the infant's life, such as first steps or learning to climb. Group photos and videos help document school activities.
2. Daily diaries and records	The teacher or caregiver makes notes about children's daily life in the classroom. Information can be related to the schedule, eating patterns, child interactions, or play incidents that might be important to record.
3. Stories about children	Anecdotes about daily events bring infant and toddler's engagement in classroom participation to life. A story is told about amusing verbalizations or other occurrences that might be of interest to parents.
4. Developmental checklists	The teacher frequently assesses progress the child has made in areas of development. When a toddler learns new words or initiates a conversation with another child, the teacher records it on the child's developmental checklist.
5. Reports	The teacher makes periodic reports to the family. The report can include information gathered using the first four documentation strategies described above. Reports can be oral when teacher and parents are able to meet and talk. Reports can also be written and given or sent to parents.

Documentation has commonly been described as pictures, photographs, and written explanations mounted on a wall. However, documentation can be expanded to a variety of formats. Documentation assessment strategies can include portfolios, products of investigations, videotapes, class books, and slide shows (Helm, Beneke, & Steinheimer, 2007; Seitz, 2008). Although the original descriptions of documentation referred to wall displays related to projects, the process has been enriched to include more possibilities on how and where documentation is used to demonstrate what children have learned through their own work. Figure 6-2 shows a comprehensive web of types of documentation. Some are teacher led, while others reflect the individual child's work products. Some documentation originates from teacher-led lessons, while observations of the child's play or learning center activities can demonstrate the child's successful learning of a skill or concept. For example, a child's accurate actions in a game based on mathematics can serve as documentation of the performance of a basic state or national mathematics goal.

There are five categories of documentation supporting the web depicted in Figure 6-2: narratives, observations of progress and performance, child self-reflections, results of work and play activities, and individual portfolios. Each of these categories of documentation is discussed below.

Suzanne Clouzeau/Pearson Education, Inc.

Observations of children's daily activities can assess their skill development.

Figure 6-2 Documentation Web

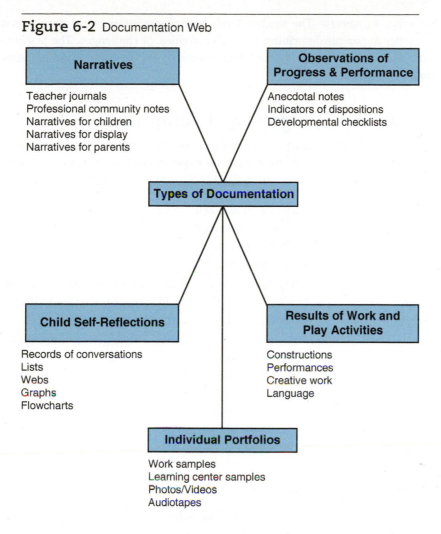

Narratives

Teacher journals
Professional community notes
Narratives for children
Narratives for display
Narratives for parents

Observations of Progress & Performance

Anecdotal notes
Indicators of dispositions
Developmental checklists

Types of Documentation

Child Self-Reflections

Records of conversations
Lists
Webs
Graphs
Flowcharts

Results of Work and Play Activities

Constructions
Performances
Creative work
Language

Individual Portfolios

Work samples
Learning center samples
Photos/Videos
Audiotapes

Narratives

Teachers mostly write **narratives** when working with young children. The narratives can have different purposes:

Teacher journal—The teacher keeps a daily record of the day's events and relevant events that occurred.

Professional community notes—The teacher takes notes in important meetings, parent interviews, collaborative teacher conversations, etc.

Narratives for children—The teacher and the children compose a story about a classroom activity. The children contribute items for the story, while the teacher writes the story.

Narratives for display—After the class has completed a project that took place over a period of time, the teacher constructs a display of the products constructed for the project. The narrative is displayed as part of the progress of the projects. The narrative might be one piece, or several sections focusing on the steps used to conduct project activities.

Narratives for parents—The teacher sends home newsletters about class activities, or a letter to parents describing a child's activities, or challenges. The teacher can alert parents about a topic that will be explored by the class and make requests for donated materials.

Observations of Progress and Performance

The teacher develops a practice of observing children during lessons, time in centers, whole group discussions, and other activities experienced during the day. The main interest is documenting children's progress and accomplishments.

Anecdotal notes—The teacher jots down activities observed in the classroom. The notes might become part of the daily journal or a record of child behaviors, or serve some other purpose. There might be an interesting event involving a child or several children that indicates developmental or social progress.

Indicators of dispositions—The teacher is aware of how children are feeling about themselves and others. Notes are taken about child behaviors that are indicators of joy, sadness, empathy, persistence, curiosity, or frustration in individual children.

Developmental checklists—The teacher uses checklists of categories of development to monitor the child's progress. Physical development might be observed on the playground and in the classroom. Cognitive developmental indicators might be observed during lessons, while children are engaged in assignments, or when children encounter opportunities to solve problems. Child interactions provide information on social development and the effective or ineffective strategies children use to engage with other children.

Child Self-Reflections

The children think about their work, ideas, and activities. This type of documentation is generated by the child, but might require help from the teacher to record it.

Records of conversations—The child or a group of children engage in a discussion of conversations they have had about an event or topic. This might take place as children discuss a field trip, an event in the classroom, or a discussion that was part of a lesson.

Lists—Children engage in making lists for various purposes. There might be a list of new words that children are learning in their emergent literacy activities. The class might make a list of groceries for a unit on the grocery store. A class cooking activity might need a list of ingredients for the recipe. Some lists are generated by an individual child, but more frequently they are generated by a group of children.

Webs—Teachers originate the use of webs with children when planning and conducting projects. After some experiences with web construction, the children can successfully help develop a web for each project. The web can include the major activities needed for the project and contributions as to what will be learned. The teacher provides constant guidance and suggestions for the children to consider.

Graphs—Teachers also initiate the use of graphs with preschool children; however, young children can also develop their own graphs with some assistance. Graphs are used with learning objectives in mathematics (see Figure 6-3).

Search and Share 6.2

Children Documenting Their Own Learning

Search online to locate examples of how children can document their own learning activities and progress. What are the benefits and drawbacks of self-documentation? How would you set up a system of self-documentation in your classroom?

Flowcharts—The plan for a learning theme or project needs to include a map of how it will progress. A web maps the objectives and plans; the flowchart maps the chronology of the progress of the theme. Again, the teacher guides the children in mapping out on a calendar how the activities will be scheduled and completed. The flowchart becomes a source of documentation of the project at the end of the learning period.

Results of Work and Play Activities

Results in this context refer to things a child can do or make. It can include play activities, art products, language arts, performing arts, or written presentations.

Constructions—A young child can use constructions for various purposes. The web for types of documentation in Figure 6-2 includes sculptures, blocks or Legos, models, and organization of the play environment. Children might make models of houses for a project on homes. They might use boxes to construct buildings. Blocks, Legos, and other activities that involve putting materials together represent constructions.

Performances—Young children engage in singing, dancing, moving to music, playing instruments, producing simple plays, or performing actions to a story. In these types of activities the children's actions are the products. The children may create their own actions or physical expressions.

Creative work—Young children become interested in making marks on paper at a very early age. This ability to document their ideas or thoughts becomes more understandable as they gain skills in using art materials to produce pictures. This interest grows as they experience more opportunities to express reactions to events on paper. Children in Reggio Emilia make extensive use of art and pictures to document what they are learning. They begin at a very young age and demonstrate skills beyond those of children from other cultures before they leave the preschool program. Children also create in other types of art media. Molding with clay and using a variety of materials for art activities can result in individual expressions and ideas.

Data collection—We might think of science when we talk about collections. Young children learn about collections that can be made from leaves, stones, shells, nuts, and other types of natural objects. But collections of other types are also used to document learning. Children might keep a record of vehicles that pass on the street, ideas for activities such as birthdays, and kinds of fruits and vegetables. Some of the collections can be real objects, but others can be collections that are documented in lists or pictures. Data is the important term for collections. Children collect data of many types to document their understanding of a topic.

> ### Using Boxes to Represent Community Buildings
>
> Mara's kindergarten class is learning about the community that surrounds their school. One of the objectives is to make a representation of some of the buildings that are nearby. The school is in a rural area; therefore, most of the buildings are fairly small compared to city structures. The class was divided into groups to plan and construct models of buildings near the school. They used a large collection of boxes that was gathered by the children's parents. One group chose to make a model of a small church, while another made a model of a farmhouse with a chicken coop behind it. A third group constructed a representation of a home located across the street from the school. The groups visited their chosen structures and made drawings. Then they worked with boxes to construct their models. When the project was finished, children from other classes came to see the models and hear children in the groups describe their chosen structure and why it was important to the community.

Data collection can be represented on graphs. Young children can easily use bar graphs, line graphs, and picture graphs. If children were to gather data on favorite fruit choices, they could use any of the three types of graphs. Larson and Whitin (2010) suggest that two different types of graphs be used to analyze the same data. Figure 6-3 illustrates the use of line graphs and bar graphs.

Language—Oral and written language becomes the most common form of documentation of learning, especially as children enter and move through the primary grades. Nevertheless, the process starts with preschool children as they use letters, labels, and books to begin the process of learning written language. They can advance to captions and signs for visual representation or documentation, and finally can write extended comments and ideas as they progress in reading and writing. They can learn to respond orally to classroom questions, which evolves into the ability to make reports and presentations about the information studied.

Individual Portfolios

Portfolios are the most comprehensive approach to documentation. Each portfolio can contain a variety of types of documentation. In a sense, portfolios are a method of recording and storing documentation rather than a single type. Portfolios begin as a teacher activity when working with infants and toddlers, and progress to child-initiated entries as children broaden the ways that they can demonstrate what they have learned. Later, children themselves will use cameras and other media to document and explain what they have learned. Children's work samples, as well as art examples, become an important element in documentation for portfolio purposes.

Enhanced eText: Application Exercise 6.1

Figure 6-3 Bar graph and line graph

Bar Graph

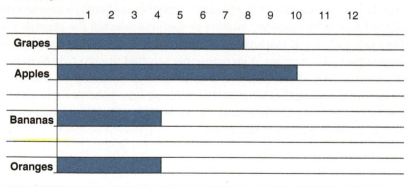

Graph of Favorite Fruits

If a total of 25 children made these choices, they could be represented
on the bar graph above.
Grapes 8
Apples 10
Bananas 4
Oranges 2

Line Graph

The same data could be represented on a line graph.

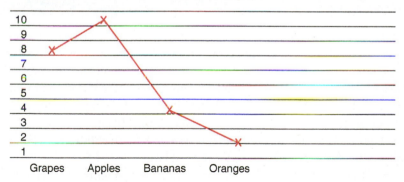

Collecting Data on Lunch Selections

The first grade class taught by Henry Clarkson is studying what children select
for a meal. There are three choices of the main dish—broiled chicken strips,
macaroni and cheese with ground beef, and lasagna with vegetables. As children
pass through the lunch line, they can choose which main dish they want. The
lunch trays also come with a banana, small salad, and ice cream. As the class
passed through the lunch line, two teams of two students worked together to
tally how many children in a class selected each choice.

After the class had finished eating, the teams returned to the classroom to
analyze their data. They added up the number for each choice and posted the
totals on the board. The total for chicken strips was 10, the total for macaroni and
cheese with beef was 17, and the total for vegetable lasagna was 2. The two teams

(Continued)

reached the same totals. There were 29 children present that day in school. Mr. Clarkson helped the children to write a report about their collection and analysis of the data. They determined that the largest number of students chose macaroni and cheese with beef. The smallest number of students selected the vegetable lasagna. They concluded that macaroni and cheese with beef was the favorite food for the largest group in the class. A large number selected the broiled chicken strips. Mr. Clarkson asked the class why they did not choose lasagna. The responses varied, but most indicated that it didn't look very good or there was not enough cheese on top. Mr. Clarkson and the students finished their discussion by making a bar graph of the lunch selections.

Enhanced eText: Video Example 6.3

Enhanced eText: Self-Check 6.3

Summary

This chapter marks a new direction in how assessment data is used to inform decisions about children's education. The era of accountability testing, technological advances that make documentation of children's learning more accessible, and an emphasis on evidence-based practices in early childhood education have all contributed to the idea of data-driven decision making. While there are distinct advantages in documenting children's progress, there can be disadvantages that detract from focusing on the children's needs. For example, the same data that is used to benefit children can be used to judge teachers, schools, and our public education at large.

Standardized assessments and teacher-designed assessments are two types of data used in data-driven decision making. At the beginning of the year, assessment for placement informs the teacher of students' abilities and what they are ready to learn. Class placement can be conducted periodically during the year for small group instruction, when students are regrouped to meet individual needs more successfully, depending on individual progress in proceeding through the curriculum.

Diagnostic assessment becomes important when students are having difficulty that might be due to a physical or intellectual impairment that is preventing appropriate progress. The teacher might administer a diagnostic test if specific areas of the curriculum seem to be affected. Students can be referred for more technical diagnostic testing conducted by a school counselor or school psychologist when diagnosis is needed for formal referral to special education or another intervention program.

Formative and summative assessments are typically conducted by teachers. Summative assessment is particularly important at the end of the school year or at the end of grading periods in the elementary grades.

Documentation moves beyond standardized and teacher-designed assessments in developing a comprehensive picture of a child's progress. Documentation is used to keep a record of the child's learning that is demonstrated through things the child has accomplished. Documentation adds to information provided by assessment results because the teacher can include a variety of class activities to present the child's work products and other indicators of what has been accomplished. Documentation strategies range from art and work samples to conversations that are documented with notes, photos, and video recordings.

Group accomplishments can be documented through wall displays and explanations of group projects or thematic studies. Students in a class can develop presentations for family members or other students in the school to summarize what has been learned over a period of classroom work.

> **Enhanced eText:** **Self-Check: Chapter Review**

Key Terms

Data-driven decision making 138	Formative evaluation 141	Summative evaluation 141
Diagnostic evaluation 139	Narratives 145	Teacher-designed assessment 139
Documentation 141	Placement evaluation 139	

Selected Organizations

Search for the following organizations online:
Educational Testing Service
National Council for Curriculum and Assessment
National Institute for Early Education Research

The Center for Comprehensive School Reform and
  Improvement
North American Reggio Emilia Alliance
Early Childhood Research & Practice

References

Goldstein, J., & Flake, J. K. (2016). Towards a framework for the validation of early childhood assessment systems. *Educational Assessment, Evaluation and Accountability, 28*, 273–293.

Guyevsky, V. (2005). Interpreting the Reggio Emilia approach. Documentation and emergent curriculum in a preschool setting. Unpublished master's thesis. Faculty of Education, York University, Toronto, Canada.

Helm, J. H., Beneke, S., & Steinheimer, K. (2007). *Windows on learning: Documenting young children's work, second edition*. New York, NY: Teacher's College Press.

Ikemoto, G. S., & Marsh, J. A. (2007). Cutting through the "data-driven" mantra: Different conceptions of data-driven decision making. *Evidence and Decision Making: Yearbook of the National Society of Education, 106*, 105–131.

Katz, L. G., & Chard, S. C. (1996). The contributions of documentation to the quality of early childhood education. (ERIC Digest). Urbana, IL: ERIC Clearinghouse on Elementary and Early Childhood Education.

Larson, M. J., & Whitin, D. J. (2010). Young children use graphs to build mathematical reasoning. Retrieved from https://www.southernearlychildhood.org/upload/pdf/Young_Children_Use_Graphs_1.pdf.

Mandinach, E. B. (2012). A perfect time for data use: Using data-driven decision making to inform practice, *Educational Psychologist, 47*, 71–85, DOI: 10.1080/00461520.2012.667064.

McDonald, B. (2006, November/December). Observation—The path to documentation. *Exchange, 172*, 45–49.

Merewether, J. (2018). Listening to young children outdoors with pedagogical documentation. *International Journal of Early Years Education.* DOI: 10.1080/09669760.2017.1421525.

Mertler, C. A. (2018). *Introduction to data-driven educational decision making.* Retrieved from http://www.ascd.org/publications/books/sf114082/chapters/Introduction_to_Data-Driven_Educational_Decision_Making.aspx.

National Council for Curriculum and Assessment. (2009). *Supporting learning and development through assessment.* Retrieved from www.ncca.biz/pdfs/guidelineseng/assessment_eng.pdf.

Seitz, H. (2008, March). The power of documentation in the early childhood classroom. *Young Children, 63*, 88–93.

Snow, C. T., & Van Hemel, S. B. (Eds.). (2008). *Early childhood assessment. Why, what, and how.* Washington, DC: The National Academies Press.

U.S. Department of Education. (2016, September 23). *Non-regulatory guidance: English learners and title III of the elementary and secondary education act (ESEA), as amended by the every student succeeds act (ESSA).* Washington, DC: Author. Retrieved from https://www2.ed.gov/policy/elsec/leg/essa/essatitleii-iguidenglishlearners92016.pdf.

Wein, C. A., with V. Guyevskey & N. Berdoussis. (2011). Learning to document in Reggio-inspired education. *Early Childhood Research and Practice, 13*, 1–16.

Chapter 7
Observation

Studio 8/Pearson Education Ltd

 Chapter Learning Outcomes

As a result of reading this chapter, you will be able to:

7.1 Explain the purposes of observation.

7.2 Describe different types of observation.

7.3 Conduct observations of physical, social, cognitive, and language development by using appropriate observation strategies.

7.4 Discuss advantages and disadvantages of using observation for assessment.

This chapter includes information about the purposes of observation and how it can be used to understand young children's development and behaviors. Different types of observation are described as well as how observation can help inform teachers and parents about specific areas of development. Advantages and disadvantages of observation are also discussed.

Purposes of Observation

Observation is the most direct method of becoming familiar with the learning and development of the young child. Because it requires a focus on the child's behaviors, observation allows the teacher to get to know the child as a unique individual, rather than as a member of a group. It is very important for teachers of young children to have training in early childhood development in order to understand appropriate behaviors when observing children. Further, such training is a prerequisite for teachers to understand what they are seeing in the context of all types of development.

Learning the characteristics of observation is important, as is developing the skills of how to observe. After the significance of observation is understood, teachers need to develop observational skills appropriate to the objectives of the observation and the information they desire from the observation (Bentzen, 2009; Pelo, 2006). Observation can be used for three major purposes: (1) to understand children's behavior, (2) to evaluate children's development, and (3) to evaluate learning progress.

Understanding Children's Behavior

Because young children have not yet mastered language and the ability to read and write, they are unable to express themselves as clearly as older children and adults. They cannot fully demonstrate how much they know or understand through formal or informal assessments involving tasks and standardized tests. According to child development specialists, one of the most accurate ways to learn about children is to observe them in daily activities. Because children cannot explain themselves sufficiently through language, evidence of why they behave as they do is obtained through on-the-spot recording of their actions. Children who are English Language Learners especially need observations of their activities for clues about what they understand, even if they cannot express themselves adequately in English. Observation of this population of children reveals information about them that may not be obvious within the larger group of students.

Skilled observation is important to correctly determine the reasons for a child's classroom behavior also. Misinterpretation leads to difficulties for both the teacher and child if the teacher makes an assumption about the cause that has led to the child's behavior (Jablon, 2010/2012; MacDonald, 2006).

Children communicate through their bodies. Their physical actions reveal as much about them as the things they say. Cohen, Stern, and Balaban (1997) described how observing children's behavior provides information or clues to their thoughts and feelings:

> Children communicate with us through their eyes, the quality of their voices, their body postures, their gestures, their mannerisms, their smiles, their jumping up and down, and their listlessness. They show us, by the way they do things as well as by what they do, what is going on inside them. When we come to see children's behavior through the eyes of its meaning to them, from the inside out, we shall be well on our way to understanding them. Recording their ways of communicating helps us to see them as they are. (p. 5)

The development of social skills is a major accomplishment during the early childhood years. Beginning as toddlers and preschoolers, young children evolve into social beings who learn to interact with each other. First efforts to become part of a social group are often ineffective, but with continued opportunities to engage in group activities, most young children develop the ability to work and play with each other (O'Neil, 2013). Observation of children at play or interacting in classroom centers reveals how social development and behavior are progressing. Social behavior is part of social development, discussed in the next section.

Evaluating Children's Development

A second major purpose of observing children is to evaluate their development. When teachers study development, observation is specific. Rather than considering behavior in general, the observer's purpose is to determine the child's progress in physical, cognitive, language, social, or emotional development. Observing development not only makes it easy to understand sequences of development but also helps teachers of young children to be aware of individual growth and aid children who have delays in specific areas of development. Skilled observation of developmental domains requires a sound foundation in child development. The ability to conduct developmental observations increases with practice when a teacher is able to match the developmental characteristics and norms with the activities of the children he or she observes (Frost, Wortham, & Reifel, 2008; Gronlund & James, 2013).

Forman and Hall (2005) describe children as spontaneous, sometimes reserved; joyful now, sad later; friendly and reserved; competent and naive; talkative and quiet (p. 1). They proposed that we can learn at least five attributes of children when we observe them closely:

- Their interests and preferences
- Their levels of cognitive and social development
- Their strategies for creating desired effects
- Their skills and accomplishments
- Their personalities and temperaments (p. 2)

Muniru

Muniru has had a "no good, very bad day" in the toddler room at the Delgado Child Enrichment Center. His regular teacher was delayed for part of the day and the substitute teacher was very impatient with him. First, Muniru's father was late for work and he did not get to finish his breakfast. Later, he bit a child, which is unusual behavior for him. He fussed and cried all morning and did not enjoy any of the play activities. By the time the regular teacher returned in the afternoon, the substitute was exasperated with Muniru. The regular teacher observed Muniru for a few minutes and noticed that he was drooling. When she checked his mouth, she discovered that a new tooth was erupting. She put some ice in a clean cloth and let Muniru suck on it. Before Muniru's father returned to pick him up, Muniru had been able to participate in classroom play and story time.

OBSERVING INFANT AND TODDLER DEVELOPMENT   The years between birth and age 2 are the most rapid period of development. They are also the years when the infant and toddler are least able to communicate verbally with others. Observation is the primary means to interpret the meaning of a very young child's behaviors. Mothers learn the differences in their baby's cries to be able to respond to their needs. Infant caregivers observe the infants in their care throughout the day to understand when the infants are tired, hungry, wet, or not feeling well. Observation of changes in an infant's daily sleeping and eating patterns might signal advances in development or an impending illness. Opportunities for adult–child interactions are also determined by observing the infant's readiness to be attentive.

Observation is an important ongoing process with infants and toddlers. Because their development changes frequently, the observer needs to document what is observed. The observer also needs to be objective and factual. Factual observations would include:

- Descriptions of actions
- Quotations of language
- Descriptions of gestures
- Descriptions of creations (U.S. Department of Health and Human Services, 2014, p.22)

Families need to be engaged in their child's developmental progress. Parents provide a perspective of their child's growth that is not available to infant and toddler caregivers. Therefore, the families should feel that they are equal partners in the observation process. This inclusion of the family's perspectives extends to screening through observation and assessments for early intervention programs.

Enhanced eText: Video Example 7.1

Developmental monitoring uses observation to record typical developmental milestones. It can be conducted by parents and grandparents, child care providers, and medical personnel. When the child goes for a visit to the doctor or nurse, they might ask questions about the child's development or interact with the child to determine appropriate development indicators. Likewise, they can provide valuable information on the nature of development.

Developmental screening is used to identify children who are at risk for development as we have already learned when discussing screening instruments used with infants and toddlers. Observers can initiate the screening process by attending to all domains of development that might raise a red flag that indicates a need for further observation and established screening techniques. This process can include careful selection of screening instruments (Centers for Disease Control and Prevention, 2014, 2017; U.S. Department of Health and Human Services, 2014).

OBSERVING ENGLISH LANGUAGE LEARNERS   Children entering preschools in the United States represent hundreds of different spoken languages. Children who enter a preschool program or elementary school with limited English proficiency have a special need to acquire or expand their language. Observation by the classroom teacher and other staff members provides input on what the child understands and is learning to express. Often a language limitation is hidden because a child seems extremely shy, when in reality he or she does not understand the language being spoken. Although tests are commonly administered to admit a child into an English language development program or a bilingual program, daily observation is key to knowing what the child needs to learn to become proficient in English. The teacher can provide instant feedback and amplification of the child's speaking attempts to further expand vocabulary and functional use of language.

It is important to remember that there are stages of second language acquisition. Though individual children may differ in how quickly they move through one or more of these stages, there is general agreement on the stages of second language acquisition, including:

- Silent/Receptive or Preproduction—In this stage, children may speak very little or not at all in the new language (e.g., English). However, the children are very busy observing how language is used in conversations to identify objects or actions, and so forth in the new surroundings. During this stage children may point, nod, or use other methods of body language to communicate. They may have a receptive vocabulary of up to 500 words but be uncomfortable trying to express them.

- Early Production—Children start to use one word or 2–3 word phrases to express themselves.

- Speech Emergence—Children speak in short phrases or sentences. They may respond to questions but still make numerous mistakes when using their second language and may have trouble communicating their thoughts or ideas.

- Intermediate Language Proficiency—Children can express themselves in longer, more complex sentences and ask for help in using the second language if they need it.

- Advanced Language Proficiency—Children can speak with fluency and express ideas with confidence. Their language functions the same as a native speaker. (The IRIS Center/Vanderbilt University, 2018)

Observation is an essential component of how a teacher can know what stage of second language acquisition a child may be experiencing and, thus, how to support the child's efforts. In this way, the teacher can help ensure that children who a English learners, for example, are not erroneously referred for a special education evaluation. For instance, if a child is in the silent/receptive or preproduction stage, the teacher can observe and document that the child uses body language to communicate or that he or she can understand receptive language. Thus, the silence is not a learning problem but, rather, a stage of language development. Children sometimes stay in the silent stage for prolonged periods of time, especially if there are extenuating circumstances such as poverty, less integration by the family into mainstream society, or poor school-family relationships (Le Pichon & de Jonge, 2016).

As a child moves through each stage, the teacher can further document how the child's second language is progressing through audio records, video records, or other means so that the child's abilities with the second language is clear. In other words, if a child is using single words or 2–3 word expressions, then he or she would be in the early production stage, or if the child is using complex sentences and expressing ideas without help, then he or she may be in the advanced language proficiency stage. This information can be shared with parents so they know how the child's second language is progressing and what they can do at home to reinforce it. Even if the parents do not speak English as a second language, for example, they can expose their child to appropriate television programs (e.g., Sesame Street), audio recordings of children's books in English, or recordings of music in English to help the child's vocabulary and language usage further develop. The communication between school and home is important to note. One study by Hindman and Wasik (2015) showed that not only did exposure to both languages (e.g., Spanish and English) at home impact Head Start children's ability to learn the second language, but also if teachers used high quality language in their practices (e.g., more details in explaining information, larger vocabularies), children learned the second language more rapidly.

It is important to remember that there is a difference between basic interpersonal communication skills (BICS), the ability to speak a language with others during daily activities, and Cognitive Academic Language Proficiency (CALP), the ability to compare, classify, synthesize, evaluate, and infer ideas and concepts in a second language (Cummins, 1981; 2000). Observation can be used to distinguish these types of skill acquisitions in the second language also. If a child can ask questions or make statements about his or her daily needs but cannot read or write or compose ideas in the second language, that would be BICS. Whereas, if a child can express ideas that demonstrate an ability to think and synthesize in the second language, that would be CALP. For example, if a kindergarten child creates a story with a plot, in a sequence of events, and writes down this story or audio records it in the second language, that would be CALP.

Enhanced eText: Video Example 7.2

Identifying the needs of young English language learners can be challenging (Soltero, 2014). Screening and assessment tools must be culturally and linguistically appropriate for the young children being served. Problems with assessment sometimes lead to overidentification of children with language delays. The mislabeling can be frustrating for teachers and parents, and damaging for the child. Observation and documentation are two of the tools for effective assessment of young English language learners (U.S. Department of Health and Human Services, 2014). As practitioners search for effective and appropriate linguistic and cultural strategies for identification and serving young English language learners, observations are recommended as one solution to address these challenges (NAEYC & NAECS/SDE, 2005). The NAEYC recommendations on screening and assessment include the following:

> 3a. Programs rely on systematic observational assessments, using culturally and linguistically appropriate tools as the primary source of guidance to inform instruction and to improve outcomes for young English-language learners (NAEYC & NAECS/ SDE, 2005, p. 4).

OBSERVING YOUNG CHILDREN WITH DISABILITIES   Educators who work with children who have developmental delays or disabilities use observation as a tool for assessing their development and academic progress. Traditionally, standardized tests for infants, toddlers, and preschool children were used almost exclusively to identify and diagnose the development of children with disabilities or at risk to develop disabilities. Today, teachers are aware that observation is a key strategy in conducting an assessment. Observations can help establish the child's current level of performance and the skills that have been mastered. The teacher should not assume that the child is not capable of using a skill, but should determine how to move the child forward toward acquiring the skill. Further, the teacher uses observation to determine whether the child's self concept, classroom management skills, or other factors are affecting mastery of a skill or completion of a task. Any method of observation used should be appropriate for the child's current development, cultural background, and life circumstances (Wall, 2011).

Observation is used to assess learning characteristics of individual children.

When using observation to identify the needs of a child with learning disabilities, the observer should be able to observe and record child behaviors objectively. Because children with disabilities communicate through their gestures, mannerisms, facial expressions, and postures, the observer must be able to sit, look, and listen. During the observation, the observer is looking for the source of a problem as well as getting a better understanding of the child's purposes, behavior, and feelings (WETA, 2018).

PLAY-BASED ASSESSMENT   Assessment during child play, or **play-based assessment**, is particularly useful for learning about development in children with disabilities. Observation of play has been found more effective than standardized testing for some situations. Both structured and nonstructured observations can be used to assess the young child's developmental strengths and needs (Kelly-Vance & Ryalls, 2008).

The procedures described in this chapter can be used with children without disabilities; however, play observation provides unique ways to assess children who may be delayed in development. For example, children with disabilities and children who are developing normally can be presented with the same toys. The observer can then compare how the two groups play with the toys to determine strengths and possible deficits in children's development. Toys can also be given to a child to observe and rate the developmental sequences of play (Fewell & Glick, 1998; Groard, Mchaffie, McCall, & Greenberg, 2007).

A team of adults usually serves children with disabilities. Assessment and intervention teams have different specializations and purposes of assessment. Parents are included on each child's play-based assessment team. The play session is flexible enough to be adapted to individual interests (Linder, 1993; Linder, 1998; Linder, 2010). The play activities are conducted with a facilitator, the child's parents, and a peer.

Both structured and unstructured play activities are included within five phases of play taking place for about 60–70 minutes. The phases are as follows:

Phase 1: Unstructured Facilitation (20–25 minutes)

The child initiates the activities. The facilitator follows along in playing and conversations using the toys the child selects. The facilitator can model slightly higher play skills but should avoid trying to teach the child.

Phase 2: Structured Facilitation (10–15 minutes)

The facilitator leads the activities and asks the child to perform spatial tasks (games) that provide an additional opportunity to observe language and cognitive development. The child should be allowed to initiate activities as well.

Phase 3: Child–Child Interaction (5–10 minutes)

The child plays with another child who is slightly older, familiar to the child being assessed, and developing typically. The children play wherever they choose, with the facilitator encouraging interaction. The team observes the child's play interactions and social patterns.

Phase 4: Parent–Child Interaction (5 minutes)

The parent and child engage in the play activities that they do at home. The team observes how the child interacts with the parent and if behaviors are different than in other phases in the assessment. At the end, the parents are asked to leave the room and then return in a few minutes. The child's behavior during separation and return is observed. The parents again play with the child in a more structured activity or teach the child a new task.

Phase 5: Motor Play (10–20 minutes)

Again, the child engages in unstructured play for a few minutes followed by specific motor activities guided by the facilitator. This phase may include an occupational or physical therapist.

Phase 6: Snack (5–10 minutes)

The child is given a snack. The team observes self-help skills, adaptive behavior, and oral motor skills. The snack can include the peer play partner from Phase 3.

The entire session is recorded using a video camera so that team members can observe it again later (Brookes Publishing, 2002).

There are other similar assessment tools that use play-based assessment. *The Play Assessment Scale (PAS)* was developed to assess the developing skills in children from 2 months to 3 years. Likewise, the *Infant-Preschool Play Assessment Scale (I-PAS)* (Flagler, 1996) is used with children from birth to age 5. Another play assessment scale is the *Play in Early Childhood Evaluation System (PIECES)* (Cherney, Kelly-Vance, Gill-Glover, Ruane, & Ryalls, 2003). Also similar to Linder's Transdisciplinary Play-Based Assessment (TPBA), the PIECES involves observation of a child at play and can be conducted in settings with adequate toys to elicit play behaviors (Kelly-Vance & Ryalls, 2008).

The 2004 reauthorization of the Individuals with Disabilities Education Improvement Act required response to intervention (RTI) activities that are effective in evaluating the needs of children with disabilities. Play-based assessment is an effective approach to acquire the needed information (Kelly-Vance & Ryalls, 2008; National Association of School Psychologists, 2005). **Play-based intervention** that follows play-based assessment is defined by the U.S. Department of Education (2012) as follows:

Observing Infants and Toddlers with Visual Impairments

Assessments of infants and toddlers with visual impairments depend heavily on observations and interviews. To provide appropriate intervention for visually impaired children, intervention providers must understand how the children learn most effectively. Children are observed in various types of activities, including familiar and unfamiliar activities, challenging or new activities, individual and group activities, and indoor and outdoor activities. Interventionists must become familiar with health and nutrition factors as well as interests, motivation, and preferences. For example, how does the child respond to music, or what makes the child happy? What are the child's favorite activities or least favorite activities? The child's response to routines, transitions, and learning activities are also important factors. Extensive observation of the child is necessary to provide the most effective interventions.

SOURCE: Deborah Gleason, Observations of Learning Styles of Infants and Toddlers with Visual Impairments or Deafblindness: Using Information About How Children Learn to Plan Effective Intervention. (2010). Austin, TX: Texas School for the Blind and Visually Impaired.

Play-based interventions are practices designed to improve socio-emotional, physical, language, and cognitive development through guided interactive play. During play sessions, an interventionist uses strategies including modeling, verbal redirection, reinforcement, and indirect instruction to sustain and encourage child play activities. Through the use of appropriate play materials and the direction of the interventionist, the goal is for young children with disabilities to be better able to explore, experiment, interact and express themselves. (p.1)

Play intervention procedures are designed for the individual needs and disabilities of young children. For example, play-based intervention programs for children with ADHD have been developed in Australia (Cordier, Bundy, Hocking, & Enfield, 2009; Wilkes, Cordier, Bunday, Docking, & Munro, 2011). Informal play intervention has been developed using improvisational play to encourage social-emotional development in a preschool program (O'Neill, 2013).

Numerous studies have been conducted to establish the effectiveness of play-based interventions. However, as of April 2012, the desired effectiveness had not been established. According to the What Works Clearinghouse:

No studies of *play-based interventions* that fall within the scope of the Early Childhood Education Interventions for Children with Disabilities review protocol meet What Works Clearinghouse (WWC) evidence standards. The lack of studies meeting WWC evidence standards means that, at this time, the WWC is unable to draw any conclusions based on research about the effectiveness or ineffectiveness of *play-based interventions* on preschool children with disabilities in early education studies. Additional research is needed to determine the effectiveness or ineffectiveness of this intervention (U.S. Department of Education, What Works Clearinghouse, 2012, p. 1).

FUNCTIONAL BEHAVIORAL ASSESSMENT   A **Functional Behavioral Assessment** is used to understand underlying causes of inappropriate behavior by looking beyond obvious behavior interpretations to determine what function it might be serving for the child. The assessment is conducted by a behavioral specialist. The assessment then becomes the basis for a behavior intervention plan that is designed especially for a particular child, including children with disabilities (Mauro, 2017). The assessment uses a problem-solving process that is integrated with the process of using IEPs. A variety of techniques is used to identify the causes of the behavior. IDEA requires schools to use functional behavior assessment when addressing challenging behaviors in children with special needs.

The inappropriate behavior is examined to identify the purpose or function of the behavior. The child might be using the behavior to get something, avoid something, or make something happen. After the behavior and function are identified, the child is helped to succeed in a more positive, appropriate way (Bundrick, 2010; Jordan, 2006). There is good reason to believe that the success of behavior interventions that teach and promote appropriate replacement behaviors serve the same role as the problem behaviors (New Mexico Public Education Department Technical Assistance Manual: Addressing Student Behavior, 2010).

The process of using a Behavioral Assessment Plan and Behavioral Intervention Plan includes the following steps (New York State Education [NYSED], 2011):

1. Collect information on the problem behavior and the conditions when it is observed. It includes a description of the problem behavior and hypotheses as to why the behavior occurs.
2. Develop testable hypotheses about changing the problem behavior to an acceptable behavior.
3. Collect information through direct observation.
4. Develop a behavioral intervention plan.
5. Develop implementation strategies.
6. Develop a plan to measure the effectiveness of the intervention.

Functional Behavioral Assessment is similar to Event Sampling discussed later in the chapter. Both use a process identified as ABC analysis, but event sampling is a simpler method used with more common classroom behaviors.

Evaluating Learning Progress

After children have entered any type of early learning program or school setting, teachers need to acquire information on what they have learned from classroom instruction and learning activities. Although other strategies, such as teacher-designed tasks and standardized tests, are commonly used, observation is also a useful

Search and Share 7.1:

Functional Behavioral Assessments and Behavior Intervention Plans

Search online to find an example of a Functional Behavioral Assessment and a Behavioral Intervention Plan. After reviewing these examples, what aspects of each type of document do you feel are most important? What strategies would you use to implement this process in your local area?

tool, especially to understand the individual learning styles used by children. The teacher might use a planned observation such as the strategies described later in the chapter or an incidental observation that is employed when the teacher notices a child's activity or behavior that can provide insight into the child's learning. One effective type of activity is a performance activity whereby the child demonstrates learning through some type of performance, such as motor skills on the playground or the ability to put together a complex puzzle. This type of performance assessment will be discussed in more detail in Chapter 9.

A teacher can use Vygotsky's zone of proximal development (ZPD) in observations to determine the child's progress toward mastery of skills (Bodrova & Leong, 2007; McLeod, 2012). Vygotsky (1978) proposed that there is a range or zone between what the child cannot do, can do with assistance, and can do independently. The teacher observes the child's activities and works to determine where the child's progress lies in the ZPD. An example in kindergarten or first grade might be the student's ability to use fine motor skills to construct a model or make a collage. The teacher observes the child at work to determine the level of competency in drawing, cutting, and putting materials together to determine his or her ZPD in fine motor skills needed for the task.

Because what is observed must be interpreted, the observer must know how to use observation to gather specific data. Background information on how children develop and learn is important if the observer is to convert the child's behaviors into information that can be used to understand the child's level of development and the need for experiences that will further this development.

Obviously, the quality of the information gained from an observation depends on the skills of the observer. The sophisticated observer uses knowledge of developmental theories and stages of development to identify the significant events of an observation and to interpret these events in a way that is useful in understanding the child. For example, a teacher may notice that a child is exploring or playing with a collection of buttons by making a pile of all the buttons with four holes. Knowledge of Piaget's cognitive developmental theory enables the teacher to interpret this activity as the ability to classify objects.

Young children develop rapidly, and their level of development changes continually. By observing frequently, teachers can track the child's development and respond to changes and advances in development with new opportunities and challenges.

OBSERVATION TO IMPROVE THE CLASSROOM ENVIRONMENT AND INSTRUCTION Teachers of toddler groups closely observe to see what their children enjoy and take clues for adding to or changing the environment to reflect the children's interest in play. What teachers think children will do and how they interact with the environment can be very different. A teacher of toddlers was interested in generating an outdoor area especially for toddlers. A track was set up for wheeled toys, a variety of clothing articles for role-play were placed in a plastic container, and small vehicles were located nearby. To the teacher's surprise, the children did not ride or play with wheeled toys on the track. Instead, they took some headbands out of the clothes items, put them on, and jogged around the track as they had experienced with their parents. The teacher learned from her observation to respond to the children's interests and introduced additional items that might enhance role-play as well as physical play.

Seeing from the Child's Point of View

One morning, the toddler teacher brought a bucket full of sparkly plastic bracelets into the classroom. As she observed the children, they used the bracelets for several purposes. Some children waved the bracelets about and noticed how they glittered in the light. One child put as many bracelets on his arm as possible. Another child threw the bracelets on the floor so that they twirled in circles. After many practice throws, the child learned that they would spin like a top if he threw them in a certain way. Finally, some children just enjoyed taking the bracelets out of the bucket and then putting them back in over and over. As the teacher observed the children, and they observed each other, they learned new ideas about how they could play with the bracelets. The teacher learned more about individual children as they experimented with the bracelets. She used some of their ideas when the bracelets were introduced to the play environment again.

SOURCE: Curtis, D. (2006, November/December). No ordinary moments: Using observations with toddlers to invite further engagement. *Exchange, 172,* 36–40.

Enhanced eText: Self-Check 7.1

Types of Observation

What happens during an observation? What does the observer actually do? When conducting an observation, the student, teacher, or researcher visits a classroom or other place where a group of children may be observed as they engage in routine activities. The observer, having already determined the objectives or purpose of the observation, the time to be spent studying the child or children, and the form in which the observation will be conducted and recorded, sits at the side or in an observation booth and watches the children. The types of observations used include anecdotal records, running records, specimen records, time sampling, event sampling, and checklists and rating scales.

Anecdotal Record

An **anecdotal record** is a written description of a child's behavior. It is an objective account of an incident that tells what happened, when it happened, and where it happened. The record may be used to understand some aspect of behavior. A physician, parents, or a teacher may use anecdotal records to track the development of an infant or a young child in order to explain unusual behavior. Although the narrative itself is an objective description, comments may be added as an explanation or interpretation of the meaning of the recorded incident, and the comments are subjective because each observer will interpret the event from their individual perspective.

An anecdotal record tells the story of what an observer has seen. Anecdotal records have the following characteristics:

1. Anecdotes are a useful strategy for taking quick notes throughout the day.

2. Anecdotes are generally written in the past tense and can be written when the teacher has time.

3. When taking anecdotes, the date, time, place, and relevant background information are included.

4. Observers should avoid using too much interpretation so that future reflection is not inhibited (Higgens, 2011).

Figure 7-1 is an example of the form and content of an anecdotal record. Teachers can use anecdotal records in the classroom to record observed behaviors. The caregiver in an infant or toddler classroom might keep a daily logbook or index cards on a child's eating or health patterns or acquisition of a new skill to share with parents. A preschool teacher might use blank address labels to record significant or changing behaviors to note and place them in a child's folder. Likewise, a primary-grade teacher might note a child's daily work habits in the classroom on sticky notes to record and document the ability or inability to focus on tasks, dependency on others, or improvements in a child's social behavior (Fields, Groth, & Spangler, 2008; Morrison, 2013).

ADVANTAGES AND DISADVANTAGES OF USING ANECDOTAL RECORDS

Anecdotal records are quick and easy to use. It takes just a moment or two for the teacher to record the information that has been observed. The teacher can later reflect on the observation and its importance. A disadvantage of using anecdotal records is that they might not contain enough information for the teacher to analyze the content of the observation. Likewise, the teacher might overlook an important behavior while focusing on a target behavior. The teacher will also have to be creative when determining how to develop a system to keep the observations organized.

Figure 7.1 Example of an anecdotal record

Child Name(s): Robbie, Mary, Janie
Age: 4
Location: Sunnyside Preschool
Observer: Sue
Type of Development Observed: Social/Emotional
Date: October 5, 2015

Incident	Social/Emotional Notes or Comments
Mary and Janie were in the House-keeping Area pretending to fix a meal. Robbie came to the center and said he wanted to eat. The girls looked at him. Janie said, "You can't play here, we're busy." Robbie stood watching the girls as they moved plastic fruit on the table. Robbie said, "I could be the Daddy and do the dishes." Mary thought for a minute, looked at Janie, and replied, "Oh, all right, you can play."	The girls play together frequently and tend to discourage others from entering their play. Robbie has learned how to enter a play group. He was careful not to upset the girls. They relented when he offered to be helpful. Robbie is usually successful in being accepted into play activities.

Running Record

Using a **running record** is another method of recording behavior. It is a more detailed narrative of a child's behavior that includes the sequence of events. The running record includes everything that occurred over a period of time—that is, all behavior observed—rather than the particular incidents that are used for the anecdotal record. The description is objective. An effort is made to record everything that happened or was said during the observation period. Running records may be recorded over a period ranging from a few minutes to a few weeks or even months.

The observer comments on or analyzes the behaviors separately after studying the record. His or her task is to record the situation so that future readers can visualize what occurred (Wall, 2011). Figure 7-2 is an example of a running record.

Figure 7.2 Example of a running record

Child Name(s): <u>Christopher</u>
Age: <u>4</u>
Location: <u>KinderKare</u>
Date and Time: <u>June 21, 2017</u>   <u>8:40–9:10</u>
Observer: <u>Perlita</u>
Type of Development Observed: <u>Social and Cognitive</u>

Observation	Notes or Comments
Chris is playing with a toy. He says, "Kelly, can I keep it?" several times until he gets an answer. He moves on to a toy guitar and plays it while he supervises the other children by walking around the room. He tells everyone to sit down at the tables after the teacher says to.	Chris is polite to others. Chris is helping his classmates follow the rules.
Chris sits by a friend and talks about eating granola bars. He watches and listens to the conversation on either side of him. He's still unaffected by the loud temper tantrum of another child. Then he notices her and watches. He tries to explain this behavior to the others by saying a plant was spilled.	Chris is interested in what others have to say. Chris tries to make sense of a child's behavior.
He follows the teacher's directions. Then he decides he wants to be in on a secret. A boy shoves him away. Chris informs him that he *can* hear if he wants to. This has caused him to disobey the teacher. He has to sit out of the circle. He walks over to the chair, sits down, gets up immediately, and comes back to the circle undetected by the teacher. He joins the circle.	Chris chooses appropriate ways to assert himself.

Figure 7.2 (*Continued*)

Observation	Notes or Comments
Chris tattles on a child hiding money. He is told to switch places and wants to know why. He gets up to push the chairs under the table without being asked directly. He wants to explain the temper tantrum to another child (it is still going on) who is curious.	Chris needs to know why he does some things.
Chris attends to the teacher's questions and the story that she is now reading. He begins to look around the circle and then back to the book. He plays with his socks and participates in the group answers to questions about the story (*Now One Foot, Now the Other Foot* by Tomie dePaola [he is in continuous motion with some part of his body during the story]). Now he becomes very still and attends to the story. He puts both hands over his ears when students remark about events in the story. He immediately makes his own remarks. He becomes very still again. The whole circle is quiet for the ending of the book.	Chris shows he has self-control.

Chris responds to and sympathizes with the characters in the story. |
| As soon as the story is finished, Chris says, "I got a cut from a thorn bush." He sits very quietly but moves around. "How do we kill our plants over there?" he asks the teacher. (A plant was knocked off earlier.) "Not mine, not me!" he says. | |

Running records are also used to assess emergent literacy. When the teacher desires to acquire information about the child's current abilities and weaknesses in reading, the teacher may listen to the child read, and record errors and corrections that are made as the child reads the passage. The teacher might mark on a copy of the material that the child is reading and use a systematic method of identifying errors such as reversals, substitutions, self-corrections, or omissions. As an alternative, the teacher might use a running record form separate from the passage being read. The intent is to conduct an informal assessment when the child is actually reading.

Running records may be used for reading instruction. A teacher might observe a child's oral reading and write down unknown words, fluency changes, or difficulty in pronouncing some words. At the end of the reading activity, the teacher has needed information to help the child immediately and in succeeding instructional periods.

Marie Clay (1993) developed a standardized running record to document oral reading behaviors in the Reading Recovery Program. In this program, designed to detect and correct problems at early reading stages, checks are used to mark words read correctly, while a dash is used for words missed. Figure 7-3 shows an adaptation of a running record and analysis of errors in a story for beginning readers. The left-hand side of the page shows the sentences in the story. Errors, self-corrections, and strategies used for identifying words are recorded in the columns at the right-hand side of the page. The check marks on each line record words the child read correctly. Where one word is written above the other, the child either self-corrected the word or made an error. Figure 7-3 is a simple running record used with a beginning reader.

ADVANTAGES AND DISADVANTAGES OF USING RUNNING RECORDS   Running records are adaptable to different purposes, as demonstrated in Figure 7-2 and Figure 7-3. They include more information than an anecdotal record and provide a snapshot of what occurred over a period of time. Other interested staff members can use the information to better understand the child. A disadvantage is that this type of observation must be scheduled and time must be designated for this purpose. In the case of beginning reading, the observation can be built into instructional time. Other types of running record observations might be more difficult to manage.

Enhanced eText: Application Exercise 7.1

Figure 7.3 Example of a running record for beginning reading

SOURCE: Based on D. S. Seymour. (1965). *The Tent*. New York: Wonder Books.

Time Sampling

The purpose of **time sampling** is to record the frequency of a behavior for a designated period of time. The observer decides ahead of time what behaviors will be observed, what the time interval will be, and how the behaviors will be recorded. The observer records how many times a behavior occurs during preset, uniform time periods. Other behaviors that occur during the observation are ignored. After a number of samplings have been completed, the data are studied to determine when and perhaps why a behavior is occurring. The observer can use the information to help the child if a change in behavior is desired.

Time sampling may be used with young children because many of their behaviors are brief. By using time sampling, the observer can gain comprehensive information about the behavior. The length of the observation can be affected by the target behavior, the children's familiarity with the observer, the nature of the situation, and the number of children to be observed (Morrison, 2013; Beaty, 2014).

Teachers or other school staff members frequently use time sampling when a child is behaving inappropriately at school—for example, when a child behaves aggressively with other children and does not cooperate in classroom routines at certain times. It is used over a period of time during the hours of the daily schedule when the unwanted behavior occurs. After the time samples are studied, the teacher can determine what to do to modify the behavior. Figure 7-4 is an example of time sampling as an observation method.

Figure 7.4 Example of time sampling

Child Name(s): Joanie
Age: 5
Location: Rosewood School Kindergarten
Date and Time: May 17, 10:45–11:00
Observer: Susanna
Type of Development Observed: Joanie Has Difficulty Completing Tasks

Event	Time	Notes or Comments
Art Center—leaves coloring activity on table unfinished	10:45	Some of Joanie's behaviors seem to be resulting from failure to follow procedures for use of materials.
Library—looks at book, returns it to shelf.	10:50	
Manipulative Center—gets frustrated with puzzle, piles pieces in center—leaves on table. Pulls out Lego blocks, starts to play. When teacher signals to put toys away, Joanie leaves Lego blocks on table and joins other children.	10:55	Behavior with the puzzles may come from frustration.
	11:00	Joanie may need help in putting away with verbal rewards for finishing a task and putting materials away.
		Encourage Joanie to get help with materials that are too hard.

ADVANTAGES AND DISADVANTAGES OF USING TIME SAMPLING   The primary advantage of using time sampling is that the purpose is very clear. The teacher is concerned about a behavior and wants to observe the child to determine how often it occurs. The framework for the observation is planned ahead of time and only the target behavior is recorded. It also gives the teacher the opportunity to focus on what is happening without being distracted by other events occurring in the classroom. A disadvantage is that time for the observation may be difficult to manage on a regular timed schedule. It is a skill that has to be practiced and learned. Observing a behavior on the playground might be much easier than observing during classroom instruction.

Event Sampling

Event sampling is used instead of time sampling when a behavior tends to occur in a particular setting, rather than during a predictable time period. The behavior may occur at odd times or infrequently; event sampling is commonly used to discover its causes or results (Beaty, 2014). The observer determines when the behavior is likely to occur and waits for it to take place. The drawback of this method is that if the event does not occur readily, the observer's time will be wasted.

Because event sampling is a cause-and-effect type of observation, the observer is looking for clues that will help solve the child's problem. Bell and Low (1977) used *ABC analysis* with the observed incident to understand the cause of the behavior. *A* is the antecedent event, *B* is the target behavior, and *C* is the consequent event. Using ABC analysis with event sampling permits the observer to learn how to address the problem with the child. Figure 7-5 is an example of event sampling with ABC analysis to interpret the incident. Because event sampling is used typically for inappropriate behaviors, its primary usefulness is to determine the cause of the behavior and to address the problem. For example, Sheila, age 4, frequently approached the teacher on the playground because she had "nothing to do." The teacher assumed Sheila just

Figure 7-5 Example of event sampling

Child Name(s): <u>Tamika</u>
Age: <u>4</u>
Location: <u>May's Child Enrichment Center</u>
Date and Time: <u>2/4</u>   <u>2:30–3:30</u>
Observer: <u>Marcy</u>
Type of Development Observed: <u>Social/Emotional</u>
   Tamika uses frequent hitting behavior

Time	Antecedent Event	Behavior	Consequent Event
2:41	Tamika and Rosie are eating a snack. Rosie takes part of Tamika's cracker.	Tamika hits Rosie.	Rosie calls to the teacher.
3:20	John is looking at a book in the Library Center. Tamika asks for the book. John refuses.	Tamika grabs the book and hits John.	John hits back and takes back the book. Tamika gets another book and sits down.

Observing Bullying Behavior

Oscar enjoys teasing his fellow first-graders and challenging them to a fight. Although he usually picks on other boys in his own classroom, his teacher, Mary Oltorf, has been getting complaints from other teachers. Mary decides to observe how often Oscar exhibits this kind of behavior. She records how often Oscar bullies other children while supervising her class during recess. Each time Oscar uses an aggressive or teasing behavior, she marks down the time that it occurred and the behavior used. At the end of the recess period, she evaluates the frequency of Oscar's behavior and finds that he disturbed children five times during the play period. After making these observed time recordings every day for a week, she and the other teachers determine that Oscar bullies other children regularly, and they plan how to intervene and guide Oscar to more acceptable play behaviors. Mary found that she was vaguely aware that Oscar upset other children, but until she made a timed observation, she was not aware of how serious the problem was for Oscar and the other children on the playground.

wanted attention until she observed Sheila's play using the ABC process and realized that she approached the teacher after being rejected by her playmates. Moreover, the other girls had noticed that Sheila "tattled" to the teacher and enjoyed the success of their actions. By probing the cause of Sheila's difficulty in group play, the teacher realized that both Sheila and the other playmates needed to change their behaviors. She helped Sheila learn acceptable ways to be a part of the play group. At the same time, the other girls were redirected to more positive interactions with Sheila.

In the activity described below, the teacher did not observe Oscar at regular time intervals as shown in Figure 7-5. Instead, she marked the times that the targeted behavior occurred during the recess period each day. Nevertheless, she was able to record the frequency of Oscar's bullying behavior for a designated period of time.

Advantages and Disadvantages of Using Event Sampling

Like the time sampling observation, event sampling focuses on a particular purpose: to find out why a child uses a particular behavior. The teacher focuses on what triggers the behavior rather than on all behaviors. The teacher is able to anticipate when a behavior occurs and observe why it occurs. A disadvantage is that the targeted behavior may be difficult to anticipate and the time spent observing could be used for another purpose.

Search and Share 7.2:
Time Sampling vs. Event Sampling

Search online to locate examples of time sampling observations and event sampling observations. Contrast the similarities and differences of these two observation methods. And give an example of why you would use each one.

Checklists and Rating Scales

Although Chapter 8 is devoted to checklists and rating scales, it is useful to include checklists and rating scales in this discussion of observation techniques. A **checklist** is a list of sequential behaviors arranged in a system of categories. The observer can use the checklist to determine whether the child exhibits the behaviors or skills listed. The checklist is useful when many behaviors are to be observed. It can also be used fairly quickly and easily.

Figure 7-6 is an observation form that is adaptable to various types of observations. The summary of important behaviors at the bottom of the page can be expanded into a narrative report if desired. Narrative reports will be discussed in Chapter 11.

The **rating scale** provides a means to determine the degree to which the child exhibits a behavior or the quality of that behavior. Each trait is rated on a continuum, allowing the observer to decide where the child fits on the scale. Rating scales are helpful when the teacher needs to evaluate a wide range of behaviors at one time. For example, a rating scale of social skills might be used to record social behaviors not yet exhibited by a child in conjunction with an observation of social play. A checklist of independent work behaviors might be used during an observation of children in the classroom to identify problematic behaviors, such as attention seeking or actions used to delay completing assigned work.

Observations and Technology

In each of the types of observations discussed in this chapter, suggestions have been offered for how observations can be recorded and analyzed. With the constant evolution of new technologies, much of the observation results can be stored in an electronic form. Notebook computers, electronic tablets, and smartphones are becoming more powerful and lighter in weight. It is easier to keep such a device close at hand to record information. Observation forms can be transferred to an electronic device, with entries quickly typed in.

It is important to remember that parental permission is required prior to recording observations. Audio recordings are helpful when children's language is important to the observation. Instead of writing down what children say, the observer can use the audio recorder to document the language used. Later, the recording can be reviewed to analyze children's conversations.

Video recordings can also be helpful to augment an observation. Although the observer can record significant events during the observation, the video can provide opportunities for further study and analysis after the observation has been completed. It can also help in interpretation and analysis when several observers are working together. Smartphone and digital cameras are especially useful in displaying results of an observation for teachers and children to share together. This is an immediate response to observations that can then be printed out in a more permanent form for future use. A recent Seventh National Summit on Quality in Home Visiting Practices featured presentations on how videos can be used to support home visits. Attendees discussed ways that videos can support program goals (The Ounce.Org, 2018).

A newer electronic device is the digital whiteboard. The whiteboard is a large interactive display screen that can be connected to a computer or projector. The teacher can project observation information to share with parents and other teachers. Photo documentation can be displayed as well. The teacher can use a finger or digital pen to write or draw on the screen. Information displayed on the screen can be saved in the computer (Lisenbee, 2009).

Figure 7-6 Sample observation form

Name _____
Date _____
Time_____
Location _____
Child(ren) Observed _____

_____
Age(s) _____
Type of Development Observed: _____
Type of Observation Used: _____

Purposes of Observation:
1.
2.
3.

Questions Answered:
1.
2.
3.

Description of Observation (Anecdotal, Time Sampling, Running Record,
        Event Sampling):

Summary of Important Behaviors Recorded and Comments:

Photo documentation also can be effective in sharing examples of children's work and activities in the classroom. Face-to-face communications can be conducted through interactive computers. Programs such as Google+, Face Time, and Skype can be used for one-to-one or group interactions.

There is a concern about how much young children should be using technology. Some of the tools available to preschoolers besides television and smartphones can include video games, DVD and music players, web-based programming, and eReaders. Fifty-two percent of children aged birth to eight years old have access to a smartphone, tablet, or other electronic device (Epstein, 2015).

Benefits and Disadvantages of Using Technology for Observations

Electronic devices such as smartphones and electronic tablets of various sizes make recording observations an instant process. Notes can be made quickly without needing to carry a pen and pad of paper. Information can be shared among the electronic tools. Teachers now are very comfortable with smartphones, computers, and tablets. They can download observation forms into an electronic format and store information more effectively.

A possible problem with electronic recording and storage can be the question of security and privacy of the children in the teacher's records. It is always possible for information to fall into the wrong hands or an inappropriate location. If the school and district have a system for using electronic information, these problems can possibly be avoided. It is inevitable that electronic recording and storage will expand in the future. Future applications may be unknown, but they will be developed as technology continues to evolve.

Enhanced eText: Self-Check 7.2

Observing Development

Young children develop rapidly. At this time, we need to consider the meaning of development in more detail. Development is continuous and sequential and involves change over time. **Development** can be defined, in part, as the process of change in an individual over time. As the individual ages, certain changes take place. Development is thus affected by the child's chronological age, rate of maturation, and individual experiences. Children of the same chronological age are not necessarily at the same stage or level of development, possibly because they mature at different rates and have different experiences and opportunities. The child who has many opportunities to climb, run, and jump in outdoor play may demonstrate advanced motor development skills, compared to the child who spends most play periods indoors.

Developmental change can be both quantitative and qualitative. Physical growth is quantitative and cumulative. New physical skills are added to those already present. Developmental change can also be qualitative. When changes in psychological characteristics such as speech, emotions, or intelligence occur, development is reorganized at a higher level.

Development is characterized as continuous. The individual is constantly changing. In quantitative change, the individual is continually adding new skills or abilities. In qualitative change, the individual is incorporating new development with existing characteristics to create more sophisticated psychological traits. In the following sections, information is provided on how children can be observed using the four domains of development: physical development, social and emotional development, cognitive development, and language development.

Enhanced eText: Video Example 7.3

Physical Development

Preschool children are in the most important period of physical and motor development. Beginning with babies, who are in the initial stages of learning to control their bodies, physical development is rapid and continues into the primary school years.

Observations of physical development focus on both types of motor development: gross and fine motor skills. *Gross motor skills* involve the movements and abilities of the large muscles of the body in physical activities. Gross motor development includes locomotor dexterity movements that permit the child to move about in some manner, such as jumping, hopping, running, and climbing. This basic list can be extended to include rolling, creeping, crawling, stepping up and down, bouncing, hurdling, pumping a swing, galloping, and skipping. In the preschool years, gross motor skills advance from riding a tricycle to a bicycle. Some older preschoolers are able to roller-skate and kick a soccer ball (Head Start, 2003).

Fine motor skills involve the body's small muscles, specifically the hands and fingers. Preschool children gain more control of finger movement, which allows them to become more proficient in using materials that require grasping and manipulating. These skills are used for eating, dressing, writing, using small construction toys, and performing other tasks. Preschool children learn to work with puzzles; cut with scissors; use brushes, pens, pencils, and markers; and manipulate small blocks, counters, and modeling clay.

PURPOSES FOR OBSERVING PHYSICAL DEVELOPMENT Physical development is observed for the following reasons:

1. To learn how children develop gross and fine motor skills

2. To become familiar with the kinds of physical activities young children engage in as they practice the use of gross and fine motor skills

3. To become familiar with individual differences in physical development

QUESTIONS ANSWERED BY OBSERVATION OF PHYSICAL DEVELOPMENT
Physical development is observed to answer the following questions:

1. Observe a six-month-old baby. What gross motor movements do you see?

2. Observe a toddler. What gross motor skills have developed after the first year? Make a list.

3. Observe a child on the playground. What gross motor movements can you record?

4. What types of large motor activities does the child enjoy using play equipment?

5. Observe a child working or playing in activity centers in the classroom. What kinds of fine motor movements can you record?

6. Observe two children engaged in art activities. Can you see differences in fine motor development and dexterity? Describe them.

Social and Emotional Development

Social development and emotional development are significant areas of development during the early years. The infant shows the first signs of social interactions with parents, siblings, and other caregivers. Smiling is joined with intentional visual interactions and sounds. Later, the toddler who is mobile can physically approach other children and adults. In the preschool period, the child moves from egocentricity to social interaction with others. When a child is able to use social behaviors, he or she influences others and is influenced by them. As children interact in various contexts, they develop and expand their repertoire of social skills.

Emotional development parallels and affects social development. The preschool child refines behaviors as he or she experiences such emotions as happiness, anger, joy, jealousy, and fear. The most common emotions in preschool children are aggression, dependency, and fear (Bentzen, 2009). *Aggression* is a behavior intended to hurt another person or property. *Dependency* causes such behaviors as clinging; seeking approval, assistance, and reassurance; and demands for attention. *Fear* includes behaviors such as crying and avoiding the feared situation.

Important characteristics of social and emotional development are self-concept, self-esteem, and self-regulation of emotions. In self-concept, young children develop awareness that they are different from other children and have individual characteristics that are defined by mastery of skills and competencies (Berger, 2008; Berk, 2010).

Self-regulation of emotions results when children develop an awareness of their feelings and can initiate behaviors that permit them to cope. Self-esteem emerges when children begin to make judgments about their own worth and competencies. They feel they are liked or disliked depending on how well they can do things, and they are influenced by parental and peer approval or disapproval. They translate accomplishments and new skills into positive or negative feelings about themselves.

PURPOSES FOR OBSERVING SOCIAL AND EMOTIONAL DEVELOPMENT   Social and emotional development is observed for the following reasons:

1. To learn how children develop social skills
2. To become familiar with how children learn about social interactions
3. To understand how children differ in social skill development
4. To become familiar with the ways preschool children handle their emotions
5. To be aware of differences in children's emotional behaviors and responses

QUESTIONS ANSWERED BY OBSERVATIONS OF SOCIAL AND EMOTIONAL DEVELOPMENT   Social and emotional development are observed to answer the following questions:

1. Observe an infant between 4 months and 12 months old engaged with a parent. What social actions does the infant use to interact with the parent?
2. Watch a toddler playing in a group. What social behaviors does the toddler use with other children?
3. How has a preschool child demonstrated social awareness and prosocial skills?
4. How do children develop leadership skills? Observe a child who is able to lead peers in play and describe how that role was initiated.

5. How does the child resolve conflict? Observe children dealing with a problem and describe how the conflict was handled.

6. How do children use and handle aggressive behavior? Observe a child who is behaving aggressively. How does this child use aggression and what is the response of the victim?

7. What kinds of events trigger dependence or fear? Observe a child who has encountered either situation and describe how the child reacts.

Cognitive Development

Cognitive development, which stems from mental functioning, is concerned with how the child learns about and understands the world. Cognitive abilities develop as the child interacts with the environment. Our descriptions of cognitive development are derived largely from Piaget's theory of development.

Piaget described cognitive development in terms of stages. The quality of the child's thinking progresses as the child moves through the stages. The infant is in the sensorimotor stage from birth until about age 18 months. During this stage, intellectual growth occurs through the senses and innate reflexive actions. In the latter part of the sensorimotor stage, symbolic thought develops, which is characterized by improved memory.

Between ages 2 and 6, the child moves through the preoperational stage. In this stage, the ability to use language is developed. The child is egocentric, unable to view another person's perspective. Thinking is bounded by perception. Later, when the child reaches the stage of concrete operations, he or she is able to move beyond perceptual thinking. Cognitive abilities become qualitatively different. The child is now able to grasp concepts such as classification, seriation, one-to-one correspondence, and causality through conservation. For example, the child with conservation thinking can now understand that objects that are the same size and shape are still the same after one of the objects is given a different shape.

The child's use of mental processes to understand knowledge develops gradually, and cognitive abilities evolve over a long period of time. Piaget attributed cognitive development to maturity, experiences, and social transmission. Therefore, the child's family, environment, and opportunities for experiences affect the development of cognitive abilities. Knowledge is reconstructed as the child organizes and restructures experiences to refine and expand his or her own understanding.

PURPOSES FOR OBSERVING COGNITIVE DEVELOPMENT   Cognitive development is observed for the following reasons:

1. To understand how children use their cognitive abilities to learn

2. To understand the differences in children's cognitive styles

3. To become familiar with how children develop the ability to use classification, seriation, and one-to-one correspondence

4. To understand how children use play and interaction with materials to extend their cognitive abilities

5. To become familiar with how children think and what they are capable of learning

6. To evaluate what children have learned

QUESTIONS ANSWERED BY OBSERVATION OF COGNITIVE DEVELOPMENT
Cognitive development is observed to answer the following questions:

1. Observe an infant who is able to sit and grasp toys. What behaviors are used that indicate the child might be thinking?

2. Observe a toddler playing with toys in a group setting. What do you notice that indicates the child is thinking during play?

3. How is the child's learning affected by cognitive abilities? Observe two children and compare how they address an activity that requires solving a problem.

4. How does the child use emerging cognitive abilities? Find examples of children using conservation, one-to-one correspondence, or seriation and describe their activities.

5. How do children differ in cognitive development and cognitive characteristics? Observe two children who seem to have different levels of cognition and compare how they work with drawings, work a puzzle, or make a construction.

6. How do classroom experiences affect opportunities for cognitive development? Study learning centers in a preschool classroom and describe opportunities for learning.

7. How is a child's cognitive knowledge demonstrated nonverbally? Observe a child and describe how the child's actions reveal that learning is occurring or being applied to an activity.

Language Development

Acquisition of language is a major accomplishment of children during the preschool and primary-grade years. During the first eight years of life, the child rapidly acquires vocabulary, grammar, and syntax. As in other types of development, the child's use of language changes, increases, and is refined over a period of time.

Whereas babies begin using speech as single utterances, toddlers and preschoolers expand their repertoire into two words, three words, and increasingly complex statements. As the child's ability to use language expands to include questions and other grammatical elements, the child uses trial and error to more closely approximate the syntax and grammar of adult speech.

Language development is also related to cognitive development. When the child's thinking is egocentric, his or her language reflects this pattern. The egocentric child talks to herself or himself and does not use language to communicate with other children. The child who is shedding egocentric thinking uses socialized speech to communicate with others. He or she not only shares conversations with peers and adults, but also listens and responds to what others are saying.

During the preschool years, young children learn about 10,000 words. Concurrent with the acquisition of a remarkable number of words, they learn the rules of their language: morphology rules, syntax rules, and semantic rules. Morphology and syntax rules relate to understanding the sounds and grammar of language, and semantic rules explain vocabulary and meaning development.

Preschool children also learn the rules of conversation, or the pragmatics of language. The ability to participate in a conversation develops at an early age and is extended and refined with expanded language abilities and experiences with conversations. By age 4, preschool children understand how to carry on a conversation in their language, community, and culture.

PURPOSES FOR OBSERVING LANGUAGE DEVELOPMENT   Language
development is observed for the following reasons:

1. To become aware of the child's ability to use language to communicate
2. To understand the difference between egocentric and socialized speech
3. To learn how the child uses syntax, grammar, and vocabulary in the process of expanding and refining his or her language
4. To become aware of differences in language development among individual children, particularly children from homes where another language or dialect is spoken
5. To determine how children are progressing in learning English as their second language and to determine their individual needs for language experiences
6. To determine a child's dominant language when placed in a bilingual program (Which language does the child use in the classroom, with friends at school, and at home?)

QUESTIONS ANSWERED BY OBSERVATION OF LANGUAGE DEVELOPMENT
Language development is observed to answer the following questions:

1. How does an infant communicate before words can be used?
2. Observe a toddler when talking. How many words can the child put together to communicate?
3. How does the child use language to communicate? Describe how two different children use language to communicate with a friend.
4. When do children tend to use egocentric speech? Socialized speech? Describe events when children use each type.
5. What can be observed about the child's use of sentence structure? Record several of a child's utterances and describe the sentence structure used.
6. How can errors in the use of language reveal the child's progress in refining language? Record some child conversations. Describe utterances that reveal an error that will later be expressed correctly.

Enhanced eText: Self-Check 7.3

Advantages and Disadvantages of Using Observation for Assessment

Observation is a valuable evaluation tool. Teachers may use it to gather the kind of information that may not be available from structured methods of measurement.

When observed, children are engaged in daily activities that are a natural part of the classroom routine. The observer sees the typical ways children respond to learning tasks, play activities, and individual and group lessons. The observer can notice the child's behaviors and the background factors that influence the behaviors.

Learning can also be evaluated by observation. The teacher can observe the child's responses in a group during a lesson or while the child engages in exploration with construction materials. Areas of development such as gross motor skills can be observed on the playground, and language skills can be noted by listening to the language of two children in the art center.

An advantage of observation is that the observer can focus on the behavior or information that is needed. If a child is exhibiting aggression, the observer can focus on aggressive incidents to help the child to use more appropriate behaviors in interactions with other children. If a child is beginning to use prosocial skills more effectively, the teacher can observe group interactions and encourage the child to continue to improve.

Although observation allows one to concentrate on specific behaviors, it can also cause difficulties. The observer can miss details that make a significant difference in the quality of the data gathered. Because many incidents and behaviors may occur during the observation, the danger is that the observer may focus on the wrong behaviors. Or the observer may become less attentive during the observation period, resulting in variations in the information obtained.

Observation bias is another disadvantage. If the observer has preconceived notions about how the child behaves or performs, these ideas can affect the observer's interpretation of the information obtained from watching the child.

Observations can be misleading when the incident observed is taken out of context. Although an observed behavior is often brief, it must be understood in context. For example, the observer who witnesses a teacher losing patience with a child may interpret the incident as that teacher's normal behavior. In reality, however, this behavior may be rare. The presence of the observer can also affect children's behavior. Because children are aware that they are being watched, their behaviors may not be typical. As a result, the validity of the observation may be doubtful (Bentzen, 2009).

Observation Guidelines

For college students and teachers who have limited experience in conducting observations or wish to improve their observation skills, certain guidelines are now presented. The student seeking a site for observation needs to know how to go about finding a school or early childhood center and how to observe effectively once it has been selected. Classroom teachers have a ready site in their own classroom or in the classroom of a colleague. However, teachers may want to observe a different type of program and may need to visit a different setting. Although observation is valuable for many reasons, it is usually the least used evaluation method by teachers because of time constraints. Therefore, new teachers may need specific training on how to accomplish successful observation times.

Determining the Observation Site

The observation site depends on the type of observation to be done. First, the observer must determine the purpose of the observation. He or she will want to know that children at the school or early childhood center engage in the activities of interest to the observer. For example, if the observer wishes to see activities typical of a Montessori classroom, it would be wise to find out whether these activities will be taking place during the observation period. Once the purpose of the observation has been determined, the observer must decide on an optimum location. If the objective is to learn about creativity in the young child, it is frustrating to spend time in a program in which art experiences are limited or infrequent. Likewise, if the purpose is to observe behaviors in a child-centered environment, it would be inappropriate to visit a structured program directed by the teacher.

After the center or school has been selected, the observer should contact it ahead of time. Although many settings welcome observers on a walk-in basis, most early childhood programs request or require advance notification. Some settings do not allow observers or schedule them in ways designed to protect children from interruptions. Some schools allow observations on certain days. Others wish to be contacted well in advance because many people wish to observe their program. Many child-care centers schedule field trips frequently and wish to avoid inconveniencing their observers. Whatever the reason, it is best to contact the observation site before scheduling the observation.

Observer Behaviors during the Observation Visit

The observer is a guest of the center or school. Although the opportunity to study the children is important, it is also important to avoid disrupting activities in progress. The observer may want to share the purpose of the observation with staff members or the teacher in the classroom being visited. In addition, the observer should conduct the observation in a manner that is compatible with the teacher's style of leadership in the type of program being observed. For example, Montessori schools frequently restrict visitors to certain areas of the classroom and may discourage any interaction with the children. Another school or program may encourage the observer to talk to the children or to take part in their activities.

Most schools and preschool centers require that all who will be working in the building undergo a background check. In addition, observers are required to check in at the office when arriving at the location to be observed. Identification badges are usually required so that the observer's approved presence is readily apparent to teachers and other staff members.

In most cases, the observer should be unobtrusive. Because children are sensitive to the presence of visitors and may alter their behaviors when a stranger is in the room, observers can minimize such changes by drawing as little attention to their presence as possible. Observers may seat themselves in a position that does not draw the children's attention. Sometimes it is helpful to avoid looking at the children for a few minutes, until they become acclimated. Postponing the writing of observation notes for a few minutes may also help prevent disruption.

Dress can make a difference. Observers dressed in simple clothing of one color rather than bright garments with bold patterns are less likely to draw undue attention to their presence. Dress should also be appropriate. Clothing that is too casual may be offensive to the adults in the early childhood center. Observers should err on the side of being dressed too formally, rather than in an unprofessional manner.

Ethics during the Observation Visit

Observers must be alert to the proper way to use the information gathered during an observation. The privacy of the children, the children's families, and school staff members must be considered. When individual children are observed, only the child's first name should be used. Information from any observation should be considered confidential and safeguarded from casual perusal by others. The child should not be discussed in an unprofessional manner with other observers, school staff members, or outsiders. The child should not be discussed when the child is present. It may be necessary to obtain permission from the child's family prior to making an observation. If this is necessary, the observer should acquire the necessary forms and have them sent to the parents for their approval prior to conducting any observations.

Teachers in training and professional teachers should be very aware of the ethics of the profession. The NAEYC position statement or *NAEYC Code of Ethical Conduct and Statement of Commitment* (2011) is a comprehensive document that serves as a professional guide for ethical behavior. It has sections on ethical responsibilities to children, to families, to colleagues, and to community and society. Each section has description of principles that give examples of indicators for that section. Individuals engaged in conducting observations can find many items that refer to ethical behaviors.

Avoiding Personal Bias

Personal bias can affect the observer's reaction to, and report of, an observation. If observers are aware of how their background and previous experiences can influence their report, they can avoid using personal opinion when analyzing the data collected during an observation.

One cause of observer bias is differences in value systems. It is easy to apply one's own value system when observing in a school. For example, a middle-class observer may misunderstand the nature of aggression exhibited by young children in an inner-city school. It is also possible to impose personal values on the language of a child from a home where cursing is a common form of communication. The observer can be biased about a child's home life or family issues. Bias against poverty and ethnicity can affect the observer's objectivity. The observer needs to be aware of such possible biases and avoid them when interpreting observational information.

The observer's reaction to the site can also distort his or her use of observational data. Each observer has a perception of the characteristics of a "good" school or center. When observing an early childhood program that does not fit this definition, the observer may impose a negative interpretation on the information gathered. The reaction to the setting affects how the observer perceives the behaviors observed.

An observation can also be biased by the time of the observation or by the briefness of the visit. Observers frequently react to a teacher's behavior and conclude that the teacher always engages in practices that the observer considers inappropriate. Observers need to understand that what they see during a short visit may give them an incomplete, distorted perception of the teacher or setting. The observer would have to make many visits during different times of the day over a long period of time before being able to draw conclusions about the quality of teaching or the environment. One or two brief observations provide only a small glimpse of the nature of the teacher and the classroom visited.

Enhanced eText: Self-Check 7.4

Summary

Although standardized tests are used to evaluate children's learning, informal assessment strategies are also essential, particularly for use by classroom teachers. They provide a variety of evaluation methods by which teachers can acquire comprehensive information about their students' development and learning.

Observation is used to assess learning and to gather information regarding children's development. Because young children cannot demonstrate knowledge in a written test, teachers of preschool children use observation to learn about children's development, as well as about the knowledge the children have acquired.

Observations are of several types, each with a specific purpose. Observers can use anecdotal records, running records, time sampling, event sampling, and checklists and rating scales to gather information about young children.

Observation of young children who are learning English or have disabilities afford the observer insight into the nature of their development and how they can be helped to make developmental progress. Often the inappropriate behavior of some children masks some need that they have. Sometimes they are seeking attention and do not know how to approach the teacher or another child in a positive manner. Behavioral intervention practices can assist each child to learn how to interact more appropriately.

Enhanced eText: Self-Check: Chapter Review

Key Terms

anecdotal record 164

checklist 172

development 174

event sampling 170

functional behavioral assessment 161

play-based assessment 159

play-based intervention 160

rating scale 172

running record 166

time sampling 169

Organizations

Search for the following organizations online:

Center for Effective Collaboration and Practice Functional Behavioral Assessment

Earlychildhood NEWS

Frank Porter Graham Child Development Institute

Pearson Achievement Solutions

National Association for the Education of Young Children

The IRIS Center/Vanderbilt University

TESOL International Association

References

Beaty, J. J. (2014). *Observing development of the young child* (8th ed.). Upper Saddle River, NJ: Pearson.

Bell, D., & Low, R. M. (1977). *Observing and recording children's behavior.* Richland, WA: Performance Associates.

Bentzen, W. R. (2009). *Seeing young children: A guide to observing and recording behavior* (6th ed.). Belmont, CA: Wadsworth.

Berger, K. S. (2008). *The developing person through childhood and adolescence* (6th ed.). New York, NY: Worth.

Berk, L. E. (2010). *Infants, children, and adolescents* (7th ed.). Upper Saddle River, NJ: Pearson.

Bodrova, E., & Leong, D. J. (2007). *Tools of the mind: The Vygotskian approach to early childhood education* (2nd ed.). Upper Saddle River, NJ: Merrill/Prentice Hall.

Brookes Publishing. (2002, July). Newsletter Archive. *Using transdisciplinary play-based assessment: Structuring a play session.* Retrieved October 20, 2009, from http://www.brookespublishing.com/email/archive . . . july02EC4.htm

Bundrick, L. (2010, April 5). Functional behavior assessments & behavior intervention plans. *The New Social Worker.* Retrieved from http://www.socialworker.com/feature-articles-practice/function

Centers for Disease Control and Prevention. (2014, March 11). *Developmental monitoring and screening for health professionals.* Retrieved from http://eee.vrv.hob/ncbddd/childdevelopment/screening-hcp.html

Centers for Disease Control and Prevention. (2017). *Developmental monitoring and screening.* Retrieved from https://www.cdc.gov/ncbddd/childdevelpment/screening.html

Cherney, I. C., Kelly-Vance, L., Gill-Glover, K., Ruane, A., & Ryalls, B. O. (2003). The effects of stereotyped toys and gender on play assessment in children 18–47 months. *Educational Psychology, 23,* 95–106.

Clay, M. (1993). *An observation survey of early literacy achievement.* Portsmouth, NH: Heinemann.

Cohen, D. H., Stern, V., & Balaban, N. (1997). *Observing and recording the behavior of young children* (4th ed.). New York, NY: Teachers College Press.

Cordier, R., Bundy, P., Hocking, C., & Enfield, S. (2009, October). A model for play-based intervention for children with ADHD. *Australia Occupational Therapy Journal, 56,* 332–340.

Cummins, J. (1981) The role of primary language development in promoting educational success for language minority students. In California State Department of Education (Ed.), *Schooling and language minority students: A theoretical framework.* Evaluation, Dissemination and Assessment Center, California State University, Los Angeles.

Cummins, J. (2000). *Language, power, and pedagogy. Bilingual children in the crossfire.* Clevedon, England: Multilingual Matters.

Curtis, D. (2006, November/December). No ordinary moments: Using observations with toddlers to invite further engagement. *Exchange, 172,* 36–40.

Epstein, A. S. (2015, February 3). *Using technology appropriately in the preschool classroom.* Retrieved from. www.ChildCareExchange.com

Fewell, R., & Glick, M. (1998). The role of play in assessment. In D. Fromberg & D. Bergen (Eds.), *Play from birth to twelve and beyond* (pp. 202–207). New York, NY: Garland.

Fields, M. V., Groth, L., & Spangler, K. L. (2008). *Let's begin reading right: A developmental approach to emergent literacy* (6th ed.). Upper Saddle River, NJ: Pearson.

Flagler, S. (1996). *Infant-Preschool Assessment Scale.* Chapel Hill, NC: CHTOP.

Forman, G., & Hall, E. (2005). Wondering with children: The importance of observation in early education. *Early Childhood Research and Practice, 7,* 1–12.

Frost, J. L., Wortham, S., & Reifel, S. (2008). *Play and child development* (3rd ed.). Upper Saddle River, NJ: Pearson.

Gleason, D. (2010, October). *Observations of learning styles of infants and toddlers with visual impairments or deafblindness: Using information about how children learn to plan effective intervention.* Austin, TX: Texas School for the Blind and Visually Impaired. Retrieved from http://www.tdbvi.rfu/trdoutvrd/2267-observations-of-learning-styles

Groard, C. J., Mchaffie, K. E., McCall, R. B., & Greenberg, M. I. (Eds.). (2007). *Evidence-based practices and program for early childhood care and education.* Thousand Oaks, CA: Corwin Press.

Gronlund, G., & James, M. (2013). Focused observations: How to observe young children for assessment and curriculum planning. 2nd ed. St. Paul: Redleaf Press.

Head Start. (2003). Domain 8: Physical health and development. *The Head Start Leaders' guide to positive child outcomes.* Washington, DC: Author.

Higgins, N. (2011, February 26). *Back to basics—A brief summary of early childhood observation methods and techniques.* Retrieved from http://www.raiselearning.com.au/blogs/news/2765692-back-tobasics

Hindman, A. H., & Wasik, B. A. (2015). Building vocabulary in two languages: An examination of Spanish-speaking dual language learners in Head Start. *Early Childhood Research Quarterly, 31,* 19–33.

Jablon, J. (2010/2012). Taking it all in: Observation in the classroom. *Teaching Young Children, 4,* 24–27.

Jordan, D. (2006). *Functional behavioral assessment and positive interventions: What parents need to know.* Retrieved from http://www.pacer.org/parent/php-c29.pdf

Kelly-Vance, L., & Ryalls, B. L. (2008). Best practices in play assessment and intervention. *National Association of School Psychologists. Best Practices in School Psychology,* Chapter 3.

Le Pichon, E., & de Jonge, M. (2016). Linguistic and psychological perspectives on prolonged periods of silence in dual-language learners. *International Journal of Bilingual Education and Bilingualism, 19,* 426–441.

Linder, T. W. (1993). *Transdisciplinary play-based assessment (TPBA): A functional approach to working with young children* (Rev. ed.). Baltimore, MD: Brookes.

Linder, T. W. (1998). *Transdisciplinary play-based assessment* (Rev. ed.). Baltimore, MD: Brookes.

Linder, T. (2010). *Observing Kassandra DVD: A transdisciplinary play-based assessment of a child with severe disabilities* (Rev. Ed.). Baltimore, MD: Brookes Publishing.

Lisenbee, P. (2009, November). Whiteboards and Websites. *Young Children, 64,* 92–95.

MacDonald, B. (2006, November/December). Observation—The path to documentation. *Exchange, 172,* 45–49.

McLeod, S. (2012). *Zone of proximal development.* Retrieved from http://www.simiplypsychologoy.org/Zone-of-Proximal-Development.html

Mauro, T. (2017, December 22). *Functional behaviour assessment for classroom problems.* Retrieved from https://www.verywell.com/what-is-an-fba?

Morrison, G. S. (2013). *Fundamentals of early childhood education* (7th ed.). Upper Saddle River, NJ: Pearson.

National Association for the Education of Young Children. (2011). *NAEYC code of ethical conduct and statement of commitment. A position statement of the National Association for the Education of Young Children.* Washington, DC: Author.

National Association for the Education of Young Children (NAEYC) & National Association of Early Childhood Specialists in State Departments of Education (NAECS/SDE). (2005). *Joint position statement on early childhood curriculum, assessment, and program evaluation.* Washington, DC: NAEYC.

National Association of School Psychologists. (2005). *Position statement on early childhood assessment.* Bethesda, MD: Author. Retrieved from http://naponline.org/about_nasp/pospaper/cca.aspx

New Mexico Public Education Department. (2010). *Addressing student behavior: A guide for all educators.* Retrieved from http://ped.state.nm.us/RtI/dl10/Addressing%20Student%20Behavior%20Guide%202010.pdf

New York State Department of Education (NYSED). (2011, May). Behavioral intervention plans: Special Education: AMSC: NYSED. Retrieved from http://www.p.2.nysed.gov/specialed/publications/topicalbriefs/B.n

O'Neill, B. E. (2013, July). Improvisational play interventions: Fostering social-emotional development in inclusive classrooms. *Young Children, 68,* 62–89.

Pelo, A. (2006, November/December). Growing a culture of inquiry: Observation as professional development. *Exchange, 172,* 50–53.

Soltero, S. (2014). *English language learners: Teacher and leadership guide.* Chicago, IL: Logan Square Neighborhood Association, lsha.net.

The IRIS Center/Vanderbilt University. (2018). *What do teachers need to know about students who are learning to speak English?: Second language acquisition.* Retrieved from https://iris.peabody.vanderbilt.edu/module/ell/cresource/q1/p02/#content

theounce.org. (2018). *Using technology & observation to support effective home visiting practices.* Retrieved from https://www.theounce.org/sessions/using-technology-observation-su . . .

U.S. Department of Education, Institute of Education Sciences, What Works Clearinghouse. (2012, April). *Early childhood interventions for children with disabilities: Intervention report: Play-based interventions.* Retrieved from http://whatworks.ed.gov

U.S. Department of Health and Human Services. (2014, March). *Birth to five: Watch me thrive! / A compendium of screening measures for young children.*

Vygotsky, L. S. (1978). *Mind and society:The development of higher mental processes.* Cambridge, MA: Harvard University Press.

Wall, K. (2011). *Special needs and early years: A practitioner guide.* Thousand Oaks, CA: Sage Publications.

WETA (2018). *Early identification-observation of an individual child.* Retrieved from http:www.ldonline.org/article/6048

Wilkes, S., Cordier, R., Bunday, A., Docking, K., & Munro, N. (2011). A play-based intervention for children with ADHD: A pilot study. *Australia Occupational Therapy Journal, 58,* 231–240.

Chapter 8
Checklists, Rating Scales, and Rubrics

Stylephotographs/123RF

 ## Chapter Learning Outcomes

As a result of reading this chapter, you will be able to:

8.1 Discuss how checklists are designed and used with young children.

8.2 Describe types of rating scales and how they are used with young children.

8.3 Explain the types of rubrics and how they are designed and used with young children.

In this chapter, we discuss additional types of evaluation strategies that involve the use of teacher-designed instruments: checklists, rating scales, and rubrics. Because checklists are used more extensively than rating scales by infant–toddler, early childhood, and primary school teachers, we discuss them first. A description of rating scales follows, so that the reader can understand how they are designed and used and how they differ from checklists. Rubrics are used most commonly with performance assessments. They will be discussed in that context.

How Checklists Are Designed and Used with Young Children

Checklists are made from a collection of learning objectives or indicators of development. The lists of items are arranged to give the user an overview of their sequence and of how they relate to each other. The lists of items are then organized into a checklist format so that the teacher can use them for various purposes in the instructional program. Because checklists are representative of the curriculum for a particular age level, they become a framework for assessment and evaluation, instructional planning, record keeping, and communicating with parents about what is being taught and how their child is progressing.

Using Checklists with Infants, Toddlers, and Preschool Children

Children in the years from birth to age 8 move rapidly through different stages of development. Doctors, psychologists, parents, and developmental specialists want to understand and monitor the development of individual children and groups of children. The developmental indicators for children at different stages and ages have been established, and lists and checklists of these milestone indicators can be used to monitor development. Many types of professionals use a **developmental checklist** format to evaluate a child's development and record the results. Several national organizations have produced infant development checklists that are readily available to parents and professionals (Centers for Disease and Control and Prevention, 2014; Mid-State Early Childhood Direction Center, Syracuse University, 2012). Infant checklists are described in terms of milestones that become developmental indicators in checklists for older infants and toddlers (Centers for Disease Control and Prevention, 2014).

Developmental checklists for young children are usually organized into areas of development: physical, cognitive, language, and social and emotional. Physical development is frequently organized into fine motor skills and gross motor skills. Cognitive, or intellectual, development might include language development. Some checklists have language development as a separate category. Social development checklists can also be organized to include emotional development and development of social skills. Figure 8-1 shows developmental milestones at 6 months.

When a special needs population is being assessed, adaptive developmental skills such as feeding skills, dressing skills, etc., are part of the checklist. As checklists have become popular their use is expanding. The Early Childhood Direction Center at Syracuse University developmental checklist for birth to age 5 includes developmental red flags to guide parents in how to identify indicators of developmental delay. For example, the developmental red flags between 4 to 7 months can include not rolling over from stomach to back or not actively reaching for an object by 6 months (Mid-State Early Direction Center, Syracuse University, 2012). The California School for the Deaf has developed a checklist using American Sign Language (ASL) to track sign language development between birth and 6 years (California School for the Deaf, n.d.).

Preschool teachers use checklists to evaluate and record preschoolers' developmental progress. The individual child's developmental progress provides important clues to the kinds of experiences he or she needs and can enjoy. For instance, the teacher may monitor the child's use of fine motor skills. After the child is able to use

Figure 8.1 Important milestones at six months

Important Milestones: Your Baby at Six Months
What most babies do at this age:

Social and Emotional

- Knows familiar faces and begins to know if someone is a stranger
- Likes to play with others, especially parents
- Responds to other people's emotions and often seems happy
- Likes to look at self in a mirror

Language/Communication

- Responds to sounds by making sounds
- Strings vowels together when babbling ("ah," "eh," "oh") and likes taking turns with parent while making sounds
- Responds to own name
- Makes sounds to show joy and displeasure
- Begins to say consonant sounds (jabbering with "m," "b")

Cognitive (learning, thinking, problem-solving)

- Looks around at things nearby
- Brings things to mouth
- Shows curiosity about things and tries to get things that are out of reach
- Begins to pass things from one hand to the other

Movement/Physical Development

- Begins to sit without support
- When standing, supports weight on legs and might bounce
- Rocks back and forth, sometimes crawling backward before moving forward

SOURCE: Centers for Disease Control and Prevention. (2014). Important milestones: Your baby at six months. Retrieved from http://www.cdc.gov/ncbddd/actearly/milestones/milestones-6mo.html

the fingers to grasp small objects, cutting activities may be introduced. In language development, the teacher may evaluate the child's speaking vocabulary and use of syntax and thus choose the best stories to read to the child.

Teachers sometimes use checklists to screen children who enter preschool programs. Developmental or cognitive tasks, including adaptive skills, are used to better understand the strengths and emerging skills of children, and the challenges of children with special needs. Because these checklists include behaviors that are characteristic of a stage of development, children who do not exhibit these behaviors can be referred for additional screening and testing (National Training Institute for Child Care Health Consultants, 2010).

Checklists are also used to design learning experiences at the preschool level. The teacher surveys the list of learning objectives appropriate for that age group of children and uses the list to plan learning activities in the classroom. These checklists can be used to assess the child's progress in learning the objectives and to keep records of progress and further instructional needs. When talking to parents about the instructional program, the teacher can discuss what is being taught and how their child is benefiting from the learning experiences.

Using Checklists with School-Age Children

The use of checklists for primary-grade children is very similar to their use with preschool children. In fact, curriculum checklists can be a continuation of those used in the preschool grades to monitor progress. However, there are two differences. First, fewer developmental characteristics are recorded, and cognitive or academic objectives become more important. Second, school-age checklists become more differentiated in areas of learning. Whereas teachers are concerned with motor development, language development, social and emotional development, and cognitive development at the preschool level, at the primary level, curriculum content areas become more important. Thus, with primary-grade checklists, objectives are more likely to be organized in terms of mathematics, language arts, science, social studies, and physical education (Centers for Disease Control and Prevention, 2014; Gerber, Wilks, & Erdie-Lalena, 2010). Checklists that can be used quickly are a particular advantage to classroom teachers because of time restraints in the daily schedule.

Curriculum objectives become more important in the primary grades, and assessment of progress in learning may become more precise and segmented. Checklist objectives may appear on report cards as the format for reporting the child's achievement to parents. Likewise, the checklist items may be representative of achievement test objectives, state-mandated objectives, textbook objectives, and locally selected objectives.

Using Checklists to Assess Children with Special Needs

Checklists can be used with children who have exhibited developmental delays and who are served in intervention programs. The components of such a system include tracking the child's growth and development through ongoing assessment, documenting and monitoring child growth for caregivers and other professional staff, and providing a structure for families to develop and monitor goals for their children (Centers for Disease Control and Prevention, 2014). Checklists in this context can be used with a family portfolio, developmental guidelines and checklists, and summary reports of the child's progress. Because children with disabilities—especially those with moderate to severe disabilities—may progress at a slower rate than children with typical development, and gifted children may progress faster, checklists can be especially effective at monitoring children's progress in smaller increments. The ASL Stages of Development describes the steps that deaf infants and young children go through as they develop the ability to use signing (California School for the Deaf–Fremont, n.d.). Figure 8-2 shows American Sign Language stages of development from 3 months to 2 years. The ASL scale continues on to 6 years.

Enhanced eText: Video Example 8.1

Using Checklists to Assess English Language Learners (ELLs)

Checklists can be used to understand the first and second language development of children who are English language learners (ELLs). Checklists can be part of an integrated assessment system already used in the classroom setting that has multiple purposes, including continuous assessment of children's language development progress.

Figure 8.2 ASL stages of development

3 to 12 months

- Begins to notice signing
- First sign may emerge from 10 to 12 months
- Babbles with hands
- Points to people, objects, and places but not at self

12 to 18 months

- Uses at least 10 signs
- Begins to use points as pronouns
- Acquires new signs but does not mark with inflections

18 months to 24 months

- Signs reflect basic handshapes with simple movements (straight forward, up, or down)
- Early signs not always produced according to adult conventional forms
- Combines 2 or 3 signs including points
- Begins to distinguish and use non-manual markers (facial grammar)

SOURCE: California School for the Deaf (n.d.) *ASL Stages of Development Checklist*. Fremont Early Childhood Education Department, Fremont, CA.

An initiative sponsored by the U.S. Department of Education is called the Sheltered Instruction Observation Protocol (SIOP) model. The focus of this model was originally to develop an observation tool used by researchers to understand teachers' implementation of sheltered instruction techniques. It later grew into an approach for lesson planning. SIOP includes 30 features of instruction for ELLs with eight components—Lesson Preparation, Building Background, Comprehensible Input, Strategies, Interaction, Practice & Application, Lesson Delivery, and Review & Assessment (Kareva1 & Echevarria, 2013).

How Checklists Are Designed

Checklists of developmental and instructional objectives have been used in education for several decades. Educators and early childhood specialists worked with Head Start and other professional educational organizations to describe the framework of learning that children should experience. Since that time, checklists have been further

Search and Share 8.1

Sheltered Instruction Observation Protocol (SIOP)

Search online to find information on the Sheltered Instruction Observation Protocol (SIOP) model, including lesson-planning checklists. What types of skills do they include? How could you use this model with preschool or kindergarten children?

developed and used at all levels of education. Reading series designed for elementary grades include a scope and sequence of skills, and many school districts have a list of objectives for every course or grade level. The scope of a curriculum is the different categories that are included, while the sequence is the individual objectives that appear under each category.

Steps in Designing Checklists

A checklist is an outline or framework of development and curriculum. When designing a checklist, the developer first determines the major categories that will be included. Thereafter, development follows four basic steps:

1. Identification of the skills to be included
2. Separate listing of target behaviors
3. Sequential organization of the checklist
4. Record keeping

IDENTIFICATION OF THE SKILLS TO BE INCLUDED   The teacher studies each checklist category and determines the specific objectives or skills to be included. Using established developmental norms or learning objectives, the teacher decides how to adapt them for his or her needs. For example, on a checklist for language development and reading under the category of language and vocabulary, the following objectives might be included:

Listens to and follows verbal directions

Identifies the concept of *word*

Identifies the concept of *letter*

Invents a story for a picture book

SEPARATE LISTING OF TARGET BEHAVIORS   If a series of behaviors or items is included in an objective, the target behaviors should be listed separately so that they can be recorded separately. For the objective of identifying coins, the best way to write the item would be as follows:

Identifies:

Penny

Nickel

Dime

Quarter

When the teacher is assessing the child's knowledge of coins, he or she may find that the child knows some of the coins but not others. Information can be recorded on the mastery status of each coin such as *developing* or *mastered*.

SEQUENTIAL ORGANIZATION OF THE CHECKLIST   The checklist should be organized in a sequential manner. Checklist items should be arranged in order of difficulty or complexity. If the checklist is sequenced correctly, the order of difficulty should be obvious. For example, the ability to count on a mathematics checklist might be listed as "Counts by rote from 1 to 10." At the next higher level, the checklist item would be "Counts by rote from 1 to 50."

Conflicts about Informal Assessment Results

Mary Howell and Francesca Carrillo are having a heated argument in the teachers' lounge. Mary teaches first grade, and Francesca teaches second grade. At issue is the checklist from the first grade that is placed in students' folders at the end of the year, before they are promoted to second grade. Francesca's complaint is that the first-grade teachers' assessments are inaccurate. They have indicated that students accomplished first-grade objectives, but these objectives have to be retaught in the second grade because the students either never knew them or forgot them over the summer.

Mary clearly is offended that her professionalism has been questioned. She defends the process by which first-grade teachers determine whether the children have learned the objectives. Josie, another teacher sitting nearby, says nothing. Under her breath, she mutters, "It's all a waste of time. I wait until the end of the year and then mark them all off, anyway."

After Mary and Francesca have left, the conversation about the merits of using checklists for assessment and record keeping continues. Gunther Sachs, a third-grade teacher, supports the use of checklists for evaluating the students. He observes that he uses the checklist record when having conferences with parents. He believes that the parents gain a better understanding of what their child is learning in school when he can tell them how the child is progressing on curriculum objectives listed on the checklist. Lily Wong, another third-grade teacher, strongly disagrees. Her experience with the checklists leads her to believe that record keeping takes a great deal of time that she would rather use to plan lessons and design more interesting and challenging learning activities for her students.

RECORD KEEPING   A system of record keeping must be devised. Because a checklist indicates the objectives for curriculum development or developmental characteristics, it must have a method of recording the status of the items. Although many record-keeping strategies have been used, commonly two columns indicate that the child either has or has not mastered the skill or behavior. Two types of indicators frequently used are a simple *Yes/No* or *Mastery/Nonmastery*. Another approach is to record the date when the concept was introduced and the date when it was mastered.

The teacher can use a checklist to record individual or group progress. Whether the teacher uses observation, lesson activities, or tasks for assessment, the checklist is used to keep a record of the child's progress. Checklist information can be shared periodically with parents to keep them informed about what their child is learning or is able to do.

Checklists can also be used to keep a record of all the children in the class or group. The group record lists all the children's names, as well as the checklist objectives. By transferring information about individual children to a master or group record, the teacher can plan instruction for groups of children as the group record indicates their common needs. Figure 8-3 is an example of a checklist record for a group of students in language development.

Checklists have many purposes. They can be developed with these purposes in mind so that they are effective in meeting the needs of the children, teachers, and parents.

Figure 8.3 Language arts: Class record sheet

NAME	LANGUAGE ABILITY													FOLLOWING DIRECTIONS			
	1. Shares personal experiences	2. Voluntarily participates	3. Voluntarily answers	4. Tells observed activity	5. Answers factual questions	6. Answers probing questions	7. Answers higher-order questions	8. Answers divergent questions	9. Problem solving	10. Asks factual questions	11. Interprets story picture	12. Comprehension	13. Attention span	14. Follows simple directions	15. Carries messages	16. Two or more directions	17. Makes simple object with specified materials

Checklists and Standards

Curriculum objectives are now developed at the state and national levels. The Common Core State Standards (CCSS) are rapidly replacing standards developed by individual states or national content area organizations in English language arts, mathematics, science, and other subjects. Because today's children are exposed to a variety of nonprint media through cell phones, electronic tablets, television, videos, and computers, more sophisticated learning skills are required. Checklists can help document these new skills, also.

There are major concerns on the part of educators and parents about the rigorous nature of the CCSS. A major difference between traditional curriculum seen as separate and distinct content areas is that the CCSS "emphasize the importance of understanding complex texts, reading informational texts, writing to learn, building vocabulary skills, and creating powerful literacy connections throughout the content areas" (Altieri, 2014). Literacy instruction thus has to be reorganized to include content area literacy connections beginning with kindergarten children. Anchor standards are placed at the beginning of a reading category. They show the basic standards for all grade levels, while the indicators written below are the grade level standards. The indicators are for both reading literature and informational text. Reading skills and content area skills are integrated into the CCSS.

Developers of the Common Core State Standards Initiative have provided ongoing information on the development process and implementation of the standards. There is a section for parents on why their child benefits from the standards and another on how the standards were developed. Upon adoption of the standards in 2015, 42 states implemented the standards and continue to do so under state guidelines. The Initiative also includes a section on Myths versus Facts about the standards (Common Core State Standards Initiative, 2018). This information helps professionals and parents to understand some of the criticisms of the standards and why they are not accurate.

Preschool developmental checklists and curriculum checklists in the elementary grades are used in the same manner for the same purposes; however, developmental checklists add the developmental dimension to curriculum objectives. Because the young child's developmental level is an important factor in determining the kinds of experiences the teacher will use, our discussion of the purposes of checklists includes the implications of child development during the early childhood years. Those purposes are as follows:

1. To understand development
2. To serve as a framework for curriculum development
3. To assess learning and development

CHECKLISTS AS A GUIDE TO UNDERSTANDING DEVELOPMENT   All developmental checklists are organized to describe different areas of growth, including social, motor, and cognitive development. The checklist items in each area for each age or developmental level indicate how the child is progressing through maturation and experiences. When teachers, caregivers, and parents look at the checklists, they can trace the sequence of development and also be realistic in their expectations for children. Checklists for infant and toddler development are significant because of the rapid pace of development in the first 2 years after birth. Figure 8-1 shows an example of a simple developmental checklist for infants at 6 months.

CHECKLISTS AS A GUIDE TO DEVELOPING CURRICULUM   Because checklists are organized by developmental level or age, they can also serve as a guide for sequencing learning. Teachers can match the experiences they wish to use with the checklist to determine whether they are using the correct level of complexity or difficulty. They can determine what came before in learning or development and what should come next. The story retelling assessment sheet for early childhood classrooms shown in Figure 8-4 includes objectives and skills for retelling stories. By studying the items on the checklist and the student's level of performance in previous experiences, the teacher can plan for

Figure 8.4 Story retelling assessment sheet

Story Retelling Assessment Checklist

Child's Name _____ Date _____

Teacher _____ Grade _____

Book Title _____ Author_____

Story was read independently ☐
Story was read to the child   ☐
Type of response: oral ☐   picture ☐   written ☐

Setting/Character	Independently	With Prompting
Retells from beginning of story		
Names main character		
Plot/Events		
Includes all major events		
Tells events in order		
Identifies the plot or problem		
Resolution		
Tells how the story ended or how the problem was solved		

Assessment Comments

---

instruction and future activities. Moreover, because the checklist is not designed for a particular grade level, a range of levels of reading and writing ability is accommodated. Teachers can attach samples of the student's work to the checklist for use in a portfolio.

Developmental checklists help teachers and caregivers plan for a balance of activities. With the current emphasis on academic subjects even in preschool programs, teachers feel compelled to develop an instructional program that is limited to readiness for reading, writing, and mathematics. Preschool teachers are caught between the emphasis on academic skills and developmentally appropriate instruction that recognizes that young children learn through active learning based on interaction with concrete materials. Developmental checklists help the preschool teacher maintain a perspective between developmentally appropriate instruction and pressures to prepare children for first grade. Inclusion of developmental experiences helps the teacher ensure a balanced curriculum that is best for the children's level of development.

In planning the curriculum and instruction in early childhood or preschool programs, teachers must incorporate the use of learning centers in classroom experiences. Developmental checklists with a sequence of objectives provide guidelines for selecting the materials to place in centers to support curriculum and instruction. For example, for 5-year-olds, the sequence on a checklist for fine motor development might be similar to the following:

Cuts with scissors

Copies a triangle

Writes first name

Puts paper clip on paper

Can use clothespins to transfer small objects (Gerber et al., 2010)

By studying the sequence, the teacher can determine that activities for cutting and pasting should be part of center activities earlier in the year. Later, when fine motor skills are better developed, opportunities to copy letters and numerals should be included in centers to complement instructional activities in writing. Thus, developmental checklists help teachers decide what to select for learning centers as the year progresses. Early in the year, the teacher may introduce simple toys, puzzles, and construction materials in centers. Later, more complex, challenging activities and materials are more appropriate. As the year progresses, the materials available in the centers should be compatible with developmental growth.

Because the rate of development varies from child to child, the sequence of development reflected in the checklists allows the teacher to vary materials for individual children. Certain games, activities, and materials can be placed in the centers and designated for a particular child's needs or interests. Materials for experiences placed in centers provide a means of individualizing learning, with checklists serving as the guide for a sequence from simple to complex. The more complex concepts or objectives lead to the selection of materials for the child whose development is more advanced.

CHECKLISTS AS A GUIDE TO ASSESSING LEARNING AND DEVELOPMENT Having information on how children are growing and learning is one of the important requirements of an early childhood program. Teachers must know how children's development and learning are progressing, and must be able to discuss it with parents, other teachers, and staff members of other schools that later may teach the child.

Because the checklists cover all kinds of development, they allow teachers to track individual children and groups of children. When teachers keep consistent records on individual children, they can give parents information about the child's progress. Parents then have a clear idea of what is happening in school and what their child is accomplishing.

Teachers who use developmental checklists to assess, evaluate, and record children's progress may eventually realize that they have a better understanding of each child in the class than they had before. If a teacher uses a checklist for gross motor skills to keep track of large-muscle development in his or her students, systematic observation of students engaged in physical activities will make the teacher more aware of how each child is progressing and will reveal individual differences in development. When reporting to one child's parent, for example, the teacher may discuss the improvement in throwing and catching a ball. In another case, the teacher may focus on the child's ability to ride a bicycle or to jump rope.

How Teachers Evaluate and Assess with Checklists

If a checklist is used as a framework for curriculum development and instruction, it can also be used for evaluation and assessment. The curriculum objectives used to plan instructional experiences can also be used to evaluate the children's performance on the same objectives. After a series of activities is used to provide opportunities to work with new concepts or skills, the children are assessed to determine how successful they were in learning the new skill or information. Evaluation can be accomplished through observation, during ongoing learning activities, and through specific assessment tasks.

Evaluating Checklist Objectives by Observation

Observing young children is the most valuable method of understanding them. Because children in early childhood programs are active learners, their progress is best assessed by watching their behaviors, rather than by using a formal test. If you look at the items on developmental checklists, you will see that some objectives or indicators of development can be evaluated only by observing the child. For example, in the area of language development, if a teacher wants to know whether a child is using complete sentences, he or she observes the child in a play activity and listens for examples of language. Likewise, if the teacher is interested in evaluating social development, he or she observes the children playing outdoors to determine whether they engage mostly in solitary or parallel play or whether individual children play cooperatively as part of a group. Because very young children learn through play, the teacher can notice how a child is learning during play activities. Likewise, the infant–toddler caregiver will become aware of each child's physical and language advances at the very beginning stages of development while children explore the environment through play.

Chapter 7 included information on how observation can be incidental or planned. The teacher may decide to evaluate during center time and may determine in advance which items on a checklist can be evaluated by observing children in the art center or the manipulative center. The teacher then places materials in those centers that are needed to observe specific behaviors, and records which children are able to use the materials in the desired manner. For example, the ability to cut with scissors can be assessed by having a cutting activity in the art center. As an alternative, the teacher might use a cutting activity with an entire group and observe how each child is performing during the activity.

Evaluating Checklist Objectives with Learning Activities

Some objectives cannot be assessed through observation alone. Objectives in a cognitive area such as mathematics may require a specific learning activity for evaluation. However, instead of having a separate assessment task, the teacher can have children demonstrate their performance on a particular skill as a part of the lesson being conducted. The teacher notes which children demonstrate understanding of a concept or mastery of a skill during the lesson. If a mathematics objective to be assessed involves understanding numbers through 5, for example, the teacher might instruct a small group of children to make groups of objects ranging in number from 1 to 5 and note which children are successful.

Evaluating Checklist Objectives with Specific Tasks

Sometimes, at the beginning or end of a school year or grading period, the teacher wants to conduct a systematic assessment. He or she assesses a series of objectives at one time. In this situation, the teacher determines a number of objectives that can be evaluated at one time and devises tasks or activities to conduct with a child or a small group of children. The activities are presented in the same fashion as in a lesson, but the teacher has the additional purpose of updating and recording progress. Assessment tasks are organized on the basis of children's previous progress and vary among groups of children. Some children perform one group of activities; others have a completely different set of activities related to a different set of objectives.

There is a time and place for each type of evaluation. The more experience a teacher has in including assessment in the instructional program, the easier it becomes. It is important to use the easiest and least time-consuming strategy whenever possible.

Advantages and Disadvantages of Using Checklists with Young Children

Using checklists for assessment and evaluation has definite advantages and disadvantages or problems. Teachers must weigh both sides before deciding how extensively they will use checklists for measurement and record-keeping purposes.

Advantages of Using Checklists

Checklists are easy to use. Because they require little instruction or training, teachers can quickly learn to use them. Unlike standardized tests, they are available whenever evaluation is needed.

Checklists are flexible and can be used with a variety of assessment strategies. The teacher can evaluate in the most convenient manner and obtain the needed information. Because of this flexibility, the teacher can combine assessment strategies when more than one assessment is indicated.

Behaviors can be recorded frequently; checklists are always at hand. Whenever the teacher has new information, he or she can update records. Unlike paper-and-pencil tests or formal tests, the teacher does not have to wait for a testing opportunity to determine whether the child has mastered an objective.

Developmental checklists can be used with parents to give them an idea of which developmental steps they can support at home with preschool children. The teacher can share ideas of activities the parents can use with the child. Likewise, the teacher can provide parents of school-age children with activities to support successful learning with curriculum objectives.

Disadvantages of Using Checklists

Using checklists can be time consuming. Particularly when teachers are just beginning to use checklists, they may feel that keeping records current on checklists reduces the time spent with children. Teachers have to become proficient in using checklists without impinging on teaching time.

Teachers may find it difficult to get started. When they are accustomed to teaching without the use of checklists, teachers often find it difficult to adapt their teaching and evaluation behaviors to include checklists. In addition, teachers can have too many checklists. They can become frustrated by multiple checklists that overwhelm them with assessment and record keeping.

Some teachers may not consider assessment strategies used with checklists as valid measures of development and learning. For some teachers, particularly those in the primary grades who are accustomed to conducting a test for evaluation, the observation and activity strategies used to measure progress may seem inconclusive. These teachers may feel the need for more concrete evidence of mastery of learning objectives for accountability.

Checklists do not indicate how well a child performs. Unlike assessments that can be used to record levels of mastery, checklists indicate only whether the child can perform adequately.

A checklist is not itself an assessment instrument. It is a format for organizing learning objectives or developmental indicators and a form of observation. The teacher's implementation of evaluation strategies by using a checklist makes it a tool for evaluation. In addition, recording the presence or absence of a behavior is not the main purpose of the checklist. The significant factor is what the teacher does with the assessment information recorded. If the information gained from evaluating the objectives is not used for instructional planning and implementation followed by further ongoing evaluation, the checklist does not improve learning and development.

Enhanced eText: Application Exercise 8.1

Enhanced eText: Self-Check 8.1

Types of Rating Scales and How They Are Used with Young Children

Rating scales are similar to checklists; however, there are important differences. Whereas checklists are used to indicate whether a behavior is present or absent, rating scales require the rater to make a qualitative judgment about the extent to which a behavior is present. A rating scale consists of a set of characteristics or qualities to be judged by using a systematic procedure. Rating scales take many forms, but **numerical rating scales** and **graphic rating scales** seem to be used most frequently (McMillan, 2007).

Numerical Rating Scales

Numerical rating scales are among the easiest rating scales to use. The rater marks a number to indicate the degree to which a characteristic is present. A sequence of numbers is assigned to descriptive categories. The rater's judgment is required to rate the characteristic. One common numerical system is as follows:

1—Unsatisfactory

2—Below average

3—Average

4—Above average

5—Outstanding

The numerical rating system might be used to evaluate classroom behaviors in elementary students as follows:

1. To what extent does the student complete assigned work?

   1 2 3 4 5

2. To what extent does the student cooperate with group activities?

   1 2 3 4 5

Numerical scales become difficult to use when there is little agreement on what the numbers represent. The interpretation of the scale may vary.

Numerical rating scales are useful in recording emerging progress in mathematics. The student is usually evaluated several times during the school year. A rating scale is used to make ratings of whether the child (1) needs development, (2) is developing as expected, or (3) is advanced in development.

Graphic Rating Scales

Graphic rating scales function as continuums (Cohen & Wiener, 2003). A set of categories is described at certain points along the line, but the rater can mark his or her judgment at any location on the line. In addition, a graphic rating scale provides a visual continuum that helps locate the correct position. Commonly used descriptors for graphic rating scales are as follows:

Never

Seldom

Occasionally

Frequently

Always

The classroom behaviors described earlier would be evaluated on a graphic rating scale as follows:

1. To what extent does the student complete assigned work?

   Never   Seldom   Occasionally   Frequently   Always

2. To what extent does the student cooperate with group activities?

   Never   Seldom   Occasionally   Frequently   Always

The behavioral descriptions on graphic rating scales are used more easily than numerical descriptors. Because the descriptors are more specific, raters can be more objective and accurate when judging student behaviors; nevertheless, graphic rating scales are subject to bias because of disagreement about the meaning of the descriptors.

Uses of Rating Scales

One of the most familiar uses of rating scales is report cards. Schools often use rating scales to report characteristics of personal and social development on a report card. Such attributes as work habits, classroom conduct, neatness, and citizenship commonly appear on elementary school report cards. Students and parents often believe that such ratings are particularly subject to teacher bias and feelings about the student.

Rating scales can also be used to evaluate learning environments. In the *Early Childhood Rating Scale, Third Edition (ECERS-3)* (Harms, Clifford, & Cryer, 2014), a numerical scale for rating how the early childhood teacher provides for sand/water play and dramatic play is evaluated, as well as the quality of the daily schedule. This type of scale is intended to be used to evaluate early childhood centers and to plan for improvements in the program (Harms, 2010).

> **Enhanced eText:** Video Example 8.2

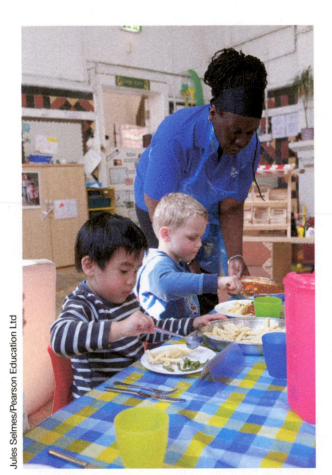

Jules Selmes/Pearson Education Ltd

Young children benefit from assessments that use real objects.

The Montessori Rating Scale—Early Childhood Environment (MRS) (montessoriratingscales.com, n.d.) is an instrument to evaluate environments that are based on Montessori classrooms and the Montessori program that serve children 2.5 to 6 years old. It focuses on the materials in the prepared environment and the experiences that are intended for self-construction of knowledge. The Montessori environment is considered to be the critical component for quality care for young children. The example of a Montessori Rating Scale pictured in Figure 8-5 includes materials needed for learning categories such as language arts, mathematics, the sciences, geography, history, and music and movement.

The *Early Learning Observation and Rating Scale (ELORS)* (Coleman, West, & Gillis, 2010) has a different approach to using a scale to measure a range of progress. The scale has four numerical categories. The lower the number assigned to the child, the higher the child's level of progress. The higher the number assigned to the child, the more concern is present about the child's progress. All scores depend on repeated observations in various contexts and activities in the classroom.

Figure 8-6 is a combination rating scale and checklist for reading (U.S. Department of Defense, n.d.). It illustrates how two types of assessments can be combined.

There are also rating scales that students use to rate themselves. In Figure 8-7 the students are able to evaluate their own work with a scale of different "happy faces." This type of scale is particularly useful with preschool and primary grade children who are still developing reading and writing skills.

Figure 8.5 Montessori rating scale-early childhood-environment

Montessori Rating Scale - Early Childhood - Environment - Scoring Sheet

Center/School: _____ Room: _____ Observer: _____ Date: _____/_____/_____
mm dd yy

	Item No.	Description	O	NA	1	2	3		Item No.	Description	O	1	2	3
I N T E R I O R - S P A C E	1.	Sound absorbing						S E N S O R I A L M A T E R I A L S	41.	Wooden cylinders/cylinder blocks (4)				
	2.	Lighting							42.	Pink tower/pink cubes				
	3.	Ventilation							43.	Brown stair/broad stair/brown prisms				
	4.	Temperature							44.	Red rods				
	5.	Size of Space							45.	Knobless cylinders, colored cylinder boxes (4)				
	6.	Surfaces - Maintenance and repairs							46.	Geometric solids (10), bases (11) & mystery bag				
	7.	Plumbing fixtures - Maintenance, repairs and cleaning							47.	Geometry cabinet with demonstration tray and matching cards				
	8.	Clean surfaces							49.	Constructive triangles boxes (5)				
	9.	Health Issues - Environmental							49.	Power of two - OPTIONAL	▓	▓		
	10.	Safety Issues - Environmental							50.	Binomial cube				
	11.	Special/exceptional needs sensitivity							51.	Trinomial cube				
F U R N I S H I N G S	12.	Cubbies/Personal Items Area							52.	Square of pythagorus - OPTIONAL	▓			
	13.	Tables							53.	Color box #1 – primary colors				
	14.	Chairs							54.	Color box #2 – primary and secondary colors				
	15.	Cabinets							55.	Color box #3 – color grading				
	16.	Rug and holder/rug area							56.	Color box #4 – color matching/grading OPTIONAL	▓	▓		
	17.	Reading/library area							57.	Fabric box w/matching pairs of fabric squares				
	18.	Soft Items - Additional furnishings							58.	Rough & smooth boards/tactile boards				
	19.	Sleeping - Cots/mats							59.	Tactile tablets/Touching tablets				
	20.	Sleeping - Cots/mats/sleeping bags - storage and hygiene							60.	Baric tablets				
	21.	Lunch – accouterments, hygiene and storage							61.	Thermic tablets				
	22.	Special/exceptional needs sensitive							62.	Thermic bottles - OPTIONAL	▓	▓		
	23.	Storage and supply area							63.	Sound boxes/Sound cylinders				
P R A C T I C A L L I F E M A T E R I A L S	24.	Pouring solids: Dry transfer with whole hand, large and small spoons							64.	Smelling bottles/Smelling cylinders/exercises				
	25.	Pouring liquids: Wet transfer with different size							65.	Tasting bottles/exercises - OPTIONAL	▓	▓		
	26.	Folding cloth – half (2), quarter (2), third (1)							66.	Tasting activities - OPTIONAL	▓	▓		
	27.	Dressing frames: small button, zipper, snap, hook and eye, bow tie						M A T H E M A T I C S M A T E R I A L S	67.	Number rods and numerals cards				
	28.	Polishing – wood, metal, mirror, shoe							68.	Spindle box with spindles (45)				
	29.	Washing – hand, shell, table, chair, dishes, clothes, baby, etc.							69.	Numerals and counters				
	30.	Scissors exercises							70.	Bead stair and numerals				
	31.	Opening and closing jars and bottles							71.	Teen Board and beads				
	32.	Flower arranging with flowers and vases							72.	Ten Board and beads				
	33.	Locks/lock box							73.	Hundred Board and numeral tiles (1–100) and control chart OPTIONAL	▓			
	34.	Food preparation – carrots, celery, peas (in shell), banana, apple, etc.							74.	Short bead chain (1–10) and numeral arrows				
	35.	Sewing sequence – bead stringing, card sowing, button sewing, material – OPTIONAL	▓	▓					75.	Long bead chain (1–10) and numeral arrows OPTIONAL	▓			
	36.	Weaving sequence – OPTIONAL	▓						76.	Golden bead introduction trays (3)				
	37.	Carpentry tools and activities – OPTIONAL	▓						77.	Golden bead materials: Bank Game				
	38.	Plant Care - watering, leaf cleaning, feeding (nutrients), re-potting							78.	Golden bead decimal cards				
	39.	Animal Care - feeding, cleaning, etc.							79.	Stamp game				
	40.	House keeping materials							80.	Dot board - wood, plastic or paper OPTIONAL	▓			
		Total for column #1 - Exclude Optionals	▓							**Total for column #2 - Exclude Optionals**	▓			
		Total for column #1 - Optionals Only		▓						**Total for column #2 - Optionals Only**				

SOURCE: Montessori Rating Scales. (n.d.). *The Montessori Rating Scale-Early Childhood Environment*. Retrieved from http://montessoriratingscales.com/node/15

Figure 8.6 Reading skills rating scale

Grade 1 - First Quarter Skills Checklist

Child's Name: _____

Teacher's Name: _____

Checked items below in Reading and Writing indicate:
M = Mastery   S = Steady Progress   L = Limited   N/A = Not Assessed
Checked items below in Mathematics indicate:
A = Adequate Progress   N = Not Adequate Progess   N/A = Not Assessed

M = Mastery S = Steady Progress L = Limited N/A = Not Assessed	M	S	L	N/A
READING				
Concepts of Print				
Identifies cover, title, author and illustrator.				
Identifies title page.				
Identifies table of contents.				
Identifies end of book.				
Demonstrates left-to-right and top to bottom page.				
Demonstrates one-to-one word correspondence.				
Understands that print tells the story.				
Phonemic Awareness and Phonics				
Recognizes letters. (alphabet)				
Understands blending and segmentation.				
Identifies rhyming words.				
Identifies beginning, middle, and ending sounds.				
Identifies consonant sounds.				
Identifies short vowel sounds.				
Identifies one-syllable consonant-vowel-consonant words.				
Word Recognition				
Reads 40 kindergarten review words with fluency.				
Reads 51 high frequency words with fluency.				
Comprehension				
Understands beginning, middle, and end to a story.				
Uses pre-reading strategies. (ex. makes predications)				
Understands character.				
Understands setting.				
Reads and comprehends appropriate text. (reading levels 6–8)				

SOURCE: U.S. Department of Defense Education Activities. (n.d.). Grade 1 First Quarter Skills Checklist (Reading). Retrieved from www.am.dodea

Figure 8.7 Self-assessment rating scale

Rating Scale for Self-Assessment of an Assignment		
1. Did I put the name and date on my work?		
2. Did I finish the assignment?		
3. Did I follow the instructions correctly?		
4. Is my work neat?		
5. Did I do my best work?		
Excellent	O.K.	Needs Work
🙂	🙂	😐

Advantages of Using Rating Scales

Rating scales are a unique form of evaluation. They serve a function not provided by other measurement strategies. Although some of the limitations of rating scales have already been discussed, it is useful to review their strengths and weaknesses.

Rating scales can be used for behaviors not easily measured by other means. In the area of social development, for example, a scale might have indicators of cooperative behavior. When the teacher is trying to determine the child's ability to work with children and adults in the classroom, the scale of indicators is more usable than a yes/no response category on a checklist. Unlike an observation, which might be completely open ended, the rating scale indicators have clues to behaviors that describe the child's level of cooperation.

Rating scales are quick and easy to complete. Because the rater is provided with the descriptors of the child's behavior, it is possible to complete the scale with minimum effort. The descriptors also make it possible to complete the scale some time after an observation (Jablon, Dombro, & Dichtelmiller, 2007). The user can apply knowledge about the child after an observation or as a result of working with the child on a daily basis and will not always need a separate time period to acquire the needed information.

Minimum training is required to use rating scales. The successful rating scale is easy to understand and use. Paraprofessionals and students can complete some rating scales. The scale's indicators offer the information needed to complete the scale.

Rating scales are easy to develop and use. Because descriptors remain consistent on some rating scales, teachers find them easy to design. When using rating indicators such as *always, sometimes, rarely,* and *never,* the teacher can add the statements for rating without having to think of rating categories for each one.

Finally, rating scales are a useful strategy for assessing progress in the child's journey into understanding the world or in reconstructing knowledge. A rating scale permits the teacher to describe the child's steps toward understanding or mastery, instead of whether the child has achieved a predetermined level, as is the case in the use of checklists.

Disadvantages of Using Rating Scales

Rating scales are highly subjective; therefore, rater error and bias are common problems. Teachers and other raters may rate a child on the basis of their previous interactions or on an emotional rather than an objective basis. The subsequent rating will reflect the teacher's attitude toward the child (Linn & Miller, 2005). There are possibilities when the teacher rates the level of concern for a child's progress that the rating can be subject to the teacher's impressions of the child. There are no indicators for a rating, and the teacher has to use individual judgment of the child's progress.

Ambiguous terms cause rating scales to be unreliable sources of information. Raters disagree on the descriptors of characteristics. Therefore, raters are likely to mark characteristics by using different interpretations. For example, it is easy to have different interpretations of the indicator *sometimes or rarely.*

Rating scales tell little about the causes of behavior. Like checklists that indicate whether the behavior is present or absent, rating scales provide no additional information to clarify the circumstances in which the behavior occurred. Unlike observations that result in more comprehensive information about the context surrounding behaviors, rating scales provide a different type of information from checklists, but include no causal clues for the observer, unless notes are taken beyond the rating scale itself.

Quick Check Rating Scales for Self-Assessment

In this chapter, information on children using rating scales for self-assessment has included examples using faces for children to rate themselves and their work. A second-grade teacher decided to avoid frustrations children experienced when they had to mark a "sad" face. The teacher devised a simple scale with four ratings and indicators. The children used different colors to fill in the circles attached to numerical ratings. Called a "quick check," the scale could be used several times, with children progressing to higher ratings. The teacher also developed four desired teaching behaviors that complemented the use of the quick checks:

1. Helping children set or accept and record individualized goals
2. Teaching, modeling, and planning ways the children may progress toward goals
3. Showing the children evidence of their progress with carefully kept records
4. Helping the children celebrate goal achievement and attributing positive feelings to their own efforts

SOURCE: Brown, W. (2008). Young children assess their learning. The power of the quick check strategy. *Young Children, 63,* 14–20.

Enhanced eText: Self-Check 8.2

Types of Rubrics and How They Are Designed and Used

Like rating scales, rubrics are qualitative instruments that can be used for assessing student progress or scoring student work. Perhaps this purpose for scoring student work distinguishes rubrics from other types of assessment instruments such as checklists and rating scales. A rubric can be defined as follows:

> A rubric is a scoring tool that explicitly represents the performance expectations for an assignment or piece of work. A rubric divides the assigned work into component parts and provides clear descriptions of the characteristics of the work associated with each component at varying levels of mastery (Eberly Center, Carnegie Mellon University, n.d., p. 1).

It is clear from the definition just cited that rubrics are related to performance assessments. They provide guidelines to distinguish performance from one level to another. Although rubrics are used most frequently with students in later elementary grades and secondary schools, they can also be useful for students in kindergarten and the primary grades (Brookhart, 2013).

Indicators of performance can also be called the criteria for scoring. That is, they set the criteria for the score at each level. Indicators can also describe dimensions of performance—different categories of indicators leading to the desired score. In Figure 8-8, four categories of an emergent writing rubric for kindergarten children are listed and rated at four levels: Beginning Emergent Writing, 1 point; Some Emergent Writing, 2 points; Adequate Emergent Writing, 3 points; and Advanced Emergent Writing, 4 points. Each child is rated on the five elements with a total score at the bottom of the rubric.

Figure 8.8 Emergent Writing

Beginning Emergent Writing 1 point	Some Emergent Writing 2 points	Adequate Emergent Writing 3 points	Advanced Emergent Writing 4 points
1. Demonstrates interest in writing tools and tries to hold them	Holds writing tool with fist	Holds writing tool with pincer grasp	Holds writing tool with pincer grasp and uses to write name
2. Attempts to scribble on paper	Scribbles on paper	Makes individual marks	Makes recognizable marks as requested
3. Attempts to write letters	Writes random letters	Writes letters from name	Writes name consistently
4. Attempts to write beginning sounds of words	Writes beginning sounds of words	Writes ending sounds of words	Writes words
5. Attempts to write 2-3 word phrase	Writes 2-3 word phrases	Writes 3-4 word phrases about topic	Writes paragraph
Total _____	_____	_____	_____

Types of Rubrics

There are generally three types of rubrics: **holistic rubric**, **analytic rubric**, and **developmental rubric**. Each type has characteristics that distinguish it from the others.

HOLISTIC RUBRIC   This type of rubric assigns a single score to a student's overall performance. These rubrics usually have competency labels that define the level of performance. A number of indicators describe the quality of work or performance at each level (Cohen & Wiener, 2003; Payne, 1997; Wiggins, 2013). Figure 8-9 is an example of a simple holistic rubric in emergent writing. It has four levels of competence. The student's work is assessed using the descriptors under each level of competence.

ANALYTIC RUBRIC   An analytic rubric resembles a grid and includes a range of descriptors, uses limited descriptors for each attribute, describes and scores each of the task attributes separately, and uses a scale such as 1. Needs Improvement, 2. Developing, 3. Sufficient, and 4. Above Average (Cohen & Weiner, 2003). Analytic rubrics are more specific than holistic rubrics, can be used for diagnostic purposes, and can be more efficient for grading purposes. Figure 8-10 is an example of an analytic rubric for problem solving. It has three dimensions: understanding the problem, solving the problem, and answering the problem. The descriptors for each are listed with a numerical scale. This particular rubric is useful for students in the latter stages of early childhood, when reading and writing skills are well developed.

Figure 8.9 Holistic rubric for writing

Inexperienced Writer

- Makes letter-like marks on paper or scribbles
- May dictate statements to the teacher
- Dictates "story" to go with drawn picture

Beginning Writer

- Writes own name
- Attempts to write words on paper
- May copy words or sentences

Developing Writer

- Uses spaces when writing words
- May use some conventions of print (e.g., punctuation or capitalization)
- Uses inventive spelling

Mature Writer

- May write multiple sentences
- Writes to a topic
- Develops fluency and confidence
- May show accuracy in capitalization and punctuation
- Still makes some errors

Figure 8.10 Analytic rubric

Problem Solving for an Assignment
Understanding the assignment
0—No attempt
1—Misunderstands the assignment
2—Understands part of the assignment
3—Understands most of the assignment
4—Understands all of the assignment
Planning the assignment
0—No attempt
1—Inappropriate plan to complete the assignment
2—Partial plan to complete the assignment
3—Almost complete plan to complete the assignment
4—Complete plan to complete the assignment
Completing the assignment
0—No attempt
1—Inappropriate attempt
2—Partial attempt
3—Assignment mostly completed
4—Assignment completed correctly

DEVELOPMENTAL RUBRIC A developmental rubric is designed to serve a multiage group of students or to span several grade levels. The intention is to abandon mastery of skills at a particular grade level; rather, the student is assessed on a continuum that shows developmental progress. Figure 8-11 shows the progression in reading skills across elementary grade levels.

Figure 8.11 Developmental rubric

READING RUBRIC K–2
Competent Reader Grade 2
• Applies grade-level phonics
• Decodes words with common prefixes and suffixes
• Uses context to self-correct word recognition
• Reads with accuracy and fluency
Developing Reader Grade 1
• Understands features of a sentence (e.g., capitalization and punctuation)
• Recognizes long and short vowels in spoken words
• Decodes regularly spelled one-syllable words
• Reads words with inflectional endings
Beginning Reader
• Follows words from left to right on a page
• Recognizes that spoken words are represented in written language
• Understands that written words are separated by spaces
• Can name all upper and lower-case letters of the alphabet

Search and Share 8.2

Rubrics for Children with Special Needs

Search online for examples of rubrics developed for young children with special needs. What types of skills do they include? How could they be advantageous for understanding the skill development of young children with disabilities?

How Rubrics Are Designed and Used

Rubrics are frequently discussed as part of performance assessment and the use of portfolios. This is because they are used to assess a performance task. When an overall, general judgment is made about the performance, a holistic rubric is used. An analytic rubric applies a detailed set of criteria, usually after a holistic evaluation has been made. A developmental rubric is designed to measure evolving competencies over a span of grade levels. Each type of rubric is designed for a different type of application, but the design process is similar (McMillan, 2007).

SELECTING RUBRIC TYPE   There are two major steps in designing a rubric. The first step is to decide what type of rubric is to be used and then design the type of rubric selected. If an overall rating is needed, then a holistic rubric scale is indicated. An analytic rubric is designed if each part of a task needs to be assessed separately, as in Figure 8-10. The three tasks to be assessed in that rubric are (1) understanding the problem, (2) solving the problem, and (3) answering the problem. Each category of the problem has different dimensions. Figure 8-9, in contrast, is holistic. The descriptors support levels of competence, but the focus is on overall proficiency at each level.

DEVELOPING SCORING CRITERIA   Teachers who are beginners at rubric design might find a generalized rubric useful as a guide to start their own rubric. The rubric can first be divided into levels of performance common to many rubrics:

> No attempt
>
> Inadequate response
>
> Satisfactory response
>
> Demonstrated competence

Each level has descriptions of the scoring criteria for that level of competence.

Enhanced eText: Video Example 8.3

Unlike the objectives on checklists and descriptors on rating scales, levels of performance or dimensions cannot always be predetermined when the rubric is designed. The dimensions of performance must be based on reasonable expectations of the students to be assessed using existing samples of student work and revised as necessary (McMillan, 2007; Wiggins, 2013).

Rubrics have many uses and purposes. They can be created to assess processes such as cooperative learning and other group strategies. They are most commonly used with student work or products. Examples are individual and group projects, exhibits, and artistic products. They are also used to evaluate performances of all types. In the classroom, they can be used for oral presentations and discussions. As can be seen from the examples presented in this section of the chapter, in early childhood classrooms, rubrics are commonly used to evaluate progress in development and learning.

Can Preschoolers Learn to Use Rubrics?

Throughout this chapter, the subject of rubrics refers to the teacher designing and using rubrics with preschool children. The children engage in the process with the teacher, but the teacher makes the basic decisions of rubric design and implementation. Teachers used their knowledge of the children's cognitive development as the foundation for their effort to teach the process to their 4- and 5-year-old preschoolers.

The children were enabled to use rubrics through a series of steps that built the children's readiness for rubric design. The first step was to engage the children in planning for their play each day. At first the children were introduced to several activities in a play period. They could make choices among those activities and discuss their play within the selected activities. The children were also introduced to the use of contracts. The teacher prepared a drawing of each possible activity on the contract. Each child selected an activity on the contract and marked it off as it was completed. The children could engage in more than one activity during the play period. The children decided when to end one activity and move to another. At the end of the play period the choices were discussed in a group activity.

The next step was to select a long-term goal and determine the steps to reach the goal. Over a period of weeks, the children could mark when they completed a step on their plan. The developers of the project proposed that children learned to work toward a goal by completing and marking each step. There were several benefits to goal accomplishment. First, the children learned they could set long-term goals and achieve them. The children were deciding on a goal, planning how to reach the goal, and assessing their progress toward the goal. When this was accomplished, they were using a rubric to plan and achieve their goals.

SOURCE: B.G. Warash & M. Workman. (2016). Teaching Preschoolers to Self-Assess Their Choices in Pre–K. *Journal of Educational Research and Practice, Volume 6, Issue 1*, pp. 97–104.

Advantages of Using Rubrics

One of the many advantages of using rubrics is that they provide guidelines for quality student work or performance. Given this characteristic, other advantages can be added.

Rubrics are flexible. They can be designed for many uses and ability levels. Although teachers conduct most of the assessments using rubrics with very young children, student self-assessment increases as students mature.

Rubrics are adaptable. They are dynamic and subject to revision and refinement. Because they are easily modified and changed, they can meet changing classroom and student needs.

Rubrics can be used by both teacher and student to guide the student's efforts toward completing a task or product. The teacher and student can review the expectations for quality during the process of an assignment or project so that the student is clear about what needs to be done to improve work.

Rubrics can be translated into grades if needed. If grades are not used, the rubrics can be used to discuss student work with parents and students. Periodic review of student efforts and comparison with a rubric such as a developmental rubric adds to the understanding of the student's progress.

Disadvantages of Using Rubrics

Despite the strengths of rubrics, rubric design and use are not without difficulties. One difficulty is that teachers just beginning to develop rubrics may have trouble determining assessment or scoring criteria.

Teachers may focus on excessively general or inappropriate criteria for a rubric. In a similar fashion, a teacher may use predetermined criteria for rubric design rather than basing rubrics on examples of student work or modifying them as needed.

A common mistake in designing and using rubrics is to inappropriately focus on the quantity of characteristics found, rather than the indicators of quality work. The teacher focuses on the wrong characteristics of student work.

Holistic rubrics may lack validity and reliability. The teacher is forced to analyze the criteria for quality when designing an analytic rubric. The descriptors for the holistic rubric can be too general and lack specificity.

Enhanced eText: Self-Check 8.3

Summary

Informal evaluation measures are useful for teachers who need specific information about their students to use when planning instruction. Checklists and rating scales are informal instruments that can be designed and used by teachers to obtain specific diagnostic and assessment data that will help them develop learning experiences for their children.

Checklists are used for more than assessment or evaluation. They are a form of curriculum outline or a framework of curriculum objectives. With checklists, teachers can plan instruction, develop learning-center activities, and evaluate children's progress and achievement on specific objectives.

Rating scales allow teachers to evaluate behaviors qualitatively. Raters can indicate the extent to which the child exhibits certain behaviors.

Checklists and rating scales are practical and easy to use. Teachers can develop them to fit the curriculum and administer them at their convenience. Unlike standardized tests, checklists and rating scales are current and provide the teacher with immediate feedback on student progress.

Using checklists and rating scales also has disadvantages. Because they are not standardized, they are subject to error and teacher bias. Checklists do not include the level or quality of performance on the objectives measured. Rating scales in particular are subject to rater bias. Rating-scale descriptors are ambiguous in definition. Differing interpretations of descriptors by raters lead to different responses and interpretations of children's behaviors.

Rating scales provide a multidimensional format for assessing student products and performances. They include the most complex format for assessing quality in student work. They are particularly useful in helping students understand the expectations for quality in an assignment and to review quality indicators while a project or learning assignment is in progress. Rating scales are also useful in helping parents understand the nature of student assignments and the criteria for quality that were developed for that assignment.

Rating scales can have drawbacks. One possible weakness occurs when teachers predetermine characteristics of quality, rather than using examples of typical student work to determine the indicators. Likewise, teachers can focus on less appropriate indicators of quality work or look at quantity rather than quality of work.

Rubrics permit the teacher and students to assess student progress toward a goal. The rubric divides an assignment into parts and provides a clear description of the sections of the assignment by explaining different levels of mastery for each section.

A holistic rubric uses a single score to determine the student's overall performance. It describes a level of performance such as beginning, developing, or mature.

An analytic rubric has descriptors that use a scale of performance such as beginning, developing, and competent. The descriptors of each category characterize where the student ranks on the overall rubric.

All four of these assessment instruments can be weakened by teacher bias and subjective judgment. Reliability in conducting an assessment with these instruments can be improved if teachers work to achieve consistency in conducting and scoring the assessments.

Enhanced eText: Self-Check: Chapter Review

Key Terms

analytic rubric 208	developmental rubric 208	holistic rubric 208
developmental checklist 188	graphic rating scale 200	numerical rating scale 200

Selected Organizations

Search for the following organizations online:
About Special Education
California School for the Deaf, Fremont, CA
Centers for Disease Control and Prevention
Eberly Center, Carnegie Mellon University

Frank Porter Graham Child Development Institute/
  Environment Rating Scale
National Training Institute for Child Care Health
  Consultants
RCampus

References

Altieri, J. L. (2014). *Powerful content connections: Nurturing readers, writers, and thinkers in grades k–3.* Dover, DE: International Reading Association.

Brookhart, S. M. (2013). *How to create and use rubrics for formative assessment and grading.* Retrieved from http://www.ascd.org/publications/books/112001/chapters/What-Are-Rubrics-and-why-are-they-important?

Brown, W. (2008, November). Young children assess their learning. The power of the quick check strategy. *Young Children, 63*, 14–20.

California School for the Deaf (n.d.). *ASL stages of development checklist.* Fremont Early Childhood Education Department, Fremont, CA. Retrieved from https://successforkidswithhearingloss.com/wp-content/uploads/2011/12/ASL-Stages-of-Development-Assmt.pdf

Centers for Disease Control and Prevention. (2014). *Important milestones: Your baby at six months.* Retrieved from http://www.cdc.gov/ncbddd/actearly/milestones/milestones-6mo.html

Cohen, J. H., & Wiener, R. B. (2003). *Literacy portfolios: Improving assessment, teaching and learning* (2nd ed.). Upper Saddle River, NJ: Merrill/Prentice Hall.

Coleman, R., West, T., & Gillis, M. (2010.). *Early learning observation and rating scales (ELORS).* Retrieved from http://www.getreadytoread.org/screening-tools/early-learning-observation-forms

Common Core State Standards Initiative. (2018). Retrieved from www.cotestandards.org.

Eberly Center, Carnegie Mellon University. (n.d.). Grading and performance rubrics. Retrieved from Http://www.cmu/teaching/designteach/rubrics.html

Gerber, R. I., Wilks, T., & Erdie-Lalena, C. (2010). Developmental milestones: Motor development. *Pediatrics in Review, 31*, 67. Retrieved from http://pedsinreview.aappublications.org/content/31/7/267

Harms, T. (2010, January/February). Making long-lasting changes with the environment rating scales. *Exchange*, 12–15.

Harms, T., Clifford, R. M., & Cryer, D. (2014). *Early childhood environment rating scale, third edition (ECERS-3).* New York, NY: Teachers College Press.

Jablon, J. R., Dombro, A. L., & Dichtelmiller, M. L. (2007). *The power of observation for birth through eight* (2nd ed.). Washington, DC: National Association for the Education of Young Children and Teaching Strategies, Inc.

Kareva1, V., & Echevarria, J. (2013). Using the SIOP model for effective content teaching with second and foreign language learners. *Journal of Education and Training Studies.*1, 239–248.

Linn, R. L., & Miller, M. D. (2005). *Measurement and assessment in teaching* (9th ed.). Upper Saddle River, NJ: Merrill/Prentice Hall.

McMillan, J. H. (2007). *Classroom assessment: Principles and practice for effective instruction* (4th ed.). Upper Saddle River, NJ: Pearson.

Mid-State Early Childhood Direction Center. (2012). *Developmental checklist birth to five.* Syracuse, University, Syracuse, NY.

Montessori Rating Scales.com. (n.d.). *Montessori Rating Scales—Early Childhood—Environment Scoring Sheet.* Retrieved from http://www.montessoriratingscales.com/node/15

National Training Institute for Child Care Health Consultants. (2010, April). *Infant/toddler development, screening and assessment.* Chapel Hill, NC: Author.

Payne, D. A. (1997). *Applied educational assessment.* Belmont, CA: Wadsworth.

U.S. Department of Defense. (n.d.). U.S. Department of Defense education activities grade 1—first quarter skills checklist. Retrieved from www.am.dodea

Warash, B. G., & Workman, M. (2016). Teaching pre-schoolers to self-assess their choices in pre-k. *Journal of Educational Research and Practice*, Vol.6, Issue 1, pp. 97–104.

Wiggins, G. (2013, January). *Intelligent vs. thoughtless use of rubrics and models (Part 1).* Retrieved from http://grantwiggins.wordpress.com/2013/17/

Chapter 9
Teacher-Designed Assessment Strategies

Dotshock/123RF

 ## Chapter Learning Outcomes

As a result of reading this chapter, you will be able to:

9.1 Explain the purposes of teacher-designed assessments and tests.

9.2 Describe the types of teacher-designed assessments used with preschool and primary grade children.

9.3 Describe how to develop quality teacher-designed assessments.

9.4 Discuss the advantages and disadvantages of using teacher-designed assessments.

Another type of classroom evaluation is teacher-designed assessments. In assessing and evaluating children from birth through the primary grades, measures other than paper-and-pencil tests are generally more appropriate. As children progress through the primary grades, however, they develop skills in reading and writing that make it possible for them to demonstrate learning on a written test. In this chapter, we discuss how teachers design their own assessments of classroom instruction and how they can use commercially designed classroom tests to evaluate learning progress.

Purposes of Teacher-Designed Assessments and Tests

Although all types of evaluation, both formal and informal, are used to measure and evaluate children's behavior and learning, there are circumstances under which teacher-designed assessments or written classroom tests are especially useful for the teacher. Paper-and-pencil tests can supplement other types of evaluation and provide teachers with information that the other types lack. The purposes of these tests include providing objective data on student learning and accountability as well as additional information for making instructional decisions.

Teacher-designed assessments support other evaluation measures (e.g., standardized tests), enabling the teacher to make more accurate decisions for the instruction of individual students. Teacher-designed assessments can provide input that other types of assessment lack (Edutopia Staff, 2014; Epstein, Schweinhart, Debruin-Parecki, & Robin, 2004; Furger, 2014). For example, a teacher can use observation, tasks completed during group instruction, and manipulative activities to determine a child's learning progress. A written test used with older children can reinforce or support the teacher's evaluation of learning objectives.

Teacher-designed assessments can also support teachers' decisions that may be questioned by parents or school staff members. The teacher may understand, from ongoing work with a child, that the child needs to be instructed at a different level or requires extended experiences with a concept that other children have mastered. Although a teacher may be confident in making the decision, the results of a completed task or paper-and-pencil assessment can support that decision and, at the same time, help parents understand the nature of a child's problem and/or accomplishments. The teacher-designed assessment thus can increase the teacher's accountability for decisions that affect students' learning.

Teacher-designed assessments support data-driven decision making. Teachers must make instructional decisions, both immediate and long term. Data should be collected for each instructional decision using concrete tasks or written tests that support these decisions. By using informal, teacher-designed evaluation strategies, such as individual tasks and ongoing observations of class progress, teachers can obtain information that will help them decide whether to include additional experiences for a learning objective, use review activities, skip planned activities, or conclude the current topic and move on to a new one.

Unfortunately, at present, there is increased emphasis on assigning grades to young children. Although kindergarten children may be exempt, primary-grade students are being given letter or numerical grades in many schools, and the practice has expanded with the recent emphasis on higher instructional and grading standards.

Stylephotographs/123RF

Teachers can design games to be used to teach concepts and for assessment.

Teachers find it difficult to assign letter grades to primary-grade children. Whether the practice should continue is debatable; nevertheless, testing can help the teacher make decisions about student achievement. To use only written evaluations for grading would be inappropriate for all the reasons discussed throughout this book; however, when combined with other developmentally appropriate evaluation strategies, paper-and-pencil tests add supporting information on which grades can be based.

In the same fashion, teacher-designed tests can be used to support diagnostic decisions about student needs. The classroom teacher can supplement information from standardized tests to determine student strengths and needs in content areas. Assessments can be designed that correspond to local instructional objectives and that provide specific information on these accomplishments and needs. Once diagnostic information has been analyzed, the teacher can place students more accurately into instructional groups and regroup periodically as students move through the program at different rates.

Finally, teacher-designed assessments allow evaluation of the local instructional program. Unlike standardized tests, which reflect general objectives suitable for a broad range of school programs at a state, regional, or national level, the teacher-designed test assesses specific or local learning objectives. These outcome-based tests evaluate more closely the effectiveness of the local educational program. Without evaluation measures designed for the classroom, there is no ready method to assess local curriculum objectives.

Enhanced eText: **Self-Check 9.1**

Portfolios can be used to share a child's performance with parents.

Types of Teacher-Designed Assessments Used with Preschool and Primary-Grade Children

Teacher-designed assessments for preschool children must match the way these children learn—through active interaction with concrete materials. Children who do not yet read cannot demonstrate their learning effectively with a paper-and-pencil test. The teacher constructs assessment activities that allow the child to manipulate materials, explain understanding orally, or point to the correct response if expressive language is limited.

Teacher-designed assessments using tasks or oral responses can be conducted during a teaching activity, as part of a learning-center experience, or as a separate assessment or series of assessments. For example, to determine whether children can recognize uppercase and lowercase letters, the teacher can select letters from concrete classroom materials or cards with five letters and ask the child to match the upper- and lowercase. Figure 9-1 pictures an array of cards that can be used for this purpose. The alphabet cards are cut into individual cards. The teacher selects five letters to work with at a time and has the children match the uppercase and lowercase letters. There can be sets of cards for each child, or several sets for small group activities.

To demonstrate an understanding of counting, the preschool child is given objects to count. The teacher can conduct the assessment in two ways. For instance, the teacher may either select five objects and ask the child to count them or ask the child to group five of the objects. To assess knowledge of shapes, an array of basic shapes could be used. If the objective is to identify shapes, the teacher can ask the child to find a given shape by saying, "Show me a triangle." The teacher can also point to the shape and ask the child to name it if the objective is to be able to name shapes. It is important that the shapes are all the same color so that the child is focused on identifying shapes and is not distracted or confused by the colors of the shapes. Figure 9-2 shows basic shape cards that can be used to identify circles, squares, triangles, and rectangles.

Figure 9.1 Uppercase and lowercase letters

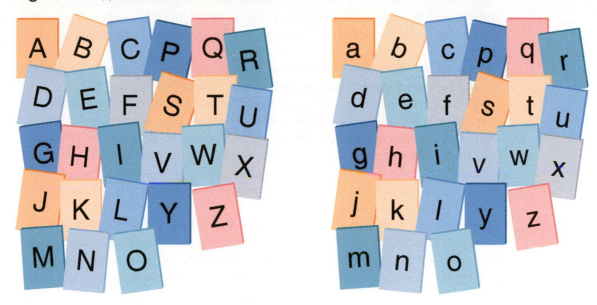

After preschoolers can name the four basic geometric shapes, other familiar shapes, such as a star or heart, can be added. After more experience with shapes, the children can do a simple shape-matching activity sheet (Figure 9-3).

For some preschool assessments, an oral response may be most appropriate. For example, a common preschool objective is for the child to know his or her first and last name. The teacher could ask the child to give this information.

Figure 9.2 Basic shapes

Circle   Square

Star   Rectangle

Heart   Triangle

For the objective of sequencing events in a story, the teacher might show a child a set of three to five picture cards that have a logical sequence and ask the child to put them in order. The child then is asked to tell the story. Figure 9-4 shows a series of pictures that can be used for sequencing and providing verbal descriptions.

As children learn to read, the teacher's assessments begin to include printed test activities with pictures and some written words. Instead of a physical response using concrete materials or an oral response, the child uses a pencil with a printed test. The best option is for teachers to design their own assessments to complement the curriculum being used in the classroom. Teachers must be able to design their own tests to evaluate their own or individual learning objectives most effectively. Commercially produced materials are also frequently used. Figure 9-5 shows a worksheet on which beginning readers can match sequence pictures with sequence words by drawing lines between pictures and words.

Paper-and-pencil tests must be adapted to the child's reading and writing skills. Therefore, tests designed for children in the primary grades use a format that provides pictorial or visual clues to help the student select or write the correct response. To prepare beginning readers and writers for written tests, the teacher introduces key words

Figure 9.3 Basic shapes worksheet

Name: _____

Draw a line to connect the shapes that match.

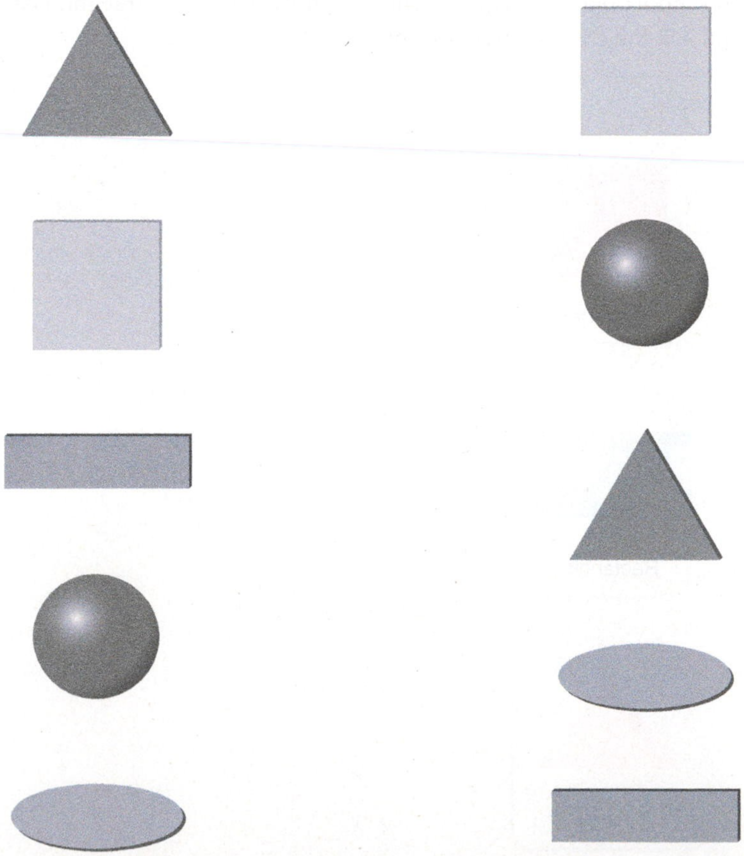

Figure 9.4 Sequencing cards

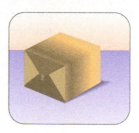

such as *circle* or *draw* that are commonly used in paper-and-pencil assessments. More words are taught until the child is able to read written instructions. Throughout the primary grades, the teacher introduces the assessment page to the children before asking them to complete the page independently.

Figure 9.5 Sequencing worksheet

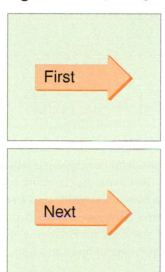

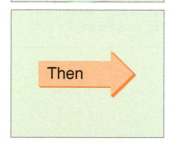

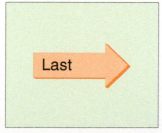

The most common beginning written tasks include *marking or circling a response, drawing a line to a response, marking a response with an X,* and *writing simple numeral or word answers.* Children can circle pictures in response to questions before they have learned to read and write. This type of response is continued in the grade levels where beginning reading skills are acquired.

As reading and writing progress, words can be selected or written for assessment tasks. In Figure 9-6, the student circles the word that fits the blank in a sentence, using a multiple-choice format. In Figure 9-7, a teacher-designed assessment for reading vocabulary, the student must determine whether to write each word under the "People" category or the "Places" category.

All the examples of written assessments for the primary grades follow the same guidelines. Not only must the child have visual clues to be able to respond, but also an example is usually given to help the child understand the task. Also, although there are written instructions for the child to read, the teacher may need to read and discuss the instructions with the students to ensure that they understand what is required. In the following section, the design of teacher-constructed assessments and written tests is discussed.

Enhanced eText: Self-Check 9.2

Developing Quality Teacher-Designed Assessments

The steps in test design described in this chapter provide a guide to developing quality assessments that are directly linked to the learning process. Test items and learning activities are linked to the same learning objectives so that teachers are teaching and testing to the same levels of knowledge on Bloom's taxonomy (discussed later in the chapter). Similar steps can be taken for all teacher-designed assessments. Following are some suggestions for teachers to consider when designing assessment tasks and tests.

Figure 9.6 Assessment in which a student selects a word for a sentence

Growing Flowers

Circle the word that fits in the blank for each sentence.

1. Planting a _____ is the first step in growing flowers.

   seed   nut   leaf

2. The flower plant next grows a stem and _____.

   trunk   leaves   bud

3. The _____ carries water for the plant.

   flower   leaves   stem

Figure 9.7 Teacher-designed assessment for reading vocabulary

PEOPLE AND PLACES

Write each vocabulary word under People or Places below.

People	Places	Words
		bank
		firefighter
		friend
		grocery store
		neighbor
		park
		police officer
		post office
		school
		sister

Concrete Tasks for Preschool

- Be sure that the task is at the same level of difficulty as the learning activities designed for the learning objective. For example, if the learning objective is identifying colors, then specific tasks could include identifying colors of crayons when drawing a picture or the colors on a puzzle when putting it together.

- Have a variety of objects and/or concrete materials available so that the assessment task can be administered several times. For example, when learning to count objects of 5 or less, materials could vary to include counting blocks during center time, counting utensils during meal time, or counting the number of steps up to the sliding board at recess.

- When possible, administer tasks for a number of learning objectives. Have materials for a number of tasks organized and available. This approach is called **integrated curriculum**, the practice providing "curriculum experiences that integrate children's learning *within* and *across* the domains (physical, social, emotional, cognitive) and the disciplines (including language, literacy, mathematics, social studies, science, art, music, physical education, and health)" (NAEYC, 2009, p. 21).

Tests for Primary-Grade Children

- Be sure that test items match the child's reading level. Use the lowest possible reading level to help ensure success.

- Use clear directions, even if they will be read by the teacher. Make sure the directions are simple and to the point. For English Language Learners (ELLs), it is important to use pictures or other concrete cues when giving directions.

- Ensure that response items for multiple-choice-type assessments have one correct answer. Once the multiple-choice-type assessment is drafted, ask another teacher to review the questions to check the clarity of correct answers.

- Ensure that response options for multiple-choice-type assessments are the same length and are brief. The more succinct and uniform the choices, the more likely the child will be concentrating on finding the correct answer rather than the longest or most complex.

- Keep the list of items brief for matching exercises. It is better to have a few key matching items that represent the learning objective being assessed than a long list in which the child may feel overwhelmed or suffer from test fatigue.

- Be sure that the list of items for matching exercises is homogeneous. Include possible choices that are logical and consistent with the content and grade level of the children.

- Ensure that the length of blanks is the same for completion test items. Thus, the length of the blanks does not give away the answers.

- Use only one blank for each completion item. It is better to separate content in multiple items than to try to lump them together.

Unlike standardized tests that provide general information about student achievement, teacher-designed tests measure student accomplishment and learning needs in relation to specific classroom objectives. These tests can be used to support formative and summative testing (Linn & Miller, 2005).

Formative and summative tests are related to **mastery learning** (Bloom, Madaus, & Hastings, 1981). Benjamin Bloom believed that nearly all students could reach high achievement if teachers could provide sufficient time and quality learning conditions (Guskey, 2009, 2010). To achieve mastery learning, teachers need to monitor children's knowledge before, during, and after the learning process. This process may include pre-assessment information as well as formative and summative testing. **Pre-assessment** is one type of teacher-designed measure used to understand children's skills, knowledge, and approaches to learning *before* instruction (Guskey, 2018; Guskey & McTighe, 2016). Data from pre-assessments help guide teachers in their decisions about where to start instruction for new skills or content. Pre-assessments can be narrow or broad in their focus. For example, a pre-assessment with a narrow focus might be given to a classroom of children before starting a new unit in mathematics to see what math skills *each child* already knows, those which are emerging, and the skills they do not yet understand. Or, a broadly focused pre-assessment might be given to a group of children at the beginning of the year to determine their general knowledge in relation to grade level goals. These data-driven decisions are prevalent in today's classroom settings where informed instructional decisions and differentiated instruction are considered a best practice.

Formative tests are given periodically while teaching specific objectives to monitor student progress. These tests measure a limited number of objectives at a time so that the teacher can identify which objectives have been mastered and which call for additional work or activities. They provide feedback and are not used for grading purposes.

Enhanced eText: Video Example 9.1

A **summative test**, in contrast, is the final test given on completion of a unit of work. The unit of work may be organized for a single objective or for a small group of objectives. The summative test is given after instruction and formative testing reveal that the material has been mastered. It is administered as the final step to verify the student's achievement on the material covered in the unit or by a group of objectives.

The information gained from formative and summative testing provides the teacher with current, relevant information for instructional planning. It allows the teacher not only to group students for instruction effectively but also to determine how long the class needs to continue working on objectives and whether alternative types of experiences are needed to correct learning needs in particular students. Unlike standardized tests that are administered once a year, teacher-designed tests provide ongoing, criterion-related information about student progress on objectives being covered in a particular classroom. To use classroom testing effectively, the teacher must know how to design appropriate tasks that match the students' ability to use paper-and-pencil tests. The teacher must also know what kinds of tests will accurately measure the students' progress or mastery of each learning objective.

Steps in Test Design

Teacher-designed classroom assessments, although less rigorously constructed than standardized tests, must accurately measure objectives for classroom instruction. Whether the teacher is organizing assessment strategies for preschool or primary-grade students, tests are carefully designed to fit the learning objectives. In this section of the chapter we discuss teacher-designed assessment in terms of test design and refer to evaluation strategies for preschool students who are nonreaders, as well as for students in the primary grades who are beginning to read and write.

Several steps in test design must be followed if a test is to measure student learning accurately. Based on Bloom's model of mastery learning (Block, 1971; Block, Efthin, & Burns, 1989), the process includes the following:

1. Determining instructional objectives
2. Constructing a table of specifications
3. Designing formative and summative evaluations
4. Designing learning experiences
5. Designing correctives and enrichment activities

Determining Instructional Objectives

In Chapter 6, we discussed objectives relative to skills continuums and checklists. Similar to objectives in relation to skills continuums and checklists, the same types of sources are used to develop instructional objectives that will be used to design classroom tests. Although the term *learning outcomes* has replaced *instructional objectives* in many states and school districts, they have the same purpose. School districts have various sources to draw from when determining curriculum objectives for each grade level.

During the 20th century, the common source of curriculum objectives was basal textbook series used in the classroom. Most textbooks in reading, mathematics, social studies, and science were based on learning objectives appropriate for that grade level in school districts in many states. A commonly accepted pool of learning objectives could be found in the content areas for each grade level; however, objectives could vary markedly among different basal series. Textbooks were organized around these objectives, and teacher's editions of the textbooks contained activities to implement instruction for the objectives and tests to evaluate student learning on the objectives.

In more recent decades, national and state standards are often the framework for curriculum and instruction. Standards were developed to clarify educational objectives and raise the learning achievement of students in public schools overall. The Common Core State Standards (CCSS) are used as a primary source of learning standards for grades K–12 in public schools (National Governors Association Center for

Best Practices and Council of Chief State School Officers, 2018). Standards from either of the two areas of CCSS (English Language Arts/Literacy or Mathematics) can be a good beginning point for developing a learning objective for school-age children. Commercial materials are rapidly becoming available based on the CCSS. Abundant resources on the Internet can be used to assist teachers in developing curriculum and assessments in their classrooms. Similarly, states have developed early learning standards to help guide care and education of children prior to school entrance.

WRITING BEHAVIORAL OBJECTIVES. **Behavioral objectives**, or **instructional objectives**, provide the framework for curriculum and instruction and the measurement of the effectiveness of instruction and learning. Many states and school districts require that behavioral objectives that specify the measurement of the effectiveness of instruction and learning be included in instructional planning. The objective is stated in observable, behavioral terms to include the following:

- An observable behavior (action verb specifying the learning outcome)
- Any special conditions under which the behaviors must by displayed
- A performance level considered sufficient to demonstrate mastery (Kubiszyn & Borich, 2003)

Another approach to understanding the elements of a behavioral objective would be to use an ABCD acronym:

- A is the audience
- B is the behavior
- C is the condition
- D is the degree or level of mastery

For example, a common objective for preschool children is to be able to sort objects into two groups by using some type of criterion. An instructional or behavioral objective could be written as follows:

> Given an array of nuts, the student will be able to sort the nuts correctly into two groups—nuts with smooth shells and nuts with rough shells—nine of ten times.

An analysis of the objective would identify the components of an instructional objective as follows:

> Given an array of nuts (C, condition), the student (A, audience) will be able to sort the nuts correctly into two groups—nuts with smooth shells and nuts with rough shells (B, behavior)—nine of ten times (D, degree of mastery).

An objective for physical development might include the ability to catch a ball with both hands. Stated behaviorally, the objective might be worded as follows:

Search and Share 9.1

CCSS and Learning Objectives

Search online to find your state's Common Core State Standards. How can these standards be used to develop appropriate learning objectives? What type of formative assessment might you design to determine a child's progress in learning this content?

Following a series of activities throwing and catching large rubber balls, the child will be able to catch the ball with both hands in four out of six tries.

To analyze the parts of this objective, it would be described as follows:

Following a series of activities throwing and catching large rubber balls (C), the child (A) will be able to catch the ball with both hands (B) in four out of six tries (D).

Before a learning objective or outcome can be measured, then, it must be stated clearly in terms of its content and the desired behavior. The *content* refers to the knowledge or skill to be learned. The *behavior* is what the student does to demonstrate that the knowledge or skill has been attained.

Enhanced eText: Application Exercise 9.1

ANALYZING OBJECTIVES TO DETERMINE PREREQUISITE SKILLS.   The teacher must not only develop the learning objective but also determine what must be taught to the student to master it. Part of planning for instruction involves studying the learning objective to decide what prior knowledge or skills the student must have to be able to learn the new information (pre-assessment). For the objective "Recall addition facts through sums to 5," the teacher plans instruction to help students to learn to combine all possible groups of numbers that equal 5. In addition, the teacher determines what the student must already know to understand and use addition skills. Prior skills to be considered include the following:

1. Knowledge of numbers through 5
2. Identification of numerals through 5
3. Understanding that small groups can be combined to make a larger group

The teacher must decide whether the students have the prerequisite skills to be able to master the targeted learning objective. If not, the prior skills will have to be taught, or retaught if necessary, before the new objective is introduced. A pre-assessment or a diagnostic test may be used to determine student readiness for the learning objective.

SETTING A STANDARD FOR MASTERY   The final step in determining the instructional objectives is to set the level of mastery that will be expected for the student to learn the objective. In the section on writing behavioral objectives, information was included on how to include the performance level for the objective. In this context, the process for determining the level of performance desired or required is discussed. The teacher, the school district, or the state department of education may set the level of accomplishment. This is the minimum standard required to pass the objective. The learning objective can reflect the established standard for mastery. If 80 percent is established as the minimum standard for mastery, the learning objective can be stated to reflect the standard.

Enhanced eText: Video Example 9.2

Constructing a Table of Specifications

After the learning objectives for a unit of study or the content of an entire course of study has been described behaviorally, the teacher or curriculum developer is ready to outline the course content. Before a test can be organized to measure the curriculum objectives, it is necessary to understand more accurately what concepts or skills are to be measured and to what extent the student will be expected to perform to demonstrate mastery of the objective. Will the student be expected to remember information, use the information to solve problems, or evaluate the information? The test items will reflect the level of understanding that is required to master the objective.

Analysis of objectives to determine the level of understanding is commonly done by constructing a **table of specifications** (Linn & Miller, 2005). Here, learning objectives are charted by using Bloom's *Taxonomy of Educational Objectives* (Bloom, 1956). This work describes levels of understanding in the cognitive domain, ranging from the ability to recall information (the knowledge level) to the highest level of understanding (evaluation). Figure 9-8 explains the levels of Bloom's taxonomy, with examples of terms that characterize each level. In Figure 9-9, an adaptation of the taxonomy is used to make a table of specifications for the mathematics unit covering addition sums to 5. The two objectives for the unit are listed to the left of the figure. The columns to the right describe how the objectives are charted on the taxonomy. The first objective requires that the student be able to recall addition facts and problems, understand the facts and problems, and apply that understanding. The second objective also requires that the student be

Figure 9.8 Explanation of Bloom's taxonomy

Level of Understanding	Descriptive Terms	
Knowledge Recognition and recall The ability to remember or recognize information	Tell List Name	Define Identify Locate
Comprehension The ability to translate information in your own words Show that you understand	Restate Discuss Explain Review	Describe Summarize Interpret
Application The ability to use information or apply learning to new situations and real-life circumstances	Demonstrate Construct Imply	Dramatize Practice Illustrate
Analysis The ability to break down information into parts To identify parts of information and its relationship to the whole	Organize Differentiate Compare Distinguish	Solve Experiment Relate
Synthesis The ability to assemble separate parts into a new whole The ability to take information from various sources and present it in a created form	Design Plan Develop	Compile Create Compose
Evaluation The ability to make judgments about information To be able to evaluate based on criteria or standards	Decide Conclude Appraise Choose	Judge Assess Select

Figure 9.9 Table of specifications for a unit on sums to 5

Sums to 5	Know	Comprehend	Apply	Analyze	Synthesize	Evaluate
2.1 Recall addition facts through sums to 5	X	X	X			
2.2 Solve problems using cumulative computational skills	X	X	X	X		

able to analyze or solve problems. When designing test or assessment items, the teacher must know the type and level of understanding that test items will reflect and must organize the test so that the described levels of understanding are adequately sampled.

More recent work similar to mastery learning is Response to Intervention (RTI), which seeks to provide high-quality, individualized instruction to all students, particularly students with learning and behavior challenges (Conroy, Sutherland, Snyder, & Marsh, 2008; Fuchs & Fuchs, 2006; Guskey, 2010). Though originally included in federal legislation to offer a model of instruction for children with learning disabilities in public schools, RTI is also applied to early childhood educational settings (DEC/ NAEYC, 2013). RTI includes three levels or tiers of instruction. Tier 1 contains instruction and learning outcomes for all children in a classroom similar to mastery learning (RTI Action Network, n.d.). If individual children are unable to make appropriate progress in the general curriculum and assessment program, then they are referred to Tier 2 instruction where they receive targeted instruction based on individual needs but are not referred to special education. The targeted instruction is usually provided by the classroom teacher with input from specialists. If Tier 2 instruction does not sufficiently help the child progress, then Tier 3 instruction is provided. Tier 3 instruction is highly specialized instruction that may include special education services. Throughout each tier of instruction in RTI, children are individually assessed to determine if they have achieved expected outcomes. Frequently, teacher-designed assessments are used in Tiers 1 and 2 to monitor children's progress or rate of improvement as well as the effectiveness of the instruction; this is sometimes called **progress monitoring** (American Institutes for Research, 2018; DEC, 2013).

Another system, called Depth of Knowledge (DOK), was developed to provide a guide to teachers as they supported children's learning to higher levels (Webb, 2002). Soon after its introduction, state departments of education were using DOK in their curriculum and instruction standards (Webb, Alt, Ely, Cormier, & Vesperman, 2005; Wyoming School Health and Physical Education Network, 2001).

Search and Share 9.2

Response to Intervention (RTI) for Early Childhood Settings

Search online to find information about how RTI is used in early childhood care and education settings. Do you feel this approach is effective in meeting the needs of children with learning challenges? What barriers to the implementation might occur?

Figure 9.10 Depth of Knowledge (DOK) levels

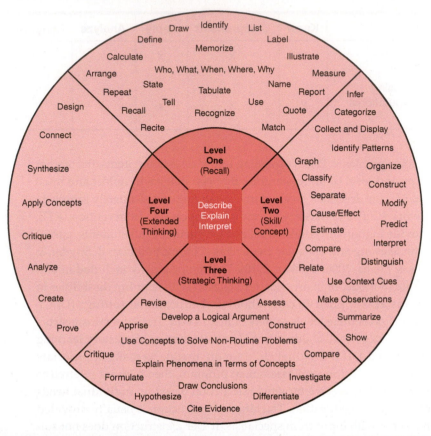

Level One Activities	Level Two Activities	Level Three Activities	Level Four Activities
Recall elements and details of story structure, such as sequence of events, character, plot, and setting. Conduct basic mathematical calculations. Label locations on a map. Represent in words or diagrams a scientific concept or relationship. Perform routine procedures like measuring length or using punctuation marks correctly. Describe the features of a place or people.	Identify and summarize the major events in a narrative. Use context cues to identify the meaning of unfamiliar words. Solve routine multiple-step problems. Describe the cause/effect of a particular event. Identify patterns in events or behavior. Formulate a routine problem given data and conditions. Organize, represent, and interpret data.	Support ideas with details and examples. Use voice appropriate to the purpose and audience. Identify research questions and design investigations for a scientific problem. Develop a scientific model for a complex situation. Determine the author's purpose and describe how it affects the interpretation of a reading selection. Apply a concept in other contexts.	Conduct a project that requires specifying a problem, designing and conducting an experiment, analyzing its data, and reporting results/solutions. Apply mathematical model to illuminate a problem or situation. Analyze and synthesize information from multiple sources. Describe and illustrate how common themes are found across texts from different cultures. Design a mathematical model to inform and solve a practical or abstract situation.

The DOK is very similar to Bloom's taxonomy. Instead of Bloom's five levels of understanding, DOK has four. Level 1 is titled recall; Level 2, skill and concept; Level 3, strategic thinking; and Level 4, extended thinking. In addition, there are many more descriptors of student behaviors for each level. Figure 9-10 provides a chart of the DOK levels and descriptors. At the bottom of the figure, suggested activities are matched with the four levels. Figure 9-11 compares Bloom's taxonomy and Webb's Depth of Knowledge levels.

Figure 9.11 Comparison of Bloom's Taxonomy and Webb's Depth of Knowledge levels

Bloom's Taxonomy	Depth of Knowledge
KNOWLEDGE Recalls facts, retells events COMPREHENSION Shows understanding, can explain information	RECALL Recall of a fact, information, or procedure
APPLICATION Is able to use information or apply to new situations	SKILL/CONCEPT Use of information, conceptual knowledge, or procedures
ANALYSIS Can break down a situation or information into parts or components	STRATEGIC THINKING Develops a plan or sequence of steps; uses more than one possible answer
SYNTHESIS AND EVALUATION Can assemble parts into a whole and make value judgments about the process	EXTENDED THINKING Uses time to think and process multiple conditions; investigates

Designing Formative and Summative Evaluations

After the teacher has determined what is to be measured by designing a table of specifications for the learning objectives to be taught, it is time to design the formative and summative evaluations. Both types of evaluations are derived from the table of specifications. Assessment items will be designed to measure the student's achievement at the levels of Bloom's taxonomy, as described in the table of specifications. The assessment items on the two forms are equivalent, but the evaluation purposes differ. The formative evaluation is not a test; it is a progress report on the student. The teacher uses the formative evaluation to decide whether the student needs further work with the objective.

If the student needs additional experiences, more activities, known as **corrective activities**, are implemented. Correctives are learning resources designed to approach the objective differently from the original instruction. The intent is to provide various kinds of activities to meet individual students' needs.

If the student's responses indicate mastery on the formative evaluation, the teacher provides **enrichment activities**. The student engages in activities that are at a higher level on Bloom's taxonomy than are required for mastery. Thus, if the mastery level in the table of specifications is at the application level, students who master the information after an initial period of instruction may benefit from activities at the analysis, synthesis, or evaluation levels (Bloom et al., 1981). Corrective and enrichment activities are discussed in more detail later in this chapter.

The summative evaluation is the final assessment or test of what the student has learned or accomplished. It is given after all instruction has been concluded. Although formative and summative evaluations are interchangeable in content, only the summative form is used as a test. The decisions to be made about both assessments include the format, selection of assessment items, determination of length, and assembly of the assessment.

TEST FORMATS AND ASSESSMENT ITEMS   Earlier in the chapter, we talked about test formats for use with children in preschool and primary grades. When the teacher is ready to design classroom assessments, the appropriate format will have to be determined. Most preschool children respond best to concrete tasks and oral questions. Assessment items reflect the table of specifications and use appropriate concrete strategies for preschool children. Figure 9-12 shows a table of specifications for a preschool

Figure 9.12 Unit objective: Classifying objects by common attributes in a table of specifications

Behavioral Objectives	Knowledge	Comprehension	Application	Analysis	Synthesis	Evaluation
A. Classifying 1. The student will describe the object by naming one of its attributes.	X	X				
2. The student will construct a set from various objects by classifying together those with common attributes.	X	X	X			
B. Noting Differences 1. From a set of four objects, the student will remove the one object that is different from the others.	X	X	X	X		
C. Classifying by Name 1. The student will classify a group of pictures into two categories, using class names.	X	X	X			
D. Classifying by Design 1. The student will classify objects into sets according to design, such as stripes, dots, etc.	X	X	X			

unit on classification. Objective B specifies that the student will be able to remove the object that is different from a set of four objects. Figure 9-13 pictures a group of objects that may be used to evaluate the child's performance on the objective. The child chooses or points to the object that does not belong to the group.

Concrete tasks should also be used with children in the primary grades, along with activities using reading and writing. When a teacher moves to a written test for first graders, the teacher should limit student responses to tasks that require little or no reading or writing, such as circling pictures, marking the correct response, and drawing lines to correct responses, as introduced earlier in the chapter. In the unit on coins described in Figure 9-14, children will have a variety of experiences using real coins to learn the objectives. More writing and reading can be incorporated into the test format. If several different tasks are to be used, more than one format can be included on a test. Figure 9-14 shows the table of specifications for the unit on coins. The teacher must develop test items that reflect the objectives to be tested.

Figure 9.13 Classification of objects: Array of objects

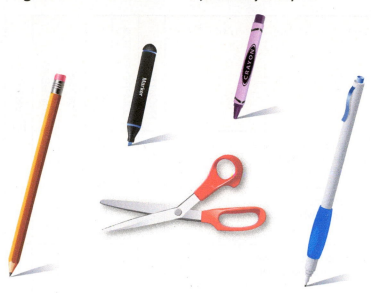

Figures 9-15 and 9-16 are examples of an assessment that includes reading and writing. In Figure 9-15, the student is asked to draw a line from each coin to its letter name, as well as write the value of each coin. In Figure 9-16, the student adds the value of collections of coins and writes the total value of the collections.

TEST LENGTH   After determining the format and developing a pool of items to provide the levels of understanding expected from the table of specifications, the test developer must determine how many test items or tasks will be included in the test. For young children, a balance is reached between the number of items needed to demonstrate and determine the child's understanding and a reasonable length that will not overtax the child's ability to attend to the task. For preschool and primary grades, the test length should not exceed the time normally needed to complete classroom activities and assignments. A maximum of 20 to 30 minutes is reasonable in testing primary-grade students. Commercial tests designed to evaluate these students are commonly one page long.

ASSEMBLY   The final step in test design is to assemble test items into both a formative and a summative form. The teacher should construct enough items so that both forms of the test can be put together at the same time. The formative evaluation, conducted after the students have had some work with the objective, will enable the teacher to assess how well the students are learning the information. After the formative assessment has been examined, the teacher can reteach, provide different types of experiences or practice for some students, or move on to the summative test if the students show adequate progress. The teacher should have enough items to obtain the feedback needed to monitor student learning and mastery. The formative and summative assessments should be equivalent in terms of the level of understanding required and the types of items used.

When assembling the tests, the teacher must decide how instructions will be given to the students. If written instructions requiring reading skills will be used, they must be simply stated to match the students' reading ability. Pictures used must be

Figure 9.14 Unit on coins: Table of specifications

OBJECTIVES	KNOWLEDGE	COMPREHENSION	APPLICATION	ANALYSIS	SYNTHESIS	EVALUATION
1. The student will be able to identify the five coins (half-dollar, quarter, dime, nickel, penny) by sight with 100% accuracy.	X					
2. The student will be able to match the five coins with their letter names with 100% accuracy.	X					
3. The student will be able to match the five coins to their number value using a cent sign (¢) with 100% accuracy.	X	X				
4. The student will be able to classify like coins by counting: pennies by ones, nickels by fives, dimes by tens, and quarters by twenty-fives, with 80% accuracy.	X	X	X	X		
5. The student will be able to differentiate like/unlike coins by switch counting from twenty-fives to tens to fives to ones in necessary order to count collections of coins up to 99¢ with 80% accuracy.	X	X	X	X		
6. The student will be able to analyze and solve story problems by counting coins with 80% accuracy.	X	X	X	X		

clear and easily interpreted. Poorly drawn or inappropriate pictures will hamper the child's ability to respond correctly and distort the child's performance on the test. If the teacher is unable to draw simple pictures, he or she should obtain them from another source or ask a colleague for help.

Designing Learning Experiences

After the table of specifications and the formative and summative evaluations have been constructed, the teacher collects and prepares the activities and instruction that will enable the student to learn the information designed in the objective. Instruction also matches the level given in the table of specifications. Instruction to introduce and work with the objectives includes teacher instruction and other resources normally used by the teacher to help children practice and master new concepts and skills.

The instructional objective contains the structure for the learning experiences that will be provided for the students to interact with and master concepts. The teacher-directed lessons and child-centered activities enable the child to work with information

Figure 9.15 Teacher-designed test on coins

Summative Evaluation

Name _____

1. Draw a line to match the coins with their names.

Quarter   Dime   Half Dollar   Penny   Nickel

2. Write the value of each coin on the line below it.

_____   _____   _____   _____   <u>1 C</u>

Half dollar, backs of dime and nickel: © Asafellason/Fotolia; quarter and penny: © Chris Hill/Fotolia; dime: © Spiroview Inc./Fotolia; nickel: © Vladimir Wrangel/Fotolia.

and skills. When planning the activities, the teacher establishes some type of format to describe each activity and how it will be used. The activity description includes the objective, the materials needed, and any other relevant information.

For example, one objective of the unit on classifying objects discussed earlier could be used to describe appropriate activities. Figure 9-12 had the objective under "B. Noting Differences" as follows: From a set of four objects, the student will remove the one object that is different from the others. Figure 9-13 shows an assessment task that uses an array of objects to permit the child to demonstrate understanding of the objective. Figure 9-17 describes an activity that can be used for young children to experience the same concepts, first as a teacher-directed activity and later in a learning center.

Designing Correctives and Enrichment Activities

Corrective activities provide learning alternatives for children who need additional work after initial instruction and formative evaluation. Three general characteristics of correctives are: (a) presenting the content using a method different than the initial

---

Figure 9.16 Test on coins

Test on Coins

Name _____

Count the value of the coins. Write the total on the line.

Half dollar, backs of dime and nickel: © Asafeliason/Fotolia; quarter and penny: © Chris Hill/Fotolia; dime: © Spiroview Inc./Fotolia; nickel: © Vladimir Wrangel/Fotolia.

method; (b) actively engaging children in learning the concept in a variety of ways; and (c) making sure children experience successful learning (DeWeese & Randolph, 2011). Correctives can include instructional strategies such as audiovisual resources, games, workbooks, peer tutoring, student–teacher discussions, and other opportunities that are different from the original instruction and activities. According to DeWeese and Randolph (2011), the most effective types of corrective activities include tutoring, small-group activities, technological activities such as computer games, paper-based activities such as concept maps, flashcards, or outlines. Most importantly, the purpose of any corrective is to provide different or alternative ways for the student to learn the information in the learning objective.

Examples of corrective activities and enrichment activities may use the objective cited previously: *From a set of four objects, the student will remove the one object that is different from the others in nine out of ten attempts.* A child who needs additional corrective activities to internalize this concept would benefit from opportunities to practice

Figure 9.17 Example of a learning activity

Objective
From a set of four objects, the student will remove the one object that is different from the others.

Materials Needed
A group of 2-inch blocks, 5 of one color, 1 of a different color
Several socks of different types and sizes, 1 shoe
An array of leaves of one type, 1 leaf of a different shape and size

Type of Activity
Teacher-directed, to be placed later in the math–science center. Small group.

Activity Description
The teacher will introduce the concept by using the group of blocks. The words *alike* and *different* will be modeled to describe the blocks.

Next, the socks and the shoe will be explored, with children encouraged to identify the one that is different. The leaves will then be used for the same activity.

As a final step, the teacher will ask each child to find examples in the classroom that are alike and different and to make a group similar to the examples that have been used: three things that are identical and one that is different. Each child is encouraged to describe his or her collection.

---

this skill, but with alternative types of experiences. For example, if the initial teacher-directed activity was focused on concrete objects, a corrective activity might consist of a picture card game of several sets of four cards that include one card that does not belong to the set of four. This game could be played by two children or with another adult. The teacher can record the child's progress with the card game to determine if additional correctives are needed (formative assessment). Another example of a corrective activity for this objective might be to use a flannel board and ask the child to remove the item that is different from an array of four items. Again, the teacher can record the child's responses to determine if further correctives are needed. This cycle of a corrective activity and then a formative assessment to determine the child's progress can continue as long as needed until the objective is met.

Correctives are particularly important for children who are English Language Learners (ELLs) and children with special learning needs. For example, an ELL may benefit from opportunities to use the vocabulary associated with the concept during the card game or flannel activity described above. The terms *alike* and *different* would be basic to understanding the concept. Then, if colors, shoes, blocks, leaves, and so on were used in lessons, those words would also be used so that they could become part of the child's vocabulary. The incorporation of this vocabulary in a variety of contexts but with the same learning objective can provide the repetition needed to learn new vocabulary. A formative assessment (e.g., checklist with targeted vocabulary) of each child's progress should be completed after each corrective activity. In recent years, research focused on strategies for teaching ELLs has brought into focus the need for correctives. For example, studies show that children who are ELLs and at risk for reading problems benefit from small group instructional experiences with one or more peers that include numerous opportunities to respond to questions, practice speaking or reading words and sentences, receive explicit feedback from teachers, and participate in direct instruction in reading (U.S. Department of Education, 2018).

An example might include having an ELL work with an English-speaking peer on counting ten objects using a different corrective for each of these types of experiences with formative assessment informing the next activity for each one.

A similar process would be important for children with special needs. Children with intellectual delays, in particular, might need many extra experiences on a one-to-one basis with the concept, while children with visual difficulties may need to have the lesson adapted with items that can be differentiated by touch. Teachers and support staff for children with special needs must plan ahead how concepts can be presented for individual children.

Enhanced eText: Video Example 9.3

Enrichment activities provide opportunities for higher-level thinking for students who have demonstrated mastery of the learning objective on formative assessments and do not need corrective activities (Guskey, 2010). Enrichment activities offer meaningful learning experiences that challenge students while other children are still working on the learning objective. Peers of children needing Tier 2 instruction in RTI, for example, can further their learning by engaging in enrichment activities without going to another topic. For instance, if additional complexity is desired in the example described above, the number of items may be increased with two items that are different, rather than one. Another way to increase complexity is to make the difference in the item more difficult to identify. For example, if four pictured items are gift-wrapped boxes, the ribbon on one of the boxes is a different color or texture or part of the ribbon is missing as the one that is different.

Enrichment activities also allow students who easily mastered the objective initially to engage in challenging and more creative activities. The students can work on individual projects that allow them to problem-solve and apply their own ideas in various types of activities that emerge from their own efforts (Block, 1977). Students may develop pictures of items that are alike and different or write a story in which each page has a different category of items with one that is different.

Phyllis and Amy

Phyllis and Amy are both in the first grade. Phyllis is an accelerated learner who grasps classroom information with little effort. Amy has cognitive delay. She works at a much simpler cognitive level than the other children in the classroom. During the mastery learning process used in the classroom, Amy often works with a teacher's aide who has activities designed for her learning needs. When the class works on the concept of *alike* and *different,* Amy has activities that concentrate on two colors. She and the aide have large discs that are red and blue. After many lessons, Amy is able to say which disc is different in an array of three red discs and one blue disc.

When the class is working on correctives and enrichment activities, Phyllis often asks to work with Amy. Phyllis is given classroom objects that Amy is familiar with and can name. Together, they practice the concepts of *alike* and *different* with pairs of objects. Phyllis alternates using like objects and different objects with Amy as if they are playing a game. Amy loves having Phyllis work with her, and Phyllis enjoys helping Amy feel that she is part of the class.

Enhanced eText: Self-Check 9.3

Advantages and Disadvantages of Using Teacher-Designed Assessments

Teacher-designed assessments in the classroom have several advantages over commercially produced tests developed for the same purpose. The advantages are related to the flexibility of the tests constructed for the teacher's own classroom.

When a teacher plans an assessment activity or test, the objective or objectives to be tested may be selected to suit individual class needs. Unlike commercial tests, which may be programmed to fit student progress in a grade-level textbook, the teacher-designed test can vary from the structure or plan of the book. A teacher may be concerned about an objective outside the textbook sequence and feel compelled to conduct an evaluation. Because he or she is developing tests to fit classroom needs, the targeted objective can be tested within the teacher's assessment plans whenever needed.

In addition, teacher-constructed assessments can be designed for a particular class. If the children are nonreaders but have advanced concepts that are normally introduced to children who have reading skills, the teacher can write the test to accommodate their

Assessments for Instructional Objectives:

How Useful Are They?

Norris teaches kindergarten. He and the other kindergarten teachers have been sent to a training session on designing assessments for instructional objectives using mastery learning. In the session, the teachers have reviewed how to write behavioral objectives and how to construct a table of specifications based on Bloom's taxonomy of educational objectives. Working with the table of specifications prepares them to design assessment strategies for the objectives.

On the way home after the training session, Norris and the other teachers voice skepticism. How can this kind of testing be used with kindergarten children? Norris comments, "I can see how some areas, such as math, can be organized and assessed by behavioral objectives, but how do you decide what 80 percent accuracy is on learning the Pledge of Allegiance, or what they learn from art or using concepts in science?" Norris finally decides that it is a matter of common sense. The teacher can apply the strategies with some parts of the curriculum in kindergarten but not others. The question is whether the school's principal and the kindergarten coordinator will share Norris's perspective. He and the other kindergarten teachers decide to talk to teachers at other grade levels to determine how they are implementing the assessment strategies. Afterward, they want to study their curriculum and decide where they can use assessments based on a table of specifications. They want to meet with the principal and the coordinator to discuss where the process will work and which parts of the curriculum do not lend themselves to that type of assessment.

When Norris and the other teachers meet with the principal and the kindergarten coordinator, they present tables of specifications and assessments for mathematics and units in science. After they explain their reluctance to use the process with their reading program and other curriculum components, the kindergarten coordinator supports their position. The principal is more reluctant but decides to let the coordinator work with the teachers to determine how and where the assessment strategies will be implemented at the kindergarten level.

abilities. If the students are advanced readers, the test can be designed to take advantage of their reading skills. The most common difficulty with commercial classroom tests is that they are set for a certain reading level or penalize the child for being unable to perform well because pencil-and-paper skills are required. The teacher can modify test tasks to include manipulative activities, oral responses, and assessment within instructional periods if the child understands concepts but cannot yet respond on a written test.

Teacher-designed assessments can be improved whenever needed. Each time the teacher administers a test, student responses provide feedback on its effectiveness. The test can be changed and improved whenever students' responses indicate problems with the format or test items.

Teacher-designed tests also have disadvantages; potential weaknesses generally focus on the teacher's skill in designing classroom assessments. Because teachers do not generally have extensive experience in developing their own tests, the evaluations they design may not be effective in evaluating student learning.

Because of the abundance of commercially designed tests that accompany curriculum texts and kits, teachers are not always required to construct their own tests. Teachers become dependent on commercial tests and do not consider the necessity of designing their own. As a result, the teacher may not clearly understand the purpose of the tests or the levels of knowledge that are tested.

Teachers may lack the training in test design that affects both understanding of the purpose of the commercial tests and the skills needed to construct tests. For example, teachers may not have learned how to use a table of specifications for curriculum objectives. When they design tests, they are not aware of the levels of knowledge in the curriculum that need to be part of the evaluation process.

Finally, the process of developing good classroom tests, especially for younger students, is time consuming. Because test items must be developed to accommodate emerging reading and writing skills, each item must be carefully considered for both content and method or format. This consideration takes more time than developing items for students who have good reading and writing skills. The method of presentation is as important as the concepts and skills being tested.

A discussion of the weaknesses of teacher-designed assessments must include mention of the issues surrounding the use of mastery learning in early childhood education. Because mastery learning requires that the teacher analyze learning objectives and determine the level of mastery to be achieved, it would seem to conflict with the philosophy that early childhood educators should provide developmentally appropriate classroom experiences; that is, the teacher is encouraged to provide learning experiences that are consistent with the child's level of development, rather than to ask the child to fit into a predetermined style of learning that requires specific types of responses to achieve mastery.

The interest in providing developmentally appropriate practices also extends to the use of behavioral or instructional objectives specifically. One criticism of the objectives is the division of learning into small, skill-based objectives, rather than more global constructivist learning. The performance standard or level of mastery seems limiting when compared to the emphasis on child-centered learning that emerges from the child's interests and previous experiences.

Although these issues first applied to preschool classrooms, they are also a concern with primary-grade teachers. Constructivist learning or a "thinking curriculum" (Linn & Miller, 2005) focuses on the student's active involvement in constructing meaning, rather than mastery of specific skills. Thus, students should be engaged in more divergent types of learning and more complex types of outcomes. Performance assessment, discussed in Chapter 10, addresses this issue.

Certain components of the preschool classroom curriculum lend themselves to the mastery learning approach. Concept development, particularly in mathematics, has sequential objectives that can be taught within the mastery learning format. Nevertheless, many early childhood educators object to attempts to limit early childhood programs to this approach. Exploratory and inquiry-based experiences, originating from the child's opportunity to initiate activities both indoors and outdoors and using self-directed learning, are essential in early childhood classrooms. In fact, these experiences are essential for both preschool and primary-grade levels.

Teachers must ultimately be able to understand and use their own assessments appropriately to match the curriculum and their students' development. Mastery learning must also be used appropriately in early childhood programs.

Despite their weaknesses, teacher-designed evaluations have an important place in early childhood classrooms. An answer to the difficulties in using these assessments may be to help teachers understand the process of test design and to support their efforts to develop tests.

Enhanced eText: Self-Check 9.4

Summary

Although written tests are the least commonly used method of evaluating the learning of young students, there is a place for these tests once children have mastered some reading and writing skills. Teachers and parents can use written tests as sources of objective information of student progress.

Like standardized tests, teacher-designed and commercially produced classroom assessments are developed through the use of procedures that ensure they are correct in content and method of evaluation. Test design begins with careful analysis and description of learning objectives for the curriculum. The objectives are examined for the prerequisite skills that must be mastered prior to their use and for how the content and skills must be taught. In addition to determining the level of mastery for the learning objectives, the test developer must use a developmentally appropriate test format that will maximize the performance of students who are learning to read and write.

Before test items are constructed, the test designer must describe the level at which the student must demonstrate the new knowledge. A table of specifications organized for the learning objectives is used for this purpose. While constructing the formative and summative evaluations, the teacher must consider length, equivalent items for both evaluations, and what types of test instructions are most appropriate.

Because paper-and-pencil tests may not be the most effective way to evaluate or assess children in the primary grades, teachers must understand when and how such tests are appropriate. Teachers must have acquired the skills to develop such tests if they are to measure learning accurately and appropriately. Teachers of young students must also understand the limitations of written tests and become skilled in combining them with alternative evaluation methods to ensure that each student is tested with procedures that are most appropriate for his or her own level of development and ability to respond.

> **Enhanced eText:** Self-Check: Chapter Review

Key Terms

behavioral objective 226
corrective activities 231
enrichment activities 231
formative test 224

instructional objective 226
integrated curriculum 223
mastery learning 224
pre-assessment 224

progress monitoring 229
summative test 224
table of specifications 228

Selected Organizations

Search for the following organizations online:
Educational Testing Service
National Institute for Early Education Research (NIEER)

Learning Resources
RTI Action Network
Edutopia: What Works in Education

References

American Institutes for Research. (2018). *Progress monitoring*. Retrieved from https://www.rti4success.org/essential-components-rti/progress-monitoring

Block, J. H. (1971). Introduction. In J. H. Block (Ed.), *Mastery learning: Theory and practice* (pp. 2–12). New York, NY: Holt, Rinehart, & Winston.

Block, J. H. (1977). Individualized instruction: A mastery learning perspective. *Educational Leadership, 34*, 337–341.

Block, J. H., Efthim, H. E., & Burns, R. B. (1989). *Building effective mastery learning schools*. New York, NY: Longman.

Bloom, B. S. (Ed.). (1956). *Taxonomy of educational objectives: The classification of educational goals. Handbook I: Cognitive domain*. New York, NY: McKay.

Bloom, B. S., Madaus, G. F., & Hastings, J.T. (1981). *Evaluation to improve learning*. New York: McGraw-Hill.

Conroy, M. A., Sutherland, K. S., Snyder, A. L., & Marsh, S. (2008). Classroom interventions: Effective instruction makes a difference. *Teaching Exceptional Children, 40*, 24–30.

DeWeese, S. V., & Randolph, J. J. (2011, February 14). *Effective use of correctives in mastery learning*. Paper presented at The Association of Teacher Educators National Conference, Orlando.

Edutopia Staff. (2014). Grant Wiggins: Defining assessment. Retrieved from http://www.edutopia.org/grant-wiggins-assessment

Epstein, A. S., Schweinhart, L. J., Debruin-Parecki, A., & Robin, K. B. (2004, July). Preschool Assessment: A guide to developing a balanced approach. National Institute for Early Education Research (NIEER). *Preschool policy facts*. Retrieved from http://www.nieer.org

Fuchs, D., & Fuchs, L. S. (2006). Introduction to Response to Intervention: What, why, and how valid is it? *Reading Research Quarterly, 41*, 93–99.

Furger, R. (2014). Assessments. What teachers can do. Retrieved from http://www.edutopia.org/what-teachers-can-do

Guskey, T. R. (2009). Mastery learning. In T. L. Good (Ed.), *21st Century education: A reference handbook* (Vol. 1, pp. 104–202). Thousand Oaks, CA: Sage.

Guskey, T. R. (2010). Lessons of mastery learning. Retrieved from www.asce.org/publications/educational/ . . . /oct.10/ . . . /lessons-.of.-mastery-learning

Guskey, T. R. (2018). Does pre-assessment work? *Educational Leadership, 75*, 52–57.

Guskey, T. R., & McTighe, J. (2016). Pre-assessment: Promises and cautions. *Educational Leadership, 73*, 38–43.

Kubiszyuin, T., & Borich, G. (2003). *Educational testing and measurement: Classroom application and practice* (7th ed.). Hoboken, NJ: John Wiley and Sons.

Linn, R. L., & Miller, M. D. (2005). *Measurement and assessment in teaching* (9th ed.). Upper Saddle River, NJ: Pearson.

National Association for the Education of Young Children (NAEYC). (2009). Developmentally appropriate practice in early childhood programs serving children from birth through age 8. Washington, DC: Author.

National Governors Association Center for Best Practices and Council of Chief State School Officers. (2018). *Common core state standards initiative*. Retrieved from http://www.corestandards.org

RTI Action Network (n.d.). Response to Intervention Tiers for Instruction. Retrieved from www.rtinetwork.org/essential/tieredinstruction.

The Division for Early Childhood of the Council for Exceptional Children (DEC)/ National Association for the Education of Young Children (NAEYC). (2013). *Frameworks for response to intervention in early childhood: Description and implications*. Washington, DC: Author.

U.S. Department of Education. (2018). *Best practice for ELLs: Small-group interventions*. Retrieved from http://www.readingrockets.org/article/best-practice-ells-small-group-interventions

Webb, N. L. (2002, March 28). *Depth-of-knowledge levels for four content areas*. Madison, WI: University of Wisconsin Center for Educational Resources.

Webb, N. L., Alt, M., Ely, R., Cormier, M., & Vesperman, B. (2005). *Web alignment tool*. Madison, WI: University of Wisconsin Center for Educational Resources.

Wyoming School Health and Physical Education Network. (2001). Standards, assessment, and beyond. Retrieved March 10, 2010, from http://www.uwyo.edu/wyhpenet

Chapter 10
Performance-Based Assessment Strategies

Carla Mestas/Pearson Education, Inc.

 ## Chapter Learning Outcomes

As a result of reading this chapter, you will be able to:

10.1 Describe performance-based strategies and how they are used.

10.2 Describe different types of performance-based assessment strategies.

10.3 Discuss how to categorize and organize performance assessments.

10.4 Discuss the advantages and disadvantages of using performance-based assessments.

Performance-Based Strategies and How They Are Used

In previous chapters we discussed the many ways that teachers can assess children's learning. We emphasized how to determine what and how children are learning.

In this chapter we add another dimension. We need to work with what children can do with what they have learned. How can they extend their knowledge by applying it in some form? In the content that follows there is discussion of what performance assessment means and the performance strategies that facilitate understanding and using new information.

Understanding Performance Assessment

We have discussed a variety of types of informal and formal assessments such as observation, checklists, rating scales, and teacher-designed assessments. In this chapter, we discuss how assessments contribute to a broader strategy—performance-based assessment. Each assessment discussed previously contributes to the collection of assessment information that is part of performance-based assessment. The strategies used to conduct these assessments permit the teacher to measure a child's performance.

Before proceeding further, we should explain what is meant by performance-based assessment and how it is seen as a positive alternative to the use of standardized tests to measure children's development and learning. Traditional formal methods of measuring learning have focused on assessing what the child knows. Achievement tests are accurately labeled in that they measure what the child has achieved. Performance assessment is advocated as a contrast to high-stakes testing. Early childhood educators such as Meisels (2000, 2014) deplored the situation in which tests determine what teachers teach, what children learn, and whether children fail or are promoted. Rather than depend on tests that are a single indicator of what a child has learned, Meisels proposed that the teacher should have a generative or transformed role with children. The teacher–learner process permits the learner to use his or her own skills to learn new skills.

Enhanced eText: Video Example 10.1

Performance assessments require more in that they measure what the child can do or apply, in addition to what the child knows. Moreover, performance assessment includes completion of a task in a realistic context. Performance assessments require the student to perform some action or activity that demonstrates understanding and application.

Performance-based assessment is considered particularly useful with young children because it measures progress as well as achievement. Children in the early childhood years are proceeding through rapid changes in development that are described as complex because of the interactions among maturation, experience, and learning (Illinois State Board of Education: Early Childhood Education, 2012).

Current needs in the workforce require the kinds of learning reflected in performance assessment. The needs of businesses and other workplaces in the 21st century require that workers be able to solve problems that are at odds with the fact-oriented curriculum found in public schools. The workplace of the future will require that workers find new ways to get work done, and students will need to be able to think critically and analytically rather than simply demonstrate content knowledge (Fadel, Honey, & Pasnick, 2007; Lai, 2011; New Commission on the Skills of the American Workforce, 2007; Stanford Redesign Network, 2008). Supporters of performance-based assessment propose that it reflects higher-order thinking skills, informs teacher instruction, is done in real-world contexts, and can be used for formative and summative judgments (Stanford Redesign Network, 2008).

Authentic Learning and Assessment

Another term frequently used for performance assessment is **authentic learning**, or **authentic performance assessment**. The Illinois State Board of Education: Early Childhood Education (2012) describes **authentic assessment** as "the documentation and analysis of a student's actual work collected over time in his or her real world environment. It tracks students' successes rather than failures. Most importantly, work sample portfolios combined with well-trained teacher observations and knowledge about research-based authentic assessment programs drives instruction" (p. 3). An important element in authentic assessment is that it is linked directly to authentic learning (Baldwin, Adams, & Kelly, 2009). State and national standards for early childhood and elementary school are also significant when considering performance assessments. Current standards require the use of application of learning beyond understanding information.

Advocates of authentic assessment propose that **authentic achievement** must accompany authentic assessment. If we are to use authentic or performance assessment to understand how children can apply or use what they have learned, the learning experiences they are provided must also be authentic or meaningful. Meaningful learning includes intellectual accomplishments that are similar to those undertaken by successful adults and involve tasks and objectives that engage the mind. Meaningful learning provides information on how children function in real-life environments (Riley, Miller, & Sorenson, 2016). When children are engaged in authentic learning, they are given opportunities to link new information to prior knowledge and engage in problem solving.

Authentic learning is based on construction of knowledge and focuses on higher-order thinking. The purpose is to move beyond the knowledge level and to construct new knowledge. This type of learning includes children's communication of their construction of knowledge and application of knowledge in meaningful contexts, such as some type of performance (Illinois State Board of Education: Early Childhood Education, 2012).

Like authentic learning, authentic assessment is meaningful. It requires the teacher to have continual interaction with student work. The teacher engages in dialogues, questioning, suggesting, observing, and guiding to encourage children. The purpose of this approach is to enable children to demonstrate how they can use what they understand and to represent that learning in some type of product or performance. Teachers not only use performance assessments to reflect authentic learning, but also use the results of these assessments as resources to extend and deepen student learning (Kleinert, Green, & Harte, 2002; The Glossary of Education Reform, 2013).

Interrelated Nature of Performance-Based Assessments

Different types of informal and performance-based assessments have been discussed in both this chapter and earlier chapters. At this point, it is important to describe how these assessments are used in an interrelated manner to understand the characteristics of a child's performance. For example, observation can be the basis for assessing a child's performance on a directed assignment, whereas a checklist might be used to record the child's progress on the same assignment. In the following sections, we explore the characteristics of performance assessments and how the teacher uses them to evaluate the development and achievement of the whole child.

THE ROLE OF THE TEACHER   The teacher has the primary role in selecting the types of performance assessments to be used and how they will be used. Because teachers evaluate and use the assessment information, they also have the responsibility to decide which strategies will be most effective for their purposes.

Performance assessment occurs continually in the early childhood classroom. Information is collected throughout the day when children are working in centers, playing outdoors, participating in small-group instruction, and performing whole-group activities. The teacher observes and participates in these activities to acquire the information about each child's progress and the child's own thinking about what and how he or she is learning. Actual examples of children's work and observations of individual growth and development demonstrate the benefits of performance assessments (Meisels, 2014).

Collecting information is only a part of the teacher's role. Interpreting and using the data are another responsibility. First, the teacher must obtain enough information to know the child's abilities and needs so that appropriate planning can further growth and development. Second, the teacher must collect comprehensive information about each child so that all areas of development and learning are addressed. The teacher's goal is to design and implement a program that is appropriate for the child's physical, intellectual, and social development. Likewise, the program should be developmentally appropriate for all the children. The program also should have relevant, real-world application (Hilliard, 2015).

Meisels (2000) adds another dimension to the teaching role. The teacher's role is transformed, in that the teacher's approach to teaching is different in authentic learning and assessment. The teacher provides meaningful learning experiences that children would have never experienced otherwise. At the same time, the teacher empowers the children to learn more independently and spontaneously.

The challenges of the Common Core Standards (CCSS) have also raised the expectations that teachers will have to improve their teaching and assessment practices. Performance assessments themselves assist teachers to learn about the standards and gain the necessary tools to teach knowledge demanded by the CCSS (Darling-Hammond & Falk, 2013). Teachers gained the most expertise when "designing, scoring, and evaluating the results of the assessments" (p. 6). Darling-Hammond and Falk further explained as follows:

> Researchers found that teachers scoring the assessments led to teachers working on instruction, which makes it excellent professional development. Examining and assessing students' work helps teachers learn more about what the students know and can do, as well as what they think. Doing this in the context of standards and well-designed performance tasks stimulates teachers to consider their own curriculum and teaching. (p. 6)

Assessments that are consistent with a relationship of trust and authority between teachers and children also have a different approach. Early childhood educators should be aware of the following (Meisels, 2000):

- In an early childhood setting, it is essential to address yourself to the personal and unique attributes of the children in your care.

- You need to learn to listen, diagnose, examine, hypothesize, intervene, evaluate, and then reflect and redesign.
- Your goal should be to try to create a relationship of trust with children—one upon which learning is based. (p. 18)

Thus, in performance assessment, teaching, learning, and evaluation result from a partnership relationship between teacher and child. Moreover, the teacher uses performance assessment strategies to collaborate with children on the nature of their accomplishments and the next steps in their learning.

The teacher in the classroom described in the box feature about a pizza project is focusing on emerging literacy skills. The strategies that are being used for performance assessment are checklists, observations, videos, digital recordings, and work samples.

The teacher uses checklists to document reading and writing skills. Children drawing an illustration for a big book demonstrate their understanding between pictures and text. As children write menus for the "Pizza Hut," the teacher can observe and document left-to-right skills in their writing skills or their use of uppercase and lowercase letters.

Observations with anecdotal notes can provide more detail about the process a child uses in reading or writing. A video or digital recording can document an entire episode. This type of documentation provides information on various children engaged in an activity that can be analyzed for assessment of what children can do.

Finally, work samples provide the teacher with specific evidence of accomplishment. In the classroom activities described in the scenario, the teacher would have work samples of big-book illustrations, menus, and a Pizza Hut sign for documentation of performance.

Purposes for Performance-Based Assessment

What, then, are the purposes of using **performance-based assessment** with young children? First, the importance of measuring young children appropriately has been an

A Teacher's Assessment Role in a Kindergarten Classroom

Upon entering the classroom of 5-year-olds, a buzz of activity captures the visitor's attention. Children working in small groups are busily pursuing a number of activities. One group is drawing illustrations for the big book that the class wrote describing their trip to Pizza Hut. Another group is creating menus for the restaurant they are setting up in the dramatic play area. "Don't forget to put 'We have pepperoni' on your menu," one child says. The other children nod their heads and continue drawing and writing on their papers. One child is bent over a large sheet of construction paper, with marker in hand. He is carefully copying the words "Pizza Hut" from the word wall the children have created. When finished, he tapes the paper to two chairs he has placed in front of the dramatic area. "Here's the sign," he tells the others. Three other children are looking at a recipe book and discussing the "gredients" they will need to make the pizzas. Another group is looking at books about restaurants in the literacy corner.

SOURCE: Ratcliff, N. J. (2001/2002). Using authentic assessment to document the emerging literacy skills of young children. *Childhood Education, 78,* 66–69. Used with permission from Association for Childhood Education International

ongoing theme in this text. Contrary to many of the standardized tests and more formal strategies that have been criticized as inappropriate to the young child's development, performance assessments can be good tools for evaluating progress in development. Because they are designed to measure a child's performance of a real or designed task or activity relevant to the desired learning, performance observations are directly related to the child's development and achievement (Baldwin, Adams, & Kelly, 2009).

Second, performance assessments are integrally related to instruction. The performance activity is a natural outcome of ongoing curriculum and instruction and not a separate, unrelated type of experience that is unfamiliar to the child. When using performance-based evaluation, the classroom teacher needs to know how to design appropriate, related assessment tools, interpret assessment results to understand the child's progress and plan for further instruction, and interpret performance assessment results to parents and administrators (Adamson & Darling-Hammond, 2010).

Finally, performance assessments are used to evaluate whether early education programs are meeting the needs of young students. Effective performance assessment tools help clarify the goals of preschool programs to provide developmental curriculum. Progress assessment reflects both individual developmental progress and the accomplishment of developmental program goals. The teacher then has the responsibility to report program accomplishments in a meaningful way to administrators (Adamson & Darling-Hammond, 2010; Caffrey, 2009).

Enhanced eText: **Video Example 10.2**

In the next sections, we discuss the types of evaluation strategies that use performance assessments. Although most of the tools are selected or created by the teacher, others use examples of the child's work. Both the teacher and the child plan some of the assessment activities, while others occur spontaneously when the teacher takes advantage of an ongoing activity or event to conduct an assessment.

All of the evaluation strategies discussed are adapted to the individual differences in children. Children who are ELLs may be assessed differently according to their progress in learning English. The child who cannot hear may be interviewed using sign language, while a child without vision may have many sensory materials included in the assessments. Directed assignments are modified according to the needs and abilities of each child. Likewise, contracts (see below) would reflect individual learning abilities, and games are adapted to make it possible for children with special needs, including second-language needs, to participate.

Enhanced eText: **Self-Check 10.1**

Types of Performance-Based Assessments

Many strategies can be used to conduct performance-based assessments. Like checklists and observations, performance-based evaluation has been used for many decades; however, in this context, it may have a broadened purpose or a more comprehensive role as part of a system of evaluation. The assessment strategies appropriate

XiXinXing/Shutterstock

A teacher studies a child's performance on tasks to understand progress.

for use with young children are interviews, contracts, directed assignments, games, work samples, projects, and portfolios.

Interviews

Teachers use interviews to find out what children understand about concepts. Interviews are especially appropriate for young children who are just beginning to develop literacy skills and cannot yet express themselves with a paper-and-pencil activity. The strategies followed in interviews complement the techniques used by Piaget to understand children's thinking. By questioning and asking more questions based on children's responses, Piaget determined not only what the child understood but also the thinking processes used to organize responses to the questions (Seefeldt, 2005). The *Early Childhood Assessment Mathematics Manual* produced by the New York City Board of Education (2009) described a mathematics interview as follows:

> The mathematics interview is a rich assessment technique. The teacher asks the child to solve several mathematical tasks and to explain their thinking as they proceed. The teacher observes and questions the child. This gives the teacher access to how each child figures out particular mathematical problems. Each child's understandings and current strategies can be identified as well as any misconceptions they may have. (p. 2)

Interviews can be described as **unstructured**, **structured**, or **diagnostic**. An *unstructured interview* can occur when children are playing, working in centers, or otherwise engaged in classroom activities. The teacher becomes aware that it is an opportune time to engage the child in an interview and takes a few minutes to question the child (Morrison, 2013).

Structured interviews are planned by the teacher and conducted to acquire specific understandings about the child. For example, the teacher might want to determine the beginning reader's understanding of a story. After a reading of the story, the teacher asks probing questions to elicit the child's thoughts about the meaning of the story. Likewise, concepts in mathematics can be assessed through a structured interview when the teacher asks oral questions about a concept or process and explores the child's responses with further questions. Kamii and Rosenblum (1990) described an activity to determine the kindergarten child's understanding of small addends by dropping beads into two glasses. The child was interviewed about the sum of the two groups of beads to assess the child's progress in mental arithmetic.

Diagnostic interviews serve an additional purpose: to determine the child's instructional needs. The interview may be informal or structured. The teacher's questioning is directed more at understanding what kind of help the child needs through responses to questions. If the teacher notices that the child is confused or making errors, the diagnostic interview can reveal the difficulty the child is experiencing in thinking about the concept or skill.

Teachers can use several techniques to enhance the effectiveness of interviewing for assessment. In addition to taking notes when conducting an interview, teachers can make digital recordings of the child's responses for later review. Seefeldt (2005) suggests that when interviewing children about a social studies concept, responses need not be limited to talking. The child could act out a concept, find an example of the concept in pictures, or draw the things he or she knows about the concept. These possibilities would be helpful for children who are native speakers of another language or otherwise have difficulty expressing themselves verbally.

Interviews with young children should be short. One tip is to limit interviews to 10 minutes. Other tips are (1) to continue questions after the child's initial responses to find out more than whether the child's response is correct and (2) to give the child plenty of time to think about and respond to the questions. The child needs to feel comfortable with the process if pertinent responses are to be elicited.

A Structured Interview to Assess Classification Skills

Nykesha Hillmon's kindergarten class has been studying classification skills. Over a period of weeks, Nykesha has conducted lessons on sorting objects into two groups by using the physical characteristics the objects have in common. The children have worked with the classification of nuts, rocks, and classroom plants. Today, Nykesha has placed an assortment of beans in the science center. She is interviewing Tyrone, who has been asked to make two groups of beans. As Tyrone is in the process of forming the groups, Nykesha begins the interview with questions she has planned earlier:

NYKESHA: Tyrone, can you explain how you decided to make the two groups of beans?

TYRONE: Well, one group of beans is round. They are all round.

NYKESHA: And the other group?

TYRONE: They are all the same as this one (lima bean). I don't know what to call them.

NYKESHA: Good. You have one group of beans that are round and another group of beans that have the same shape. You have made your groups by using their shape. Can you think of another way you could make two groups?

TYRONE: (After some hesitation) I could make groups of big ones and little ones.

NYKESHA: Could you think of another way?

TYRONE: I don't think so.

NYKESHA: How about using their color?

TYRONE: Oh, yes. I could put the ones that have brown together, and the rest that don't have brown together.

Contracts

Contracts serve a dual purpose. They provide a plan between the teacher and the child and a record of the child's progress. Contracts of activities the child will engage in are designed for a period during a day, for the whole day, or for several days. Preschool children need pictures or other visual representations of activities to be completed. Primary-grade children can follow simple written instructions. After the child has completed an activity, some type of check-off system can be used to record the accomplishment.

Contracts can also be used to record accomplishment of skills and concepts. The teacher and the child can use the contract as a guide for conferences and interviews or as a recording system for the teacher to indicate when the child has completed an objective or needs more opportunities to interact with a concept. Over a period of time, completed contracts can provide information on progress and accomplishments.

Directed Assignments

Directed assignments are an extension of teacher-designed assessments, discussed earlier. They are also similar to interviews, except that a specific task is involved in acquiring the child's understanding, rather than an interview. Children who

Using Contracts to Assess Performance

Graciela, a second-grade student, is discussing her mathematics contract with her teacher, Luis Garza. Luis plans contracts with the students on Monday of each week and conducts conferences with the students throughout the week to monitor their progress. Graciela has worked on her contract for 2 days. Her contract on Monday and Tuesday included the following:

Monday:

1. Small-group lesson on subtraction
2. Center activity solving subtraction problems
3. Worksheet of subtraction problems

Tuesday:

1. Game with a partner solving subtraction problems
2. Subtraction worksheet
3. Conference with Mr. Garza

Luis discusses Graciela's work to date. They review her work, which includes the worksheets and problems solved in the math center. Luis notices that Graciela has made several subtraction errors. He questions Graciela and then gives her blocks to help her to work out the subtraction problem. After she has described how she arrived at her answer, he tells her to work out the problem with the blocks again. After the conference, Luis makes a note to observe Graciela the following day to determine whether she needs further help with the subtraction process.

are beginning to read independently might be asked to read a story and discuss it. Preschool children might be asked to use concrete objects to solve a problem in mathematical thinking. The important point is that the teacher makes a specific assignment or task for the purposes of assessment. Discussion and questioning may be a part of the process, but the child's ability to carry out the assignment is the focus of the assessment process (State of Connecticut State Board of Education, 2007).

Games

Games can be used to understand children's progress with a skill or a concept. Although more than one child may be playing a game at one time, the teacher can use observation to assess each child's abilities and thinking. Kamii and Rosenblum (1990) suggest that the teacher use games for systematic observation of an entire class. Two children or a slightly larger group play the game until all the children have been assessed. The ability to make 10 with two numbers is one example of a skill that can be assessed through the child's performance in a game. Cards from 1 to 9 are arranged in groups of nine at one time. The child shows all the pairs that can be combined to make 10. In addition to determining whether the child has mastered the skill, the teacher can observe the process the child uses to solve the problem. If the child arranges combinations quickly, a higher level of progress of mental addition has been achieved than that of a child who must count up from the first card to get the sum with the second card.

Games may be used for concepts and skills in other content areas and with very young children. For example, playing peek-a-boo with an older infant or toddler can inform the teacher about the child's attention span, ability to maintain eye contact, and the appropriateness of his or her emotional reactions.

Over many decades, games have been developed for reading skills. Card games to identify letter knowledge are one ready example. Board games can be adapted or developed for language arts, mathematics, and social studies. A game similar to Trivial Pursuit, in which children must respond to an oral or a written question related to a topic being studied, is an example of how games can be used as an assessment activity to test the child's ability to perform a task or solve a problem.

Enhanced eText: Video Example 10.3

Work Samples

Teachers and children are equal participants in the use of **work samples** for performance assessment. Work samples are examples of all types of children's work that can demonstrate the child's developmental progress or accomplishments (Morrison, 2013). For preschool children, work samples may be clay models of animals that reflect the child's understanding of concepts in a thematic study related to animals. Other work samples include paintings, emergent writing, and dictated interpretations of wordless books. Primary-grade children might have samples of book reports, creative writing that has been illustrated, and work pages of computation problems. Other media, such as photographs, videos, and digital recordings on electronic tablets or computers, might be used.

Digital cameras and electronic tablets are especially useful for this purpose. They can be used to document children's work, as well as a mechanism for transferring work into an electronic form. When classes engage in project work, photographic samples can be made of the project's progress from the beginning to the end of the topic being studied (Howe, 2016).

Work samples are often included in discussions about portfolios because portfolios become the means through which work samples and other types of information related to performance assessment are stored. A system for selecting and organizing work samples is important if the collection is to serve appropriately for performance assessment (Meisels et al., 2010).

Projects

A **project** is an activity conducted by a child or a group of children that is lengthier than a classroom activity conducted during a single class period. The project can be part of a unit of study, such as a science or social studies unit, or part of a theme that is studied by a class. A product of some type results from the project. For example, a second-grade class may study spring wildflowers. A group of students may gather samples of the flowers, identify them, and describe their characteristics. Each flower is dried and attached to the completed information. The completed booklet of wildflowers becomes the product of the project that could be evaluated.

Projects are flexible in terms of meeting student needs. Children with limited English skills may engage in projects that expand language while working with new concepts. Student interests are a part of the project; therefore, different groups may vary in how they conduct a project. For children with disabilities, a project approach can be used to tailor learning opportunities according to a child's abilities and needs.

Search and Share 10.1

Work Samples & Performance Assessment

Search online to find examples of how to use children's work samples as a type of performance assessment. What ideas seemed the most feasible to you? What challenges might occur in using these examples and how would you address these challenges?

Assessing Progress with Games

Joan Harrison, a first-grade teacher, is using a board game to assess reading words. The purpose of the game is to assess children's knowledge of words that have been used in reading activities. Each student has an individual bank of words from books he or she has read. Kim Soo and Martha are playing the game. The children take turns drawing a word card. If they name the word correctly, they can advance one square on the board. The first child to reach the end wins the game. Words that are missed are put in a separate pile, and Joan notes them in her notebook so that she can work with the words in small-group activities.

Portfolios

The **portfolio** was one of the most popular methods of documenting authentic assessment in the 1990s. In looking for alternatives to standardized tests, drill worksheets, and other assessment measures that reflect skills development rather than developmental progress evolving from the student's own demonstrations of performance, school districts across the United States have implemented portfolios as a preferred type of reporting performance-based evaluation. Some states have initiated the use of portfolios in early childhood education programs (Illinois State Board of Education, 2012).

Portfolios are a process or method whereby student performance information can be stored and interpreted. Portfolios may be a folder very similar to collections of student work that many teachers have used for decades for reporting to parents. They may contain examples of papers that students have completed, as well as checklists, anecdotal records, summary reports for a grading period, and any other materials that students and teachers think are relevant to demonstrate the student's performance (Morrison, 2013).

Portfolios may also be the vehicle used for assessing and reporting the student's progress and accomplishments to parents and administrators. How portfolios are designed and used will be discussed in Chapter 11.

Enhanced eText: Self-Check 10.2

Categorizing and Organizing Performance Assessments

Although all performance assessments are considered informal measures, they can be categorized as structured or unstructured and direct or indirect. These organizational patterns are similar to structured and unstructured interviews but are more comprehensive in the types of assessments that are included.

One approach to categorizing assessments is by the type of activity used for assessment. **Unstructured** (or nonstructured) **performance assessments** are those that are part of regular classroom learning activities, such as writing samples, projects, checklists, and teacher-designed tasks and tests. **Structured performance assessments** are predetermined or designed to include questions or tasks that require problem solving, synthesis, and analysis. Questions are open ended, and all students are administered the questions through similar test administration procedures.

Another perspective of the two classifications is as spontaneous or structured. Spontaneous assessments evolve from the teacher's natural day-to-day interactions and observations in the classroom. Structured performance assessment is not only planned but also must meet the standards for reliability and validity required of standardized measurement instruments. Such assessments are carefully designed and have specified scoring criteria, as well as well-defined behaviors that are to be measured.

Performance assessments can also be classified as direct or indirect. **Direct performance measures** require students to use knowledge in some type of application; **indirect performance measures** measure what students know about a topic (Stiggins, 2005). An example of an indirect measure is a paper-and-pencil test. An example of a direct measure is taking measurements of a table to determine how large to make a tablecloth to fit the table. The distinction between these performance measures is assessing knowledge versus assessing application of knowledge.

The Role of Observation

Strategies for observation were discussed in Chapter 7, and the importance of using observation to evaluate the development of young children was emphasized. A discussion of the role of observation within performance assessments reinforces that importance. When considering the measurement of the young child's performance, observation is the most effective strategy (Frost, Wortham, & Reifel, 2008; Jablon, 2010/2011; Reifel, 2011). Observation behaviors such as attending, examining, heeding, considering, investigating, monitoring, studying, and watching enable the teacher to understand and know the child and what the child can do in real-life circumstances and common learning situations (Jablon, 2010/2011).

Observation should occur throughout the day in all types of classroom activities. Strategies for recording observation, including anecdotal records, running records, observation with checklists and rating scales, and time and event sampling, can all have a role in performance assessment. To ensure that the desired performance is observed and recorded, the following components should be determined prior to conducting the observation:

- **Purpose**—What do we want to know?
- **Main Emphasis**—Who or what is being observed? What behaviors might be exhibited? Why is the observation needed?
- **Method of Documentation**—What information is needed? How will it be recorded? How frequently?
- **Use of the Observation**—How will observation results be used? What next steps would be taken to further the child's development?

Gathering and documenting information through observation is not enough. Analysis and use of assessment data must also be facilitated as a result of the observation. Therefore, the child should be observed at different times and places and using different materials before determining whether new knowledge has been developed (Frost, Wortham, & Reifel, 2008). In addition, teachers should spend time reflecting on the information that has been gathered. The purpose of this reflection is so that teachers will use assessment in an intentional manner to plan for children's future learning opportunities. To properly collect and reflect on observation data, teachers might include planning for observations with individual children and groups of children. After data is collected and analyzed, teachers can plan for future instruction based on their findings.

Observation is the foundation of performance assessment. It is used with interviews when the teacher observes the child's responses and behaviors. It is integral to directed assignments as the teacher observes the child completing the assignment or task. Observation enables the teacher to understand the child's thinking and knowledge when engaging in assessment games. Observation complements other strategies used for unstructured and structured and direct and indirect performance assessments. Finally, checklists, rating scales, and teacher-designed assessments of various types incorporate observation as part of, or all of, the process of understanding the child's performance (Baldwin et al., 2009).

Enhanced eText: Application Exercise 10.1

The Role of Documentation

The term *documentation* has been used throughout this text to mean a method of recording a child's progress or accomplishments. Thus, observation, checklists, rating scales, and rubrics can document development and learning, as can assessments related to mastery learning.

In the context of performance assessment, documentation can take a broader meaning, particularly when it is linked to an early childhood program and child-centered or constructivist learning experiences. In Reggio Emilia schools (Wurm, 2005) and early childhood programs using the Project Approach (Helm & Beneke, 2003), the curriculum is child initiated. Although teachers have a major role in preparing curriculum, what is to be learned is not predetermined. Rather, as projects proceed in both programs, children's ideas and questions for exploration take the work in more than one direction or the lessons are expanded from the original plan. Documentation in these curriculum approaches is a process of documenting the progress of the activities to better understand the children's interests, thinking, and problem solving within their activities (Wien, 2011). A major purpose of observation and videos, digital photographs, and children's work is to note how children reacted to experiences and to record the chronological progress of a period of work (Wurm, 2005). The displays and sharing of work at the end of a project is a culminating activity. Displays of the work accomplished by the child serve as documentation of what was accomplished

---

Documenting Infant Development

Sugar is 6 months old. She is in the infant room in a corporate-sponsored child-care center near a large insurance company. Her parents both work for the company.

Caregivers at the center observe the children daily. They are tracing the infant's development toward developmental milestones. Sugar recently learned to roll over. She is now enjoying rolling over frequently during her periods of play. Now she is developing the skills to be able to sit up by herself. She is in the process of using her arms to lift her upper body to an upright position. Each day, the caregiver notes what actions Sugar uses to learn to sit. These will be reported to the parents at the end of the day. When Sugar is consistent in being able to move to a sitting position, she will have reached another physical milestone. The caregivers and parents will have a chronological documentation of this stage of Sugar's development.

that can be shared with parents, other teachers, and students in the school or preschool program. A child's diary is used as an example of documentation of a child's progress in a Reggio Emilia school (Edwards & Rinaldi, 2009).

USING DOCUMENTATION WITH INFANTS AND TODDLERS   Individual forms can be used daily to track routine care and anecdotal notes with infants and toddlers. The forms can include eating, diapering, and nap routines during the day. This information can assist parents and teachers to adapt schedules to individual needs. Journals provide more in-depth information about very young children. The journal focuses on the child's development over a period of time and can include information from observations as well as teacher interpretations of the child's learning (Shabazian, 2016).

CURRICULUM DOCUMENTATION   Curriculum documentation is the teacher's description of what the children are doing over a period of time and includes reflections by the teacher. Curriculum documentation includes photographs of the children engaging in the learning process and their own words. It typically is mounted on wall panels and helps parents to understand and follow the learning progression. The documents include all children in the classroom and their individual attributes and abilities, thus helping parents to appreciate their experiences. Developmental journal entries are kept in a binder for each child. They can be sent home for parental perusal and contributions, and are given to the family at the end of the year. Parents can learn more about their child through teacher observations and interpretations included in the journal entries (Caldwell, 2016; Shabazian, 2016).

DOCUMENTATION THROUGH PHOTOGRAPHS, SOUND RECORDINGS, AND FIELD NOTES   Teachers can understand a child's thinking through photographs and sound recordings. The child feels appreciated and valued when there are records of activities and examples of verbalizations in daily activities. The teacher's participation in documenting children's activities through photographs, the child's thoughts about experiences through recordings, and field notes about class activities increases the teacher's understanding of each child that improves the relationship between teacher and child (Turner & Wilson, 2010).

The Role of Rubrics

In Chapter 8 rubrics were described as being essential to performance assessment. Different types of rubrics were defined and the process used to develop rubrics was discussed. Examples of different kinds of rubrics were provided to demonstrate their flexibility and adaptability to different developmental stages and content areas in preschool and primary grades. In this section, it might be helpful to reemphasize why rubrics are essential for performance assessment. Checklists, rating scales, and teacher-designed assessments tend to focus on whether a developmental milestone or skill has been achieved or how well it has been achieved. Performance assessments, on the contrary, focus on process and progress in development and learning. Teachers must be grounded in how children develop as well as how children use emerging mental processes to acquire knowledge and new concepts. Rubrics provide the framework to assess processes of learning that focus on child-initiated accomplishments. The assessment strategies discussed earlier in the chapter—interviews, contracts, directed assignments, games, work samples, portfolios, and projects—can be used with rubrics. (See Chapter 8 for examples of rubrics.)

Teachers and Children Use Cameras in the Nursery School

The use of photographs to document individual and group experiences has been discussed in various contexts in this text. Photographs of children, teachers, and parents are included in every chapter. In most examples, adults have been responsible for the photographs. One nursery school reported how children were also engaged in taking pictures to reflect their interests and experiences.

Each classroom was given a camera for the children to use. Teachers responded to the children's growing interest in cameras and how they work by introducing various cameras, including older examples so that the children could experience how the cameras were operated and the purpose of various parts in the process. After the children had many opportunities to take pictures and see the results of their efforts, both teachers and children had new perspectives on what the children learned and how they demonstrated what they could understand and do.

Children growing up in the current environment are very familiar with taking photographs with cellphones. Taking cellphone photographs is a constant in the American and world cultures. Very young children are able to view stories and games on cellphones. They can talk with others using social media programs approved by teachers or parents. Using cameras in a preschool enriches their understanding of how to take photographs and share them with others.

SOURCE: Howe, N. (2016). Cameras in the Early Childhood Classroom: A Powerful Tool for Documentation and Reflection. Retrieved from https://bingschool.stanford.edu/news/cameras-early-childhood-classroom . . .

Understanding stories can be assessed in structured interviews. The teacher may read a story to the class and then interview children individually to discuss the story. By asking questions such as "What happened [to a character] in the story?" or "Can you tell me the story in your own words?" the teacher can assess comprehension of text in an emerging reader.

When working with children who engage in thematic projects, the teacher may use the following range of four points or levels to establish the structure of a rubric to evaluate the projects:

- Begin again
- Revision needed
- Acceptable
- Well done

For example, a kindergarten class may study the topic of "homes." After investigating different types of homes in the surrounding neighborhood, small groups select a type of home to study. Construction of a model of a type of home is the task of small groups to represent what they have learned. The teacher designs the following rubric to establish performance standards:

1. *Begin again*
   Group is unable to initiate task.
   Teacher redirection is needed to initiate an appropriate approach.
   Initial efforts show little evidence of understanding the task.

2. *Revision needed*

Project work is incomplete; needs elaboration.

Project does not reflect the information learned.

Additional planning is needed to achieve the desired results.

3. *Acceptable*

Project is completed.

Project reflects the purpose of the task, although details and elements are missing.

Information about the project could be expressed more clearly.

4. *Well done*

Project shows clear understanding of the concepts learned.

Project fully accomplishes the purposes of the task.

Project includes details and elements essential to communicate learned information.

This rubric is generic in that it can be applied to different types of thematic studies. Although it can be applied to projects reflecting the study of homes, it can also be adapted to other projects and topics. It can be simplified or made more detailed as circumstances indicate.

Standards and Performance-Based Assessment

How do state standards for early childhood affect authentic learning and performance-based strategies? Because standards for learning achievement might be linked to mandated standardized tests for accountability in public education and Head Start programs, many educators may assume that authentic learning and authentic assessment are not compatible with mastering state standards. There has been much information on documenting achievement and accountability through such testing, but performance assessment should not be overlooked as the major tool in verifying what children have learned. Performance assessment is particularly important for understanding development in the early childhood years.

To link standards and performance-based assessments, teachers must understand how standards are integrated into the curriculum and how assessment emerges from the implementation of learning experiences. Meeting standards is accomplished by making them a part of best practices rather than as a separate part of the curriculum.

Connecting Standards to Authentic Learning

The first step in linking standards with performance assessments is to connect standards to the curriculum. The task is to develop a relationship between the standards and best practices for young children in quality early childhood programs. Child-centered learning in an environment rich with opportunities for a variety of activities, both indoors and outdoors, can be used to address standards (Baldwin et al., 2009; Drew, Christie, Johnson, Meckley, & Nell, 2008).

One approach is to relate state standards to content areas in the curriculum. Teachers study the standards and match them to the instructional activities planned for the children. The content areas of the curriculum and the standards are organized so that the relationship is mapped out for the teachers.

If curriculum is planned within projects or the study of topics, the state standards are analyzed and matched to the topic being planned (Jacobs & Crowley, 2010). One way to chart the relationship is to use a curriculum web for a topic or project.

Figure 10.1 Planning web correlated with standards

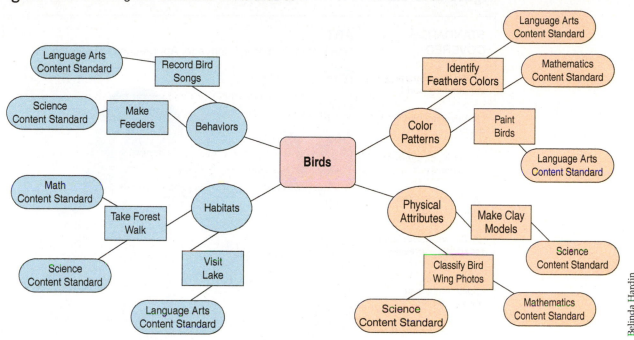

Belinda Hardin

Figure 10-1 shows a planning web for a study of birds with the content standards to be addressed (Baldwin et al., 2009).

Connecting Standards to Performance Assessment

Assessment related to standards incorporates all of the strategies that have been discussed in this book, and especially in this chapter. Whatever type of assessment is used is matched to a standard or several standards. Evidence of a child's accomplishments in activities planned for a project is also evaluated based on applicable state standards. Figure 10-2 shows an example of assessment of a child's performance while doing an art activity based on the teacher's observation, the child's explanation, and the early learning standards in fine motor, cognitive, language, and approaches to learning that were addressed. The teacher maintains a child-centered, developmentally appropriate classroom, an integrated curriculum, and performance assessment that has a direct relationship with state standards (Baldwin et al., 2009).

Learning is a process, and children experience many learning activities before they accomplish a standard. Authentic performance assessments conducted over a period of time demonstrate the child's path to learning (Gronlund, 2006). Moreover, because advances in development are of primary importance in the early years, performance assessments are the best indicators of progress toward meeting early childhood standards.

As discussed earlier in the chapter, the Common Core State Standards are the most recent effort to improve student learning. The standards are intended to serve as a national approach to learning that will replace individual state standards. The CCSS have been adopted by a majority of the states, but concerns about the rigor of the standards have caused some states to question the move. Nevertheless, the higher standards required by CCSS encourage the use of performance assessments both as training for teachers, and

Figure 10.2 Standards correlated to anecdotal observation

STANDARDS COVERED

_X_ Try to understand surrounding world

_X_ Develops pincer grasp

_X_ Develops eye-hand coordination

_X_ Expresses ideas and thoughts clearly

_X_ Shows appreciation for artistic expression

_X_ Describes characteristics of physical world

_X_ Explores objects in surroundings

ART
Fine Motor, Cognitive, Language, Approaches to Learning

Mixing red paint with yellow paint makes green paint.
—Cindy J. (4-21-17)

Teacher Reflections: Cindy is curious about mixing paints. She experimented with putting red paint into containers of other colors. She described the color changes and asked questions about them.

Wortham, Hardin, Assessment in Early Childhood Education, 8e

Poznyakov/Shutterstock

to accomplish problem solving and creative thinking on the part of the students (Darling-Hammond & Falk, 2013; Darling-Hammond & Hyler, 2013; McTighe, 2012).

Enhanced eText: Self-Check 10.3

Advantages and Disadvantages of Using Performance-Based Assessment

Advantages of Using Performance-Based Assessment

Performance-based evaluation for assessment of young children has definite advantages. Although performance assessment is recommended for children of all ages, it is particularly suitable for children in preoperational and concrete operational stages of development. Because young children learn best by acting on the environment, it logically follows that assessment that permits the child to demonstrate ability by performing some action is most compatible with developmental capabilities. Performance assessments, then, are fitting for the development of children in the early childhood years. Some arguments for using performance assessments for evaluation are the following:

1. Performance assessments are conducted in the context of what children are experiencing, rather than in isolation from classroom curriculum. In addition, they are conducted within the teacher's knowledge of families and what is authentic to them. Assessments are adapted to differences in language, culture, and ability. Earlier in the chapter, it was recommended that assessment be an integral part of curriculum and instruction. Whenever possible, performance assessments are conducted as part of a lesson, during center activities, or serendipitously when the teacher observes desired learning demonstrated spontaneously. Performance assessments are meaningful and timely (Meisels, 2014).

2. Performance assessments take advantage of the premise that children construct their own understanding. Early childhood educators today prepare curriculum activities with the comprehension that the teacher does not transmit knowledge; instead, the child gradually forms or produces new knowledge through repeated encounters with concepts and information. Performance assessment provides the teacher with tools to observe and document the child's progress. This provision means that assessment goes beyond assessing whether the child has mastered the teacher's learning objectives. The child's progress toward mastery using Vygotsky's (1983) zone of proximal development can also be evaluated. The zone described by Vygotsky refers to the variability between what the child can currently do and what the child can master potentially in the future. The teacher can determine whether the child is unable to demonstrate an ability or understanding, whether the child can show some of the desired behaviors with assistance, or whether the child can perform independently. Also, the focus of the assessment is on the child, and not on the child's responding to the teacher. The teacher still plays a major role in the assessment, but the child's performance is the key and the teacher responds to what the child is doing. Moreover, performance-based assessments serve as a model for what teachers should be teaching as well as what children should be learning (Lai, 2011).

3. Performance assessments provide a variety of means whereby the child can demonstrate what he or she understands or can do. The child's ongoing work examples, art products, play, conversations, emergent writing, and dictated stories are a few examples of ways that children can perform. Some of the performances can be recorded as a result of the teacher's observation or interviews, whereas others can be documented by work samples. Because assessment is integrated with instruction and daily activities, the possibilities for observing and interpreting accomplishments are almost unlimited.

4. Performance assessment is continuous or ongoing. Unlike more formal assessments such as tests, end-of-chapter assessments, and reporting-period evaluations, performance assessments reflect daily opportunities to be aware of the child's thinking and work. They provide extended performances over time rather than during grading periods (Lai, 2011).

5. Performance assessments provide meaningful information for parents to understand their child's progress and accomplishments. The information is more in-depth than in more traditional assessments (Meisels, 2014). They also enable parents to contribute to, and participate in, the assessment process. Teachers can use performance assessments of all types in parent conferences. Because teachers have visited the homes and are familiar with the parents (see Chapter 3), they can adapt the conferences to be most meaningful for the parents. Likewise, parents can become more aware of behaviors their child is using at home that demonstrate developmental advancement and share their observations with the teacher. Once parents understand the significance of the child's activities and their relationship to development and learning, they can be partners with the teacher and child in facilitating opportunities for the child.

Enhanced eText: Video Example 10.4

Meisels (2014) summarized the benefits of performance assessment for teachers of young children. The teacher should be able to:

- Recognize that children can express what they know and can do it in many different ways
- Evaluate progress as well as performance
- Evaluate the whole child
- Involve children in the process of assessing their own growth
- Establish a framework for observing children that is consistent with the principles of child development
- Contribute to meaningful curriculum planning and the design of developmentally appropriate educational interventions
- Give parents specific, direct, and understandable information about their child
- Collaborate with other teachers, thus enhancing their own professional skills (p. 2)

Disadvantages of Using Performance-Based Assessment

Performance assessments have disadvantages or limitations. Like all other informal assessments, they are subjective; teacher bias and interpretation are part of the process. Teachers must be constantly alert to the need for objectivity when evaluating young

---

Search and Share 10.2
The Role of Parents in Performance Assessment

Search online to find information about the benefits of performance assessment. How can you use this information to help educate parents on the benefits of performance assessment? How can you engage parents in the process of collecting data for performance assessments?

children. Also, performance assessments increase the responsibility and accountability of the teacher in administering and interpreting evaluations. This opportunity for more meaningful assessments is accompanied by the need for teachers to be skilled in the assessment process.

Although some of the strategies used to evaluate children in performance assessments are not new, the approach as the primary means to assess and give grades to students is considered an innovation. Like any educational innovation, problems and difficulties can cause teachers and administrators to become disenchanted with the process and to doubt the effectiveness of the practice. This is the case with the current concerns about the Common Core State Standards. Therefore, it is important to be aware of, and understand, the implications and limitations of performance assessment, as well as the benefits. Following are some of the concerns that measurement specialists propose about the use of performance assessments:

1. Performance assessments are time consuming. Teachers need time to conduct observations, record data, and interpret information in planning future instruction. All performance assessments require extensive involvement of the teacher. Record keeping adds to paperwork responsibilities; moreover, teachers must consider how to fit assessment into otherwise busy days. Teachers must develop the ability to do several things at once and to keep up with reflection on information and ideas they gain from studying the child's performance activities. For example, the teacher can keep a notepad handy to jot down notes during the course of the day. Assessments can be made using observation in the course of teaching lessons to note which children are consistently accurate and which students are struggling with a concept. During project work, the teacher can observe children's actions and note advances in physical and language development. All of these methods are integrated into the school day, making specific assessment activities needed less often.

2. Authentic assessment can be more complex than more traditional types of assessment. Because assessment is integrated into instruction, teachers must clearly understand what they are looking for in an assessment. Assessment with young children might be interdisciplinary or measure more than one type of development when it is a part of integrated curriculum and child-centered activities. The teacher must determine explicit standards of performance for development and learning objectives, no matter how incidental or integrated the assessment process is. The more complex and integrated the curriculum is, the more difficult the performance assessment process will be in terms of interpreting the implications of the child's performance. A related issue is in scoring performance assessments. A common concern is who will determine the quality of performance assessments when they are used for grading or state-level evaluations. Another related issue is the possibility of rater error (Givens, 1997; Lai, 2011).

3. More traditional forms of assessment have had the goal of evaluating the child's achievement. Performance assessment has the goal of evaluating progress as well as achievement. Teachers may have difficulty incorporating this new role of understanding the child's progress and implications for curriculum planning for that child. Teachers must not only develop new competencies in acquiring assessment information but also become more competent in using progress information to further the child's development. Teachers may find this requirement very confusing and be uncertain about how skillfully and appropriately they are using performance assessments (Adamson & Darling-Hammond, 2010; Caffrey, 2009).

4. There are also concerns about the validity and reliability of performance assessments. Early childhood assessment tools must be developmentally appropriate, valid, reliable, and user friendly. As described in the previous section, the difficulty of using performance assessments would raise doubts about how user friendly they are. To be valid, the tools must correlate with concurrent measures being used to assess young children. Likewise, assessments should be internally consistent and assessed similarly by various assessors. Informal procedures used in performance assessments must provide evidence of validity, reliability, objectivity, and freedom from bias if they are to be considered feasible (Darling-Hammond & Hyler, 2013).

5. Parental involvement and education are a requirement when implementing performance-based evaluation. Parents are familiar with traditional evaluation and reporting practices. School districts must plan to educate and prepare parents before moving into performance assessments. Parents need to be knowledgeable and comfortable with how the innovative assessment process is used before they encounter it in their child's grade report or in a parent–teacher conference. Unfamiliar terminology and assessment procedures can cause a lack of confidence in, and support for, the school and teachers.

Most of the disadvantages and limitations discussed previously seem to be related to proper preparation and training for performance assessments. Too often in the past, schools have embraced and implemented curriculum and instruction innovations without training teachers and administrators properly. Some of the authors cited in this chapter consistently discuss the need for extensive training and preparation prior to using new performance assessments. As with any other change or new approach to curriculum or assessment, adequate training and knowledge about performance assessments can do much to ensure that they will be a successful and appropriate alternative for the assessment of young children. Because performance assessments inherently have the potential to measure young children's development and learning in a realistic and meaningful way, the limitations can become either difficult obstacles or perceptive cautions that can be used to facilitate the appropriate and skilled use of new tools.

Quality performance assessments are part of a quality assessment system. In the United States today, a comprehensive system is important to prepare for the implementation of Common Core State Standards at national and state levels. At the early childhood level, the Rhode Island Department of Education and the National Center for the Improvement of Educational Assessment, Inc. (n.d.) proposes a: "Assessments include a variety of different methods that allow children to demonstrate evidence of learning and can range from observations, student writing samples, performance tasks, to large scale standardized tests" (p. 2). Further, "A well-constructed comprehensive assessment system provides continuous, coherent, and high-quality information on student performance that teachers, school leaders, and district and state administrators could use to improve teaching and learning . . . (Rhode Island Department of Education & the National Center for the Improvement of Education Assessment, Inc., n.d., p. 4). This approach to assessment in early childhood programs is consistent with practices for appropriate assessment first supported in the 1990s and now advocated for all levels of education in the new century. Performance assessment was neglected with the focus on standardized tests in recent decades; however, it is now a key to reaching the higher goals set for Common Core State Standards.

The Council of Chief State School Officers (CCSSO) initiated the development of the Common Core State Standards. Author Linda Darling-Hammond (2010) proposed a comprehensive student assessment system to meet the principles of CCSS to be addressed at state and district levels. In a paper written for CCSSO, Darling-Hammond used examples of high-achieving educational systems both in the United States and beyond to provide a framework for assessment systems addressing CCSS. Darling-Hammond (2010) characterized high-achieving systems as ones that, "Seek to implement their standards with assessments that measure performance in authentic ways and with intensive teacher engagement process as teachers work with others to develop, review, score, and use the results of assessments" (p. 2).

Earlier in this text on assessment in early childhood education, characteristics of quality for individual components of performance assessment were discussed. High-quality components of performance are then combined to design a comprehensive assessment.

Enhanced eText: Self-Check 10.4

Summary

The word "perform" is a key to understanding performance assessments. A child performs or demonstrates what is understood and what the child can do with that knowledge. In traditional assessments, the child shows understanding of knowledge. In performance assessments the child is able to apply what has been learned.

In this chapter we discussed the merits of performance assessment as a process that deepens understanding of the child's learning. We have discussed performance-based evaluation as an alternative or authentic method of assessing young children.

A number of methods or strategies can be used to evaluate a child's development or learning through performance of what he or she understands and can do. Interviews, contracts, directed assignments, games, work samples, projects, and portfolios are among the assessment activities that permit young children to demonstrate their ability to understand and apply new skills and information.

Performance assessments complement each other in how they focus on the child's progress and accomplishments. In addition, informal assessment methods, such as observation, checklists and rating scales, and teacher-designed assessments, are used in the process of assessing through performance.

Performance assessment transfers responsibility to teachers for the instructional and assessment process. This empowerment of the teacher facilitates the teacher's opportunity to design assessment that includes all areas of development and that is appropriate for the level of development of each child. It also allows the teacher to make a close connection between curriculum and evaluation. It also permits the teacher to consider learning and assessment within the family backgrounds of the children. Knowing that performance assessment should be meaningful, the teacher interacts with the family and home frequently to understand what type of performance is suitable for individual students.

Although performance assessment is more relevant and appropriate than traditional formal methods of measuring learning, it can also be more difficult. Teachers must accept the time that is needed to organize and conduct this type of evaluation; moreover, they must overcome limitations related to validity, reliability, and accountability. Care must be exercised in planning and implementing performance assessment if it is not to become an educational fad that fades after a few years.

Recent years have brought changing expectations for evaluating learning under the Common Core of State Standards (CCSS). The Common Core is the first effort to establish national standards that can be applied in any state. The Common Core requires a more rigorous curriculum and assessment. The standards bring a new meaning to performance assessments. Teachers must learn how to instruct, assess, and interpret what the student has learned. Through working with this process, the teacher develops a deeper understanding of levels of performance and how they are graded.

Enhanced eText: Self-Check: Chapter Review

Key Terms

authentic achievement 246

authentic learning 246

authentic performance
    assessment 246

contract 252

diagnostic interview 250

direct performance measure 255

directed assignment 252

game 253

indirect performance measure 256

performance-based
    assessment 248

portfolio 255

project 254

structured interview 250

structured performance
    assessment 255

unstructured interview 250

unstructured performance
    assessment 255

work sample 253

Selected Organizations

Search for the following organizations online:

Association for Childhood Education International

Association for Supervision and Curriculum
    Development (ASCD)

National Association for the Education of Young Children

Springer

Zero to Three

George Lucas Educational Foundation (Edutopia)

References

Adamson, F., & Darling-Hammond, L. (2010, April). *Beyond basic skills. The role of performance assessment in achieving 21st century standards of learning.* Stanford, CA: Stanford Center for Opportunity Policy in Education.

Baldwin, J. L., Adams, S. M., & Kelly, K. M. (2009). Science at the center: An emergent, standards-based, child-centered framework for early learners. *Early Childhood Education Journal, 37*, 71–77.

Caffrey, E. D. (2009). *Assessment in elementary and secondary education: A primer.* Washington, DC: Congressional Research Service.

Caldwell, J. (2016, December 5). *Meaningful Documentation in the early childhood classroom.* Retrieved from https://fairydustteaching.com/20106/12/meaningful-documentation-ece/

Darling-Hammond, L., (2010). *Performance counts: Assessment systems that support high-quality learning.* Washington, DC: Council of Chief State School Officers.

Darling-Hammond, L., & Falk, B. (2013, September). *Teacher learning through assessment. How student performance assessments can support teacher learning.* Washington, DC: Center for American Progress.

Darling-Hammond, L., & Hyler, M. E. (2013, Summer). *The role of performance assessment in developing teaching as a profession.* Retrieved from http://www.rethinkingschools.org/archive/27_04/27_darling

Drew, W. F., Christie, J., Johnson, J. E., Meckley, A. M., & Nell, M. L. (2008). Constructive play. A value-added strategy for meeting early learning standards. *Young Children, 63,* 38–44.

Edwards, C., & Rinaldi, C. (Eds.). (2009). *The diary of Laura: Perspectives on a Reggio Emilia diary.* Reggio Emilia, Italy: Reggio Children.

Fadel, C., Honey, M., & Pasnick, S. (2007, May 18). Assessment in the age of innovation. *Education Week, 26,* 34, 40.

Frost, J. F., Wortham, S., & Reifel, S. (2008). *Play and child development* (3rd ed.). Upper Saddle River, NJ: Pearson.

Givens, K. (1997). Performance assessment tests: A problematic panacea. *Contemporary Education, 69,* 27–29.

Gronlund, G. (2006). *Make early learning standards come alive: Connecting your practice and curriculum to state guidelines.* St. Paul, MN: Redleaf Press.

Helm, J. H., & Beneke, S. (2003). *The power of projects: Meeting contemporary challenges in early childhood classrooms—Strategies and solutions.* New York, NY: Teachers College Press.

Hilliard, P. (2015, December 7). *Performance-based assessment: Reviewing the basics.* Retrieved from https://www.edutopia.org/blog/performance-based-assessment-reviewing-the-basics

Howe, N. (2016, Oct. 20). *Cameras in the Early Childhood classroom: A powerful tool for documentation and reflection.* Retrieved from https://bingschool.stanford.edu/news/cameras-early childhood-classroom

Illinois State Board of Education: Early Childhood Education. (2012, May). *Authentic assessment and early childhood education—An update and resources.* Springfield, IL: Author.

Jablon, J. (2010/2011). Taking it all in: Observation in the Classroom. *Teaching Young Children 4,* 24–27.

Jacobs, G., & Crowley, K. (2010). *Reading standards and beyond in kindergarten.* Washington, DC: National Association for the Education of Young Children, and Thousand Oaks, CA: Corwin, a Sage Company.

Kamii, C., & Rosenblum, V. (1990). An approach to assessment in mathematics. In C. Kamii (Ed.), *Achievement testing in the early grades: The games grown-ups play* (pp. 146–162). Washington, DC: National Association for the Education of Young Children.

Kleinert, H., Greene, P., & Harte, M. (2002). Creating and using meaningful alternative assessments. *Teaching Exceptional Children, 34,* 40–47.

Lai, E. R. (2011, May). Performance assessment: Some new thoughts on an old idea. Retrieved from www.pearsonassessments.com

McTighe, J. (2012, December 6). *Common core big idea 4: Map backward from intended results.* Retrieved from https://www.edutopia.org.blog.common-core-map-backwards-Jay-McTighe

Meisels, S. J. (2000). On the side of the child. *Young Children, 55,* 16–19.

Meisels, S. J., Wen, X., & Beachy, K. (2010). Authentic assessment for infants and toddlers: Exploring the reliability and validity of the ounce scale. *Applied Developmental Science, 14,* 55–71.

Meisels, S. J. (2014). Performance assessment. *Scholastic.com.* Retrieved from http://www.teacher.Scholastic.com/professional/assessment/perfassess.htm

Morrison, G. S. (2013). *Fundamentals of early childhood education* (7th ed.). Upper Saddle River, NJ: Pearson.

New Commission on the Skills of the American Workforce. *Tough choices or tough times.* Rochester, NY: National Center on Education and the Economy.

New York City Board of Education: Department of Science, Technology, Engineering, and Mathematics. (2009). *Early Childhood Assessment in Mathematics Manual.* New York, NY: Author.

Ratcliff, N. J. (2001/2002). Using authentic assessment to document the emerging literacy skills of young children. *Childhood Education, 78,* 66–69.

Reifel, S. (2011, March). Observation and early childhood teaching. *Young Children, 4,* 62–65.

Rhode Island Department of Education & the National Center for the Improvement of Educational Assessment, Inc. (n.d.). *Guidance for developing and selecting quality assessments in the primary classroom.* Providence, RI: Author.

Riley, K., Miller, G. E., & Sorenson, C. (2016, September). *Early childhood authentic and performance-based assessment.* Retrieved from https://link.springer.com/Chapter 10.1007/978-1-4939-6349–5

Seefeldt, C. (2005). *Social studies for the preschool-primary child* (7th ed.). Upper Saddle River, NJ: Merrill/Prentice Hall.

Shabazian, A. N. (2016, July). The role of documentation in fostering learning. *Young Children, 71,* 73–79.

Stanford Redesign Network. (2008). *What is performance-based assessment?* Stanford SRN informational booklet. Retrieved from https://www.edpolicy.stanford.edu/sitesdefault/files/events/materials/2011-06/linked-learning-performance-based-assessment.pdf

State of Connecticut State Board of Education. (2007). *Early childhood: A guide to early childhood program development.* Hartford, CT: Author.

Stiggins, R. (2005). From formative assessment to assessment FOR learning: A path to success in standards-based schools. *Phi Delta Kappan, 85,* 324–328.

The Glossary of Education Reform. (2013, September 16). *Authentic learning.* Retrieved from http://www.edglossary.org/authentic-learning/

Turner, T., & D. G. Wilson (2010). Reflections of documentation: A discussion with thought leaders from Reggio Emilia. *Theory into Practice, 49 (1):* 5–18.

Vygotsky, L. (1983). School instruction and mental development. In M. Donaldson, R. Grieve, & C. Pratt (Eds.), *Early childhood development and education: Readings in psychology* (pp. 263–269). New York, NY: Guilford.

Wien, C. A. (2011). Learning to document in Reggio-inspired education. *Early Childhood Research and Practice, 13,* 1–16. Retrieved from http://ecrp.uiuc.edu/v13n2/wien.html

Wurm, J. P. (2005). *Working in the Reggio way.* St. Paul, MN: Redleaf Press.

Chapter 11
Portfolio Assessment

Rob Hainer/Shutterstock

 ## Chapter Learning Outcomes

As a result of reading this chapter, you will be able to:

11.1 Discuss the purposes and types of portfolios for assessing and reporting student progress.

11.2 Describe strategies to organize portfolio assessment.

11.3 Explain how to set up and use a quality portfolio assessment system.

11.4 Discuss how narrative reports and model portfolio assessment systems are used for reporting progress.

In this chapter, we address how to take data collected by using informal or performance assessments to construct a holistic picture of a child's progress that can be reported to parents and school district administrators periodically throughout the school year. These alternative types of reporting are suggested as more suitable for communicating the development and learning of children in the early childhood years. They are equally important for children in elementary schools.

Purposes and Types of Portfolio Assessments

Currently, teachers in school districts all over the United States are reviewing and redesigning report cards. A primary motive for this endeavor was the difficulty teachers faced in following trends in curriculum and instruction based on the No Child Left Behind movement. More recently, Common Core State Standards are focused on higher levels of learning, as well as more meaningful assessments (Etale, 2013;). Although letter grades have limitations, they are still in use (Epstein, Schweinhart, DeBruin-Parecki, & Robin, 2004; Furger, 2014). Alternative systems of reporting that use authentic or **performance assessments** provide more than letter grades. Report cards are changing as teachers and administrators find more flexible and meaningful types of reporting. Figure 11-1 shows a continuum or hierarchy of skills for language arts, math, science, and social studies. Progress is the important factor, rather than simply a letter grade.

Alternative systems of reporting that use authentic or performance assessments can include (1) a continuum of development and learning, (2) information about the whole child, not just about skills that have been mastered, (3) diagnostic information that allows the teacher to adjust instruction and activities, and, most important, (4) examples of what the child has done to demonstrate learning (Morrison, 2013). After school district policy makers, administrators, and teachers determine that performance assessments are to be included in the evaluation process, decisions are then made on how to use them and develop a comprehensive picture of the child's

Figure 11.1 A first-grade reporting system

	Language Arts	Math	Science	Social Studies
	FIRST GRADE			
6.0	❑ Recognizes vowels ❑ Reads primer-level simple sentences ❑ Understands antonyms ❑ Writes phrases ❑ Arranges events in sequential order ❑ Alphabetizes according to initial letter ❑ Acquires basic sight vocabulary ❑ Engages in creative dramatic activities and nonverbal communication ❑ Responds to nonverbal cues	❑ Knows greater than/less than ❑ Writes numerals 1–20 ❑ Recognizes simple color and size patterns ❑ Recognizes and sorts plane figures ❑ Finds differences by separating and comparing objects ❑ Solves problems involving addition and subtraction with manipulatives ❑ Uses numeral sentences	❑ Acquires data through the use of senses ❑ Identifies careers related to theme (mayor, construction workers, business people) ❑ Identifies internal organs and their functions (brain, heart, lungs) ❑ Identifies skeletal parts (skull, ribs, pelvis, spine) ❑ Classifies food into pyramid levels ❑ Classifies events in a consistent, organized fashion while making observations (plant growth)	❑ Is aware of others' needs ❑ Identifies kinds of work of school personnel and family members ❑ Knows birth date ❑ Knows geography of school campus ❑ Identifies name of school ❑ Knows geographical location of home in relation to school/community ❑ Identifies and accepts one's classroom responsibilities ❑ Completes assigned tasks ❑ Identifies positive traits of self and others
6.3	❑ Selects topics of interest to self and others ❑ Understands opposites ❑ Understands naming words (people, places, things, animals) ❑ Recognizes a sentence ❑ Understands action words ❑ Identifies the main idea in speaker's words ❑ Uses basic phonics: media/message/ final consonants ❑ Uses pronouns properly ❑ Contributes ideas and information in group discussion	❑ Finds sums by combining groups and counting ❑ Finds differences by separating and comparing objects ❑ Estimates and predicts quantities ❑ Identifies lines of symmetry ❑ Measures/estimates mass using standard units ❑ Develops concept of conservation (measuring capacity using containers) ❑ Constructs picture graphs	❑ Creates an order of events in a logical continuum while making observations ❑ Collects information to make reasonable interpretations ❑ Makes accurate measurements and uses them appropriately as descriptors ❑ Manipulates laboratory materials and equipment ❑ Uses information and observations to make reasonable interpretations	❑ Contributes to group activities ❑ Understands food processing ❑ Discusses visuals (pictures, charts) ❑ Knows how animals are used for clothing, food, etc. ❑ Understands and distinguishes animal habitats ❑ Uses terms concerning time (today, tomorrow, yesterday) ❑ Knows months of the year ❑ Knows the days of the week ❑ Knows N, S, E, W ❑ Knows the four seasons

progress. Collection and interpretation of data relevant to the child's performance require organization of an evaluation system that permits the teacher to describe growth in a meaningful manner. Portfolios are one such assessment.

Portfolios are a collection of a child's work and teacher data from informal and performance assessments to evaluate development and learning. A portfolio may be kept just by and for the child, with samples of work over a period of time. It may also be organized by the teacher and contain observation reports, checklists, work samples, records of directed assignments, interviews, or other evidence of achievement. There are child portfolios, teacher portfolios, and combinations that include entries made by both the child and teacher.

Purposes of Portfolio Assessment

How the contents of a portfolio are used depends on the purpose. Portfolios can be used for assessment and evaluation, for self-assessment and reflection, and for reporting progress. These different purposes are described below.

USING PORTFOLIOS FOR ASSESSMENT AND EVALUATION   A portfolio collection is used to develop a holistic picture of activities the student has engaged in over a period of time. The portfolio should include many examples of a student's work that will provide multiple assessments of concepts, skills, and projects that result in an accurate picture of what the student understands and is able to use in a meaningful context (Fernsten, 2009; Peters, Hartly, Rogers, Smith, & Carr, 2009). In addition to the child and the teacher assessing the child's achievement, the portfolio can be used to evaluate the teacher. The child is given an opportunity to provide feedback to the teacher.

Enhanced eText: Video Example 11.1

USING PORTFOLIOS FOR SELF-ASSESSMENT AND REFLECTION   Portfolios, particularly those that are used over a period of several years, make it possible for the student to observe growth and progress by comparing work samples and drawings longitudinally (Hebert & Schultz, 1996). For example, many teachers in kindergarten and primary grades have children make a drawing of themselves at the beginning of a school year. At the beginning of each subsequent reporting period, another drawing is made. Students can look back and see how their efforts have improved. Samples of writing provide the same type of comparison. Students at the end of second or third grade may not even recognize their earlier efforts at the beginning of the year.

USING PORTFOLIOS FOR REPORTING PROGRESS   At the beginning of the chapter, we discussed how alternative reporting methods to report cards are needed to report student progress to parents. Portfolios are a comprehensive alternative approach. When parents are engaged with their child and teacher in selecting and reviewing what has been completed during a grading period, they are able to see the work and assessment examples that have been used (Damiani, 2004; Gilkerson & Hanson, 2000). If grades are required, the work in the portfolio can document the assessments used to determine the grade.

Types of Portfolios

Portfolios have become a popular trend in elementary schools in the last few years, particularly in the language arts. Although abundant literature is available on how to use the portfolio for assessment in language arts, particularly for the whole language and emergent literacy approaches, less has been offered for other developmental or content-area categories. More recently, portfolios have been used for many content areas in the curriculum. It is now just as appropriate to use portfolios for social studies, science, and mathematics as it is to use alternative or authentic strategies for assessment for all types of curriculum and instruction.

As teachers and students use portfolios to fulfill the three purposes of portfolio assessment described earlier, they make decisions about the type of portfolio that best serves their purposes. Among these possibilities are working portfolios, evaluative portfolios, showcase portfolios, and archival portfolios.

Decisions must be made about who will determine portfolio contents and purpose. Will the portfolio be maintained and used by the teacher alone? Will the teacher and child make choices for the portfolio together? What role will parents play in the process? Will parents be encouraged to make selections for a portfolio and bring samples of work done at home to be included? These considerations can be included for each of the types of portfolios described next (Cohen, 2014).

WORKING PORTFOLIOS   A **working portfolio** is used to collect examples of students' work for future evaluation. During an interval of a reporting period, the work is collected without making final decisions as to what will be kept and what will be discarded. Samples are collected by both the teacher and the child. Progress notes and planning for subsequent work are important components (Fernsten, 2009; Gronlund & Engel, 2002; Gronlund & James, 2013). The items in the working portfolio later can become part of another type of portfolio.

EVALUATIVE PORTFOLIOS   This is the most commonly understood type of portfolio. An **evaluative portfolio** permits the teacher to make an assessment of the student's progress, both formative and summative. The teacher uses the materials included to evaluate the student's developmental advances and needs for future growth and learning. The evaluative portfolio is used for reporting to parents and administrators and for planning for curriculum and instruction (Barbour & Desjean-Perrotta, 1998; Fernsten, 2009).

SHOWCASE PORTFOLIOS   A **showcase portfolio** is used to exhibit the child's best work. Showcase portfolios are most frequently used to share the child's accomplishments with his or her parents. They can also be used for school open-house events or occasions when children from different classrooms and grade levels share what they are learning and doing. Showcase portfolio contents are frequently chosen by the child (Gronlund & Engel, 2002).

Graham Oliver/123RF

Parents need opportunities to engage in the assessment process.

ARCHIVAL PORTFOLIOS In some preschools and elementary schools, student portfolios follow students from year to year. This type of portfolio is sometimes called an **archival portfolio** or *pass-along portfolio* because it can provide information to the child's next teacher and/or other future teachers (Puckett & Black, 2008; Seitz & Bartholomew, 2008).

Portfolios can be organized by developmental category, by content area, or by topics or themes if an integrated curriculum is followed. As is true for curriculum design, the goals of the program and objectives for development and learning serve as the foundation for instruction and assessment. As teachers understand more about the emergent nature of cognition and development, their task is to become comfortable with using characteristics of emerging development and how that is reflected in the work they and the children can collect for assessment. In this respect, understanding the principles and characteristics of development become essential if the teacher is to comprehend how to assess the child's developmental progress. In the following sections, examples of organization of a **developmental portfolio** and content-area portfolio are provided.

PRESCHOOL PORTFOLIOS The use of portfolios with preschool children has received more attention in recent years. The focus of describing the benefits of portfolio use has been documented in studies of portfolio use with very young children (Alacam & Olgan, 2016; Loop, 2017; Smith, 2000; Smith, Brewer, Heffner, 2014). Early childhood teachers have been pleasantly surprised to learn that preschool children can discuss their portfolios and explain their accomplishments (Smith, 2000). Smith reported that preschool children could use portfolios to reflect about their work over the school year.

Two studies of preschool portfolio projects looked at whether portfolios were beneficial for teachers. Shu-Chin, Chen, & Cheng (2011) documented the development of a curriculum-based learning model in a preschool in Taiwan. They found that systemized documentation of children's learning can reduce the workload for teachers, but they still had to organize anecdotal records outside the school day. Alacam & Olgan (2015) also studied the possible benefits of portfolio assessment for early childhood and first-grade teachers. These teachers discussed how they communicated with parents using portfolios. They discussed portfolios differently with different parents.

Loop (2017) explained the advantages of using portfolios in the preschool classroom to document children's progress. She stressed how the products of children's activities allowed the teacher to assess student progress. She discussed progression portfolios that permit the teacher and children to see the progression of their work. Portfolios permitted student progress to be personalized instead of comparing one child's work with another. Parents also gained insight from the portfolio that documented the entire school year with notes, photographs, audio recordings, and samples of student work.

ELECTRONIC PORTFOLIOS When the first ideas about portfolios were being developed in the 1990s, the focus was on paper portfolios and containers for portfolios. Much of the information in this text focuses on this type of portfolio. But even in the beginning, there were ideas presented for storing portfolios on a CD-ROM.

The rapid revolution of electronic tools, such as cellphones, electronic pads, and small computers, has transformed the strategies used for portfolios. First grade children can enter information on their individual pads or notebooks in Internet blogs (Cassidy, 2013). Teachers use their cell phones to record child observations for portfolios.

There are now many examples of **electronic portfolios** available for educators to adapt and use in their classrooms. There are various online tools that can be used to transition to "e-portfolios." Some tool or platform options are Evernote, Dropbox, Google Sites, and eBackpack (Hertz, 2013). Cloud-based websites like Evernote are popular (Cassidy, 2013; Van Nood, 2012). These tools help the teacher to collect, organize, and share student work. A teacher of first and second grade (Cassidy, 2013) shared how she used blog-based portfolios in her classroom. She believed that online portfolios encouraged parent engagement and the creation of an online community. Van Nood (2012), teacher of 8- to 11-year-olds, blogged instructions on how to use Evernote to create a portfolio system and get the system started.

Electronic portfolios are now being used at every level of education. Teachers in higher education are using them to track student progress in many fields; however, state education departments have led the way with professional development portfolios that followed future teachers through their college preparation and preparation for job interviews.

The flexibility of portfolios has enhanced their advantages. They can encourage access to wider examples of student-created content such as written work, scanned work, videos and audiotapes, and photos. Student work can easily be shared with parents, and parents find it easy to access their student's work (Cool Tools for School, 2018). However, portfolio assessment is subjective and that can make it unsuitable for making comparisons between schools (Davis, 2017).

Enhanced eText: Self-Check 11.1

Strategies for Organizing Portfolios

After the decision has been made as to the type of portfolio that will best suit the children in a classroom or groups of classrooms, the teacher can begin the process of organizing the portfolio that is most suitable. A combination of strategies can be used to include paper entries as well as electronic entries. The organization will depend on the age of the students and how advanced they are in developing literacy and writing skills. After the organizational strategy has been selected, the teacher is ready to make decisions about implementing the process.

Organizing Portfolios Using a Developmental Approach

A sensible approach to organizing portfolios for preschool and primary-grade children is by developmental category. Thus, the teacher might provide dividers in the portfolio for motor development, cognitive development, language and literacy development, and social development. The following suggestions are examples rather than all possibilities for portfolio entries.

Cognitive Development

Cognitive development includes experiences that support the child in learning new concepts. Although the focus might be on math and science, learning about new concepts occurs in most categories of development.

Photos or Videos

Visual records of the child engaging in math and science activities such as mixing colors, participating in preparing a recipe, and recording weather changes on a chart

Work Samples

Samples of math activities recorded on paper, child drawings, pasting items to represent a numeral, or construction of a class chart showing two groups of items combined to make a larger group (pre-addition)

Classroom Assessments

Recorded results from checklists, teacher observations, and child interviews

Results of planned assessment tasks to document a child's progress in cognitive tasks

Language and Literacy Development (Photos or Videos)

Visual records of the child participating in language development activities such as learning rhymes and finger plays

Visual records of the child participating in developing a story recorded on an experience chart

Audio Recordings

Recordings documenting the child retelling a story, participating in a class discussion, and child-to-child conversations

Work Samples

Child journal entries

Copies of child-dictated stories, songs, or poems

Copies of signs and labels the child has constructed

Copies of child's attempts at writing

Classroom Assessments

A log of books "read" by the child or read to the child

Audio recordings to assess progress in vocabulary development and the skills in using language

Motor Development—Fine Motor (Photos and Videos)

Photos of child's work with puzzles, small construction materials, and clay

Videos of child engaged in fine motor activities such as painting, manuscript printing

Work Samples

> Copies of child's work in art activities such as a collage and cutting and pasting
>
> Samples of drawing activities using different tools such as crayons, chalk, and markers

Classroom Assessments

> Teacher observation of daily fine motor activities to assess progress on a checklist or teacher notes
>
> Teacher-led activities in writing lessons using letters, names, and words

Motor Development—Gross Motor (Photos and Videos)

> Videos of the child's gross motor movements in the classroom and outdoors
>
> Photos and anecdotal records that demonstrate the child's progress in large motor skills
>
> Photos of musical activities that use movement or dancing

Classroom Assessments

> Notes from teacher observations of the child's active play to determine progress in motor development
>
> Child interviews about favorite outdoor games at school

Social Development (Photos and Videos)

> Photos of child in play and classroom interactions with other children
>
> Videos documenting field trips and other school outings and activities that demonstrate the child's interactions with other children

Organizing Portfolios Using a Subject-Area Approach

The teacher may prefer to organize portfolios using a subject-area approach. If so, the teacher must choose whether to include all subject areas or to dedicate a portfolio to a single content area. If a comprehensive collection of the child's work, teacher assessments, and other evaluation data is desired, Batzle (1992) recommended the following contents for the portfolio:

1. *Required Tests and Accountability Measures*
   Standardized tests
   Minimum competency tests
   Criterion-referenced tests
   Chapter or unit tests

2. *Samples across the Curriculum*
   Language arts
   Reading responses
   Reading logs

Home reading logs
Oral reading tapes
Writing folders
Writing samples
Spelling work
Math
Fine arts
Content areas

3. *Teacher Observations and Measures*
Kid watching and anecdotal records
Running records
Retellings
Progress checks
Teacher-made tests
Rubrics
Conference records
Summary of findings

4. *Inventories and Other Forms*
Reading inventory
Informal reading inventory
Writing inventory
Parent surveys, comments, and evaluations

5. *Additional Items*
Cassette or photo of drama presentations
Oral presentation, book talk
Oral language inventory
Oral "publishing" (p. 35)

This example includes possibilities for several subject areas to be included; nevertheless, some subjects, such as social studies, are omitted. Moreover, the predominant categories suggested are related to language arts. Note that inclusion of results of standardized tests is recommended.

Enhanced eText: Self-Check 11.2

Setting Up and Using a Portfolio Assessment System

The decision to initiate the use of portfolio assessment should be approached thoughtfully. If the process of implementing portfolio assessment is to succeed, the early childhood center or school must have a good climate that will support the change (Cohen, 2014; Damiani, 2004). The purposes of portfolio assessment and how they are associated with a philosophy of learning and instruction need to be understood and accepted by the teachers before embarking on a new and complex assessment approach (Harris, 2009; Seitz & Bartholomew, 2008).

Steps in Getting Started

After the decision has been made to use portfolio assessment and the teacher understands the implications of undertaking the changes, several decisions must be made prior to beginning the process of setting up a portfolio assessment system. The first steps are to select the purpose, format, and storage system for portfolios. Then the teacher must determine what will go into the portfolio by selecting portfolio contents and decide how student work will be collected, organized, and reviewed. Finally, the teacher must decide how assessment of student progress will be reported.

WHAT IS THE PURPOSE?   The purpose of the portfolio is determined by the teacher's objectives for assessment. If the purpose is to assess development for a reporting period, an evaluative portfolio with a developmental format is chosen. If the purpose is for the student to initiate learning objectives and engage in reflection and self-evaluation, a working portfolio may be the obvious choice. If portfolios are implemented for parent conferences and are not the major sources of assessment, a showcase portfolio might be indicated.

The teacher may determine multiple purposes for a portfolio. The portfolio may be used both for assessment and as a showcase. For this type of portfolio, both the teacher and the student may have sections of student work. As an alternative, there may be a section for assessment and another for showcase entries. There are all kinds of possibilities. The teacher will want to consider what purpose or purposes will best serve his or her objectives for assessment.

HOW WILL IT BE ORGANIZED?   After the teacher has decided why and how the portfolio is to be used for assessment, some decisions will be made as to how to organize the contents (Seitz & Bartholomew, 2008). For an evaluative portfolio in preschool, a chronological organization may be the best choice to display student progress in developmental domains. If the teacher uses a thematic curriculum, the materials placed in the portfolio may be organized by thematic topic. If a portfolio is to serve as the assessment system for a single content area, the genre approach to organization permits division of the contents into reading, writing, skills practice, and so forth. Organization by difficulty may be preferred for a mathematics portfolio.

After the format has been determined, it can be further organized using a table of contents. The following can be used for various formats:

- A table of contents
- A title page that identifies the student, explains what can be found in the collection, and describes the purpose of the portfolio
- Dividers with labels that identify contents of each section
- Dates on all entries
- A review or assessment section that includes both teacher and child assessments to include teacher comments

WHERE WILL IT BE STORED?   An important decision is how to store portfolios. The purposes for the portfolio and types of materials to be stored influence the type of ll5

storage containers to be used. A writing portfolio composed primarily of student writing samples can be housed in a file folder; in contrast, a portfolio that contains project work or videos and audio recordings may require a box. Some suggested storage containers include the following (Barbour & Desjean-Perrotta, 1998; Grace & Shores, 1991):

- Expandable file folders
- X-ray folders
- Pizza boxes
- Grocery bags stapled inside each other
- Large mailing envelopes
- Office supply boxes
- Paper briefcases
- Shoeboxes containing file folders
- Plastic crates
- CD-ROM
- Computer program

Portfolio assessment has now become so widespread that there are commercial sources for portfolio storage. One can find boxes, shelving, racks, and other commercial containers on the Internet, as well as at storage companies such as The Container Store. School furniture supply companies also offer storage pieces that can be used for portfolios. However, because the trend is away from paper portfolios and toward electronic portfolios, much of the need for storage systems is becoming dated.

WHAT WILL GO IN THE PORTFOLIO?   Based on the purposes and format of the portfolio, decisions must now be made about portfolio contents. Will the portfolio for 4-year-olds include all developmental domains or just literacy? Will the content-area portfolio be for math and science or language arts? Will the portfolio include only student work, or will teacher assessments be included? There are many possibilities for determining what will go into the portfolio that will vary according to the developmental level of the child and the purposes of the portfolio. As the use of portfolios evolves, teachers will modify the components portfolios include. In some cases, they may find that they are collecting too many types of materials. In other cases, they may find that they need to expand the examples that are to be included.

Teachers may find it useful to develop a checklist for reviewing the steps they have taken in getting started in using portfolio assessment. One model for such a checklist is pictured in Figure 11-2.

Search and Share 11.1

Portfolios & English Language Learners

Search online to find examples of portfolios used with young children who are English Language Learners. What types of information are contained in the portfolios? How might portfolios be beneficial for children who are learning English and for parents whose first language may be a language other than English?

Figure 11.2 Checklist for portfolio design

PORTFOLIO DESIGN WORKSHEET

1. **What will be included in your portfolio?**

   - Work samples
   - Journal
   - Teacher assessment
   - Self-assessment
   - Examples of your best work
   - Assessment progress reports

2. **How will your portfolio be organized?**

   _____

   _____

3. How will portfolio entries be collected?

   _____

   _____

4. Who will be included in assessment of your portfolio?

   _____

   _____

5. How will your portfolio be shared? How will assessment results be reported?

   _____

   _____

   _____

Collecting and Organizing Work

When the portfolio process is getting underway, the teacher and children decide how they will collect and organize entries for the portfolio. Periodically, during a grading period or another designated time, pieces are selected for the portfolio. The teacher can likewise select samples for the portfolio from assessment activities or tests that have been administered, checklists, rating scales, essays, and other evidence of work. Rubrics for individual and group work are included in the assignments. When it is time to finalize the portfolio, the teacher, child, or teacher and child make final choices for the portfolio.

Over the duration of the school year, more decisions are made as to which materials will remain for the entire year and which will be replaced by better or more advanced work. If a longitudinal review is desired at the end of the year, work completed at intervals throughout the year is retained for comparison over time. If the portfolio is for archival purposes, decisions are made about what will be passed on to the next teacher and what will be eliminated. Size and amount become important factors in all portfolio collections, but archival portfolios require careful selection (Seitz & Bartholomew, 2008).

Selecting Portfolio Assessments

A major task for the teacher is to determine which assessments will be included in the portfolio, depending on the purpose of the portfolio. There should be a balance between process and product. Process work will be the work that reflects the student's progress toward a developmental goal or cognitive skill. Product is the final step in the process, where the child has achieved success. Therefore, there should be a balance between examples of both types of assessments. The portfolio contents should include traditional assessment measures, performance assessments, and observation results. The assessments that are chosen should correspond to the possibilities or purposes of their use. At this point, all the assessment possibilities that have been included in this text can be analyzed and considered for the portfolio. Although most of the assessment types are performance based, teacher-designed tests and tasks and other assessment instruments are included in the total range of possibilities. Figure 11-3 shows a range of assessments and the purposes they can serve for portfolio assessment.

A kindergarten teacher selecting assessments for a comprehensive preschool or kindergarten portfolio may consider several types. For example, the pattern of emergence in writing and reading can be organized into a checklist, rubric, or other record-keeping form to determine the child's progress in emergent literacy. Figure 11-4 is a form for keeping a record of a child's emergent and conventional reading, and Figure 11-5 is a rubric that can be used to select materials for a learning center and assess emergent writing. Figure 11-6 is an example of an interview form that might be used with a child in kindergarten or first grade. Figure 11-7 provides for self-assessment by the child.

Analyzing Portfolio Assessments

Periodically, the teacher, child, and parents review portfolio contents to determine the child's progress and how appropriate experiences should be planned for further growth and development. To prepare for discussions, the teacher first conducts an analysis based on established learning objectives, indicators of developmental progress, and other criteria that demonstrate learning accomplishment. Work samples, interview results, checklists, rating scales, rubrics, teacher-designed assessments, and performance tasks are studied to determine what the child has learned. The child's work as presented in the portfolio is evaluated in terms of developmental domains, sequences of skills, and objectives established by the teachers and school. Using such established criteria, the teacher develops a profile of the child's strengths and weaknesses, as well as the interests and creative expressions revealed in various types of work samples.

The teacher and child can then use the portfolio as a vehicle for the child to reflect on progress and interests. Parents can also interact with the teacher and child on accomplishments and discuss future plans and goals together (Smith, 2000).

Strategies for Developing Quality Portfolios

Teachers who are beginning the process of using portfolios should consider why and how they help children benefit from the process. Understanding what they wish to accomplish will help them initiate their efforts correctly.

1. Determine a theme, subject area(s), or which developmental categories will be assessed.
2. Determine what type of container or storage method will be most useful. This can include digital storage for long-term use.
3. Choose a location for portfolios in the classroom.

Figure 11.3 Portfolio assessment purposes

PURPOSES OF PORTFOLIO ASSESSMENTS

Work Samples
To assess and evaluate
To make a diagnosis
To assess longitudinal progress
To conduct student self-evaluation
To understand student thinking processes
For self-selection of important work

Diaries
For student reflection
To trace progress
To express understanding
For problem solving
For self-evaluation
For self-expression

Interviews
For specific feedback
To evaluate conceptual understanding
To observe thinking processes
To assess skills
To assess progress

Interactive Journals
For communication and feedback
For peer editing
For building support
To stimulate creativity
For problem solving

Checklists and Rating Scales
To assess and report progress and mastery
To assess and report development
To record task list results
For instructional planning
To assess teaching processes

*Teacher-Designed Tests, Tasks,
    and Observations*
To assess skills
To assess cognitive processes
To document progress
To determine eligibility for special programs
For screening
To establish zone of proximal development (ZPD)

Contracts
For behavior management
To conduct student self-assessment
To assess student work habits
To conduct student self-initiated planning
For student management of learning activities
For feedback on student activities
For feedback on student interests
For recordkeeping

*Audio/Video/Photographs/Computer
    Assessments*
For assessment through observation
To determine progress
To assess learning processes
For self-assessment
For reporting to parents
To demonstrate skills
To maintain an electronic portfolio

Performance/Criterion-Related Tasks
To conduct a demonstration or exhibit
To conduct application of learning in context

Group Assessments
To assess group performance
To evaluate instruction
To evaluate program progress
To assess skills
To assess student progress in learning how to learn
To assess student progress in cooperative group
    learning

Narrative Summary
For teacher reflection on student progress
For summative assessment
For reporting to parents
To screen for special programs

---

4. Decide the types of samples or artifacts that will be included.

5. Have a clear understanding of how the portfolios will be evaluated. Communicate this information to other staff members, students, and parents.

6. Determine the process of student interaction with the portfolio process (Arter & Spandel, 1992; Cohen, 2014; Damiani, 2004; Fernsten, 2009).

After the portfolio process has been established, the teacher must consider what practices will ensure a quality assessment outcome. Management strategies are important.

Figure 11.4 Teacher's record of child's reading

Student:	
BOOKS THE CHILD HAS READ INDEPENDENTLY	
Title	Date Read
BOOKS THE CHILD HAS READ WITH ASSISTANCE	
Title	Date Read
Comments/Instruction needed:	

Portfolios should include meaningful assessments. The teacher should establish a system of observation and recording observations that reflects authentic information.

1. Develop a plan for collecting and analyzing children's portfolio entries. A system for evaluating each child will ensure that all children are considered and included in the analysis of their work.

2. The selected entries for portfolios should reflect the student's progress and accomplishments over a period of time. All entries should provide evidence that instructional goals and objectives have been met.

Figure 11.5 Learning center writing rubric

LEARNING CENTER DEVELOPMENT GUIDE SHEET		
Objective(s): *The student will use descriptive language*		
Materials: *paper, pencils, markers, pens*		
Duration: *1 week*		
Addressing different levels and assessment:		
Level	**Activity/Expectation**	**Assessment**
Pre-writer	*The student will describe a picture using words*	*Rubric uses pictures May copy letters or words Can write some familiar words*
Developing Writer	*The student will describe a picture using sentences.* • *Upper and lower case letters* • *Some punctuation*	*Understands sound-symbol relationship uses indented spelling Can read own writing*
Experienced Writer	*The student will describe a picture using sentences in a paragraph* • *Capitals used correctly* • *Correct punctuation*	*using conventions of print in spelling Demonstrates sentence sense Can use correct punctuation and use of upper and lower case letters*

LEARNING CENTER DEVELOPMENT GUIDE SHEET		
Objective(s): _____		
Materials: _____		
Duration: _____		
Addressing different levels and assessment:		
Level	**Activity/Expectation**	**Assessment**

3. Rubrics that are used for assessment should include the required components and expectations for specific criteria for grading.

4. Rubrics should include the goals, obligations, and expectations for the assignment (Cohen, 2014; Fernsten, 2009; Hanson & Gilkerson, 1999).

In sum, portfolio assessment systems can provide in-depth information for planning and implementing quality instruction. Also, they can be used as an effective means of recording and reporting student progress to parents, school administrators, and others.

> **Enhanced eText:** Application Exercise 11.1

Advantages and Disadvantages of Using Portfolios to Report Student Progress

The advantages of using portfolios for assessment and reporting were discussed earlier. Portfolios permit a wide range of assessment methods and a variety of ways that children can demonstrate mastery and growth in development. They allow for

Figure 11.6 Teacher interview form

Reading Interview with **Name** _____ **Date** _____

1. **What kinds of books do you like?**

_____

_____

2. **What is your favorite book?**

_____

_____

3. **Do you have books to read at home?**

_____

_____

4. **Does someone read to you at home?**

_____

_____

5. **Do others read at home? What do they like to read?**

_____

_____

_____

_____

_____

flexibility in how the teacher documents student progress; at the same time, they provide parents with extensive information about their child's experiences in school that facilitate learning and accomplishments.

Portfolios provide evaluation above and beyond letter grades on a report card. Children can be tracked on a continuum of development. In addition, assessment can be used for diagnostic purposes, as well as to document learning. Teachers can meet the individual needs of each child by examining portfolio contents and discussing progress and problems with the child through interviews and conferences (Harris, 2009).

Portfolios include input from the child, making the child an active partner in the evaluation process. The child not only makes selections for portfolio contents but also participates in the assessment process. This participation includes discussing progress with parents during parent–teacher conferences. Damiani (2004) summarized the advantages of portfolio assessment:

- Assesses what students can do and not just what they know
- Engages students actively
- Fosters student–teacher communication and depth of exploration
- Enhances understanding of the educational process among parents and in the community
- Provides goals for student learning
- Offers an alternative to traditional tests for students with special needs (pp. 2–3)

The most obvious challenge in organizing and maintaining portfolios is the issue of time. Both the teacher and the children need time to implement and maintain portfolios. It is important for the teacher and the children to work regularly with portfolios, review

Figure 11.7 Reviewing my portfolio

Reviewing My Portfolio

name _____

date _____

teacher _____

1. The work I like best in my portfolio is _____

I will draw or write about it here

```



```

2. I have the most work in _____

I will draw or write about it here

```



```

3. I would like to have more of this kind of work in my portfolio.

I will draw or write about it here

```



```

contents, discuss progress, and make changes in what is to be kept in the portfolio. If the portfolios are to be effective, they must be kept organized and current. Time is needed to work with portfolios, and teachers who are enthusiastic about the benefits of portfolios may also be concerned about the time needed to use portfolios appropriately.

Teachers are also concerned about accountability and grading portfolios. If a school district combines the use of portfolios with evaluation of the child's longitudinal progress, and if the evaluation of that progress is the primary purpose of reporting, teachers can become very comfortable with using portfolios. If, however, portfolios are used to assess and assign grades, the evaluation process is much more difficult when using portfolios. Teachers can be much more anxious about using portfolio assessment when they have to use portfolios to compare the achievement of students with each other. The issue of assigning grades can be one of the biggest challenges teachers face when initiating portfolio assessment.

A major concern when using portfolios for assessment and reporting is validity of the assessment strategies used. Earlier in the chapter, we discussed the need to predetermine standards and procedures that would be used to assess portfolio contents. In addition, steps must be taken to ensure that the assessment strategies have been checked for validity. Teachers are particularly concerned about their own accountability for the evaluation process. They may be insecure about using portfolio assessment because they are uncertain whether they will be able to grade the child's work appropriately.

Fairness can be a concern. Because access to computers and outside help in completing assignments can be a factor, not all students have the same outside influences. When children do not have computers in the home or parents who might be of assistance, it is possible that samples of student work can lack fairness.

Another issue can be the interpretation of portfolio results outside the school. Will staff members from other schools and parents have the same interpretation as the classroom teacher? Will lack of information about the assignment influence the interpretation of those outside the school system (Damiani, 2004)?

Enhanced eText: Self-Check 11.3

Reporting Progress Using Narrative Reports

Although portfolio assessment is a valuable system to report student progress, parents must be involved, particularly when teachers are transitioning from traditional reporting, such as report cards, to portfolios. Parents have typically been left out when portfolios have been initiated. In a partnership relationship, parents are invited to learn about portfolios at the beginning of the transition process. Parent training sessions can be held to explain the purposes and goals of portfolio assessment, followed by opportunities to understand how portfolio entries are selected, how the format is designed, and how entries will be evaluated (Seitz & Bartholomew, 2008).

Using Narrative Reports to Report Student Progress

Narrative or summary reports are another alternative to report cards for communicating a child's progress to parents. A *summary report* is an evaluation written by the teacher to describe the child's development and learning. A narrative report can stand alone as the periodic evaluation of progress or be combined with other assessment and reporting strategies. A narrative report can be part of a portfolio assessment or another system of assessment and reporting. Purposes of the report are to describe a review of the child's growth over a period of time and to describe that growth in a meaningful way for parents.

A summary report can describe the child's strengths, using developmental categories or subject areas. It can be organized to include (1) projects and integrated curriculum topics, (2) a profile of development and change over time, and (3) terminology that parents can understand to gain a picture of their child's progress. Using the results of observations, checklists, performance assessments, and other performance strategies, the teacher translates the information so that parents can comprehend what their child has accomplished (Meisels, 2014).

WRITING A NARRATIVE REPORT   A narrative report as described by Horm-Wingerd (1992) includes the following:

1. Descriptions of examples of the child's behaviors

2. Examples of what the child can do

3. Concerns the teacher may have about the child's progress

4. Goals and plans for the child in the future

Advocates of written summaries to report child progress express concern that teachers write reports in such a manner that parents appreciate their child and value his or her progress. Strengths, rather than weaknesses, should be stressed. When the child's weaknesses are described or concerns are expressed, the teacher should be careful not to assess blame and to use a positive tone in the report. The goal is to develop reports that promote a positive home–school partnership. Project Spectrum, described in more detail later, suggests that any home activities described for the parents for use with their child require inexpensive, readily available materials (Krechevsky, 1991).

It is important for teachers to write the narrative report carefully and accurately. It should inform the parents about the child's progress and educate them about appropriate instruction and assessment practices. Horm-Wingerd (1992) suggests the following procedure when writing narratives:

1. Open with an overall statement describing a child's progress in a broad developmental area since the last report or conference.

2. Give a specific example of behavior to serve as evidence for your global description of change and to help parents understand exactly what you are describing.

3. State your plans.

4. If appropriate, note what the parents can do at home to facilitate their child's development. (p. 14)

Teachers frequently have difficulty in reporting objectively about some children in their classroom. It is easy to write a very positive report about an attractive child who is cooperative and eager to please the teacher. The teacher may not be aware that the child's progress is being overestimated and reported because the teacher has very positive personal feelings about the child. On the other hand, teachers may have great difficulty in evaluating and reporting objectively on children who pose problems in the classroom. Children who are disruptive, rude to their peers and the teacher, or physically unattractive can have their progress underestimated. The teacher may put too much negative emphasis in the report, rather than stressing the child's accomplishments. Teachers can be unaware that they have subjective perceptions of some of their students. Additional questions a teacher might ask are these: Am I being objective about this child's progress? Are my personal feelings about this child affecting how I write the narrative report? The narrative report should stress positive information about the child first, but even negative information should be discussed accurately and fairly.

Advantages and Disadvantages of Using Narrative Reports

Many of the advantages and disadvantages of using performance assessments in general and strategies for reporting the child's performance and development discussed in terms of portfolios are true for narrative reports. Advantages are that they permit

Example of a Narrative Report

Montessori/Kindergarten Classroom

Emmanuel Felane

November 17, 2013

Overall Report

Emmanuel has adjusted very well in kindergarten during the first quarter of school. He participates well with other children, both during indoor class time and during outdoor play periods. He is particularly interested in working in the block center and focuses on complex constructions for an extended period of time. He is comfortable with the structured nature of the Montessori materials and responds well to individual lessons. Although he is a fairly quiet child, he has several good friends and has little difficulty when working in small groups.

Personal and Social Development

At the beginning of school, Emmanuel was very shy and hesitant about some of the class activities. He had some difficulties in replacing materials in an orderly manner after using them. He is working on being more responsible with these activities and others in the classroom. He tends to interact in small groups or by himself during outdoor play.

Language and Literacy

Emmanuel has a large vocabulary and a well-developed level of oral communication. These abilities are demonstrated in classroom discussions and during play activities.

His fine motor skills are developing more slowly; he finds emergent writing activities a bit difficult. He is encouraged to spend time engaged in fine motor Montessori activities during self-selected work periods.

He participates in emergent literacy activities and Montessori phonetic activities and can recognize about 20 words from class storybook reading activities.

Mathematical Thinking

Emmanuel is advanced in understanding mathematical concepts. He is well advanced in mathematical lessons and activities beyond the preschool/kindergarten level. He enjoys these activities and particularly likes the sequenced nature of the Montessori materials.

Science and Social Studies

Science and social studies are integrated within study topics and projects. During the first quarter of school, we have studied occupations near the school and weather in the fall season. Emmanuel has contributed to a mural about local jobs and engaged in individual art work demonstrating how leaves change in the fall. (Photos of Emmanuel's contributions are attached to this report.) Emmanuel has also contributed to the construction of neighborhood buildings made of cardboard boxes. They can be viewed in the project corner of the classroom.

(continued)

Physical Development and Health

It was mentioned earlier that Emmanuel's fine motor skills are still emerging slowly. However, his large motor skills are progressing normally. He loves outdoor activities and enjoys group games that require running.

His health is good, although he has trouble with allergies. He is receiving medication that is reducing the severity of this problem. He has good eating habits and enjoys all kinds of food. He is more slender than some of his classmates, but his weight is within the normal range.

Summary and Recommendations

Emmanuel is particularly suited for the Montessori activities in the classroom. He likes working by himself and usually completes activities without any problems. He seems to enjoy school. Emmanuel can be helped at home by guidance in keeping his things in order. Drawing and other activities requiring him to use his fingers will help with his fine motor development. He likes art activities such as working with clay and painting. Similar activities at home will be enjoyable for him. Reading and enjoying books will extend his language and literacy skills.

the teacher to report the child's broad range of developmental characteristics over a period of time. They can incorporate information from various sources and assessment and record-keeping strategies when the child's evaluation is reported. A unique aspect of the narrative report is that the teacher can describe in writing what the child has accomplished. Unlike the portfolio, which may be the focus of verbal exchange between the parents and the teacher, the narrative report requires the teacher to think through what is desired in the report and to write it down prior to a conference. If a face-to-face conference is not possible, the narrative report contains the essential information and interpretation the teacher wishes to communicate.

The obvious disadvantage of the narrative report is the time needed to write, edit, and finalize a narrative report in professional form. The teacher must not only collect pertinent information and organize it to reflect the advances made in all developmental or subject areas of the curriculum, but also translate these data into a coherent, comprehensive, concise narrative. The ideal is to combine the written summary with the portfolio so that contents of the report can be supported with contents of the portfolio; however, each additional component of an evaluation also adds time to the teacher's overall evaluation tasks. Perhaps if the written report is completed at the end of the school year or, at most, twice a year, the teacher will have the opportunity to write down thoughts and descriptions about the child.

Model Assessment and Reporting Systems

Attempts have been made in recent years to develop models of assessment and reporting systems that reflect the strengths of authentic or performance assessments. Educational leaders and measurement specialists for young children have worked toward designing and piloting methods of assessing and reporting children's evaluations logically and coherently. The goal is to guide teachers in connecting curriculum, instruction, assessment, and reporting via natural and meaningful strategies.

Three examples of these models are Project Spectrum, the Work Sampling System, and the Child Observation Record. Each of these systems seeks to correct the mistakes in assessment that are currently being made with young children. They also focus on strategies for informal and performance assessments differently, but with the same goal of evaluating and reporting child development and learning in a meaningful and constructive manner.

Enhanced eText: Video Example 11.3

Project Spectrum

Project Spectrum was initiated in 1984 at Harvard and Tufts Universities to better understand the linguistic and logical bases of intelligence. A major goal of the project was to produce a developmentally appropriate approach to assessment in early childhood. In addition to studying the child's individual cognitive style, the project emphasized the child's areas of strengths often not included in Piagetian approaches to education. The areas of cognitive ability examined in the project included numbers, science, music, language, visual arts, movement, and social development. The assumption was that when educators evaluated the young child's strengths in many domains, all children would exhibit performance in some domains.

Assessment is integrated into curriculum and instruction in Project Spectrum. A variety of activities are offered to the children; assessment is conducted through the child's involvement in the activities. Thus, assessment is performance based within both structured and unstructured tasks and teacher observation. Assessment is interfaced with meaningful activities provided in the classroom environment. Assessment is conducted throughout the year and documented through observation checklists, score sheets, and portfolios. Activities used for curriculum and assessment include games, puzzles, and other activities in learning areas such as obstacle courses for movement assessment, a child's activity in reporting for language assessment, and a bus game designed to evaluate the child's ability to make mental calculations and to organize numbers. Project Spectrum is also based on the work of Howard Gardner and his colleagues (1998) who have done extensive work on multiple intelligences and how their approach can be used with young children (Baum, Viens, & Slatin, 2005; Chen, 1998; Krechevsky & Chen, 1998).

Assessment data collected during the year are reported through a Spectrum Profile, a summary of the child's participation in project activities during the year in the form of a narrative report. The child's areas of strength are described, along with suggestions for follow-up activities the parents can conduct with the child.

The child's active involvement in the assessment process and the wide range of developmental domains incorporated into the curriculum are considered strengths of Project Spectrum. A concern is that parents may focus only on the child's strengths described in project assessments and focus on these strengths prematurely, thus neglecting the development of other areas (Krechevsky, 1991).

The Work Sampling System

The Work Sampling System, 5th Edition (Meisels, Marsden, Jablon, & Dichtelmiller, 2013) was designed as an alternative to the use of standardized tests for the assessment of young children. The system is based on the philosophy that performance assessments are appropriate because they (1) document the child's daily activities, (2) reflect an individualized approach to assessment, (3) integrate assessment with curriculum and instruction, (4) assess many elements of learning, and (5) allow teachers to learn how children reconstruct knowledge through interacting with materials and peers.

The first component of the Work Sampling System is teacher observation by means of developmental checklists. Because learning and instruction are integrated with assessment, the documentation of development and learning also provides information on the curriculum. Checklists cover seven domains: (1) personal and social development, (2) language and literacy, (3) mathematical thinking, (4) scientific thinking, (5) social studies, (6) art and music, and (7) physical development. Guidelines are provided for understanding the process of observation with the checklist indicators.

A second component is portfolios, which provide an assessment process that actively involves the teacher and child. Both the teacher and child select portfolio content. The activity of organizing the portfolio permits the teacher and child to review progress and plan future activities, thus integrating the teaching–learning process. Items are selected that represent the seven domains covered by the checklist. Essential or core items of work samples are selected several times during the year, in addition to other items selected that represent all domains. The portfolio becomes a tool for documenting, analyzing, and summarizing the child's learning and development through the year.

A third component of the Work Sampling System is the summary report completed for each child three times a year. The report summarizes the child's performance by means of specific criteria for the evaluation. Information from the checklists and the portfolios is used to communicate the child's progress to the parents. The child's overall progress is reported, as well as whether the child is making appropriate progress in each developmental category.

The Preschool Child Observation Record

The Preschool Child Observation Record is based on observation as the core of the assessment project with young children. The system was developed as an answer to the misassessment of young children, including those in caregiving settings during the preschool years. The goal was to produce an assessment process that is developmentally appropriate, reliable, valid, and user friendly. Also, the purpose of the system is to observe and assess children conducting child-initiated tasks for some of the activities. Because child-centered activities integrate all categories of development, children can be assessed during natural daily activities. The teacher in the assessment process uses developmental checklists combined with anecdotal recordings of observations.

Search and Share 11.2

Work Sampling System

Search online to learn more about the Work Sampling System. What components of this approach did you find most interesting? If you were using this system, what features would you include and how would you involve parents in the process?

The Preschool Child Observation Record system was developed by the High/Scope Educational Research Foundation for use in all developmentally appropriate programs. The system was studied for two years to establish validity and reliability. It assesses six areas of development: (1) initiative, (2) creative representation, (3) social relations, (4) music and movement, (5) language and literacy, and (6) logic and mathematics. The teacher rates the child several times a year on 30 items that have five levels of indicators. Anecdotal notes taken on an ongoing basis through observations are used to complete the ratings (High/Scope Educational Research Foundation, 2003; Schweinhart, 1993).

Teacher-Designed Systems

The examples of assessment and reporting systems just described provide some clues as to how teachers can design and organize their own systems. The Work Sampling System provides a sample framework for a system and provides the categories to be included in the curriculum. In this case, the developmental approach is being used and all domains are being represented. Three basic strategies are included in the system: checklists and guidelines, portfolios, and summary reports. When the teacher designs a system, state or national standards may be the framework used to determine categories. Thus, standards in mathematics, language, arts, and science, may be the categories. Strategies such as checklists, commercial and teacher-designed tests, inventories, and other assessment activities may be included in the system.

How will the portfolio support standards and objectives for learning? What will the teacher include in the portfolio for reporting periods? Will it include work samples, group reports, teacher interviews, photo documentation, and audio recordings? The teacher does not need to include all options included in this chapter, but can be selective, using strategies that provide a variety of indicators of a child's progress and achievements and that are suitable for the purposes of the portfolio.

How much material should be included in the portfolio for each reporting session? Teachers can become overwhelmed by the amount of material they have gathered and

The Work Sampling System and the Ounce Scale: Early Childhood Accountability in Pennsylvania

The *Ounce scale* was first introduced in Chapter 3 as an infant/toddler scale that measures domains of development from infancy through 3 years. When paired with the Work Sampling System, children's development can be followed from infancy through the fifth grade. The combination of the two tests has been found to be useful for measuring children's progress on early learning standards. An example of using two tests to measure development comes from the Office of Child Development and Early Learning in Pennsylvania. In 2007, the Office and the Bureau of Early Intervention Services issued an announcement that the two scales were to be used to measure child progress on the Early Childhood Accountability in Pennsylvania, or ECAP, system. The two measures were later to be used as a data collection system for early intervention programs (Department of Public Welfare Commonwealth of Pennsylvania, 2007).

the prospect of keeping it manageable. A good possibility is for the teacher to remember the difference between a working portfolio and an evaluative portfolio. Materials can be gathered in a working portfolio and reduced to significant samples for the portfolio that will be used for reporting. Much of the material can be sent home after this process has taken place.

How often should reporting be done? This will largely be controlled by how the school system or preschool center has determined reporting periods. In the Work Sampling System, reporting is done three times a year. Some schools report every 6 weeks, every 9 weeks, or twice a year. The system will be organized accordingly.

Finally, how will the child's progress and accomplishments be reported to parents? Will there be a written summary such as is used in the Work Sampling System? Will a report card be involved? Will there be a conference with the parents? Will the child be included in the conference? Will the parents have opportunities to provide input into the evaluation? Will the child be an active participant in the process?

> **Enhanced eText:** Self-Check 11.4

Summary

In this chapter, we have explored some strategies for reporting student progress to parents through performance or authentic assessments. We discussed the inherent limitations in traditional report cards that report only what the child knows. In contrast, performance assessments demonstrate what the child knows and how the child applies that knowledge in a realistic context.

A major focus of the chapter was to describe some alternative methods of constructing an evaluative profile of the child's development and learning that permits the teacher and the child to communicate to parents broad information about what the child has accomplished. Portfolios can contain many types of informal and performance assessment results to support what the child has learned.

The teacher will need to design some type of system for assessing and reporting the child's accomplishments. The system will include a portfolio, but may not be limited to the child's work. It can include tests, teacher assessments, checklists, and other strategies for documenting and summarizing the learning objectives for the instructional period.

Much progress has been made during the past decade in portfolio assessment. Teachers at all educational levels have become accustomed to the benefits of portfolio assessment. Likewise, the advent of electronic tools has made electronic portfolios accessible to students, parents, and teachers. Much of the paperwork associated with portfolios has been digitalized, saving teachers time and effort.

Narrative reports supplement portfolio information. They provide parents with an overview and summary of the child's progress and accomplishments. The narrative reports, along with portfolio contents, are useful for three-way conferences between teachers, students, and families.

Key Terms

archival portfolio 275

developmental portfolio 275

electronic portfolio 276

evaluative portfolio 274

performance assessments 272

showcase portfolio 274

working portfolio 274

Selected Organizations

Search for the following organizations online:

Association for Supervision and Curriculum Development

Centers for Disease Control

High/Scope Educational Research Foundation

North Central Regional Educational Laboratory

References

Alacam, N., & Olgan, R. (2016). Portfolio assessment: Does it really give the benefits that it purports to offer? Views of early childhood and first-grade teachers. *Early Child Development and Care, 186*, 1505–1519.

Arter, J., & Spandel, V. (Spring 1992). Using portfolios of student work in instruction and assessment. *Educational Measurement: Issues and Practice, 11*, 36–44.

Barbour, A., & Desjean-Perrotta, B. (1998). The basics of portfolio assessment. In S. C. Wortham, A. Barbour, & B. Desjean-Perrotta (Eds.), *Portfolio assessment: A handbook for preschool and elementary educators* (pp. 15–30). Olney, MD: Association for Childhood Education International.

Batzle, J. (1992). *Portfolio assessment and evaluation: Developing and using portfolios in the K–6 classroom.* Cypress, CA: Creative Teaching.

Baum, S., Viens, J., & Slatin, B. (2005). *Multiple intelligences in the elementary classroom: A teacher's toolkit- Harvard Project.* Retrieved from www.pe.harvard.edu . . . multiple-intelligences-in–the-elementary-classroom-a-teacher . . .

Cassidy, K. (2013, May 30). *A great tool to continuously assess progress.* Retrieved from http://www.plpnetwork.com/2013/05/30/digital-portfolios-thinking-assessment

Chen, J.Q. (1998). *Project spectrum: Early learning activities.* New York: Teachers College Press.

Cohen, L. (2014). The power of portfolios. *Scholastic Early Childhood Today.* Retrieved from http://www.scholastic.com/teachers/article/power-portfolios

Cool Tools for Schools. (2018). Digital portfolios for students. Retrieved from https://cooltoolsforschool.net/digital-student-portfolios

Damiani, V. B. (2004). *Portfolio assessment in the classroom.* National Association of School Psychologists. Retrieved from http://www.education.com/reference/article/portfolio-assessment

Davis, V. (2017). 11 *Essentials for Excellent Digital Portfolios.* Retrieved from https://www.edutopia.org/blog11-essentials-for-excellent-portfolios . . .

Department of Public Welfare, Commonwealth of Pennsylvania. (2007, July 13). *Announcement: ELS/EI-07 #9.* Office of Child Development and Learning, Bureau of Early Intervention Services. Retrieved from http://www.portal.state.pa.us

Epstein, A. S., Schweinhart, L., DeBruin-Parecki, J., & Robin, K. B. (2004, July). Preschool Assessment: A guide to developing a balanced approach. *Preschool Policy Facts.* Brunswick, NJ: National Institute for Early Education Research.

Etale. (2013, April 10). *5 common reasons for the importance of letter grades.* Retrieved from http://www.etale.org/main/2013/04/10/5-common-reasons-for-the-importance-of-letter-grades

Fernsten, L. (2009). *Portfolio assessment.* Retrieved from http://www.education.com/reference/article/portfolio-assessment

Furger, R. (2014). *Assessments: What teachers can do.* Retrieved from http://www.edutopia.org/what-teachers-can-do

Gardner, H., et al. (1998). *Project spectrum: Early learning activities.* New York: Teachers College Press.

Gilkerson, D., & Hanson, M. F. (2000). Family portfolios: Involving families in portfolio documentation. *Early Childhood Education Journal, 27,* 197–201.

Grace, C., & Shores, E. F. (1991). *The portfolio and its use.* Little Rock, AR: Southern Association on Children Under Six.

Gronlund, G., & Engel, B. (2002). *Focused portfolios: A complete assessment for the young child.* St. Paul, MN: Redleaf Press.

Gronlund, G., & James, M. (2013). *Focused observations: How to observe young children for assessment and curriculum planning* (2nd ed.). St. Paul, MN: Redleaf Press.

Hanson, M. F., & Gilkerson, D. (1999). Portfolio assessment: More than ABCs and 123s. *Early Childhood Education Journal, 27,* 81–86.

Harris, M. E. (2009, May). Implementing portfolio assessment. *Young Children, 64,* 82–85.

Hebert, E. A., & Schultz, L. (1996). The power of portfolios. *Educational Leadership, 53,* 70–71.

Hertz, M. B. (2013, May 30). *Using e-portfolios in the classroom.* Retrieved from http://www.edutopia.org/blog/e-portfolios-in-the-classroom

High/Scope Educational Research Foundation. (2003). *Preschool child observation record.* Ypsilanti, MI: Author.

Horm-Wingerd, D. M. (1992). Reporting children's development: The narrative report. *Dimensions of Early Childhood, 21,* 11–15.

Krechevsky, M. (1991). Project Spectrum: An innovative assessment alternative. *Educational Leadership, 48,* 43–48.

Krechevsky, M., & Chen, J. Q. (Eds.) (1998). *Project Spectrum: Preschool assessment handbook.* New York: Teachers College Press.

Loop, E. (2017). *The advantages of keeping portfolios in the preschool classroom.* Retrieved from https://classroom.synonym.com/advantages-keeping-portfolios-preschool . . .

Meisels, S. J. (2014). *Performance assessment.* New York, NY: Scholastic Press.

Meisels, S. J., Marsden, D. B., Jablon, J. R., & Dichtelmiller, M. (2013). *Work Sampling System* (5th ed.). San Antonio, TX: Pearson.

Morrison, G. (2013). *Informal methods of assessment.* Upper Saddle River, NJ: Pearson.

Peters, S., Hartly, C., Rogers, P., Smith, J., & Carr, M. (2009). Early childhood portfolios as a tool for enhancing learning during the transition to school. *International Journal of Transitions in Childhood, Vol. 3.*

Puckett, M. B., & Black, J. K. (2000). *Authentic assessment of the young child: Celebrating development and learning* (2nd ed.). Upper Saddle River, NJ: Merrill/Prentice Hall.

Schweinhart, L. J. (1993). Observing young children in action: The key to early childhood assessment. *Young Children, 48,* 29–33.

Seitz, H., & Bartholomew, C. (2008). Powerful portfolios for young children. *Early Childhood Education Journal, 36,* 82–85.

Shu-Chin Susan Chen & Yu-Pay Cheng. (2011). Implementing curriculum-based learning portfolio: A case study in Taiwan. *Early Child Development and Care, 181:2,* 149–164.

Smith, A. (2000). Reflective portfolios: Preschool possibilities. *Childhood Education, 76,* 204–208).

Smith, J., Brewer, D. M., & Heffner, T. (2014). Portfolio assessments with young children who are at risk for school failure. *Preventing School Failure: Alternative Education for Children and Youth, 48,* 38–40. Retrieved from https://www.tandfonline.com/doi/abs/10.1080/1045988X.2003.10887 . . .

Van Nood, R. (2012, February 28). *How to create a-portfolio with Evernote (Education Series).* Retrieved from http://www.blog.evernote.com/blog/2012/02/28/how-to-create-a-portfolio.

Glossary

achievement test   A test that measures the extent to which a person has acquired information or mastered certain skills, usually as a result of instruction or training.

alternative assessment   An assessment that is different from traditional written or multiple-choice tests; usually related to authentic and performance assessments.

alternative-form reliability   The correlation between results on alternative forms of a test. Reliability is the extent to which the two forms are consistent in measuring the same attributes.

analytic rubric   A rubric that provides diagnostic feedback and is more specific than a holistic rubric.

anecdotal record   A written description of an incident in a child's behavior that can be significant in understanding the child.

aptitude test   A test designed to predict future learning or performance on some task if appropriate education or training is provided.

archival portfolio   A collection of a child's work that is passed along from year to year.

assessment   The interpretation or evaluation of information about a child gathered from different sources.

assessment software   Textbook publishers and developers of early childhood assessment tools make assessment software available as an option alongside traditional assessment tools.

authentic achievement   Learning that is real and meaningful; achievement that is worthwhile.

authentic assessment (authentic performance assessment)   An assessment that uses some type of performance by a child to demonstrate understanding.

authentic learning   Another term frequently used for performance assessment.

authentic performance assessment   Another term frequently used for performance assessment.

behavioral objective   An educational or instructional statement that includes the behavior to be exhibited, the conditions under which the behavior will be exhibited, and the level of performance required for mastery.

checklist   A sequence or hierarchy of concepts and/or skills organized in a format that can be used to plan instruction and keep records.

concurrent validity   The extent to which test scores on two forms of a test measure are correlated when they are given at the same time.

construct validity   The extent to which a test measures a psychological trait or construct. Tests of personality, verbal ability, and critical thinking are examples of tests with construct validity.

content validity   The extent to which the content of a test such as an achievement test represents the objectives of the instructional program it is designed to measure.

contract   An agreement between teacher and child about activities the child will complete to achieve a specific objective or purpose.

corrective activities   Instructional materials and methods used with mastery learning that are implemented after formative evaluation to provide alternative learning strategies and resources.

criterion-referenced test   A test designed to provide information on specific knowledge or skills possessed by a student. The test measures specific skills or instructional objectives.

criterion-related validity   To establish validity of a test, scores are correlated with an external criterion, such as another established test of the same type.

data-driven decision making   The process of using assessment data to identify children's strengths and needs and then applying this information to plan appropriate learning opportunities.

development   The process of change in an individual over time, including the child's chronological age, rate of maturation, and individual behaviors.

developmental assessments   In-depth evaluations of young children to determine whether development is proceeding normally. They are used as one source to identify children whose development is delayed.

developmental checklist   A checklist that emphasizes areas and levels of development in early childhood.

developmental portfolio   A portfolio that is designed to fit the needs of preschool children.

developmental rubric   A rubric that is organized using domains of development.

developmental screening   A quick look at a young child's development to determine whether development is proceeding normally. If development is atypical, further in-depth assessment is usually recommended.

diagnostic evaluation   An evaluation to analyze an individual's areas of weaknesses or strengths and to determine the nature and causes of the weaknesses.

diagnostic interview   An interview to determine a child's learning needs or assess weaknesses. May be part of a diagnostic evaluation.

direct performance measure   A performance measure that requires the student to apply knowledge in an activity specified by the teacher.

directed assignment   A specific assignment to assess a child's performance on a learning objective or skill.

disability (learning disability)   A developmental difference or delay in a young or school-age child that interferes with the individual's ability to learn through regular methods of instruction.

documentation   A process of recording information about the progress of project activities and children's interests, ideas, thinking, and problem solving within their activities.

electronic portfolio   A portfolio that is developed and stored on an electronic device such as a computer.

enrichment activities   In the context of mastery learning, challenging activities at a higher cognitive level on Bloom's taxonomy than the instructional objective described on a table of specifications.

equivalent forms   Alternative forms of a test that are parallel. The forms of the test measure the same domain or objectives, have the same format, and are of equal difficulty.

evaluation   Assessment information gathered from multiple sources to determine a child's current level of functioning and to determine what should happen next to meet a child's developmental and/or educational needs.

evaluative portfolio   A work sample collection to assess student progress.

event sampling   An observation strategy used to determine when a particular behavior is likely to occur. The setting in which the behavior occurs is more important than the time it is likely to occur.

family-centered   Beliefs and practices on behalf of children and families that are led by family concerns and priorities.

family–professional partnerships   Mutually respectful, trusting relationships in which families and professionals work together on behalf of the child.

formal assessment   A test that has been standardized to measure developmental progress or achievement.

formative assessment   An assessment designed to measure progress on an objective rather than to give a qualitative result.

formative evaluation   Evaluation conducted during instruction to provide the teacher with information on the learning progress of the student and the effectiveness of instructional methods and materials.

formative test   A test designed to evaluate progress on specific learning objectives or a unit of study.

functional behavioral assessment   Used to understand underlying causes of inappropriate behavior by looking beyond obvious behavior interpretations to determine what function it might be serving for the child in order to plan appropriate steps for improving a child's behavior.

funds of knowledge   The information of a child's family and background that a child brings to the educational setting.

game   In the context of authentic assessment, a structured assessment whereby the student's performance progress is evaluated through engagement with the game.

grade equivalent score   The grade level for which a given score on a standardized test is the estimated average. Grade-equivalent scores, commonly used for elementary achievement tests, are expressed in terms of the grade and month.

grade norms   Norms on standardized tests based on the performance of students in given grades.

graphic rating scale   A rating scale that can be used as a continuum. The rater marks characteristics by descriptors on the scale at any point along the continuum.

group test   A test that can be administered to more than one person at a time.

holistic rubric   A rubric with competency levels that indicate levels of performance. It assigns a single score to a student's performance.

home visit   A visit by a professional to the home of a child to establish a relationship with the family and better understand the child.

inclusion   The process of including children with disabilities in a classroom where they would have been placed if they had not experienced a disability.

indirect performance measure   A measure that assesses what a student knows about a topic. The teacher's assessment is accomplished by observing a student activity or examining a written test.

individual test   A test that can be administered to only one person at a time. Many early childhood tests are individual tests because of the low maturity level of the examinees.

individualized instruction   Instruction based on the learning strengths and needs of individual students. It may be based on criterion-related assessment results and/or the child's diagnosis.

informal assessment   The use of observation, learning tasks, and other naturally occurring events to gather information about a child.

instructional objective   *See* behavioral objective.

integrated curriculum   The practice of providing curriculum experiences that integrate the child's learning *within* and *across* domains and disciplines.

intelligence quotient (IQ)   An index of intelligence expressed as the ratio of mental age to chronological age. It is derived from an individual's performance on an intelligence test as compared with that of others of the same age.

intelligence test   A test measuring developed abilities that are considered signs of intelligence. Intelligence is general potential independent of prior learning.

interest inventory   A measure used to determine interest in an occupation or vocation. Students' interest in reading may be determined by such an inventory.

internal consistency   The degree of relationship among items on a test. A type of reliability that indicates whether items on the test are positively correlated and measure the same trait or characteristic.

interview   A discussion the teacher conducts with a child to make an assessment.

item analysis   The analysis of single test items to determine their difficulty value and discriminating power. Item analysis is conducted in the process of developing a standardized test.

least restrictive environment (LRE)   Relates to the environments provided for children with disabilities; environments are arranged to encourage the child's abilities; for example, on a play structure, the entries to the structure are wide enough to accommodate a wheelchair.

mainstreaming   A process of placing children with disabilities in regular classrooms for part of the school day with children who do not have disabilities; has been replaced by inclusion or integration, in which the child is not singled out as being different.

mastery learning A theory that all students can achieve mastery of learning objectives if time and quality learning conditions are provided.

mastery testing Evaluation to determine the extent to which a test taker has mastered particular skills or learning objectives. Performance is compared to a predetermined standard of proficiency.

mean The arithmetic average of a set of test scores.

minimum-competency testing Evaluation to measure whether test takers have achieved a minimum level of proficiency in a given academic area.

multiple-choice A type of test question in which the test taker must choose the best answer from among several options.

narrative report An alternative to report cards for reporting a child's progress. The teacher writes a narrative to describe the child's growth and accomplishments.

narratives Written documentation such as teacher journals, notes, and children's stories to report progress to parents.

neonatologist A physician who specializes in babies less than 1 month old.

normal distribution The hypothetical distribution of scores that has a bell-shaped appearance. This distribution is used as a model for many scoring systems and test statistics.

norm-referenced test A test in which the test taker's performance is compared with the performance of people in a norming group.

norms Statistics that supply a frame of reference based on the actual performance of test takers in a norm group; a set of scores that represents the distribution of test performance in the norm group.

numerical rating scale A series of numerals, such as 1 to 5, that allows an observer to indicate to the degree an individual possesses a particular characteristic.

observation A type of assessment used to study and evaluate child behaviors; the teacher watches the child for evidence of the designated behavior.

obstetrician A physician who specializes in pregnancy and childbirth.

parent conferences Meetings in which professionals and family members discuss children's progress and future goals.

parent group meeting conferences Meetings for all parents in which the teacher spends time explaining assessments and information on projects or thematic study topics.

pedagogical documentation A performance assessment that is based on a child's work to determine skill development and instructional needs.

pediatrician A physician who specializes in the development, care, and diseases in young children.

percentile A point or score in a distribution at or below which falls the percentage of cases indicated by the percentile. The score scale on a normal distribution is divided into 100 segments, each containing the same number of scores.

percentile rank The test taker's test score, as expressed in terms of its position within a group of 100 scores. The percentile rank is the percentage of scores equal to or lower than the test taker's score.

performance assessment An assessment in which the child demonstrates knowledge by applying it to a task or a problem-solving activity.

performance-based assessment An assessment of development and/or learning that is based on the child's natural performance rather than on contrived tests or tasks.

personality test A test designed to obtain information on the affective characteristics of an individual (emotional, motivational, or attitudinal). The test measures psychological makeup rather than intellectual abilities.

placement evaluation Assessment to determine how to group children for instructional needs.

play-based assessment Assessment often used for children with disabilities that is conducted through observation in play environments. Play activities can be spontaneous or planned. Play-based assessment can be conducted by an individual or through arena assessment.

play-based intervention Interactive play is used to guide, model, instruct, or reinforce to encourage a child's play activity.

portfolio A format for conducting an evaluation of a child. Portfolios are a collection of a child's work, teacher assessments, and other information that contribute to a picture of a child's progress.

pre-assessment A type of teacher-designed measure used to understand children's skills, knowledge, and approaches to learning *before* instruction.

progress monitoring The process of monitoring children's progress or rate of improvement as well as the effectiveness of the instruction.

project An authentic learning activity that can also be used to indicate the degree of a characteristic that the person possesses.

rating scale A scale using categories that allow the observer to indicate the degree of a characteristic that the person possesses.

raw score The number of right answers a test taker obtains on a test.

reliability The extent to which a test is consistent in measuring over time what it is designed to measure.

rubric An instrument developed to measure authentic and performance assessments that is given to determine qualitative characteristics on a scale.

running record A description of a sequence of events in a child's behavior that includes all behaviors observed over a period of time.

scope (sequence of skills) A list of learning objectives established for areas of learning and at a particular age, grade level, or content area.

screening A brief test of a child's development to see if an in-depth assessment is needed.

screening test Provides a snapshot of children's development that indicates when a child might have a developmental problem that needs further investigation.

showcase portfolio   A portfolio that contains the student's best work.

split-half reliability   A measure of reliability whereby scores on equivalent sections of a single test are correlated for internal consistency.

standard deviation   A measure of the variability of a distribution of scores around the mean.

standard error of measurement   An estimate of the possible magnitude of error present in test scores.

standardized assessment   An assessment that has specific content, procedures, and normative data for interpreting scores.

standard score   A transformed score that reports performance in terms of the number of standard deviation units the raw score is from the mean.

stanine   A scale on the normal curve divided into nine sections, with all divisions except the first and the last being 0.5 standard deviation wide.

strengths-based   Services built on family resources and assets.

structured interview   A planned interview conducted by the teacher for assessment purposes.

structured performance assessment   A performance assessment that has been planned by the teacher to include specific tasks or activities.

student-led conferences   Conferences led by students, first with the family and later including the teacher.

summative assessment   A final assessment to assign a grade or determine mastery of an objective. Similar to summative evaluation.

summative evaluation   An evaluation obtained at the end of a cycle of instruction to determine whether students have mastered the objectives and whether the instruction has been effective.

summative test   A test to determine mastery of learning objectives administered for grading purposes.

table of specifications   A table of curriculum objectives that have been analyzed to determine to what level of Bloom's taxonomy of educational objectives the student must demonstrate mastery.

teacher-designed assessment   Measures teachers create to assess one or more subject or developmental areas.

T score   A standard score scale with a mean of 50 and a standard deviation of 10.

test–retest reliability   A type of reliability obtained by administering the same test a second time after a short interval and then correlating the two sets of scores.

three-way conferences   A student, parent, and teacher all participate in a conference to discuss the student's work through a portfolio. Each person has time to discuss progress and set goals.

time sampling   Observation to determine the frequency of a behavior. The observer records how many times the behavior occurs during uniform time periods.

true score   A hypothetical score on a test that is free of error. Because no standardized test is free of measurement error, a true score can never be obtained.

unstructured interview   An assessment interview conducted by the teacher as the result of naturally occurring performance by a child. The interview is not planned.

unstructured performance assessment   An assessment that is part of regular classroom activities.

validity   The degree to which a test serves the purpose for which it is to be used.

working portfolio   A temporary method of storage of the child's work to be used later for evaluation.

work sample   An example of a child's work. Work samples include products of all types of activities that can be used to evaluate the child's progress.

Z score   A standard score that expresses performance in terms of the number of standard deviations from the mean.

Index